BERLIN WITNESS

G. Jonathan Greenwald

BERLIN WITNESS

AN AMERICAN DIPLOMAT'S
CHRONICLE OF
EAST GERMANY'S REVOLUTION

The Pennsylvania State University Press
University Park, Pennsylvania

Library of Congress Cataloging-in-Publication Data

Greenwald, G. Jonathan.
    Berlin witness : An American diplomat's chronicle of East Germany's revolution /
G. Jonathan Greenwald.
        p.   cm.
    Includes index.
    ISBN 0-271-00932-2
    1. United States—Foreign relations—Germany (East).   2. Germany
(East)—Foreign relations—United States.   3. Germany—History—
Unification, 1990.   4. Greenwald, G. Jonathan—Diaries.   I. Title.
E183.8.G35G74   1993
327.730431—dc20   92-33261
                                                                                        CIP

Copyright © 1993 The Pennsylvania State University
All rights reserved
Printed in the United States of America

Published by The Pennsylvania State University Press,
Suite C, Barbara Building, University Park, PA 16802-1003

It is the policy of The Pennsylvania State University Press to use acid-free paper for the first printing of all clothbound books. Publications on uncoated stock satisfy the minimum requirements of American National Standard for Information Sciences—Permanence of Paper for Printed Library Materials, ANSI Z39.48–1984.

Contents

List of Figures   ix

Preface   xi

1. THE DECEPTIVE CALM, MAY AND JUNE 1989   1

May Day as in father's time. The lion of Magdeburg. Hungary opens its border. The grand old man of GDR dissent. An election 98.5% pure. Soccer Perestroika? Blood in the streets of Rostock? Turned-off youth rocks and rolls. Inner-German contacts. Tienanmen Square and non-Communist Poland. Honecker to Washington? Friend or Stasi? U.S.-GDR relations. Defending communism with the New York Philharmonic and "a rifle in the hand." Travel and potatoes. A Minister's futile life. Political humor. Berlin policy. The Central Committee stonewalls. Hungarian border dances. A might-be, could-be GDR Gorbachev. Honecker visits the Soviet heart of steel.

2. THE SILENT CRISIS, JULY AND AUGUST 1989   55

Succession sweepstakes. No table for four. A Jewish graveyard. "Poland is not yet lost." Honecker falls ill. An entrepreneur's good life. The German Question rediscovered. "Go to Mecklenburg when the world ends." Soviet-GDR relations.

Honecker's Kissinger.   Rethinking U.S. policy.   The stories of
Jürgen and Renate.   The perils of Foreign Service life.
Awakening Washington.   Theater evenings.   A day with the
Soviet and GDR armies.   Sit-ins close the West German Mission.   The unusual master spy.   "Yesterday my son crossed the
border."   Martin Luther's heir.   Honecker's troubled birthday.   Is there justification for a second German state?   Soviet
Embassy views.   The Communist Prince of Bad Salzungen.
Is Honecker dying?

3. THE FALL OF HONECKER,
SEPTEMBER 1989–OCTOBER 17, 1989   123

Civil society.   Hungary picks the West.   Small-talk at the Wall.
The church pleads with Honecker.   What are the Soviets doing?
The Opposition forms.   Is the situation explosive?   Bloc Parties
stir.   "Maybe something big is going to happen."   Would you
write a life insurance policy on the GDR?   What should the
U.S. do?   Leipzig on the march.   The Establishment begins to
speak out.   Prague sit-ins stream west.   The 40th Anniversary
arrives.   Cracks in the media.   The Embassy is stormed.
Rumors of violence.   Torches on Unter den Linden.   Gorbachev:
"Don't panic."   Berlin protests.   Dresden and Leipzig boil
over.   The Politburo digs in.   The hurricane's eye.   Glasnost.
Rock for reform.   Can Honecker survive?   Can the GDR survive?

4. THE PEACEFUL REVOLUTION,
OCTOBER 18, 1989–NOVEMBER 12, 1989   201

Honecker out.   Krenz misses a chance.   Nervous Washington.   Protests spread.   Leipzig Monday.   Socialism's last
chance?   "A red German eaglet."   Rising demands.   Church
views.   Berlin Town Meeting.   The Number Two man.   A role
for honorable Communists?   Plenum maneuvers.   Markus Wolf
again.   Miss Playboy and the Miracle Mets.   Can the SED share
power?   Krenz and Gorbachev.   *Eisbein* with Gregor Gysi.   The
Turk whets his sword.   The Party's mood.   Revolution in Alexanderplatz.   Dresden and the price of mushrooms.   Drinks with the
Opposition.   Who can govern?   Krenz's program.   The SED

rebels.   The Wall is open: "I just can't believe it."   Elections in six months?   Krenz's two-front challenge.   Trabies in West Berlin.   Seven questions, no answers.

AFTERWORD: THE YEAR OF GERMAN UNITY,
NOVEMBER 13, 1989–OCTOBER 3, 1990   277

Inevitable Unification?   The Election Campaign.   200 Days.

Glossary   325
Index   335

List of Figures

Figures 1–12 follow page 110.

FIG. 1. January 1989: Erich Honecker, the author, Ambassador Barkley, and Jerry Verner.
FIG. 2. May Day 1989.
FIG. 3. Gaby Greenwald on the island of Usedom.
FIG. 4. Wolgast, May 1989.
FIG. 5. October 4, 1989: Prayer vigil at Gethsemane Church.
FIG. 6. October 6, 1989: Torchlight parade on Unter den Linden.
FIG. 7. October 7, 1989: Erich Honecker and Mikhail Gorbachev.
FIG. 8. October 7, 1989, 5:00 P.M.: Young people begin the first demonstration in Berlin.
FIG. 9. October 7, 1989: Police move against the demonstrators.
FIG. 10. October 15, 1989. Unauthorized street dancing in front of Gethsemane Church.
FIG. 11. The GDR's new leader, Egon Krenz.
FIG. 12. October 29, 1989, Berlin Town Meeting, in front of City Hall.

Figures 13–24 follow page 238.

FIG. 13. Bitter cartoon of the *Wendehals* decorates the Wall.
FIG. 14. November 4, 1989: On the way to Alexanderplatz in Berlin.

List of Figures

Fig. 15. November 4, 1989: View of the giant demonstration that filled Alexanderplatz.
Fig. 16. Another view of the Alexanderplatz demonstration, November 4, 1989.
Fig. 17. November 11–12, 1989: Trabies stream through the open Wall.
Fig. 18. November 11–12, 1989: The Kurfürstendamm after the Wall opened.
Fig. 19. Marchers carry banners demanding a united Germany.
Fig. 20. Gregor Gysi.
Fig. 21. Ibrahim Böhme.
Fig. 22. Lothar de Maizière.
Fig. 23. Free elections in the GDR, March 1990: Party posters in Berlin.
Fig. 24. March 6, 1990: East Germans cheer Helmut Kohl.

Preface

> When that Wall went down in Germany, we said, "Hey, now anything is possible."
> —Jack Zduriencik
> *Washington Post*, August 4, 1991

Television showed the world pictures of what happened that November evening in Berlin, and life has not been the same since—not for the small, insular "second German State," the German Democratic Republic (GDR), which had celebrated its 40th Anniversary a month earlier and would be gone from the map of Europe before it knew a forty-first, not for Germany, which has returned to the family of nations as a rich, troubled giant; and not for Washington and Moscow, which live now in a world where East and West no longer mean the familiar confrontation of cold war and assured European alliances. Not even for Jack Zduriencik, scouting director of the Pittsburgh Pirates, who wants to persuade Fidel Castro to allow his baseball players to come to the land of the Yankee dollar.

My wife Gaby, a native Berliner, and I arrived in East Berlin in the GDR's Indian summer of 1987. Erich Honecker, General Secretary of the GDR, had presided with pomp and satisfaction over the Communist portion of Berlin's 750th Anniversary ceremonies and was preparing to be received in Bonn by West Germany's Chancellor Helmut Kohl, a symbolic recognition that there were indeed two sovereign German states. If the GDR was not as large, free, or rich as its West German brother, it counted for something in Europe: it was the closest thing to a success story in the still nearly monolithic Communist East, one of the world's ten largest industrial economies, the Soviet Union's most powerful ally, a cornerstone of the armed but apparently stable security order that had grown up in the aftermath of the Second World War.

I was the political counselor, the third-ranking officer, in the American Embassy to the GDR. My job was to explain the dynamics of East German society to Washington and thereby assist in the development of U.S. policy. It was certain to be fascinating and important. The regime's unlovely nature, the physical fact of the grotesque Berlin Wall, caused most Americans to pay it little attention. The diplomatic relations established in 1974 were our least developed anywhere in Europe. American business traded less only with Albania. But, a colleague who had served there in the 1970s emphasized to me as we packed, the GDR was stirring not far below its tightly controlled, deceptively placid surface. The month before our arrival, young East Germans, frustrated at being kept from a rock concert in front of the Reichstag a few hundred yards the other side of the Wall in West Berlin, had demonstrated on Unter den Linden. Their "Gorby, Gorby" shouts before they were dispersed by police showed that the personality and reforms of the new Soviet leader were electrifying East Germans, as they were Poles and Hungarians.

I anticipated spending three or four years awakening Washington's interest in important developments along Europe's most sensitive frontier. I expected to chronicle a new, more fluid, and unpredictable stage in the inner-German and East-West rapprochements that had been under way for two decades, but it was signs of evolution, not revolution, I initially searched for. Like everyone, I was surprised at the pace of events, at the East Germans' increasing boldness and the Soviet Union's willingness to accept liquidation of a nearly half-century-old security policy. I had no forewarning that by my tour's end the slogan "Come together—Try the West" would be on billboards all over East Germany, as an advertisement for a cheap cigarette and as a symbol of the materialistic side of a unification that would already be fact.

In mid-summer 1988, I wrote a provocative dispatch that asked "Will the GDR become reformist?" My thesis was that reform was brewing within the ruling Communist Party—the SED—just beneath the top leadership level and within the society at large; Honecker might adjust to it, but if he did not, the question of his successor would arise, and within a year or two significant reform could well begin to be introduced from above. Frank

Meehan, then U.S. Ambassador, one of the Foreign Service's most experienced Eastern European observers and perhaps its greatest gentleman, championed the telegram, but he edited out sentences that suggested U.S. policy should take more account of trends in this small state that could complicate our ties with West Germany and the comfortable European balance. I scribbled back to him the following note:

> I can live comfortably with the demise of the penultimate paragraph of the reform message. It was analytically open to many views and bureaucratically heretical. The development it predicted may never come to pass because the GDR either does not reform or the results prove . . . otherwise. That makes at least a 2:1 ratio against and reason enough to jettison. Let me explain . . . what I had in mind in writing (and believing) it.
>
> The common wisdom . . . in the Administration is that "reform in Eastern Europe is an all-win situation for the United States. Eastern European countries, by reforming, will (a) break away from Soviet influence; (b) rediscover capitalism; (c) adopt U.S. economic and social models and thus fall more under U.S. influence. The Doberman Pinscher school of GDR-ology would probably add a special East German postscript: The Wall will be torn down, the regime of Communists swept away, and Germany as a whole moved neatly into the West, if not NATO's corner.
>
> I am all for reform, here as in the rest of Eastern Europe, but, need it be said, it won't be that clear cut. And it will be least clear cut of all in Germany. Why? First of all, . . . the GDR has a chance, because of its relative economic and political strengths (or domestic discipline), to do reform more by itself, or really, by itself with the West Germans; it won't need U.S. assistance in the measure that, say, the Poles or Hungarians do. But the most important point is the impact in West Germany. The GDR will not make an economic miracle . . . that will greatly impress Westerners, no matter what reforms it adopts. If it begins to loosen up politically and socially, however, if it pays more attention to freedoms, in other words, it will become very interesting to West Germans. Just recall how interested West Germans were in the brief Prague Spring; think of how fascinated they are by what Gorbachev is doing. All of that will be slight in comparison to the fascination, hopes, and stirring that liberalization in the GDR would bring forth.

> The consensus in West Germany for years has been that freedom is more important than unity, and that since there was precious little freedom in the GDR, the . . . only realistic option was to be anchored firmly in the West. If the GDR becomes a freer, more open, less different from West Germany place . . . , many in West Germany will be less convinced of the immutability of that formula, more intrigued by what they see to the East, more inclined to spin ideas of system and state rapprochement.
>
> This is what I was trying to indicate by saying that once "real, existing socialism" [Honecker's phrase for what he had produced] begins to change, impulses will start flowing in both directions in the inner-German transmission belts. I did not mean that West Germans would want to be just like the GDR or that reform communism would win the next election, or that the Federal Republic would walk out of NATO one midnight. But Central Europe will not become an easier, more predictable, more "American"-like place; just the opposite. It will become much more unpredictable, and the German Question will assume a volatility that it has not had.

To this, Ambassador Meehan replied: "I share your ideas in the paragraph I took out. Why then do I hear you say, did you take them out? In a word, their hour has not yet come. We are giving the State Department and others a good many new ideas about the GDR. The dosage is important. We have to condition the little bastards. Don't throw the paragraph away. We will get to them again."

We were daring enough for 1988, but in retrospect we were both less than fully perceptive. Nevertheless, it is timely to think about those and related ideas again. Was what happened inevitable, or were there other channels down which German history might have flowed if actors or roles had been different in the months that culminated in the Peaceful Revolution? There are still practical lessons to be learned, for the drama has not yet been played out. Germany is united, but Germans find the task of stitching two very different societies together much harder than it appeared in the innocent late autumn of 1989. The United States is trying to find its way in the new landscape of a not "divided" but more fragmented Europe that no longer so obviously needs it.

This volume begins on May Day 1989, when the GDR still seemed to be a stable state with a reasonably predictable and unexceptional future. The book's heart consists of almost daily entries until immediately after the Berlin Wall was opened. I hope it will help readers both understand the what, how, and why of that extraordinary occurrence and experience vicariously the building excitement. An "Afterword" carries the story forward, with broad strokes, to October 3, 1990, the day when the two German states legally became one, and the United States Embassy to the GDR ended its existence. It rounds off the tale and suggests some interpretations, but makes no pretense at being comprehensive. The unification process during those final eleven months of the GDR requires detailed study from a wider perspective than my East Berlin address afforded me.

This is a reconstructed diary, and it is fair to ask whether the adjective calls its honesty into question. I had neither wit nor time to maintain a proper account during the period in question. I pieced together what follows from multiple sources, the most important of which was my own memory and Gaby's, but also contemporary notes and other written records, virtually all of which, however, I did draft at the time. In several instances, I refreshed my memory by consulting participants in the events described.

The product is meant to be a contribution to history that has implications for the future but concentrates on how matters looked at the moment from my vantage point on the ground in East Berlin. Some passages in the early chapters may seem irrelevant to the main theme of the drama, but they too are a part of the history, if only as illustration of how implausible early German unification seemed, even as its precursor events were upon us. Correspondingly little will be said about topics the locus of which was elsewhere, such as the calculations behind West German policy that fall and winter, or the Two-Plus-Four negotiation during the first half of 1990.

I have scrupulously tried to prevent knowledge-after-the-fact from creeping in, except where explicitly indicated in the Afterword, and I believe I have avoided making at least myself appear wiser than I was. I joked frequently with the journalists who shared the excitement of that time in Berlin. Reporters were less fortunate than diplomats, I said. They put their perceptions on the line for the public every day. We could classify our dispatches, so that only historians thirty years hence would know how often we followed false trails. This book is a way to make some advance adjustment of the balance with the Fourth Estate. Indeed, some readers may feel that its most interesting revelation is the simple one of how often a close and professional observer was surprised by what happened that summer and fall in Germany.

Obviously, though necessary to say, the views expressed are my own and do not necessarily reflect those of the Department of State. If a hero appears in its pages, however, I would hope it is the American Embassy Berlin—not any single member, but the entity, or rather the people of whom it was composed. I will be pleased if the public acquires more appreciation both for what the modern diplomat does, in the eye of the hurricane when no one can be sure in which direction the winds of history will blow next, and for the fellow citizens who make up the United States Foreign Service.

I mention many by name, but inevitably mainly those with whom I worked most closely, Ambassador Richard ("Dick") Barkley, his deputy ("DCM" in Foreign Service jargon) "J.D." Bindenagel, and my colleagues in the Political Section. When the crisis hit, however, the full embassy pulled together, working nearly round-the-clock seven days a week. It was, for me, an inspiring insight into human nature to see how diverse individuals will put aside personal preoccupations and the small frictions that are inevitably part of any institution and work unstintingly, even heroically, for the common good.

Few villains are described here. Undoubtedly they were in the background, where the Secret Police (Stasi) worked, but when we met their representatives they were on best behavior. Press and politicians regularly depict the infamous Stasi as evil incarnate, a tabloid metaphor that simplifies and demonizes the GDR even as it allows millions to avoid examining their own consciences and facilitates disavowal and disposal of a forty-year heritage. It is as much a mistake to treat the Stasi as synonymous with all that was lived in East Germany between 1949 and 1989, as it is to believe the Stasi was composed only of single-minded thugs.

In the GDR, as elsewhere in Eastern Europe, representatives of the secret police / intelligence service were among diplomats' best sources of information because they were often among the more sophisticated, self-confident, and therefore expansive of those with whom we talked. They operated under "cover," of course, so that one was not normally certain who reported to the Stasi. The prudent assumption, borne out by subsequent revelations, was that anyone might, and I sought the widest possible contacts in East German society in part at least to balance the spin that official interlocutors imparted. That an individual might be a Stasi informer or even officer did not necessarily devalue his commentary or increasingly frank remarks on the crisis engulfing the GDR. Nor could the latter mitigate the malignant impact his true employer did indeed have on the state and society it was meant to protect.

The political leadership, especially Honecker and his Politburo, will appear more as fools than knaves—mostly old and sick men who had long since lost their ideals and sense of reality in the pursuit and protection of power. They lacked the energy, intellect, and character to realize they stood on the lip of a volcano and to attempt remedial action, but for the most part—at least late in the 1980s—they were not conscious evildoers.

The great mass of East Germans—and in this I include most Party members, including many in high government and cultural positions—were neither heroes nor knaves nor fools. They were average people trying to make the best of a bad situation that they had come to believe could be improved in the Gorbachev era, and they were increasingly frustrated by the rigidity and lack of comprehension at the very top. Virtually none realized how late the hour was. They share responsibility, of course, for matters going on as long as they did while pressure in the pot rose: would-be establishment reformers bided time timidly, preferring to believe that Gorbachev or a biological solution would give them their chance soon enough without personal risk; the man in the street ignored the handful of youthful activists, leaving them isolated with only a few church walls for protection, and then turning away from them again with startling rapidity after the revolution was assured.

It is not popular to speak well of East Germans these days—and certainly not in Germany, where they are too often viewed as mendicants asking for costly handouts that could put a second holiday or car at risk for a Western taxpayer. They are seen as either maintainers or victims of a failed system who can contribute to the common weal only after they have been purged of whatever traces of socialist principles and habits they retain. Unification is unlikely to be a true partnership for at least a generation, and all too many Germans east of the old borders are suffering, not physically and rarely financially but psychologically, at the overnight loss of almost everything that was familiar and at being told they bring nothing but their poor selves to the new Germany.

How wise a formula that is for unification is not for an American to say, but those East Germans will also not appear in these pages. Readers will find, instead, people like themselves, no better and no worse, with one exception: They are the only Germans who made a great democratic and peaceful revolution, who came out of themselves and rose above themselves for one remarkable moment that changed all our lives. It was they who did it, not the Germans in the West, or the Russians or the Poles or the Americans or anyone else. No one predicted it, and it was difficult at the time to know quite how ephemeral it would be. But perhaps the reminder can help them and their well-wishers draw a fairer balance and more reliable guide for the future.

Washington, D.C., Summer 1992

1
The Deceptive Calm
May and June 1989

MAY 1

There was noticeably less tension this May Day, our second in East Berlin. Of course, there was still heavy security for the parade. A year ago, however, it was the first big public event since dissidents had touched off a month of arrests and church-supported protest by breaking into a Party demonstration. A nervous regime sealed off the route so that marchers filed between rows of Stasi. Today, bystanders could be sucked into the line of march inadvertently, as Gaby and I nearly were when we went down a side street to find a better view.

Gaby came for the first time, and we rode the subway to avoid the parking crush and observe people. Families with small children predominated, the latter with genuine anticipation of a parade and street carnival. The marchers were relaxed about a familiar routine, the fortunate ones those with low assembly numbers so they could pass the Politburo stand on Karl-Marx-Allee quickly. Once in Alexanderplatz, their obligations were over and the holiday began.

It is, for me at least, a thrill when the chimes signal the start of the parade. The old anthem, the "Internationale," recalls what it once meant for German workers to dare to assemble. That thrill dissipates with the hackneyed introduction by the alcoholic union boss, Harry Tisch, the sameness of marchers and mass-produced banners with ordained slogans, and the overwhelming sense of preplanned and practiced order. Everyone knows when to turn to Honecker and smile for the cameras. Except in the children, who enjoy the color, and the old people with memories of when carrying a red banner on this day could mean jail or worse, emotion, much less spontaneity, is absent.

After an hour, we peeled off to the street parties. Those, both the great one on Alexanderplatz in Berlin's heart and the smaller ones in each district, are nearly as perfectly planned, down to the booths selling clothes, books, or garden implements that are often hard to find in shops. But the dominant impression is of ordinary people having simple and cheap fun. Families buy the 85-pfennig (ten-cent) bockwurst and the local Margon Cola, children plead to try one more ride, oblivious that most seem to come from a 1950s amusement park, men drink too much beer and schnapps. We left while technicians were adjusting the sound system for the open-air concert, but young people stayed well into the evening. Their music is indistinguishable from the Western variety. Indeed, if the holidays here are consciously proletarian and most lifestyles are lowish middle-class consumerism, GDR pop culture is, younger colleagues assure me, mainstream: loud, hedonistic, and rebellious. The system accepts the contrast—probably by now without much inner resistance—to keep social peace. Honecker even curries popularity by exchanging gag gifts with a West German rock idol.

MAY 2

The first half of *Neues Deutschland,* the SED daily, was devoted to May Day: "Four-and-a-half-hour march of more than 700,000 Berliners, a demonstration of socialism's life force." It was identical to the 1988 issue, down to photo angles, participation estimates, and text. It will take a better "Kremlinologist" than I to spot variances in such reporting, but then that is the Party's message: There is no change. The Honecker system has celebrated another May Day with every intention of demonstrating its staying power.

Portraits of Walter Ulbricht, the SED's first leader, whom Honecker pushed aside in 1971, intrigued the Western media and diplomatic colleagues, however. Ulbricht's reappearance, the theory is, means the regime is not only digging in against Soviet-style reform but also signaling willingness to return to Stalinist repression. That goes too far. There were only a few Ulbricht portraits, about as many as of Gorbachev, and both were less numerous than those of the German socialist saints: Marx and Engels, the founders, and Luxemburg and Liebknecht, the martyrs. Ulbricht appears now with greater frequency in newspaper and academic articles, but that is consistent with the gradual introduction of a more balanced history. More is also being written about Frederick the Great, conservative July 20 anti-Hitler conspirators, and even Bismarck. If anything, the Gorbachev-Ulbricht ratio seeks to portray the GDR not as reactionary but as self-assured. The Soviet matters, but no more than figures from the GDR's past, as befits the mature, relatively successful socialism Honecker says this country will maintain without need to copy Moscow any longer.

And things do seem to be going reasonably well for Honecker. The press reported his invitation to Magnitogorsk, the Soviet "steel city," which he helped build as a youth. He may have pulled strings, but Gorbachev must now receive him. He will thus demonstrate that, despite Gorbachev's visit to Bonn next month, the GDR's ties to its protector are in order. The SED leadership will also take satisfaction that Ernst Albrecht, minister-president of Lower Saxony, has been in town. He was about the last senior West German to pay court to Honecker, something he had refused to do for years. As long as Gorbachev and West German politicians need Honecker as much as he requires their security and financial assistance, the old man can pretty well choose his course. All signs indicate it will be a steady one.

In early afternoon, I drove with Ambassador Barkley to Magdeburg, where the district chief, Werner Eberlein, will be his first leadership call outside Berlin since coming to the post in December. On the way, we agreed there were few signs of impending reform, but we both sense more diversity in the SED than *Neues Deutschland* admits. I spoke of a new book that Party intellectuals sympathetic to Gorbachev tipped me to: *Der Erste* (Number One), about an SED county chief. It includes topics normally ignored here, and some see it as a touch of Glasnost. I told Dick that on holiday next week I would read the copy I was lucky enough to buy before the shop sold out, and then try to go to Bad Salzungen in the far south to interview the characters.

After a tour of the cathedral, the oldest Gothic structure on German soil, we called on Mayor Herzig, in office twenty-four years, who smiled archly and claimed uncertainty about whether he would win Sunday's election. He should, he implied, because everything was going quite well, thank you. In the evening, we saw a spirited one-woman play, "Lola Blau," the story of a Jewish girl forced into exile by the Nazis. A success on Broadway and in Las Vegas, she is set back by drugs and rootlessness and returns after the war to pick up life in Vienna. The director was flattered that the American Ambassador came. We were impressed at the quality of provincial theater.

MAY 3

Frank Meehan, who had been ambassador in martial law Poland and Prague and knew Moscow well, called Werner Eberlein the toughest Communist he ever met. Once he told Eberlein he regretted never visiting Siberia. Eberlein, whose father had been high in the German Communist Party until Stalin murdered him in the 1930s, gave him a piercing stare and replied dismissively, "You would not have understood." "Hard as steel" was Meehan's characterization. Eberlein has too many Soviet ties, and too much respect within the SED, to be discarded, but he is probably too unbending to get along with Honecker, who likes compliant consensus and fancies himself a modern man of détente. His posting to Magdeburg after making the Politburo is exile from the real power in Berlin.

That was my briefing, but after ninety minutes Dick emerged shaking his head and saying, "You know, I rather liked the old scoundrel." So did I. Physically imposing, well over six feet (another reason why the small Honecker finds him awkward to have around?), Eberlein was by turns jovial and combative. He made a mock complaint that the conversation strayed far from Magdeburg, but he relished the chance to talk larger issues. Of course, Honecker did not mean the same thing Gorbachev did when he praised Perestroika, Eberlein said, but there had always been more Berlin-Moscow disagreements than the West acknowledged, and they were not more serious now.

The economic problem, Eberlein claimed, was that the GDR now had to deal directly with 150 Soviet enterprises instead of ten familiar ministries.

This was manageable, and self-financing for its large trusts (*Kombinate*) would soon be the rule. For Eberlein, however, philosophical dispute was more significant. He avoided criticizing Gorbachev, but Shevardnadze—guilty of sweeping and subjective rhetoric that encouraged people to give personal desires priority over the common good—was fair game.

The old lion's curious mix of materialism and idealism was most apparent when he discussed nationalism in the Communist world, something for which he had no sympathy. What would Georgia or the Baltic States be without the Soviet Union? he asked. He had passed through Estonia when the family fled Hitler, and it was "a piteous land, barely able to grow potatoes." Whatever republics had, they owed to communism and to union with Moscow. Tbilisi's demonstrations in April, when the army opened fire to restore order, and those now in Beijing, Eberlein insisted, were little different from periodic riots in West Berlin. What, after all, did Chinese students want? "Not democracy, but doubled scholarships and VCRs" was his scornful answer. Unfortunately, East Germans were also materialistic and would prefer a Mercedes or BMW to a Trabant. Who would not? he admitted, but other values must be considered.

Eberlein professed shock at the homeless in the streets of West Germany. East Germans did not realize how demeaning it was to live on a dole, and in the West two million were without jobs, he said. The GDR could offer consumers more if it listened to experts. It made economic sense to slash rent, food, and other subsidies, but to return to a have/have not society "would offend my socialist morality."

On local issues, Eberlein was equally unwilling to accept the reformers' value system. Magdeburg has troubles, especially Elbe River pollution, he conceded. "We need to do more, and we will, but we know the problems, and shouting about them would only stir people up and worry them." Siegfried Grünwald, age fifty and the head of the government apparatus, later discussed new pollution standards more pragmatically. Like many younger officials, he appears technically competent and intellectually prepared to conduct a more active problem-solving policy if the Politburo sets a new course.

But can it? It is not that an Eberlein cannot see the contradictions between rhetoric and reality, or that he lacks wit to recognize that many East Germans have other priorities. Rather, he fails to understand the motivation of youths who want democracy, of minorities who treasure uniqueness, or of citizens who call for debate. They, in turn, are ignorant of the crucible that formed him: the Weimar Republic's struggles, Hitler's persecution, Stalin, Siberia, the early cold war, and an optic that focuses idealism through a rigid ideological and materialistic prism. Eberlein offers little hope that the Honecker team, of which he is a committed if idiosyncratic member, will drop its self-satisfied opposition to reform, but at least he is the real article, a Communist with convictions. In a state where most people, certainly most Party members, go with the flow, that gives him a certain nobility.

As we checked out of the hotel, I purchased a copy of *Népszabadság*, the Hungarian Party daily that was regular reading when we were posted to Budapest. Even five years ago, the paper's relative objectivity put it in a different league from the East German media, which is perhaps the most criticized element of the Honecker system. Its lead story—Hungary has cut the barbed wire along the border to Austria—was ignored by *Neues Deutschland*. The action is mainly symbolic. Hungarians have traveled unhindered except by currency shortages for years. My Hungarian Embassy contact insists the reform Communist government will honor Warsaw Pact commitments to permit only East Germans with GDR exit stamps to cross. Still, free travel symbolism is something *Neues Deutschland* has no interest in reporting, even though East Germans will get the story from West German television or radio. If there is logic in this, it is that East Germans look to their own news outlets—to the extent that they heed them at all—only to learn the official line.

More interesting was an interview with writer and GDR dissenter Stefan Heym. A Hungarian rock opera version of his *King David Report*, a novel on the double-speak dishonesty of dictators and their publicists, had an East German premiere in Halberstadt, near Magdeburg. The regime made gestures toward Heym on his seventy-fifth birthday last year, and he told me his books may soon at last come out here. *Népszabadság* reports that GDR Radio also interviewed him—only on the opera, but still the first time in decades he could speak directly to his audience. I must ask him what it means.

MAY 5

Though the United States has had diplomatic relations here for fifteen years and there are military-to-military ties even with the Soviets, there has been no contact between U.S. and GDR armies. This reflects the American bureaucracy's distaste for the GDR. I urged an initiative last year but was shot down in Washington. Our Germanists cut their eye teeth in West Berlin in the Wall's early days and tend to be "purer" than the West Germans on the GDR. But after the Rand Corporation last fall found East German arms-control specialists worth cultivating if the United States was serious about encouraging Eastern Europe's most strategic state to think for itself, we got a green light to propose a low-key visit by students at our National Defense University (NDU). My deputy, Imre Lipping, sold the East Germans, who were at first as skeptical as Washington. The delegation is back from two days in Dresden and Leipzig and says it will support an embassy recommendation to do more next year. It is rare that we make any progress in encouraging interaction with this government, whose policies, like it or not, have considerable impact on vital American interests.

MAY 6

Posters herald tomorrow's election for thousands of local offices. GDR elections are cut from the classical Communist mode. There are no contested seats, only the single "List" of the National Front, a body that selects candidates and allocates positions to the parties and other groups like the FDJ, the youth organization. Its formula theoretically gives the SED only a plurality, but Party members predominate also in the caucuses of the FDJ, the trade unions (FDGB), and the Women's League. No one doubts where power really is. Tongue-in-cheek, Dick once remarked to Manfred Gerlach, the intelligent, cynical chairman of the Liberal Democrats (LDPD), that with the growing economic role of independent tradesmen and entrepreneurs, traditional supporters of that party, ratios should be readjusted to the Communists' detriment. "It will never happen," was the answer.

Still, I have searched the "campaign" for change, either in SED conduct or in popular response. New procedures to "further perfect our socialist democracy," which Egon Krenz, the Politburo boss supervising the elections, lauded, allowed a further handful of parochial and safe groups like gardeners and small-animal breeders to nominate National Front candidates. Meetings for voters to question proposed nominees were added to the scenario. Shortly after these "perfections" (never called reforms, lest that suggest the GDR required Perestroika) were announced, I called on officials in Cottbus, a city southeast of Berlin. Why not offer a choice, I asked, even if the National Front vetted all candidates, as the Soviet Union is now doing? "But we don't know whether the Soviet reform will work," was the surprisingly candid answer. I suspect it applies to more than electoral procedure.

Peter Pragal, an experienced West German reporter, witnessed a few lively sessions between citizens and candidates in the Saxon south, but most of my contacts dismiss the changes. Gunnar, a scientist at a prestigious Berlin hospital, could not even get a ballot to cast an absentee "no" vote. Helmut Domke, a Potsdam physicist and lay church leader, assured me the result would approximate the 99 percent approval/participation rates reported for every election in the GDR's forty-year history.

To see for myself, I applied to attend a campaign event. Gaby and I knew the advance notice would reduce spontaneity, but the Potsdam district to which we were invited was no showcase. The Am Stern suburb, a working-class area of ten-year-old high rises, has little outer charm, though I suspect the regime is proud of it as an example of tolerable, if hardly luxurious, living quarters and cultural facilities.

Herr Brust, the National Front man who was waiting at the door and invited us to dinner, and the SED chairman made sure the audience knew a diplomat was there. Our presence probably keyed several statements about system virtues, but more than a few residents did ask sharp, if narrow, questions: When will we get extension of the commuter line we have heard about for years, or when will the lake again be safe for swimming? One speaker criticized police for doing nothing to limit evening noise from this very restaurant, to prevent hooligan harassment of decent citizens, and to stop dog-walkers from allowing their charges to relieve themselves next to sidewalks. Potsdam, he said, needed cops who knew how to handle crime and nuisance, like the Americans. Genuine gripe, half-hidden expression of sympathy for the United States, or clever propaganda? Only one young man, who tried to talk about the environment, put his complaints in a broader context. The chairman brushed him off, but he stopped us later to explain he was a dissatisfied SED member attempting to publicize pollution scandals and urged us to stay in touch. Party reformer, genuine dissident, or Stasi plant?

It is hard to penetrate the propaganda and deception. The regime is sufficiently embarrassed to require an appearance of greater participation in the electoral process. The half-dozen candidates from in and near Berlin who were at the Press Club a few days ago were at pains to claim they faced newly rigorous environmental questioning. But I am skeptical that a democratic core is forming. The National Front deputy chairman assured me with straight face that East Germans had no need for the voting booths Gorbachev tells Soviet citizens to use to ensure secret elections. Nor does the media nourish my hope that the GDR is moving toward reform. "We vote May 7 for the National Front candidates," said the front page of *Neues Deutschland* yesterday. Ironically, Honecker will be judged tomorrow not by whether the List again gets virtually unanimous approval but by whether the results reflect a semblance of the unhappiness just below the surface. The SED can really win only if it acknowledges that many citizens will vote "no" or stay away from the polls.

MAY 7

The press message on Honecker's Prague visit was that whatever the world believes about the inevitability of reform in Eastern Europe, the GDR and Czechoslovakia will follow their own course. *Neues Deutschland* also ran statistics on "continuing dynamic growth in preparation for the Twelfth Party Congress." The numbers look good, as always, but Reno Harnish, our economic counselor, suspects they are cooked. The more Honecker and his guru, Günter Mittag, can make an idling if not stagnating economy look dynamic, the more easily they can withstand pressure for unproven Soviet reforms. Again, it is difficult to distinguish reality from manipulation.

I will visit polling stations before driving to Potsdam for coffee with a professor recommended by a Washington friend.

MAY 8

Neues Deutschland called it "an impressive attestation to our policy of peace and socialism" and said "98.5% voted for the candidates of the National Front." Those "facts" and pictures of a smiling Honecker and other Politburo members casting ballots in their golden Wandlitz ghetto ("Volvograd," in local wit, a double play on the leaders' favored cars and the Russian tie) suggest politics as usual. There are nuances, however. As monolithic as the results and 98.77 percent participation appear, they are below what has been reported in the past. "No" votes were five times more numerous than in any previous election, and participation was under 99 percent for the first time since 1981. Since pressures to support the National Front candidates are considerable, the independent activists who urged a "no" vote or boycott can take some heart even from reported tallies.

An affirmative ballot is the course of least resistance—more ritual than political judgment—and the results, even with marginal differences from years past, are redolent of classical Communist "democracy," which requires ratification, not participation. They do not reflect the diversity of views and interests in this society and can only mean that citizens did not engage in the process or that the apparatus actively rigged the tally. Honecker lost an opportunity and confirmed that the GDR is to the rear of those Eastern European states trying to establish a new kind of support base.

We shall ask activists whether fraud, not just apathy, played a part. They had positioned teams, especially in Berlin, to monitor returns. What my colleagues and I saw, however, suggests the National Front could have had a good result without wide-scale rigging. During several hours in a senior citizens home in Pankow, I saw no one use the booth. The voters, mostly pensioners with reason to feel beholden to the state for virtually free upkeep in a reasonably well-appointed facility, gave scarcely a glance to the ballot they picked up at a registration table and dropped in a box before going in to lunch. "J.D." Bindenagel, the ambassador's deputy (DCM), who visited other Pankow polling stations with his children, and junior officers who were downtown had similar experiences.

Our call on the Esches in Potsdam was pleasant. Annemarie is a professor at East Berlin's Humboldt University; her husband works for a Potsdam institute. Both are Asia specialists with a love for Burma. The conversation was cautious, especially when it circled back to politics, which is often the case here when both sides are feeling each other out. As always, the fact that Gaby is a Berliner helped break the ice. It is less language nuance and more that Gaby conveys the feeling that though she is from the West she is close enough to understand what does not go easily into speech. This encouraged the Esches to indicate to strangers their place within the establishment and critical distance from some of its policies.

As we ate cake and considered whether diplomatic freedom from highway police checks would allow us to take brandies, the doorbell one flight up rang. They are trying to persuade the old lady to vote, the Esches said, laughing. It is not as bad as in the old days, when refusal was a serious matter, they said, but if someone does not appear by early afternoon an effort is still made to get the missing ballot. Those who do not vote can expect a black mark in their personnel files, but probably no direct consequences.

MAY 9

At our weekly country team meeting, Dick asked me to assess political developments. There was an important story, I said, which indicated breakdown of the old order, major change in the relationship between Berlin and the provinces, perhaps even regime concessions to the demand for reform. No, I assured disbelieving colleagues, not the election, but soccer, where Dynamo Dresden has ended Dynamo Berlin's nine-year title reign. The latter is the toy of Erich Mielke, the widely detested and, of course, feared octogenarian Stasi boss. Its dominance is widely believed to have stemmed from referee decisions and player transfers inspired by Mielke's reputation for offering deals that cannot be refused. But how to explain that Berlin has also fallen behind Rostock? There are two theories. Perhaps Mielke, with his notorious sources of information, made a concession to the popular will and instigated his club's downfall to further domestic tranquillity. Or perhaps the changing of the guard is a sign that the old political order is losing its grip. After all, the Dresden Party chief is Hans Modrow, the hope for SED reform, a man rumored to have excellent credentials with Moscow.

Alfred Ironside, a junior officer, recounted to me today a remarkable evening at the GDR Section of the PEN Club. The featured speaker was Jurek Becker, a good writer victimized by the crackdown that decimated the country's cultural elite in the late 1970s. Becker lives in the West, retaining a GDR passport out of conviction, and was appearing in East Berlin for the first time in a decade. He called Sunday's election "an embarrassment," but his theme was censorship, a bulwark of dictatorship that, he said, writers should take the initiative to destroy. Christoph Hein and others broached this at the Writers Conference last fall, but an open debate was new. Before he walked out, Jürgen Rennert, a regime poet, said he was "hurt and insulted." An elderly lady said she had lived under communism since 1933 and saw no reason to be discouraged. An example of change, she claimed, was that a Volker Braun novel available only in the West for fifteen years was getting a GDR edition. That, Becker retorted, was "like trying to revive a corpse." His supporters went further: "Nothing is changing. We'll be waiting until 2000 for reforms." The division was mostly generational, Alfred said. One exception was Stefan Heym, who told the writers the only reason the state rarely had to censor a book itself these days was "the scissors in your heads."

The chairman adjourned "our version of an American talk show" without putting a resolution to a vote, but the evening was proof of growing willingness among intellectuals to raise controversial topics and label Honecker out of touch with the Gorbachev era. A few years ago, that would have brought Stasi intervention and at least severe professional punishment. Now there are few sanctions, at least for those with reputations. Clever regime tactic to deflect criticism, indication of leadership division, or first sign of the Glasnost that precedes Perestroika?

I had an appointment today with Heym, the Jew who found refuge from Hitler in the United States, became a citizen, landed in Normandy on D-Day, and wrote best-sellers in English before returning his battlefield commission to President Truman and fleeing to Socialist Germany fearful that Joe McCarthy was creating an American Fascism. When I came to know East Berlin fifteen years ago, its broad avenues easily accommodated the few cars. Today a rush-hour traffic jam made me late at the comfortable house in the rural Grünau District, not far from a section of the river used in 1936 for Olympic rowing. The GDR has become a motorized society, but its cars are unhealthy, unsafe stinkpots—the infamous, plastic Trabies and Wartburgs for which buyers wait a decade but which even Eberlein admits are unsatisfying. Once they are in them, their mobility is restricted by the Wall. Part of the journey to Heym's house is along a section almost like a factory fence, except for signs and watchtowers that make clear this is a "Forbidden Area."

I found Heym writing with his computer. He is being partly rehabilitated, he said. His novel of the 1953 East German revolt, *Five Days in June*, will appear, two decades late, in a surprisingly large edition of 30,000. One or two of his other banned books should also be published this year, but not *Collin*, the reckoning with the secret police he wrote in the 1970s, or *Obituary*, the memoirs that are a top seller in West Germany. "I sent *Obituary* to Honecker with a polite note," he said, smiling, "but he has not answered." Heym was surprised we knew about the PEN Club evening, and moderately encouraged that cultural life is opening up, but he cautioned us not to overvalue this. The regime regards the mass media as far more sensitive than elitist discussions or books that at most a few tens of thousands will read, he explained. There has been no change in press or television. The politicians, Heym judged, are still just trying to let off steam, not use Glasnost, as Gorbachev has, to prepare real reform. And exactly that, he emphasized, is what a frustrated citizenry is waiting for, if not yet demanding.

The elderly writer believes in a democratic socialism that, he argues, has never been tried in the GDR. His hope is that it will prove itself in Gorbachev's Russia, but he is bitterly scornful of Honecker, whom he charges has wasted the moral credit he earned as a Hitler opponent by embracing Stalinist structures and sacrificing idealism to careerism. Heym is vain, and some fellow writers who have not done as well in the delicate business of earning West Marks while living and criticizing in the East call him an opportunist. I admire him and others from his generation who have known the brutishness of two or three worlds and still hold the ideals of their youth. He is also a great writer, whose judgment on leadership rigidity is serious, and he has an undeniable charm. As I left, he picked a bouquet of garden wildflowers for Gaby.

MAY 10

The election story is not going away. The activists say they will go to court to prove that many more voted "no" or stayed home on Sunday than the government acknowledges. Their poll-watchers insist that official results contradict what was counted out in front of them, that negative votes in several Berlin districts reporting only 1 to 3 percent in opposition ran as high as 20 percent. That the count could be observed and that local officials passed on initially honest tallies suggests there are opportunities to use the GDR's desire to be known as a state of laws (a *Rechtsstaat*) to publicize the activists' cause. At some point, however, even though the activists themselves accept that, for whatever reason, the National List received handsome majorities, the SED is certain to block proceedings. To back down now would be interpreted less as liberalization than weakness. And, surrounded by the class enemy to the West and ideologically suspect Communists to the East, that is the last thing Honecker believes he can afford. The activists' best weapon remains West German television, which brings their arguments into virtually every East German home. Meanwhile, the Party has begun the drumbeat for the next unity demonstration, a mammoth *Pfingsttreffen* (Whitsun Meeting) that is to bring one million young people to Berlin this weekend.

Dick Cheney's comment on German unification is worrying "Americanists" in the GDR's think tanks. The U.S. defense secretary talked mostly about Gorbachev, but Sam Donaldson pressed him on whether the United States wants a united Germany. Cheney tried to pass on with the answer "We're not at the point yet where we can even talk about that," that self-determination would be possible only when the cold war ended and the Berlin Wall came down, but Donaldson persisted:

Q.: May I suggest it's extraordinary that you are not willing to say flatly that the eventual goal of our policy is the reunification of Germany?

CHENEY: Well, I think that a natural outcome if we're successful in our other efforts.

Q.: Well, a lot of people are scared about it—and I suppose—is that one of the reasons why you want to kind of duck a little on this?

CHENEY: No, I don't think people are scared about it at this point. . . . It is a kind of development that will occur perhaps many years down the road and would be the natural outgrowth of the activities, if we're successful in obtaining our objectives.

Of course, unification is taboo for the GDR, which frets that the Bush administration is signaling a desire to put the topic back on the East-West agenda. I doubt it. For reasons of history and geography, the United States has always been more relaxed than Europe about the German Question, but nothing in Cheney's remarks suggested we are abandoning the consensus that bringing the Continent back together requires living with the reality of two states for the foreseeable future. Still, in the fourth year of the Gorbachev era, so many verities are under attack that the GDR is nervous.

MAY 11

There is to be no recount. "To err is human" was *Neues Deutschland*'s headline, but its editorial accused West German reporters and GDR Protestant (Lutheran) church leaders of having tried and failed to solicit negative votes, and it warned the latter to preach God's word, not politics. Because the SED maintains an uneasy truce with the church, the tone was unusual.

MAY 12

Before Gaby and I left today on holiday, Imre predicted that the activists, whom he knows well from countless evenings in cold church basements, will not back down over the election. The support of Gottfried Forck, the Protestant bishop of Berlin-Brandenburg, is specially meaningful, he said. The church offers the country's only free space for debate, and it is divided about how far it should go in taking up causes directly or protecting the more radical groups that have secular interests. It often temporizes, but Bishop Forck has enlisted as a powerful ally. Forck is so respected that his quarrelsome constituency bent rules last year and drafted him to serve past mandatory retirement. Saintly he may be, Imre noted, but there is a stubborn, combative side to the tall, white-haired gentleman that recalls the U-Boot commander he was before he returned from a POW camp in the American South to enter the church. The bishop considers the state's treatment of young people who played by its rules to uncover fraud an affront and intends to keep protests both peaceful and active.

The election is another drop or three of poison, mistrust, and disillusionment laid down between state and citizens. While it is hard to see what even Forck's moral authority can achieve, I am curious about political fallout. For two years there have been signs that Honecker is no longer sure Krenz is the successor he wants, and the election embarrassment could change the odds in a contest with Günter Schabowski, the Berlin boss.

MAY 13

What a marvelous island Usedom is! The sea, white beaches, rocky cliffs, beech forest, farmland, and freshwater lakes are within easy walks or bicycle rides, and the sun shines until ten o'clock at night. One day I will get up early enough to bike to the cliffs and see the sun rise out of the Baltic, as Gaby does, but I never tire of watching it dip into the Achterwasser, the lake on which our cottage is situated. Other than the multihued sunset, there is nothing spectacular about the island or our rented bungalow. There is no nightlife—not even West German television, since Usedom is part of the 10 to 15 percent of the GDR that lies beyond the range of the transmitters, in the "Valleys of Ignorance." But the simplicity and harmony of life and landscape are a recipe for relaxation.

The outside world is not completely absent. *Neues Deutschland* printed János Kádár's letter accepting forced retirement—pathos mixed in it with the unaffected style that gave the Hungarian a certain popularity once the wounds of the 1956 revolution had superficially healed and before inflation ate away the base of Goulash Communism. His health was failing, Kádár wrote, and he was reflecting increasingly on his life and hoped future generations would "judge more objectively." He had made mistakes but, "Believe me, all I did was with good intentions." Kádár made better arrangements with the Soviet colossus than any other Eastern European chieftain, and he created zones of partial freedom in Hungary. An idealist and ultimate pragmatist, he did much evil, partly—I am sure he saw it—to avoid worse. His life mirrored half a continent's tragedy, and his gray compromises were probably the most his generation of Communists could achieve. Honecker never liked Kádár, whose style and policies were so different, though they occasionally made common cause—as in 1983, when both fought to keep their Western ties even as the Soviets were walking out of the Geneva arms talks. Ironically, Kádár has been more honored here as his standing fell in Budapest, after the motto "Better the familiar heretic." His farewell brings home poignantly that in Hungary a new chapter has begun, and it raises the question of how long Honecker, who is of the same generation, can hold back time.

MAY 14

The television was full of the *Pfingsttreffen*: smiling faces, enthusiastic commentaries, and marches past the leaders—everything to plan, including fireworks. Before we left Berlin, however, J.D. and I got a different perspective from Gerd Basler, a star at the Institute for International Politics and Economics (IPW), the Central Committee's think tank. Basler, who is candid about his ambition to make the Central Committee, hints that he differs with many SED policies. He was scathing about the gala. His own daughter and her friends, not to mention less-privileged teenagers, find little in the FDJ that speaks to their concerns, other than its rock concerts. Despite less-than-subtle persuasion, the organizers had difficulty getting even Party members to volunteer beds for out-of-town youths. At their dacha, Gerd and his wife sat out festivities they found grossly out of touch with GDR problems. The weekend's sole purpose, Gerd said, was to reassure old men that the world is as remembered from their youth. He was certain this irresponsibly expensive nostalgic fling will be the last of its kind.

MAY 18

West Berlin friends departed Tuesday, leaving us three days to explore. The first morning, we drove toward Peenemünde, where Wernher von Braun developed rockets for Hitler, but it is now an off-limits GDR air force base. We did find a Peenemünde history exhibit tucked in a corner of the museum in Wolgast, the small mainland port off the western tip of the island. That onetime border city (Usedom was Swedish until Napoleon) is typical of many GDR municipalities: redolent with history, slow-moving, gray, run-down architectural gems only sporadically restored or maintained, not quite overwhelmed by drab uniformity. Gaby bought a poster depicting its seventeenth-century doors, but we were otherwise depressed at the cultural riches nearly lost to poverty, neglect, and decay.

The next day, guided by Gunnar's father, a retired professor, we traced the mainland to Greifswald, the venerable university city, and Stralsund, a Hanseatic port. The former has a special place in GDR history. A Wehrmacht colonel surrendered it intact to the Soviets in 1945, thereby becoming a hero whose autobiography preaching the responsibility of anti-Fascists to build a better Germany is always in print. A few years ago, his widow complained her husband had not saved the city from being destroyed by war for it to collapse from neglect. Embarrassed, Honecker freed Greifswald from the requirement to contribute construction personnel and material to Berlin. Since then, a start has been made at repairing forty years' rot, but Greifswald remains a symbol of the scandal the activist pastor Friedrich Schorlemmer called "Ruinen schaffen, ohne Waffen" (creating ruins without weapons). It lived off capital so long without investing even in maintenance that much is past saving. Near the marketplace, a few houses have been restored; workers were mending several, and as we watched with horrified fascination, mechanical claws pulled down others, each hundreds of years old. Some of the activity has a special purpose. Honecker will attend the cathedral rededication next month; Greifswald, like every city to which he travels, must present a clean and cheerful face.

Stralsund was more of the same. The medieval city center is protected as a national treasure, but there are funds only to hold back time's worst ravages. Citizens willing to invest work and money, however, can acquire some of the old houses. A friend of the professor's is restoring the city archives, aided by money from Berthold Beitz of the West German firm Krupp, a native with an honorary doctorate from Greifswald. "You must realize," said the professor, "our economy is a disaster."

MAY 19

We drove leisurely back to Berlin, detouring through the forests of the Schorfheide and skirting a lake on which Honecker has a hunting lodge where he received Helmut Schmidt the week martial law was declared in Poland. Schmidt was criticized, but that meeting was a milestone, a signal that both Germanies wanted to insulate intensifying bilateral ties from a cold war in which each remained a superpower's strongest ally. Schmidt's fidelity was reciprocated when Honecker persevered despite the East-West recriminations of the mid-1980s. Now the relationship is an ever more important element of the European constellation. Its exact contours are kept to the Germans themselves, and its implications vaguely trouble neighbors in a manner that cuts across alliances.

On this sunny day, our preoccupation was with the surrounding beauty. Unconscionably polluted as the GDR is, there remain broad swathes of unspoiled countryside, especially in the north. Compared with thickly populated West Germany, the GDR is half empty. Narrow, tree-lined roads the West would have long since converted into six-lane highways connect villages that recall a simpler, prewar Germany. It makes West Germans nostalgic for their youth, and East Germans sensitive they are props in an open-air museum.

During our holiday, demonstrations in China's cities overshadowed Gorbachev's journey to end the thirty-year feud between the Communist world's giants, and one of East Germany's best friends, Mengistu of Ethiopia, hurried home from Berlin to face a bloody coup. For Honecker, these must be further unsettling signs of how volatile the world around his little island has become.

I returned a day early for the opening of an unusual conference. The Aspen Institute in West Berlin and the Academy of Social Sciences, the SED's cadre training school, are jointly hosting a session on the GDR in the 1990s. The first two days are at Aspen's villa on Schwanenwerder Island near where the Nazi Wannsee Conference planned the Holocaust. The final day will be in East Berlin.

MAY 21

J.D. and I are the "official" American representatives at Aspen, but most participants are Germans, East and West, who ignore foreigners and engage one another in a fascinating mixture of polemic and mutual understanding. Gaby was charmed by her partner at the opening dinner, Heinz Koziolek, a Central Committee member and a talkative old-style Berliner. The next day, however, he was hard-pressed to defend his rosy sketch of a GDR economy poised to make course adjustments without wrenching structural reforms.

The most intriguing presentation was by Rolf Reissig, the SED Academy's rector for Marx-Lenin studies. Like the others, it was based on staff papers prepared for next year's Party Congress, but his thesis was that unless the GDR makes a quantum advance in "socialist democracy," it will not meet the economic challenge. A command society would fail to stimulate initiative, and the GDR would lag ever further behind the West. Reissig was treated gently by Westerners, who recognized his paper was prescription not puffery. It was either a sign that things really are beginning to move, or an act of courage. I respect Reissig, whom I first sought out in 1987 as he became prominent in meetings with the West German Social Democrats (SPD). "You must find our GDR boring, like a Communist Switzerland," he apologized to me then, as his body language signaled that he wanted Gorbachev-style reforms. At lunch on Saturday, he said the May 7 elections would be the last of their kind. "Can you imagine a choice of candidates" when the Parliament is elected in 1991? I asked. "Of course," was his answer. "Could the other parties run against the SED?" I probed. "Why not?" he replied.

Reissig's protector, Otto Reinhold, orchestrated the proceedings, however. The academy's director, Reinhold is a powerful man: a Central Committee member who could be in the Politburo soon. He is a prominent public defender of economy-distorting subsidies, but he hinted at a serious internal debate and some modifications. Reinhold returned repeatedly to the argument that East and West have a common interest in ensuring that GDR change is evolutionary, not revolutionary. "Imagine how terrible it would be to have a Tbilisi in Rostock," he said repeatedly. Was he only reworking the old propaganda saw about the sensitive inner-German border, or does he genuinely fear street demonstrations here, and as bloody a response from Honecker as Soviet Georgia experienced from the Red Army this spring? Violent scenarios preoccupied the East Germans during coffee breaks. If force is used to resolve the Chinese confrontation, they agreed, the consequences are incalculable.

First appearances often mislead. Erich Hahn, the academy's philosopher, was the most polemical in formal sessions. During one interlude, I found him staring dreamily out the large picture window at the Wannsee. "I was born and went to school near here, and I have not seen the lake for nearly thirty years," explained this member of the privileged East German elite. How hard it is for an American to appreciate the complexities of the German division.

The sharpest Western questions came from the Green Party man. He knows reality here from young friends, not from theory or negotiation, and his human-rights criticisms were case-specific. It was a good illustration of why Honecker makes deals with the "respectable" Bonn political spectrum but blacklists most Greens.

MAY 22

On Sunday evening, Reinhold took over the second half of the seminar, beginning with an informal dinner in the Nikolaiviertel, the recreated slice of old Berlin between the Spree River and Alexanderplatz that is a new tourist attraction. A full day in East Berlin followed. Monday's lunch featured Gerald Götting, who has run the most important Bloc Party—the Christian Democratic Union (CDU)—almost from the GDR's beginning. Bloc Party chairmen must be reliable from the Communists' point of view, of course, but otherwise they differ considerably. Dick Barkley finds Gerlach (the "Liberal") perceptive, if cynical, and Homann, the eighty-year-old "nationalist" whose NDPD was originally formed to facilitate the integration of Wehrmacht officers and minor Nazis, a lively anachronism. Götting, however, is a first-order hypocrite in his protestations of Christian values, a smarmy Uriah Heep. Sensing the poor impression Götting made, Reinhold claimed the CDU had moderated SED policy—for example, by saving a lively if small private service sector. When Götting called this month's elections a triumph of democracy, I abandoned the role of careful, neutral observer more than is my custom, but I am less proud of what occurred when we piled into cars afterward. I commented unflatteringly on Götting without noticing that Heinrich Fink, dean of the university theological faculty and a CDU member, was behind me. Fink is no Götting admirer, but I should not have embarrassed him. He kept a more diplomatic silence than I.

We were on our way to a lively session with Hans Reichelt, environment minister for seventeen years and number two in the Peasants Party, another SED ally. Neither credential suggests a man in tune with a greening process that may be further advanced among citizens here than in West Germany, if only because the problems are so massive. Reichelt surely sees his task mainly as deflecting anger about growth-at-any-cost policy, but he appeared on top of his subject in informal give-and-take. I posed a case from my vacation reading. Questioned whether to build first a new factory or a system to reduce poisonous waste discharges into the Werra River, Bad Salzungen's SED secretary answered: the factory will create the wealth so we can afford the filter. Is the environment still thought to be a luxury? I asked. Reichelt was taken aback. That attitude had been widespread until recently, he admitted, but things were changing. No factory would be built today without a cleaning pool, he claimed, and if the either-or question were put, his ministry would fight for a different answer.

Many citizens are doubtful. The GDR has only begun to publish a few statistics and otherwise show awareness of environmental sensitivities. There is little evidence of new priorities, activists say. Still, our Environmental Protection Agency told us this year that a young East German lawyer sent by Reichelt's ministry was the best foreign trainee it had ever hosted—bright, dedicated, competent. Janice Weiner, one of my junior officers, knows her and says there are more like her, in and out of public life. Janice is working on proposals to expand environmental cooperation. It is the only area where bilateral prospects are encouraging. Reichelt was upbeat, and Washington's mind is open.

MAY 23

General Jaruzelski is in Berlin to sign a treaty resolving a Baltic Sea border dispute. Honecker was willing to compromise several years ago, but negotiations were turned over to the unimaginative Foreign Minister Oskar Fischer. Only desire to deprive Lech Walesa's Solidarity of an issue before the Polish election produced a sense of urgency, we hear. The gesture to Jaruzelski, like the respect shown Kádár, stems from the realization that allies once suspect for flexibility, if not weakness, are the best the GDR can get as Eastern Europe grows increasingly unstable. When Jaruzelski told Honecker power had to be shared with Walesa, Polish Embassy contacts say, the East German responded that only the Polish Party could decide the outlines of its socialism, just as no outsider could preempt his own responsibility. Honecker made the best of it, but the chat could not be more than a duty-directed respite from problems with which neither chieftain can much help the other.

MAY 24

The West German Ständige Vertretung (Permanent Mission) held its massive National Day reception yesterday. There was a smattering of high officials at a level calculated by the GDR to indicate a good working relationship with an important capitalist power. The real story, however, as always, was the semi-official and private attendance. The Ständige Vertretung—an embassy in all except name, and Bonn's legal point that two German states cannot have "foreign" relations—is the most important Western diplomatic establishment here, with contacts unparalleled except perhaps by the Soviets. As sanctions against West contacts diminish, East Germans flock to it to share culture, to get a whiff of a largely forbidden world and sometimes a helping hand to visit, or to protest their own state's policies, perhaps its very existence. The Stasi watch with special care, but, particularly on this day, the unpretentious office building in the Hannoversche Strasse, blocks removed from Unter den Linden, was the place to be.

Later that evening, at dinner in his apartment with a panoramic view of the Brandenburg Gate, my Hungarian contact denied rumors the GDR would abrogate the bilateral tourist agreement. More East Germans would holiday in his country than ever, he said, and Hungary would meet its Warsaw Pact commitments. Discreet controls would be exercised well back of the "open" border, he implied. The Hungarians want to stay everyone's friend. They made a strong play for Western support by publicizing the border opening, even giving President Bush a swatch of barbed wire, but they do not want to forfeit links with the GDR, a major trade partner. The GDR does not publicize the inconsistency. Hungary is one of few accessible vacation locations for East Germans, and talking about what happens near the border would be counterproductive. But how long can Budapest maintain the balancing act?

MAY 25

Before I went to the Baltic, I asked Heather Troutman, one of my junior officers, to coordinate the young officers so we could cover a cross section of *Pfingsttreffen* events, including the rock concerts, seminars, and discussion groups. Almost everything was open—no FDJ cards asked for—so the team sampled activity that never made the media. One went to a discussion of computer freaks. Heather, a fan, met rock idols and the director of a film that is an underground legend. *Whispering and Shouting*, pulled quickly from first-run theaters last year, documents the rock-band phenomenon that exists here at the edge of youthful protest. After a showing at the festival, the director and such singers as Tamara Danz held a lively session with fans for whom the music is a metaphor for a freedom and variety they miss in daily life.

At that gathering and others with more overtly political themes, young people were critical, and panelists, often youngish representatives from Party and government institutes, were surprisingly undogmatic. To attract youth to Berlin to profess loyalty, the FDJ had to offer more than its usual thin gruel of shows and agitprop. The organization is virtually moribund, a bloated bureaucracy existing to recruit SED cadres and provide career paths for the ambitious. But its *Pfingsttreffen* gave a further sign that this society is ready for change. Both young people and the brightest of the middle generation are deeply dissatisfied, fascinated by what they know of the West and Gorbachev's reforms.

MAY 26

The GDR will celebrate its own 40th Anniversary in October, but the press has been at pains this week to discount West Germany's jubilee. The transparent objective, to preempt German nationalism and create room for GDR patriotism to develop, leads to anomalies. Poland's election, with prospect of a Solidarity victory, has been a nontopic, but a few days ago *Neues Deutschland* ran a lengthy Warsaw press analysis, apparently because it offered the judgment that Germans East and West feel increasingly foreign to each other. A more effective economy does give Bonn more "legitimacy," conceded *Rzeczpospolita*, but "GDR watchers have the impression that also in the GDR, state awareness has begun to build." That, of course, is the great question.

Will President Bush visit the GDR? It seems farfetched, but his response to a West German interviewer has started speculation. Would he be interested? he was asked. "Yes," was the short answer, hedged by a restatement of need for more forthcoming policies from Honecker. The Foreign Ministry spokesman commented only that the remarks had been noted with interest, but Norbert Reemer, head of the U.S. Desk, told us he was busy all day coordinating that sentence. Several contacts recall that George Bush, as U.S. Ambassador to the United Nations, was the first American official to deal with the GDR. They surmise that his well-known propensity for diplomacy includes a special interest in the GDR. It sounds like wishful thinking, but our diplomatic colleagues will find it hard to believe we have no hidden agenda, especially since Mitterrand and the British foreign minister are expected here soon. The GDR's intense desire for prestige does suggest to me that if we were willing to negotiate we might extract a considerable price for a visit.

But relations are more than the plans of heads of state. I was called to the Foreign Ministry on "a matter of urgency." Werner Siegler, Reemer's deputy, told me the GDR had learned of the return of John Runnings, a septuagenarian who in 1987 mounted a personal crusade against the Wall that included running, dancing, and urinating on it, and eventually taking a hammer to it. The East Germans pushed him back to West Berlin several times before jailing him. Wolfgang Vogel, the GDR lawyer prominent in spy exchanges and delicate inner-German business, arranged a release, with the understanding he would return to Seattle. Well, said Siegler, he was back and building a battering ram. The ministry expected us to ensure there would be no provocations against "the most sensitive border in Europe." I made appropriate noises about peaceful protest and distaste for the Wall but had trouble keeping a straight face. To his credit, so did Siegler, whose preference would be to ask about the Redskins.

MAY 27

Honecker met two days ago with the Chairman of the West German Social Democrats, Hans-Joachim Vogel. Communist ties with the SPD are even more burdened by history than the ties with the Christian Democrats. Cooperation with the conservative ideological enemy has always been easier than with the half brother whose roots and natural constituency are similar. Nevertheless, Former Chancellor Willy Brandt and his idea man, Egon Bahr, resumed those links when they began *Ostpolitik* twenty years ago. They were developed further after 1982, when an SPD in opposition needed its own policy profile, and the SED sought to drive wedges into the West German consensus on NATO. Such Party-to-Party contacts, as well as the government contacts, of course, also served Bonn's fundamental purpose of insulating the inner-German relationship from cold war shocks. In the process, they helped people in need and ensured that human ties at the bedrock of common nationhood would survive the passing of the generations with direct knowledge of a single Germany.

The most daring step was the 1987 "Principles of Ideological Dispute," a document for which Reinhold and Reissig were the primary East German drafters. Both parties took risks: the SPD that it would be denounced as naive or worse, the SED that its signature to a paper acknowledging need for reform would increase pressure for Glasnost and Perestroika. Church contacts and progressive SED members insist the document has helped them. Because Honecker has so obviously drawn a line against reform, however, both the Social Democrats and the Communists seem to be pulling back. He and Vogel now only agree to disagree about the exercise's objective. Still, Honecker must be far from disappointed about the willingness of West German politicians to meet him at least halfway. Vogel favored ending support of the Salzgitter Center, which archives evidence of GDR human rights violations, and backed relations between the two Parliaments. Meanwhile, yet another member of Kohl's Cabinet, the minister for research, is in East Berlin, and a Honecker meeting with Berlin's new SPD governing mayor, Walter Momper, is being prepared.

MAY 29

Poland's astonishing election campaign is still almost a media nonevent, but efforts have begun to prepare the public for a Communist embarrassment. Until well into spring, the new Hungarian leaders, who were seen as having little idea of what kind of socialism they wanted, evoked most worry. Now Warsaw is viewed as the most dangerous source of the reform virus and threat to Eastern European stability—next to Gorbachev's Soviet Union, of course.

MAY 30

Horst Dohlus is perhaps the dullest and grayest Politburo member, the only one with whom we have met in my two years here who was so unsure in the presence of the American Ambassador that he confined himself to reading from a briefing book. As Central Committee secretary for cadre questions, however, he has a powerful behind-the-scenes role, especially to discipline those who break ranks on reform. Dohlus has been meeting with local SED chieftains to discuss the Party Congress, now officially advanced a year, to next May. No one can be certain whether the earlier date will facilitate the old men's reelection or stimulate internal pressure for new policies. One clue about its intent, however: Dohlus announced that membership cards must be turned in and revalidated, which gives the Politburo a perfect opportunity to purge the rebellious.

MAY 31

The SED is far from a monolith, but conservatives hold the high ground. Reissig tells me he was sharply criticized after a West Berlin paper described his Aspen Conference presentation. No matter how out-of-step Honecker is on human rights, however, he remains a responsible arms-control proponent. The reaction to President Bush's NATO summit speech, particularly the willingness to negotiate air reductions, has been quick and positive. The GDR is delighted to have a domestically popular subject on which to show solidarity with Gorbachev, and relieved to be able to pursue inner-German benefits in a sunnier East-West climate.

JUNE 1

To many Americans, the Conference on Security and Cooperation in Europe (CSCE), which just ended a human rights meeting in Paris, is a windy waste of time—at best irrelevant, at worst a delusion of diplomatic security that weakens European support for NATO. To me, this process, which began in 1975 when Gerald Ford, Leonid Brezhnev, and thirty-three other heads of state and government signed the Helsinki summit's Final Act, is the best mechanism for stimulating and channeling democratic change and a guarantor of a U.S. role in Europe beyond the increasingly irrelevant one of policeman.

Though the Paris meeting marked a new stage of intense human rights review, the GDR remains a firm supporter of the forum in which it made its European debut. Diplomatic contact with what used to be dismissed as "the Pankow regime" began in 1972 at the three-year negotiation that produced the Helsinki charter. The difference is that the GDR regards the CSCE as guarantor of postwar Europe's immutability, and the West as promise that its divisions will eventually be overcome. The trend favors the view that the CSCE encourages positive change, but the argument continued in Paris. Fischer insisted that practical humanitarian improvements, such as the enormous increase in travel East Germans have enjoyed in the last three years, were possible only with European stability, which required acceptance that the second German state is here to stay. Western speakers, particularly West Germany's Hans-Dietrich Genscher, countered that no society is stable unless it respects its citizens' rights. I witnessed a similar debate last June when the two German foreign ministers clashed at a program on the site of the World War II Potsdam Conference. The CSCE argument is another phrasing of the question shaking the Communist world and threatening to alienate the GDR from its Soviet sponsor: Is reform necessary for survival, or does it put survival at risk?

JUNE 2

The GDR is working hard to put the best gloss on its dispute with the Soviets. Schabowski is in Moscow to open an exhibit showcasing top-line consumer goods and technology, a less-than-subtle reminder of how important a supplier the East Germans are for the Soviet economy. Meanwhile, a Bush speech in Mainz about pulling down the Berlin Wall has produced a predictably negative response. My impression, however, is that the GDR is going through the motions with its indignation, just as it probably considers we are going through the motions in reiterating principled opposition to the Wall. I suspect the hypersensitive Honecker resented that the President failed to mention the GDR and referred only to the Federal Republic, "Germany as a whole," East and West Berlin, and the Soviet Union, as much as he resented rhetoric that every President since John Kennedy has used. Nevertheless, the GDR will follow a differentiated policy. It will acknowledge that the United States is critical to arms control, but it will concentrate its political and economic attention on the responsive West Germans.

JUNE 3

Helmut and Petra Frick, of the Ständige Vertretung, came for a drink, and I described our meeting with Eberlein. Helmut laughed and told me that Eberlein had been even more blunt with the West Germans earlier this year. He had conceded the GDR could not hold out against Gorbachev forever. When it fell into line on reforms, there would be great trouble, he said. Fortunately, he, Eberlein, would be retired and bear no share of the responsibility.

The confrontation in China between students, with their homemade Statue of Miss Liberty, and conservative Party elements has sharpened. The GDR media emphasizes the government's calls for a peaceful end to demonstrations, but goes easy on charges of outside influence. Everyone here is walking on eggs.

JUNE 4

Nothing of the bloody crackdown in Beijing has yet been reported here, apparently in anticipation of Politburo guidance. Gunnar and his wife,

Gabi, were here for coffee. When I told them, Gunnar went white and said, "That will end badly. A billion people can't be controlled by guns." His immediate worry is that use of force will confirm the GDR leadership's belief that a tough line works.

Gunnar's family is highly educated, middle class, close to the church. His father, the Greifswald professor, wanted to take them to the West in August 1961 but delayed to visit an ill sister. When the Wall went up, it was too late. Gunnar returned from a church visit to the United States last year, convinced the GDR is a backward, unfree society. His life is here, however, and he tries to make the best of it. He and his wife, a pharmacist, have a roomy apartment, a car, and most of the good things East Germany offers. Their religious involvement is an outlet for much frustration, but they worry about the children: a girl, 14, and a boy, 11. Do they endanger their prospects by raising them liberally? Can they risk their future by applying to emigrate? Dare they not give them a chance to grow up in the West? Like so many, Gunnar and his family live and work here as if in internal exile, psychologically half-disengaged but with talents this society badly needs to mobilize. Gorbachev is their hope.

JUNE 5

Joachim Herrmann, the Politburo's media czar, must have had difficulty setting today's public line. The massacre in Tienanmen Square was a minor item under the headline "China's Army Struck Down a Counterrevolutionary Uproar." There was no editorial, no government statement. That and the fact the Soviets were obviously distressed by the events suggested the GDR was at least slightly embarrassed at again finding itself isolated. However inadequately China was covered, Poland was ignored. A genuine election in which the Communists played by the rules and lost is harder to order in the SED's propaganda scheme than a military strike to save power. That gives East Germans—who read *Neues Deutschland* for signals, not news—food for somber thought.

Stephen Solarz, the New York Congressman and Democratic foreign policy expert, asks us to plan for a July visit. Some posts receive many Congressional delegations and try to avoid them. East Berlin may get one a year—a sign there is no interest at home—so, particularly with a serious figure like

Solarz, a no-frills workaholic, we seize the opportunity. Solarz can help us persuade the GDR that without concessions on bilateral issues and human rights improvement it will get neither more trade nor upgraded relations. We can lobby him on why it is important to pursue American interests with a state that is half of the German Question and Eastern Europe's most powerful economic-military entity.

JUNE 6

Still no editorial on China or coverage of the Polish vote. The day's headline was the kind the SED likes: "High Economic Performance in May in Preparation for the Party Conference." A contact at the Chinese Embassy, whom it will be difficult to see now that his government has put itself in Coventry, told me that prominent GDR economists recently tried to send a more pessimistic assessment to the Central Committee. Mittag killed it, because it reflected badly on his stewardship and could have given impetus to serious thinking about reform—as it was meant to do.

Gaby took a call last week from a man who identified himself only as "Winter from Potsdam." It was the young man who had questioned the candidates aggressively on the environment at the election meeting and then introduced himself to us in the parking lot as "Sommer." The distinctive accent, characteristic of Thuringia in the far southwest, facilitated identification better than his simple code. Would we like to visit Potsdam again? he asked. His wife, a guide at Sanssouci, Frederick the Great's summer palace, could give us a private tour.

I was tied up, but I encouraged Gaby to accept, with a caution not to play conspiratorial games. We could not know what, from curiosity to have an American friend through the Stasi, motivated the young man. Our guiding principle is simple: The more East Germans we meet informally, the more we learn about life here, and the better we do our twin job of interpreting the GDR to Washington and serving as friendly, open representatives of the American people. These are the goals of any "political officer" at an American Embassy. A spouse as good with people and the language as Gaby has a unique opportunity to share in their accomplishment. She and I are confident that as long as we are aboveboard and use common sense to avoid entrapment, our diplomatic status protects us from the omnipresent Stasi.

The East Germans face the tougher decision. If they are not authorized to have contacts with Westerners, they must assess career or other consequences for themselves and families. Only they can make that judgment, and we will respect it. Many, especially in and around the church and the arts, but also "ordinary" citizens, do feel more confident about normal relationships than a few years ago. We were only months in East Berlin when we realized we had been invited to more homes than we had been invited to in our entire Hungary tour. The liberalization aimed at by the CSCE works even in the shadow of the Berlin Wall.

Gaby returned from Potsdam still uncertain. Mrs. Sommer was a good guide. Her husband provided more anecdotal evidence that last month's vote tally was rigged. Everything was innocent enough, Gaby said, but was it her imagination that he kept a very large pen clipped at the front of his shirt? To do this job, it helps to maintain a balance between naiveté and paranoia.

JUNE 7

Jim Hoagland and Bob McCartney of the *Washington Post* took Imre and me to lunch for background before their interview with Honecker today. Katharine Graham, the *Post*'s publisher, had planned to do the interview herself in April, but Honecker pulled out at the last minute with the explanation he would be on holiday. (Probably true, though there are rumors the vacation was ordered by doctors.) Surprisingly, the GDR called back late last month. Honecker wants to crown his career by being received at the White House, and he must believe the coverage will help. More immediately, when Gorbachev visits Bonn next week he can anticipate a new round of criticism that he is out of touch with the times, and he means to make his own case to Western audiences first.

JUNE 8

Day Four, and the Polish election is still absent from *Neues Deutschland*. The paper did print a letter from Heinz Schauer, a self-described SED member for forty years, which would be satire if the SED went in for humor. To Party members increasingly bitter about the dreadful media policy dictated by Honecker and Herrmann, it was enraging and insulting. Its longtime reader wrote:

> *Neues Deutschland*'s information and its argumentation have improved. I consider its theoretical and propaganda contributions so important that I keep them ordered in folders. But the information about our brother Allies, the extensive news coverage . . . all these things . . . have impressed me favorably in recent months. Sometimes I note in discussions and also in Party meetings that Comrades ask questions which long before have been appropriately answered . . . or about which *Neues Deutschland* has already reported. Whoever reads *Neues Deutschland* thoroughly is regularly well informed and has sufficient arguments for discussions. I can always recommend that to every Comrade.

Actually, there was an article about Defense Minister Kessler's reception of the Polish Army's judge advocate general to talk military law, but if Herr Schauer gets into a discussion on Poland this week, it is unlikely to carry him far.

A meatier item in all dailies was an Associated Press claim that the American Commandant for Berlin (the major general in the Western Sectors who represents our share of the occupation regime for the former Reich capital) may restrict shopping by U.S. forces who visit the East. It included references that contradicted basic GDR positions, such as "Four-Power Berlin," and described the status rules that prevent the GDR from controlling Allied soldiers who circulate in what it considers its capital. There was much speculation at J.D.'s party for Reno, whose tour is ending, about why the propaganda apparatus highlighted the embarrassing story. The worst-case scenario had the GDR preparing to restrict Allied access under the guise of customs controls, arguing that unrestricted shopping, which frequently focuses on goods in short supply, like baby clothing and down bedding, produces economic hardship. I doubt Honecker would cut across East-West détente and his own policy of improving cooperation with West Germany at this time. A more likely reason is to persuade East Germans that because their consumer goods are attractive even to wealthy Americans, the East is better and the West less golden than they think.

I hope this affair does cause our military to exercise self-restraint. We need to show the flag in East Berlin, but our role as defender of the city's freedom is demeaned when we send buses through Checkpoint Charlie for unabashed shopping runs. Someday this might indeed be used by the GDR as the pretext to attack access rights. Many do not realize, however, the unfortunate impact on our image right now. Gaby has stood in many lines and heard the bitter remarks when the soldiers and their wives come through, and more than once she has left a store in embarrassment.

JUNE 9

Dissidents plan activities at monthly intervals to keep the memory of the rigged May 7 election fresh. Wednesday was the first "anniversary," and churches that took part had two objectives: to support the activists, but also to keep them inside, where they probably can operate with only harassment from the Stasi. The Pankow village congregation, whose pastor has been in trouble with the Stasi since the independent peace movement of the early 1980s, participated. On my drive home, I saw uniformed policemen posted at intervals for the half-mile between the village green on which the twin-towered red brick church, one of Berlin's oldest, stands and the Chinese Embassy. The latter was ringed by uniformed and plain-clothes forces backed up by paddy wagons. The show of force was meant to deter the mostly young people in the church, but dozens did march to that embassy before they were dispersed. The Stasi must worry that anger over political chicanery is fusing with the widespread disgust the Beijing bloodletting produced.

The Honecker interview broke no new ground. Before leaving, Hoagland and McCartney told Dick Barkley he was in good shape for a man two months short of his seventy-seventh birthday, alert, in command of facts, and very much a politician who intends to remain in charge. His interest in visiting the United States was obvious, but nothing suggested he has ideas for ending our bilateral impasse or his estrangement from Moscow. Indeed, Hoagland found him more rigid, if physically and intellectually impressive, than expected—an old man who will not, and probably cannot, change. Honecker's most significant venture into the American media in years only highlights that his is an increasingly anachronistic species of socialism.

At last *Neues Deutschland* reported the first round in Poland's election—120 hours late and in three spare paragraphs on page 11, without direct mention of either Solidarity or the Communist Party, much less who the real winners and losers were. That is scanty even for the GDR, which has two rules for awkward news in a Communist country. The most common practice is to relay that state's own reporting; the alternative is that, though one should not criticize, it is acceptable not to print what the friend is saying. Rule one is in force for China, rule two for Poland, and the choices reveal much about the attitude toward reform and repression. Jaruzelski said yesterday, "We try to combine our reformist determination with an evolutionary character," but Honecker must be increasingly skeptical that the general knows how to ride the tiger.

JUNE 10

The rubber-stamp Parliament yesterday approved by acclamation a resolution "against foreign intervention in China's internal affairs," the clearest indication yet that Honecker backs the crackdown despite its unpopularity here and his near isolation even in the Communist world. Few East Germans have had the courage to join the protesters, though we know high school students, not previously activists, who are standing watches during the Pankow church's vigil, and nearly every conversation brings new evidence of unhappiness. Party liberals despondently believe the Politburo views Tienanmen Square as proof that reform produces chaos and that force can restore order. Those outside the establishment are embittered that their government seems to be warning them it will do whatever necessary to repress dissent if they take their case into the streets, no matter their anger or belief in Gorbachev.

JUNE 11

It was arranged so quickly that Foreign Minister Fischer had to rush back to town, but Shevardnadze satisfied protocol by briefing the East Germans here before Gorbachev travels to Bonn. The Soviet Embassy hinted he would have been glad to skip the occasion altogether, but it was important to the GDR to be seen as still central to Moscow's diplomacy.

Shevardnadze also brought the invitation Honecker has maneuvered for:

to make a working stopover in Moscow when he goes on his nostalgic Magnitogorsk journey at month's end. It allows Honecker to flank the Kohl-Gorbachev talks and to counter the suspicion that new Kremlin thinking extends to its German interests. This suspicion is the core of the ambiguity that surrounds next week's Bonn summit, however. Vague formulations on Europe's divisions, uttered by Gorbachev advisers, titillate East and West German politicians differently. Objectively, the GDR welcomes good Soviet–West German ties. They make its own cooperation with Bonn easier, a policy that is both economically advantageous and beneficial to Honecker's domestic standing. The GDR knows Gorbachev needs it because it is part of Germany and is stable (compared with the rest of Eastern Europe), a military asset, and technologically advanced. But since the Federal Republic is all that and more, there is a nervous twitch just below the surface and deep into its psyche. The Soviets may begrudge time for hand-holding, but they understand the need. When a Western paper reported last week that Moscow was relaxed about a coming GDR crisis that could include large street protests, the Soviet Foreign Ministry answered at once: "Everyone is interested in the stability of [the GDR, which] has been and remains our reliable ally."

JUNE 12

We were in Greifswald on the same day as Honecker. He went to church for the first time since he became a Communist; we resumed our tour of the Baltic coast with Gunnar's father. It was my first glimpse of the preparations for the great man's visits outside Berlin. The political cabaret "Distel" nearly was closed last year for a skit in which cheerful peasants from a shabby village sang the refrain "Travel, Daddy, travel, travel." The point was that wherever Honecker goes cleanup brigades precede him. They do not exactly create a Potemkin Village, but do ensure that what he sees is painted, renovated, or in working order well beyond the GDR norm. We saw preparations in the main square a few weeks earlier. On this early Saturday morning, the crews were sweeping the motorcade route and streets around the cathedral, the rededication of which was the cause for his invitation. The propaganda apparatus went all out, carrying live the religious service and scenes of Honecker entering and leaving to cheers. He wants to keep the modus vivendi with the church and would cut deals that leave activists some breathing space. The church is divided about how far it can balance business-as-usual with the building anger in the country. The strong-willed local bishop exacerbated the intrachurch controversy by inviting Honecker on his own and then pitching him conversational softballs.

We left town, however, as Honecker entered, and made our way to Rügen, the large island above Stralsund. The professor again showed us much we would otherwise never have found, including pre-German Slavic sites and, from a distance, the luxurious vacation resort of "Spy and Eavesdrop Inc.," the omnipresent Stasi. At Cape Arkona, the northern tip, where young Swedes conducted an informal sing-in below the lighthouse, the professor joked: "This is the end of the GDR, at least geographically." We lunched in a Stralsund restaurant advertising "Mecklenburg specialties." The coast from here to the Polish border never belonged to Mecklenburg, the professor said heatedly. It was the western edge of Pomerania, a territory otherwise lost to Germany after 1945. The GDR had become more ready to encourage local customs in order to strengthen ties to the land, he said, but it still refused to acknowledge Pomerania, lest that imply less-than-firm commitment to the Oder-Neisse border and upset Poland. Typical manipulation of history, he complained.

The British foreign minister has postponed his visit indefinitely. The British—unlike the French, who say Mitterrand is coming soon—are leery of too forward an association as Honecker becomes more isolated. Still, they, like the other Europeans, remain far ahead of the United States in pursuing their interests in this unlovely but important country.

JUNE 13

GDR Radio claimed that the Honecker interview's "unusual prominence" in the U.S. media was causing speculation in Washington. That is surely overstated, but here the leader's every utterance is indeed put under the microscope. He was at his most reasonable, very much on the Gorbachev line, when discussing arms control. On internal reforms—or rather the lack thereof—he was as obdurate as ever. Most interesting was probably his hint that the Berlin Wall need not be forever. Responding last winter to Western criticism, Honecker had said the Wall would last "50 or 100 years," unless the conditions that had produced it changed. The conditions caveat is usually forgotten. Presumably he meant the cold war and the competition side of German-German ties, but the economic and human rights gaps would apply if he were candid. The "50 or 100 years" is now cited repeatedly to show how out of touch he is. For the American audience, he avoided the provocation and implied that the Wall could someday, though not yet, be covered by his ambiguous formulation that "we are for the disappearance of relics of the cold war, so that citizens and states can cooperate more closely."

Our diplomatic colleagues, who know such an interview usually heralds an impending trip, are skeptical when we insist nothing is in the works. It does appear that Honecker is trying to start the process. He is sensitive to the impression the GDR is less an actor in its own right than, potentially, a subject of Washington-Moscow-Bonn negotiation. Honecker would do much to be dealt into the summit game with the United States, but he has until now kept his own counsel. He may be feeling his age, or even more acutely the GDR's second-class status, as Europe enters a period of greater diplomatic activity. Whatever the motivation, his yearning for prestige, legitimacy, and a piece of the action offers us leverage. Dick wants to sit down with J.D. and me to decide whether we can exploit it.

JUNE 14

An embassy's efforts with a difficult and unpopular regime are always suspect. There is a Foreign Service tendency, as a former boss put it, to have as a policy "Good relations *über alles*." But good relations per se mean nothing; one must be able to use them to advance specific, legitimate national interests or they are useless, even harmful if they associate the United States with wrongs in the eyes of the citizens of the country concerned and the world.

I am convinced, nevertheless, that there are persuasive reasons to seek a stronger relationship with the GDR. We have an obligation to settle government and Jewish claims and so assist people who have waited decades to get even small compensation for property nationalized by the Communists or for the Holocaust's horrors. The GDR occupies a key position in Central Europe by virtue of its geography, its Germanness, and its contributions to the Soviet Bloc. If we can influence its policies and increase the tendency to think for itself (though the Honecker-Gorbachev argument shows this is not undiluted gain), we will be better positioned to advance American security and political interests in an area vital to us.

We would not be relieved of an obligation to choose appropriate objectives, but it is evident that we should not abdicate interests simply because we disapprove of the regime or believe the GDR is another's primary business. Our commitment to Berlin's freedom and alliance with West Germany will always have priority over anything we might achieve by improved GDR ties, but it should not be an either-or choice. After all, the West Germans have constructed extensive relationships they believe make the GDR more responsive to Western human rights and security concerns. There are influential old Germanists in Washington who argue that Kohl wants us to maintain implacable hostility on principle while he pursues a special German détente, but what we learn on the ground from the Ständige Vertretung suggests the contrary: Bonn would welcome signs that the Americans were moving in harmony.

From Washington, Dick brought encouraging news that seeds our embassy has tried to plant may be flowering. The State Department's European Bureau and Secretary Baker's policy-planning staff have agreed to review the bilateral relationship this summer, he says, and we need to send recommendations. It is not possible, or even desirable, to make large advances without major GDR concessions on the issues around which the deadlock has hardened, especially claims, and a different GDR stance on reform. But we believe there are areas in which forward motion can be resumed.

I put my contribution to our initial brainstorming session jointly with Jerry Verner, the press and cultural counselor, who has more Eastern Europe experience than the rest of the embassy combined. Our idea is keyed to bringing more East Germans to the United States for get-acquainted stays of at least a month. The International Visitors Program is one of the best things the United States does abroad, but it needs the Communist government's acquiescence. Jerry's targets and mine are not Politburo dons already at the top, or our regular contacts from the Party's think tanks, but local and youth officials as well as Central Committee staffers who will be the next generation of high-fliers. The trick is to persuade the SED that there is mutual interest in knowing each other better. When I was in Budapest, the Hungarian Party made a strategic decision that its best young leaders needed to experience the United States, as well as Moscow. As a result, such politicians as Imre Pozsgay, who may become the reform president, came. The way to get the SED to take this step may be to package it as expansion of the political dialogue Honecker calls for. Hermann Axen, its foreign-policy czar, is the key to convincing the Politburo.

JUNE 15

We sent the Foreign Ministry a diplomatic note requesting a meeting with Axen. We cannot go directly to the Politburo, an indication of the distance at which the SED seeks to keep us and of the control it maintains over our activities. Except to an extent with a few contacts who are familiar with American style and authorized to deal with us regularly (and required to report back), it is almost impossible to telephone officials directly. Our goal is to break through the barriers, to create a normal aura for our activities, and thus to accustom East Germans to more extensive and informal contacts with private as well as official Americans.

Almost simultaneously, I asked for appointments in Bad Salzungen with the author of *Der Erste*, Landolf Scherzer, and the county leader. The book broaches taboo subjects, including the mendacious media and attempts to "flee the Republic" to West Germany. Scherzer is giving readings around the country that turn into openly critical discussions. Getting a feel for the degree to which writers, the second level of the Party, and ordinary citizens are stirring may be more important than whatever the Politburo is willing to tell us this summer.

JUNE 16

Careful East German coverage of Gorbachev in Bonn showed little of the public adulation, "Gorby Mania." Though the Soviet Union and the Federal Republic will always be incomparably the most important countries with which the GDR must deal, its significance to each could be seriously weakened if they can work smoothly with each other without requiring facilitation by East Berlin. Honecker would then find himself cut even further out of the political and economic decisions shaping post–cold war Europe, and possibly even in a fatally weakened personal position. As antidote to Western euphoria over the week's events, however, Radio Moscow commented bluntly and no doubt accurately: "The Socialist German State is our strategic ally and loyal partner and will remain so."

The biggest East Berlin story was the Teachers Conference that filled the Palace of the Republic for three days. Honecker and much of the Politburo sat through the interminable televised sessions. The star was Education Minister Margot Honecker, who is more conservative than her husband and whose speech was old-fashioned Communist fire-and-brimstone. It is gossiped that at a recent cocktail party she exclaimed, "Who would ever have dreamed that the counterrevolution would come at us from the Soviet Union?" My Potsdam friend Helmut says the Defense Ministry would resume dialogue with the church, but the Education Ministry, which also stonewalls our modest youth exchange proposals, refuses.

School problems here—parents and high school students Gaby and I know agree—start with the strong emphasis on the political reliability of teachers and students. The latter are discouraged early from asking awkward questions or stating nonstandard views. Initiative is not always rewarded, and students learn that it rarely pays to stand out from the crowd. Many technically competent, but few exceptional, graduates are produced. The implications for society's competitiveness have been cautiously addressed in specialized articles by academics, such as the octogenarian economic historian Jürgen Kuczynski, and it was thought this might be a conference theme. However, on new ideas Mrs. Honecker never got beyond whether to end Saturday morning classes. She put an end to hope that an easing international situation would allow the state to back away from compulsory military training for high school students introduced a decade ago. GDR youth, she said, must be prepared to defend socialism "with a rifle in its hand." Perhaps in no other state would political leaders devote three days to a teachers conference, but this interest only adds to the impression that the GDR is battening down the hatches to keep out heresy that these days can affect young minds from all compass directions.

A footnote: The New York Philharmonic performed this week in the Schauspielhaus, the superbly restored auditorium on the Platz der Akademie. When the ambassador sought to show the flag, we learned that Mrs. Honecker had requisitioned all tickets for conference participants. My inclination was to shrug it off. That is how things are often done here, and if our goal is to achieve a multiplier effect for American culture throughout East German society, an audience of teachers is not the worst. I have rarely seen Dick so angry, however. He pointed out that the second Honecker had both unfairly associated the United States with her conference and deprived music-lovers of a chance to hear the orchestra. He will let the SED know how distasteful he found the fraud, and warn Americans who are considering performing here to be wary of manipulation.

JUNE 17

The Verners' dinner was late yesterday. We sat transfixed as West German television reported from Budapest the reburial of Imre Nagy, the martyred hero of 1956 who for more than thirty years had lain in an unmarked grave, the location of which was a state secret. Now, in a coincidence that must appeal deeply to the Hungarian sense of drama, János Kádár lies dying, stripped of authority and abandoned by a party casting aside the baggage of its past in a struggle to retain even a share of power. And the people in their hundreds of thousands stand in Heroes' Square and sing the "Himnusz" (the national anthem) to honor the man he betrayed and the Soviets murdered. Seeing the remarkable pictures, it was easy to believe another revolution is under way, one that Gorbachev gives every indication of tolerating. There is nothing in the East German press, of course, but how can Honecker watch and retain belief in his course? Gorbachev is unlikely to take on another headache by directly intervening in GDR politics, but is it implausible that the SED itself will begin to ask whether it does not need a new and younger leader who is more in tune with the times?

JUNE 18

Günther Krusche, Bishop Forck's deputy, described at dinner this evening the half-steps and compromises with which the church chivies concessions from the SED and seeks to keep activists from pushing hard enough to set off Stasi hard-liners. The more liberal travel policy since 1986 has backfired, he said; millions suddenly are seeing West Germany for themselves, and the comparison they share with family and fellow workers is made more painful by the antireform atmosphere at home. The result is increasing dissatisfaction, not the release of pressure the Party anticipated.

Our guests, in Berlin for an Aspen conference, were my law school classmate Walt Slocombe, deputy undersecretary of defense under President Carter, and Toni Chayes, another former senior Pentagon official. The restaurant was an unpretentious state establishment in a high-rise development. The outside promised little, but the cook, who moonlights for official dinners at our house, fulfilled his promise of a special meal. I think Walt and Toni were surprised, however, that Krusche focused on the simple delight of the spring potatoes, the like of which he said he had never seen in a GDR restaurant. Potatoes are a staple for East Germans, who probably eat more of them than their Western cousins, but artistry—that extra bit of time and effort with fresh produce—is indeed a rarity.

JUNE 19

Media coverage of an Interflug crash at Schönefeld Airport has been extensive and apparently objective. The media has been free only a few years to report single-incident bad news, such as natural disasters, accidents, and crime. This is cited as a small sign of Glasnost, but most consider it a placebo to make local news slightly more interesting and credible, and there is no suggestion that the honesty will eventually extend to politics and economics. However, a string of transport breakdowns this year may signal that the economic infrastructure is poorer than generally credited. Some economists say the government needs to shift resources massively from prestige projects, such as the computer industry, to a rebuilding of roads, railways, and telecommunications. Those of us who bounce along the *Landstrassen* in the provinces or wrestle with the telephone system—or our friends who often must wait years to get a telephone at all—can only agree.

At the Ständige Vertretung this evening, I ran into two Americans who had come from another Aspen event, which brought younger officials from a cross section of CSCE countries to Berlin. Most of their East German interlocutors were surprisingly open in off-the-record give-and-take, they said, but one meeting left them shaken. Culture Minister Hans-Joachim Hoffmann treated them to a view of the GDR that went beyond candor. "It is difficult," they quoted the sixty-year-old, who has been in the Cabinet almost from the start of the Honecker era, "to admit that what you have dedicated your life to is a failure."

JUNE 20

Neues Deutschland says a Warsaw Pact summit will convene in Bucharest "within the first ten days of July." Jaruzelski will go greatly weakened by his party's electoral disaster, and the Hungarians will be preoccupied with their ever more problematic effort to keep ahead of reform. A collective attempt to reimpose conformity is improbable, however. Honecker may fear the worst from Poland and Hungary, but he also has staked much on his own right to set a course independent of Moscow's. The summit will likely confirm rather than rein in a pluralism that is becoming fragmentation by another name.

JUNE 21

My secretary, Kirsten Christensen, is a pioneer. She is the first "Fascell Fellow," a program named for the House Foreign Affairs Committee chairman that puts young Americans with language skills into jobs in Eastern Europe formerly held by local nationals. The dual objective is to ease security concerns and expose young Americans to the Foreign Service. Kirsten, on leave from Brigham Young University, has proved its worth. Her cheerfulness keeps us positive, her energy and flawless German are invaluable for fixing schedules when we travel, and her warmth makes her a fine representative for our country with the many East Germans she knows.

Mormons constitute one of the GDR's smallest religious groups. That and the care they take to distinguish between what is Caesar's and what is God's have made their church a showcase for the SED's religious tolerance. A year ago, the GDR became the first Eastern European state to accept a Mormon mission. Technically, its members are not allowed to proselytize, Kirsten says, but if the person who opens the door on which they knock is interested, they are free to describe the church's teachings. Mormon facilities vary from city to city, she reports. Leipzig, Dresden, Freiberg, and Zwickau have new or renovated meetinghouses; Berlin has made do with a cramped apartment for forty years. New construction has been stalled in a bureaucratic runaround that is typical, not just for churches, and by an equally common lack of building materials.

JUNE 22

Political humor has special qualities in Eastern Europe. It would be hard to claim for it more than a pressure-release function, and cynics suggest the authorities are among its more assiduous creators in tough times. However, it gains relevance and impact in proportion to the lack of formal channels for comment and critique. In a society where many topics are approached only obliquely until one is sure of the other person, it is more than a conversational icebreaker. Two items heard recently:

> An SED official asked at a reception if the American Embassy had yet discovered why labor productivity was so much higher in West Germany. We had not. "Well," he said, lowering his voice conspiratorially, "it's all in *Neues Deutschland* today. Didn't you see the headline, 'Communists not permitted to work in FRG?'"

> At a joint audience in Heaven, President Bush asks what the United States will be like in the year 2000. "Communist," says God, and Bush turns away and cries bitterly. Gorbachev, confident of Perestroika, asks what the Soviet Union will be like. "Capitalist," God thunders, and Gorbachev is crushed. Then it is Honecker's turn to ask about the GDR in the new century. God turns away and cries bitterly.

More-nuanced political humor flourishes on the stage. Cabarets offer vitamin substitutes for undernourished public exposure of issues and gripes, if usually not fundamental questions. They permit the temperature of the body politic and SED toleration limits to be measured infinitely better and more enjoyably than by reading *Neues Deutschland*. We are trying to get tickets for the new program at the most famous cabaret, Berlin's Distel.

JUNE 23

Walter Momper, the new SPD governing mayor on the western side of the city, finally called on Honecker and came away with promises of improvements in the conditions under which West Berliners may visit East Berlin and the GDR proper. The warming inner-German trend has been extended to the relationship between West Berlin and the GDR in recent years. Before this meeting came off, however, there was concern that Momper did not accept Allied status red lines or would be tricked by Honecker. The not always best-tempered argument, which drew in Bonn embassies and Chancellor Kohl, was symptomatic of several recently accelerated developments. The Germans are more assertive about their ability to handle Berlin issues that are no longer the Allies' exclusive province. No politician will subordinate his political judgment to that of the three Western powers and forgo an opportunity to pursue his own interests with the GDR. The Allies worry that they are being marginalized, that their security responsibilities are viewed as ever less relevant by the Germans whose freedom they guarantee.

It is difficult for our embassy to enter the debate, because its mandate is the GDR, and the West Berlin Mission is responsible for the city, including all status issues, but Dick and I have a background in the specialized discipline called Berlinery and can put GDR policy into historical perspective.

Increasingly, East Germans and West Berliners see the other less as mortal threat than as opportunity to advance pragmatic interests. The latter show the sense of being on a roll that characterizes the West German approach to the crisis-ridden Communist world. They feel they are on history's side, that time, which once worked for the Wall's acceptance, now exposes it as an anachronism. The GDR's adjustment is more cautious, because it is grounded in grudging acceptance that it is the weaker, more vulnerable German society. In the early 1980s, when it became clear that Brezhnevism was at a dead end in Moscow and that *Ostpolitik* had achieved consensus status in Bonn, the GDR made a strategic assessment that it could get the economic assistance and international prestige it needed only from West Germany. The turn to West Berlin is part of that reorientation, from exclusively Eastern toward what is in many ways half or more Western.

Of course, the motives differ. West Germans and West Berliners are more accommodating to the GDR, not because they have been seduced but because they want to change that society, open it up, ameliorate the human costs of division, and keep alive the possibility of a new form of "togetherness" sometime in the next century. The GDR will remain a loyal Moscow ally because Soviet power and national security interests continue to be the most basic guarantees of its survival. There is, however, tacit understanding that long-range goals can be put aside—in effect, for history to judge—while pragmatic cooperation is pursued through ever-proliferating channels. Monday's Momper-Honecker conversation was but one momentarily prominent stage. Every day there are hundreds of construction workers earning hard currency for the GDR and themselves in West Berlin, academicians, institute personnel, and intellectuals interacting with counterparts and broader audiences, and of course more and more private visitors. Even a few years ago these things did not happen. The landscape looks the same; there is still a Wall, four foreign military powers with occupation rights, two antithetical political systems, and all the other paraphernalia we have come to associate with Berlin the beleaguered city. But a core change is under way.

As angst-ridden as the GDR is, it has gained enough confidence to believe that, without crisis, its East Berlin position is acknowledged de facto if not de jure. Our classical status concern, realistically grounded in early postwar history, revolved around the assumption that severance of West Berlin–Bonn ties was a priority SED objective that, once obtained, would lead quickly to incorporation of the entire city by the GDR. Honecker knows that scenario is neither consistent with European trends nor affordable. The GDR needs payment in a more practical currency than status. West Berlin's utility is precisely that it is plugged into West Germany. As the GDR is exposed to the unpredictable consequences of Western influence, its status emphasis has become defensive. It is the poor cousin when it sits down with Bonn. Geography at least gives it some leverage when it deals with West Berlin and keeps the West German powerhouse a half step in the background.

We too often fail to recognize how fundamentally all this works to the West's advantage. What the East Germans require, the Soviets can no longer provide. They have been thrown back on their own resources and those they can bargain for with the West. If two societies as different as the GDR and West Germany interact more extensively, most change, most real concessions, will come from the poorer, less free, less legitimate side. Our protection of West Berlin was designed to give the Germans just that chance. If we are willing to trust our allies as well as the direction in which history seems to be flowing just a little more, we could reduce frictions with politicians in Bonn and West Berlin and find that we have more flexibility for pursuing American interests.

The new, dependent GDR with greater interest in economic cooperation than confrontation may even occasionally have positions that are compatible with ours. It has hinted, for example, that it is more prepared than the Soviets to explore inner-German aviation improvements. Our most meaningful commitment in Central Europe is to Berlin, but with the cold war winding down, the GDR's relationship to that commitment is no longer inevitably that of threat. It has become a more nuanced player—not benign, but potentially a contributor to some solutions. The embassy's challenge is to encourage innovative thinking about that heresy.

JUNE 24

The Central Committee, formally the supreme authority in the SED but in actuality as compliant a tool as the Parliament, has ended a two-day summer session that lacked any hint of spontaneity. Herrmann's lengthy "all's well" report on behalf of the Politburo was followed by a dozen choreographed speeches. Most diplomats consider the announcement that Honecker and Prime Minister Willi Stoph have already been designated to deliver the initial reports at the Twelfth Congress next May proof that the old leadership intends to hold on for another term. That may well be the intent, but it is premature to conclude it is a done deed. The imminence of the Congress may yet stimulate maneuvering over policies and personnel. It will not be easy to spot the early signs, since what the Party does best is cloak its internal operations, but the impression of a docile monolith could prove misleading.

JUNE 26

The Polish election remains, publicly, a nontopic while the Politburo holds its collective breath and waits to see how many concessions Jaruzelski must make to Walesa. There is an effort, however, to put a positive spin on the internal shakeup the Hungarian Party has just gone through. The choice as Party Chairman of Rezső Nyers, the economist who fathered the original 1968 reforms before falling into disfavor, was reported relatively thoroughly. Nyers is apparently first among equals in a collegial leadership that includes Miklos Németh, the young prime minister; Imre Pozsgay, the putative president; and Károly Grósz, the most orthodox. The GDR has apparently decided to portray the shuffle of positions—even if it amounts to a setback for Grósz—as welcome stabilization.

Nevertheless, the concern for a spiraling Eastern European crisis remains deep. The GDR scarcely knows what to make of Hungarian events, except that it does not like them, and it has far less trust in the new team at the top than in Jaruzelski. It would be hard to imagine a Communist leader further from the pseudo-Prussian gerontocracy's ideal than the gentlemanly, scholarly Nyers, who was a Social Democrat in his youth. Even SED advisers privately sympathetic to Perestroika worry that it is fine for each Party to develop its own socialism but that the Hungarians do not know where they are heading. The problem goes deeper than national character differences between spontaneous Magyars, and Germans who are uncomfortable without a master plan (*Gesamtkonzept*).

Barring dramatic change in Soviet toleration of heresy, however, there is nothing any member of the conservative Little Entente can do, and the GDR retains practical reasons to avoid a fight. It has a parochial desire to uphold the principle of noninterference by Moscow in an ally's affairs. Also, Hungary continues to help on a sensitive matter. My Hungarian colleague says his embassy has reassured the GDR that East Germans without exit visas for Austria will be arrested if found in the expanded border security zone. This does not get to the fundamental questions so close to the surface in Heroes' Square on June 16, but it indicates that the GDR and Hungary want to avoid an open break.

JUNE 27

While the GDR tries to be restrained about trends in Poland and Hungary, it is going the extra mile to support Chinese repression. A documentary on "counterrevolutionary disturbances," taken intact from Chinese television and full of references to the crowd's gruesome violence toward soldiers, has had three prime-time screenings. This constant repetition of the official Chinese line is a good deal more than socialist protocol requires. There is widespread distaste of that line here, and sympathy for the bloodied students. Each evening as I drive home, I see the police around the Chinese Embassy, where on the weekend several dozen youths made another abortive attempt to deliver a protest letter. Even establishment figures like SED loyalist Hermann Kant, president of the Writers Association, are uneasy. The GDR is staking out a position as Beijing's most dedicated supporter from a mixture of relief that one reformist party was prepared to do whatever necessary to keep domestic discipline, and fear that the virus remains in the blood, and closer to home than China.

JUNE 28

Günter Schabowski is an intriguing contender for the Honecker succession, Krenz's most serious opposition. He has a good base in the Berlin Party, which he heads, and is intelligent, energetic, and ambitious. I observed him up close when I escorted Dick to his office earlier this year. "Like the painter?" was his question when he heard my name. Unlike most of his colleagues whose bookshelves are bare or stocked with Marx and Engels, Schabowski displayed a multivolume reprint of a postwar literary journal. It may have been a show, but he was making a statement. More than his peers, he obviously enjoyed the cut and thrust of conversation. He was outspoken and earthy in his criticism of the Soviets. Many of their reforms, he told us, were "horse manure and garbage." "The Soviets always go overboard. They used to tell us everything had to be planned. Now they think the Market is the miracle cure."

If there is a potential Gorbachev in this Politburo, it would be Schabowski. It may be a sign of the times that the former editor of *Neues Deutschland* (not a reform credential that, of course), with the heavy Berlin dialect and the quick, sharp tongue for which Berliners are known, is making an effort to give himself a populist image. A few anecdotes:

> Rock singer Tamara Danz is an enthusiastic Perestroika backer and outspoken critic of much in the GDR. She told Heather of bumping into Schabowski a few weeks ago in Moscow. Seeing her large "Gorby" button (which could get her into trouble here), he gave a thumbs up and said, "We need more like you."

> A theater director told me Schabowski is making unannounced and relatively unescorted visits around town to meet the people. This is almost a subversive concept in an SED the last of whose senior figures to talk over beer in a pub with a real worker, according to common wisdom, was Wilhelm Pieck three decades back, before construction of the golden leadership ghetto on the shores of Lake Wandlitz. Recently Schabowski went walking in Prenzlauer Berg, once a workers' district, now something of a center for artists, intellectuals of many persuasions, and social dropouts. Here are two of the more unusual encounters:

> SCHABOWSKI: "But don't you miss contact with colleagues and fellow workers?"

FEMALE PUNK: "No, my pet rat is company."
SCHABOWSKI: "Why don't you make something of your life?"
DISHEVELED YOUTH WITH BOTTLE ON PARK BENCH: "I'm ready to do anything as long as it doesn't involve work."

The politician who would have the common touch and is rarely at a loss for words reportedly left the scene without a rejoinder, presumably a bit more aware of the surprisingly numerous nooks and crannies of this city that do not fit the textbook descriptions of life in the "first Socialist state of workers and peasants on German soil." It will be interesting to see whether he keeps on with his effort to break out of the mold.

Reno and Leslie Harnish leave this week. Their dinners, topped by homemade ice cream sundaes, will not be forgotten by diplomats and the East German businessmen, trade officials, and academics in their congenial circle. For a farewell, Gaby and I reserved a table in the "1900," a bit of East Berlin chic that is more bar than restaurant and has the reputation that every third or fourth customer sends the tab to the Stasi. The "1900," however, is a private venture whose owner took years to gather its antique fittings. It is on Käthe-Kollwitz-Platz, at the end of Husemannstrasse, the short street along which every apartment house has been restored to turn-of-century splendor. Around the corner, Prenzlauer Berg reality returns—buildings, whole blocks, that look as if it is still 1945—but this small area is a regime promissory note of what is to be done to all the GDR, when there is money.

We reminisced about our recent visit to Jürgen Kuczynski—the critic of GDR society, but also staunch defender of its ideals—in his home, where books are stacked to the ceilings. The old man and the French wife, who won him to communism when both were at the Brookings Institute in Washington before the Great Depression and who now served us cakes, dream of a socialism that is more democratic and productive than Honecker's. There were stirrings, Kuczynski said. He had more opportunity to speak around the country, and *Neues Deutschland* even admitted it was receiving (though not printing) letters on both sides of the subsidy issue. But would the GDR launch major reforms soon? we asked. "I would like to believe it but I do not think so" was his answer.

Reno chose not to extend his tour for an additional twelve months. I face that decision this summer and will extend so Gaby can be near her ailing mother in West Berlin, but I share Reno's belief that the next year is likely to see more of the same here: the old men in the Politburo holding back change and holding on to their power. We both have talked with the impatient second echelon of Party and government and know it cannot last, not with reform established in Moscow and shaking the GDR's neighbors, but it can last to the Party Congress and a bit beyond. I understand why Reno opted for Rome. I reproach myself often for rejecting the Department's initial proposal to study Polish two years ago. Had I not fought to return to Berlin, I would be political counselor in Warsaw now reporting the biggest story in Europe, negotiations that are about to establish a non-Communist government.

JUNE 29

The lawyer and Honecker confidant Wolfgang Vogel tells Dick that a steady trickle of East German tourists have been refusing to leave the West German Embassy in Budapest until they get permission to emigrate. Vogel, with whom Dick has worked for years on sensitive spy exchange and human rights cases and whose word he trusts, is called in to settle these tricky matters. There are also sit-ins at the Warsaw and Prague embassies, but the most delicate situation is building in Berlin, at the Ständige Vertretung, Vogel added.

In January, when many believed a new travel law would put those who had been waiting years to the rear of the line, the number of asylum-seekers swelled, and the Ständige Vertretung was about to close its doors to the public. An appeal to Honecker, who claimed he had not been informed and who told Vogel to get involved, saved the day. The sit-ins left with assurances they could go West. The GDR continued to process emigration applications and implement the more liberal family-visit procedures of the past several years. Nevertheless, the Ständige Vertretung has become cautious about allowing East Germans to enter without an invitation or clear consular business. It is a painful but prudent precaution, because a new flood of asylum-seekers would mean a crisis. No one wants to imperil inner-German cooperation, so Vogel resolves cases while both governments play them down to keep them from multiplying. There is a revolving door, with small numbers entering West German missions almost daily, and roughly equal numbers leaving to begin a new life in the Federal Republic. It is a barely tolerable situation for all sides, and its delicate balance can easily be upset.

A letter from a Yale professor asks: "Can you tell me whether the gardens and park at Muskau, near Cottbus, which once belonged to Prince Pückler-Muskau, are open to the public? . . . Is it feasible and permissible for American citizens to visit?" I sent a positive response, probably with more information than the professor expected, because I know the park and its twin at Branitz, where Pückler is buried. We are friendly with a Cottbus pastor active in a citizens movement to protect these nineteenth-century English-style landscape gems. However, it is symptomatic of our problem in developing interest in the GDR that even a sophisticated academic is uncertain whether Americans are welcome at one of this unknown land's great cultural sites. At that, the professor is ahead of most of our countrymen, who think only of the Wall and Katarina Witt when they hear "East Germany."

JUNE 30

Honecker has been in the Soviet Union three days. The meaning of the Moscow segment was in the simple fact that the two leaders, despite obvious distaste, know they still need each other. Honecker cannot afford to offend Gorbachev and must rebut the impression that he and his state are no longer at the center of their protector's security policies. For his part, Gorbachev was as diligent at soothing East German nightmares as he had been a few weeks earlier at inspiring West German dreams. The implicit reaffirmation of mutual dependency so soon after the visit with Kohl was a reminder not only that the GDR cannot isolate itself indefinitely from Glasnost and Perestroika but also that it remains an indispensable component of the European order as seen from the Kremlin. That is Honecker's dilemma and leverage alike, and the boundary within which the Berlin-Moscow-Bonn triangle operates even in these changing times.

More revealing of the inner man was the "private" and nostalgic stop in Magnitogorsk. When both he and the Communist dream were young, Honecker worked in a brigade that stamped the city's steel mills out of frozen earth. As shrewdly as he planned the trip to meet with Gorbachev, the return moved him. Ambitious, arrogant, preoccupied with power, Honecker is also a man who has suffered for beliefs. Ten years in Nazi prisons give him a moral bonus in the SED and a degree of respect among the wider population. He never looks happier than when surrounded by old comrades and performing familiar rituals, such as the raised-fist singing of the "Internationale" in the cold of the cemetery at Friedrichshain, where Karl Liebknecht and Rosa Luxemburg are honored every January.

That Honecker is from a different age and school was illustrated for me one time in his office. He had criticized West Germany's two-million unemployment, and Deputy Secretary of State John Whitehead responded that unemployment was inevitable, even necessary, to lubricate a modern economy. Honecker's jaw muscles tightened as he scribbled a memory aide on his notepad. When his turn came, he smiled stiffly at the Wall Street banker and checked the point off his agenda with the comment that their experiences were very different and their views would remain different also.

Some of this protestation of the old values and beliefs has become only ossified ritual, but it does the man and what he has lived through no justice to deny him his ideals even if they are those that history and practice have discredited for most. Still, when he tells workers how delighted he is to be back in Magnitogorsk, "where the steel heart of the Soviet Union beats," I recall that Embassy Moscow colleagues recently referred to that city as a microcosm of much of the country's troubles: with out-of-date, unprofitable and environmentally destructive heavy industry, and grimy, rundown living quarters. Earlier this year, Honecker boasted of the "millions of apartments we have built since 1971, each with a level of luxury undreamed of in the Kaiser's time." He was visibly proud and could hardly understand, even if he was made aware, why this statement of irrelevant truth so infuriated most East Germans, whose expectations, even the purely economic ones, have moved far beyond those of their grandparents. It is a painful irony—but a fair reflection of much that makes the GDR so unhappy this summer—that Honecker is more at home in the Magnitogorsk he romanticizes than in Gorbachev's Moscow, where the real and accumulated problems of the present are at last being tackled.

2

The Silent Crisis
July and August 1989

JULY 1

My Norwegian counterpart came by to compare notes. Like the United States, Norway has for years negotiated compensation for property taken after the war. Along with the problem we call "Jewish claims" (envisioned as a symbolic GDR contribution to Holocaust survivors), and more general human rights problems of the sort dramatized by the Wall, that issue blocks significant improvement of ties. The Norwegians, I learned, held another inconclusive round in mid-June.

What did we think about military-to-military contacts? my colleague asked. Norway was being pressed to accept a meeting of defense ministers. I reviewed our small steps. They helped expose the GDR's conservative security establishment to new thinking, I said. For reasons of pride and prestige, the once secretive GDR military wants to join the détente/CSCE game. I believe we can take advantage without paying a price, but I expect reflexive resistance from traditionalists. Last month I encountered this in the French diplomat who first told me Mitterrand would pay a state visit to East Berlin and then expressed surprise that we had allowed our National Defense University students to associate with a GDR army that "violates the demilitarized status of Berlin daily." More will be heard on this subject, if only because the West Germans want to develop a new area of inner-German contacts.

JULY 2

Dick and Nina Barkley gave a pre–July 4 party today. Normally, an ambassador's Independence Day reception is anything but a holiday experience. All personnel are expected to "work the affair" to ensure that guests circulate and that as many substantive conversations as possible are held. The Administrative Section is at full stretch for weeks. The Fourth is the one day when the embassy cannot afford to let anyone take leave. The Barkleys made this Saturday our embassy celebration, and they did it in informal, at-home fashion: a garden cookout followed by games. I sprained a wrist at volleyball. The hit of the day was lip-sync, a contest in which the participants mimed words to recorded songs. A party at the ambassador's residence is not a big deal for senior officers and spouses, who frequently attend official dinners there, but it is for junior staff and non-American employees. The gesture, and the warmth with which it was carried out, will pay big morale dividends.

JULY 3

Assessing potential successors is a preoccupation in any Communist country. Eighteen years in power have established the parameters within which Honecker operates, but he will be seventy-seven this summer and, despite apparent good health, is unlikely to hold office more than a few additional years. Who comes next and what policy adjustments can be expected assume even greater significance when the Communist world is in ideological civil war. The SED, however, prides itself on discipline. Little information gets out prematurely, so we dissect tidbits about the rise or fall of political stars even when not much more substantial than gossip.

The race between Krenz and Schabowski is close, with the former probably ahead by a neck. Both politicians are capable of adjusting to new situations, which does not make me inclined to categorize either as "hard-line" or "reformist." Egon Krenz, however, the Politburo's youngest, has probably invested more to satisfy the expectations of the inner circle of old men; it would be marginally harder for him to move in a radically new direction. Günter Schabowski probably is more intelligent and unpredictable, with greater faculty to grow in the job. We know too little about them, however. It is not even certain whether Mrs. Krenz is Russian, as claimed in the West. Speculation about who is closer to Gorbachev is just that, near guesswork.

Dark horses cannot be ignored. Highly placed sources insist that, despite diabetes that has caused amputation of one and possibly both legs, Günter Mittag, the economic czar, believes he can become Honecker's Chernenko. Suddenly I am hearing Werner Jarowinsky tipped for bigger things. Successor generation age, at sixty-two, and vastly experienced at the SED's top level, he has held a key position in the Secretariat since 1963, moving papers and making decisions at the center longer than anyone except Honecker himself and the much older Kurt Hager. He made it into the Politburo in 1984, where his twin portfolios are trade and supply and the church. A few weeks ago, a well-connected Central Committee staffer surprised me with the opinion that Krenz was only one of several possibles, nowhere near the safe bet Honecker was as the Ulbricht era wound down. In fact, he was only slightly more probable than Schabowski—or Jarowinsky. Was Jarowinsky really being considered? I probed. He was beginning to be, I was assured. Soon thereafter, a retired diplomat confirmed there was increasing talk that Jarowinsky would at least take Mittag's portfolio.

That is the sort of straw with which we must make a few bricks, and I am trying to learn more about Jarowinsky the man and evaluate how he fits into the political maneuvering that I sense is beginning in earnest. There is scant evidence of strong views. Jarowinsky has been a colorless, nearly invisible political bureaucrat for so long that it is unlikely he harbors unusual reserves of drive and ambition, though every successful politician—and he is that— must have at least a share of those qualities.

The church portfolio has attracted attention for two years, partly because the church has become the focus of wider Party-society tensions, partly because the retirement of Klaus Gysi, the longtime secretary for religious questions who had direct access to Honecker, placed more of a burden on Jarowinsky. Most but not all of our sources say Jarowinsky has taken a hard line. Gysi himself, outspoken in retirement, tells us Jarowinsky is one of the most intelligent and well-read members of the Politburo, and if anything too open-minded. Allegedly, he is also habitually indecisive and quivers with uncertainty when a decision is required. Early this year, Dick Barkley judged him friendly, even jovial, uncommunicative and unexceptional on substance, except for one thing: More than any other Politburo member, Jarowinsky seemed genuinely interested in the United States. He also wanted to talk about books—history, economics, literature—he had just read on vacation.

The picture of Jarowinsky I draw from the sketchy and subjective evidence is of a man who is unlikely to try for the brass ring on his own initiative but who has the intelligence and presence to be useful to others. The relatively liberal adviser who first called my attention to him was distressed when Werner Felfe's death last fall removed the candidate in whom many would-be reformers placed hopes. He and others may prefer the open-minded Jarowinsky to either the (probably) conservative Krenz or the mercurial Schabowski. It is also tempting, however, to see third-candidate speculation as a ploy by those whose objective is to keep either Krenz or Schabowski from acquiring the aura of the inevitable successor. Were that to happen, pressure might build for an early change. Honecker himself may have most interest in sowing doubt about the main contenders.

Jarowinsky is not known to have especially close Soviet ties. He was born in Leningrad, but his return to Germany in time to serve in the Wehrmacht suggests that Stalin may have purged his father. If so, he is unlikely to be an uncritical admirer of the Soviet Union, but this does not tell us his stance on current policies. Werner Eberlein and retired master-spy-turned-Gorbachev-admirer Markus Wolf share backgrounds but not present politics. Obviously, too little is known for judgments. However, that there is now talk of a man who is so low-profile but who has a hand on several power levers indicates that pre-Congress politicking is picking up. Both those interested in blocking alternatives to the status quo and those seeking to build their own power base have reasons to court the Politburo's charming mystery man.

JULY 4

We almost committed the worst of sins: being late for the ambassador's reception. We had been showing the Sanssouci gardens in Potsdam to my cousin John, a graduate student in London, and his girlfriend and were pressed to make the start of our embassy's largest social obligation of the year. Gaby got us back, barely, by speeding around the Berliner Ring twenty miles above the 62 mph limit the GDR maintains on autobahns. Diplomats are immune from arrest but cannot ignore local law, and the traffic police near Oranienburg are sticklers for the speed limit. Gaby has already been stopped three times and given polite lectures. She gambled against a fourth, and we were lucky.

So was the embassy. The rains held off, and the Americana themes for finger food and the swing music played by an Army band from West Berlin were hits. As protocol dictates, we invited the Politburo and the Cabinet in addition to working-level official contacts and the full range of private East Germans with whom we deal, including church leaders, artists, writers, and, not least, dissidents. The GDR carefully allocates VIP acceptances. The full Politburo comes to the Soviet National Day, but we had deputy ministers, and Werner Krolikowski as sole Politburo representative. Dick took Krolikowski to a corner of the garden for an unrevealing talk.

The establishment and independent intellectuals do seem to be interacting a bit more these days. The Institute people were more ready than ever before to speak with my church friends, and Stefan Bickhardt, a young Lutheran vicar, volunteered that a few open-minded SED members wanted to establish links to the democratic opposition. Reissig was one of the boldest, Stefan said. He was trying to develop a blueprint for Glasnost and Perestroika in GDR colors after the Honecker era ended. I first met Stefan two years ago when he impressed Steny Hoyer, the Maryland Congressman who led a CSCE Commission delegation to Berlin. If the reform era dawns, he, like Reissig, could have a political future.

The prevailing atmosphere on the ambassador's lawn, however, was anxious. SED members and activists alike agreed that the country's mood has never been worse. Demonstrative support of China, the insulting elections, and the Central Committee's bland claim that all is well are taken as signals Honecker will make no concession to reform. There is a perceptible effort from above to tighten Party discipline. Is it any wonder, asked one churchman, that more are seeking asylum in West German diplomatic missions every day?

JULY 5

Until last fall, we were making incremental progress with the GDR. Then the United States decided to defer a better trade relationship until the GDR resolved both sets of claims, and the GDR reacted by accusing us of breaking an understanding to proceed on a parallel track (the "package solution"). Activity stalled across the board, but the State Department is now reviewing the bidding, Dick confirmed. We should see a draft soon, and then have our chance for input.

The day before John and his friend left, we stopped at an attractive café along a canal of the Spree for ice cream, but the waitress refused us an empty table for four. It was not in her sector, she explained, and there was no other waitress. When we sought to add two chairs, she said it was not allowed. I lost my temper and said we were trying to show two young Americans her country, but her churlish attitude confirmed their worst preconceptions. The girl was unaffected. "There is nothing I can do about the rules," she grumbled.

Gaby told me I was too hard. The waitress was overworked; like many GDR enterprises, the café was short of help. The cook for the restaurant to which we had taken Walt Slocombe told us he had only two of the five kitchen assistants he needed. Staff have little incentive to extend themselves. They know they can expect minimal tips and will not be fired. The manager could not replace them, and state ideology protects even unmotivated workers. We found a second café, but John and his friend had learned another facet of GDR reality beyond the Wall. I suspect it was less the self-confidence of the young worker than her failure to meet minimal standards of courtesy and performance that impressed them.

JULY 6

Adass Jisroel, East Berlin's smaller Jewish community, split on liturgical grounds from the majority of Germany's Jews in the last century, and the dispute astonishingly survived the Holocaust. Honecker has lately worked at establishing ties to world Jewry, both to improve his image and to increase the possibility, however remote, that he might be invited to the United States. Several years ago, he rescued Adass Jisroel's overgrown cemetery from a bulldozer and offered restoration assistance. Dr. Mario Offenberg, an Israeli whose father was the community's last prewar rabbi and who has made recovery of its rights his life's work, says Honecker is backing away from his promise to return other properties. Nevertheless, the congregation has made more progress with the GDR than in the West, where the autocratic local chairman, Heinz Galinski, maintains that German Jewry cannot afford the luxury of schism.

Today was a time for thanksgiving that the dead again rest in sanctified and protected surroundings. A dozen young GDR citizens present at the ceremonies impressed me deeply. For more than a year these students, workers, and stonemasons, of no particular religious or political persuasion, have contributed their Sundays to Adass Jisroel. Why? I asked. Because they know the tragedy of German and Jewish history, they answered; they want to learn about a part of their culture that almost died, and to make amends. Honecker still quibbles about whether the socialist GDR shares responsibility for the Holocaust. In the last year, the GDR has grudgingly acknowledged there are youths here, Skinheads, as ready to take to the streets with rowdy and sometimes anti-Semitic actions as their Western counterparts. There is justified finger-pointing at the educational system. And yet some young people here are as idealistic and generous of spirit as those anywhere in the world. What is more selfless than to devote precious weekends with no prospect of return to restoring the cemetery of strangers?

JULY 7

Rudolf Seiters, head of Helmut Kohl's office, has been in town seeking to put inner-German relations back on an even keel. Serious negotiations have resumed on the big-ticket item for the 1990s: construction of high-speed train connections between Berlin and West Germany. For legal and political reasons, Bonn's GDR policy is run from the Chancellor's desk. For the West Germans, relations with East Berlin cannot be treated as "foreign" and "diplomatic," so Genscher's Foreign Office must not lead; but the GDR will not deal formally with Bonn's Ministry for Inner-German Affairs, for its own reasons of principle. Giving responsibility to Seiters satisfies theologians and ensures that Kohl has direct control over business of the greatest domestic sensitivity. The same balancing interests are reflected in the Ständige Vertretung, which has a mix of diplomats and officials of the inner-German and other ministries. There is one common feature: they are topflight. For the Federal Republic, East Berlin may be its most important post, and it is surely its most delicate. Only the best are sent here.

JULY 8

A Stephen Solarz visit has no shopping or touring and as little downtime as possible. While we waited for bags at Schönefeld Airport, the Congressman questioned me like a machine gun on semi-automatic. In twenty-four hours, he met with the Country Team, senior churchmen, Central Committee staff, Politburo media czar Joachim Herrmann, the acting foreign minister, the Ständige Vertretung, and dissidents, and found time for a drink with George McGovern. He wanted to assess whether the Gorbachev virus would spread, and he put the same questions to everyone: Would the GDR become reformist, and what was its position on Polish and Hungarian efforts to redefine socialism? Could it accept that some Communist parties might lose power?

Party intellectuals admitted growing dissatisfaction, while church officials said they were willing to work within socialism and hoped the hundreds of thousands of would-be emigrants stayed to make East Germany better. The GDR, they argued, was important for Europe's stability. Major changes were needed, but the backdrop of economic disarray made most East Germans ambiguous about Polish and Hungarian reforms, they cautioned. The West German diplomats told Solarz that GDR society was far more dissatisfied than officials admitted, flawed by insufficient, inconsistent delivery of the social benefits on which the Party prided itself. Change was coming, but slowly, because the leadership believed only classical socialism justified a second German state. They defended Bonn's policy of cooperation because it maintained the concept of a single nation, provided leverage over policies, and aided people. Without it, the GDR would not collapse, but only become a harsher place.

The young people who received him in a church basement provided Solarz with a taste of life near the margins, where dissidents are partly protected by the church but can still come into conflict with the state. They described efforts to collect ecological information, the obstacle course faced by anyone who wants to travel, and their frustrated efforts to field candidates in the May elections. What East Germans desire most, they told him, was for the government simply to allow them more free space.

"What did you think of Herrmann?" they asked. "Full of hot air," the Congressman replied, to their delight. Even the youthful Foreign Ministry translator had been unimpressed by the Politburo man. "I think the Congressman must have been a little unhappy," he whispered to me. The questions, he said, had been to the point, but the long answers had not.

What others were attempting, Herrmann insisted smugly—to rationalize their economies—the GDR did fifteen years ago. Kohl, he said, had asked Gorbachev when the GDR would reform. Gorbachev allegedly replied that if the Soviets had followed the GDR example in the 1970s their shops would not now be empty. The SED saw no need to introduce more market elements and would maintain subsidies as a just component of the social compact, he said. The system needed only minor economic adjustments and no political reform.

Nevertheless, Herrmann was categorical that times had changed. The GDR would not interfere with Hungarian or Polish reforms, but nonintervention must be a two-way street, he said. Gorbachev had said, Herrmann recalled approvingly, that any effort to overcome Europe's division by doing away with socialism risked a new age of confrontation. Indeed, it was striking that, in contrast to many conversations with GDR leaders over the past year, Herrmann was upbeat on Gorbachev. He claimed that, while briefing Honecker on his Bonn visit, the Soviet had stressed that his reforms would strengthen socialism, not introduce capitalism. He would retain a one-party system, Herrmann said confidently. The GDR supported Soviet reforms fully, therefore, even if many were not relevant here. It appears that Honecker's Politburo realizes the GDR needs a rejuvenated Soviet Union if it is not to be hopelessly isolated on West Germany's doorstep. It grumbles and worries about the implications, but the fundamental judgment is that Gorbachev's failure would be worse for this state than his success.

"If it ain't broke, don't fix it." That is how Solarz summarized the Politburo's message. Herrmann agreed at once. And yet, despite the bluster, he and his colleagues know the stakes. When Solarz suggested they agreed on the statement "Let Poland be Poland," Herrmann shot back his preferred line from that country's anthem: "Poland is not yet lost." Reforms in the Soviet Union, he said, would be decisive for socialism's future, not whatever was happening now in Poland, Hungary—or the GDR.

JULY 9

The ADN announced yesterday that Honecker suffered an acute gall-bladder attack following Friday's Warsaw Pact summit banquet, spent the night in the hospital, and then was flown home early. I got word from a Swedish diplomat who heard it as he drove to a house party given by mutual East German friends on a lake deep in the Brandenburg countryside.

Until this embarrassingly public sign that he is not immune to human frailties, the seventy-six-year-old has appeared to be in excellent health. I have no reason to believe the attack is serious, but it will raise questions about how long this very old Politburo can keep the reins in its hands. Even if Honecker is on his feet quickly, there may be a psychological impact, in the Party and in his own mind. The deaths of Gromyko and Kádár last week had already delivered two sharp reminders of the mortality of politicians. It would be natural for thought to be given behind closed doors to scenarios for a graceful withdrawal, either in October at the GDR's 40th Anniversary or next spring at the SED Congress. If the situation does begin to loosen at the top, speculation will increase exponentially on implications for the GDR's conservative policies. No one our embassy knows has reliable information. There is poignant symbolism, however, in the fact that Honecker had to absent himself from today's Politburo in-house celebration of Prime Minister Stoph's seventy-fifth birthday. Even in the GDR not everything can be planned, and change could come faster than we have all assumed.

Our hosts, at whose summer place in Marienthal on a lake sixty minutes north of Berlin we learned of Honecker's illness, demonstrate that with talent and dedication, though at extra emotional cost, it is possible to prosper and live in the GDR in a manner that middle-class West Germans would not despise. They are the country's best hairdressers, whose clientele includes East Berlin's most fashionable women. Their fees are strictly regulated at a fraction of those in the West. Like private entrepreneurs who run half of East Berlin's restaurants, they can earn more than the average only by offering quality service.

Even many service-sector independents are not willing to sacrifice to provide that extra. Rules are stacked against them, though not as badly since the state realized that they plug gaps in an economy where quality rather than absolute scarcity is a chronic problem. Tax rates are steeply progressive but no longer blatantly confiscatory. Licenses, even state loans to assist start-up, are more available, but entrepreneurs can hire only ten employees.

That is not a problem for our hosts. Their shop is a family affair, with a daughter learning under their tutelage. They study hard to keep up with trends, have talent, and think nothing of working twelve-hour days six days a week. Like others in the small but surprisingly varied East German business elite, they put money into one of the few feasible outlets for wealth, their home. Well into fall, they weekend at their lakeside house, and they commute on long summer weekday evenings. The isolated lake is sparsely settled. Lost, we were directed by neighbors who proudly displayed their collection of monkeys and exotic birds.

Our hosts used connections to buy the choice lot from the county, and they struck another deal with the cooperative that holds exclusive commercial fishing rights. The utilities would be unacceptable in the West—electricity but no sewers, and barely paved roads—but the house is a gem. It and the garage have reed-thatched roofs. The terrace offers a panoramic lake view with the welcoming cocktail. Roast wild boar was grilled outdoors and followed by a fishing interlude from the private dock.

This religious family does not readily discuss politics. They live as much as possible within their own walls, admitting only relatives and friends to share relaxation and free talk, an example of what the Ständige Vertretung's first chief, Günter Gaus, called the GDR's pervasive "society of niches" (*Nischengesellschaft*). But reality intrudes. The husband's sister and her West Berlin fiancé were there. After two years, their application to marry and settle across the Wall had just been approved. The day was bittersweet, tinged with uncertainty about when the family would be together again.

There have been positive changes. Professional prominence has enabled our hosts to travel for years, a privilege unlikely to be cut off when millions of family visits are allowed. The sister must forfeit GDR citizenship, but a "binational marriage" case is treated better than that of an emigrant, who cannot return to visit for five years. Still, no law, at least none accessible to the public, establishes a right East Germans can rely on. In this, as in so much of their successful and not unpleasant lives, our hosts are at the mercy of arbitrary policy and bureaucracy.

JULY 10

Rabbi Israel Singer, the number-two man in the World Jewish Congress, invited me to his hotel suite Sunday for a talk before he met Foreign Minister Oskar Fischer. The effort to persuade the GDR to make a substantial humanitarian gesture for Holocaust victims is a matter of sensitivity and historical complexity. It is too late, and the GDR is too poor, to expect it would establish a payments program as extensive as the Federal Republic did in the 1950s. It is not acceptable, however, for its leaders to argue that their own anti-Nazi engagement and Hitler's persecution of Communists free this society of seventeen million from a need to reflect on the past and to assist survivors. The United States cannot formally negotiate, because international law limits a state's protective jurisdiction to wrongs suffered by those who were its citizens at the time of injury. From the day exchange of embassies was first discussed, however, we have told the GDR that relations could never be good until it made peace with World Jewry. If it doubts our motives, it should at least recognize political reality. No U.S. President or Congress will approve normal trade until the obligation is met.

The short-lived experiment of an American rabbi who ministered to the East Berlin community in 1987–88 was an effort to normalize ties between the GDR and Jews, as has been the project, launched in Honecker's presence at last year's commemoration of Kristallnacht, to rebuild Berlin's largest synagogue. There has been no concrete offer, however, since ten years ago $1 million was rejected as trivial. Figures as high as $100 million have been rumored but not confirmed, and the GDR argues that it needs improved opportunity to earn hard currency in U.S. markets before it can afford to pay. The influential president of the World Jewish Congress, Edgar Bronfman, last year in Berlin expressed public confidence that Honecker would do the right thing, but there has been no sign of it since.

I told Rabbi Singer the secretary would not see Fischer at the United Nations unless there was major progress on the familiar issues. Singer said he had heard that in Washington. He was here because the GDR had benefited from a no-interest public-relations loan for nine months, and it was time to show the color of its money. Singer said he would make it clear that Bronfman's patience was wearing thin, and also that a new attitude toward Israel was necessary. Bronfman's stature makes a threat of public criticism meaningful, but I am not optimistic. GDR style is to haggle for narrow advantage, and rarely to make a dramatic gesture without assurance of what it can get in return. Especially with Honecker convalescing, the bureaucracy is unlikely to move out of old, sterile grooves.

JULY 11

Dick convened a meeting to plan for the contingency of asylum-seekers in the American Embassy. Our West German colleagues speak softly, for fear of contributing to mass psychosis, and discourage press reports, but they have let us know that scores of people are refusing to leave the Ständige Vertretung until guaranteed they can cross the Wall. Thirty are at the Budapest Embassy, and a further handful are in Prague. These are too many for the lawyer, Wolfgang Vogel, to process without special dispensation. Honecker's illness deprives him of his access, and the Stasi and the obstructionist bureaucracy are filling the vacuum. The sit-ins, as well as hundreds of thousands who have filed emigration papers, want to settle in West Germany. The United States has essentially full success in resolving its handful of divided-family cases. Historically, however, pressure on the Ständige Vertretung has spilled over to the American Embassy, which frightened and increasingly desperate East Germans may believe is not as tightly guarded.

The United States is in an awkward position. We make human rights the centerpiece of relations, but we cannot offer embassy asylum; the concept does not exist in international law. More practically, we cannot physically help an asylum-seeker reach West Berlin without GDR assistance, and we lack space to put up more than a handful for a brief period. If we encouraged sit-ins, the GDR could call our hand by holding Vogel back. Normal work, including protection of Americans, could then become impossible, as nearly happened to the larger Ständige Vertretung in January. Of course, we would never give a desperate East German to the police or force him from the embassy. Even a case of self-defense, when the Marines a few years ago had to remove a man who threatened a consul with a knife, was highly controversial in West Germany.

Dick wants to be certain we do whatever we can to avoid problems that would have no easy, perhaps no good, solution. This includes instructing receptionists to be alert. If a family appears with children and suitcases, we will explain we cannot help directly, but a consul will pass particulars to the Ständige Vertretung so the West Germans can take up the case.

We will take common-sense precautions without allowing them to defeat the embassy's purposes. We have worked to persuade the East Germans to let their people learn more about the United States. The GDR originally objected that our U.S. Information Service Library, offering materials about the United States, was not a proper diplomatic function, and police frequently prevented East Germans from entering. After our strong objections, blatant restraint ceased, but they still often ask those leaving the building to identify themselves. Gaby was pursued down Unter den Linden just after we arrived, but the policeman backed off red-faced when he discovered she was immune to harassment. In recent years, East Germans have become less willing to be intimidated. Two years ago, the library had thirty customers weekly. Now there are two hundred each day. Once, when Gaby was librarian, an entire group of blue-uniformed youngsters stopped by to sample Madonna videos after a meeting at FDJ headquarters around the corner. The last thing we should do is destroy the small advances we have achieved in this tightly controlled society in search of our own perfect security.

JULY 12

Speculation about Honecker's illness is the name of the game among diplomats. Party contacts, who dismiss it as routine, are repeating the line developed by Politburo spin artists. *Neues Deutschland* says Honecker is on his annual holiday after brief hospital treatment for "gall-bladder colic." Hermann Axen told a Western visitor that the problem was "nothing serious." Nevertheless, the longer Honecker is out of sight, the more conjecture there will be.

JULY 13

The GDR is beginning to interest journalists who appreciate the significance of the changes brewing in the region. A CBS reporter called from New York to discuss a documentary in which the GDR would be contrasted with Poland and Hungary as Eastern Europe's conservative bastion. I urged her to come and said she might find the reality somewhat more complex.

Other correspondents are arriving. Henry Kamm, the *New York Times* veteran, called on Dick and me. It was his second time in the American Embassy Berlin, he said. The first was fifty years ago, in the old embassy building on Pariser Platz in front of the Brandenburg Gate, inside what is now the Wall's "Death Zone." A teenage Jewish boy from Breslau, he told a white lie, denying a lung disease to get a visa. Henry had never received permission to do stories from the GDR, perhaps because with his perfect German the regime knew he would probe deeply. Now the restrictive press policy has changed, at least for Western media, and he is on an extensive tour. Timothy Garton Ash, a Briton who a decade ago made himself unwelcome with a book that argued the GDR needed a dose of Polish

Solidarity, has also returned. At breakfast, he promised to test my estimate that there is a new outspokenness here, even within the SED, that the leadership must soon come to grips with.

It is beginning to dawn on reporters that the GDR can only become more important. It is the geographic, military, and technological bulwark of the Soviet position in Europe. In direct proportion to the extent East-West confrontation is built down, Europe's great unresolved matter, the German Question, will move front and center. The GDR is thus far more pivotal to any conceivable scenario for the coming decade than Hungary or even Poland. The West willfully ignored the unlovely state for a quarter-century and still understands it poorly, but now it is vital to pay attention.

One who has long recognized the GDR's significance is Peter Bender, the West German publicist who articulated an intellectual framework for Willy Brandt's innovative policies twenty years ago. The most recent issue of *Die Zeit* carried his thought-provoking analysis. The Honecker team, he pointed out, has drawn lessons from its historical experience: that the June 1953 revolt happened because the GDR's indecisive political leaders accepted Soviet-dictated reforms; and that military force has always been needed to restore order after Eastern European experiments. It is not likely now to be persuaded that the dangers Perestroika can precipitate must be braved in order to establish genuine stability. Still, Bender argues, Honecker's successor cannot delay long. The GDR is Eastern Europe's richest state, but it lives excessively on substance inherited from prewar Germany. In 1987, Kurt Hager encapsulated Politburo disdain for Gorbachev with the statement "One does not change wallpaper just because a neighbor does." But, Bender argues, "the GDR's wallpaper is rotten and in places peeling. The impetus to reform lies in the GDR itself. The leadership can delay the new beginning, but not escape it."

It is also part of Bender's thesis, however, that reform has better prospects in the GDR than in other Communist lands. There is a stronger economic foundation and a talented population that both understands something of market principles and Western ways and, arguably, has internalized some socialist values and achievements. The latter, he admits, is open to question, but, he asks, "How must a GDR with which its citizens would be satisfied look? Do the seventeen million there want a second Federal Republic, or do they want to . . . be partly their own? Was socialism only a gigantic mistake, in the manner of the familiar crack about the longest road from capitalism to capitalism? Or does it contain some things the people do not want to be without and that deserve to be developed further into a socialism freed of its Stalinist deformation?"

Bender explores more than provincial German interests. The ice in which Europe's divisions have been frozen is thawing, he points out: "Most Europeans fear a unified Germany and want the GDR to survive," but "European necessity alone can make no German state survivable." The GDR needs even more than other Communist states to make its political system democratic, its society pluralistic, its economy efficient, since it cannot outlive failure. Can socialism achieve those goals? If anywhere, the argument goes, then here. Bender again: "Does the SED have the strength to change into a party of democratic socialism, as parts of the Hungarian and Polish Parties are attempting? Such a Party would be greatly needed in a state that acquired a substantially market economy but is accustomed to socialism. Would the majority be prepared to support such an attempt? Would they give their trust to a changed SED? The GDR has no time to lose. The chance still exists to confront the crisis before it is here. The longer this does not happen, the more difficult and dangerous a new beginning will be. Perhaps that is the worst in the blind stubbornness of East Berlin's leaders: it holds Party and People back from trying their future."

JULY 14

A bemused J.D. signed my diplomatic note requesting a meeting with the GDR Soccer Association. The idea is not frivolous. To understand America, Jacques Barzun once said, it is necessary to understand baseball. Nothing tells as much as enjoyably about society as its sports. Some of my best excursions into Hungarian life included the soccer scene, and it would be fun to try this in the GDR. Even *Neues Deutschland* comes near candor when it rails against the failures of the GDR team, which has had three coaches this season. Perhaps not coincidentally, signs of major change are appearing—dare one use the "R" word?—which resemble early Soviet moves toward replacing club subsidies with self-management. It is worth a summer flier.

JULY 15

We drove north again this weekend to visit friends in their dacha. Uwe and Marianne Haus spend the summer in Fürstenberg, where Brandenburg, the "sandbox of the Holy Roman Empire of the German nation," blends into the rolling fields and lakelands of Mecklenburg, to which Bismarck recommended people go when the world ends, "because everything there happens fifty years later." It is a typical run-down, mid-sized GDR town: the few new buildings mostly of slapdash sameness; paint peeling off many older, once solidly middle-class structures; streets potholed on a par with Washington in early spring. Fürstenberg is home for a garrison of the nearly 400,000 strong Western Group of Soviet Forces. Unlike Berlin, Red Army uniforms are common in streets and shops. We walked where Soviets are the only occupants of dwellings the yellow paint of which recalls lands east and south of Germany, past playgrounds where soccer players called out in Russian.

The "Friends," as the Soviets are euphemistically known, are almost entirely isolated from German life. Fights in pubs, stimulated by alcohol or competition for girls, motivate officers to keep conscripts in the casernes, but there is surprisingly little anti-Russian feeling. East Germans feel superior to and sorry for soldiers who are too poor to partake in what for them is the GDR's well-stocked consumer society. With Gorbachev, condescending avoidance turned for many East Germans into livelier interest. Ironically, the SED discourages this and tries to confine contacts to the ubiquitous German-Soviet Friendship Society, where programs can be monitored. Last fall, when it banned the pro-reform Moscow monthly magazine *Sputnik*, the GDR prepared to close the Friendship Society's own journal until the Soviets demonstratively gave the magazine an award. It remains difficult for Germans and Russians to come together. Life is probably lonelier now for troops who might want to learn about the country where they are stationed.

Uwe Haus, a top theater director, and Marianne, a doctor, have the basement apartment of what used to be Marianne's parents' house. The state has turned the remainder over to tenants, but our friends retain use of the garden, which leads to a stream that flows into the Havel River. It offers an idyllic if hardly luxurious break from their Berlin apartment, particularly for their musically inclined son, who can fish, make friends with the neighbor's horse, and turn the garage loft into a hideaway. It is a level below the sparkling good life of West German counterparts, but still impressive. Uwe has been barred from work in the GDR for years, a result of his independent thinking, but his is a special talent that cannot be buried. He directs a theater on Cyprus, has put on Brecht at American universities, and is negotiating a long-term position in West Germany. This year, for the first time, Marianne accompanied him across the Atlantic. Despite the credit they bring the GDR, they face the same frustrations as less-fortunate citizens. Marianne's passport was issued only after a nerve-racking test of wills with the Stasi. Other artists with a similarly critical bent have been hectored into emigration. Uwe's fame provides little leverage should the security organs decide he has overstepped their bounds.

We sat in the garden, drinking Cypriot wine, eating homemade bread, grilling meats in Greek, German, and American styles, and discussing the GDR mood. All agreed that SED rigidity contrasts so dramatically with the sense of new horizons in most of Europe that discontent is very high. The signs are everywhere, from turned-off youth and the increasingly open grumbling of intellectuals, through bolder protests against rigged elections and official support for the Chinese Solution, to the sit-ins at West German embassies. At some point Honecker must react, but how? The conversation intrudes on many evenings this summer. We had no answers.

JULY 17

The Yale Whiffenpoofs' preppy style went over surprisingly well with East Germans at the Verners' informal lawn-party concert. What I keep recalling, however, is my exchange with Norbert Reemer, head of the Foreign Ministry's U.S. Section. When he approached me in a corner of the garden, he began by promising to support my request to meet the soccer officials, provided I told him if I learned what was wrong with the GDR team. "It's a deal," I said. Reemer is a regularly disappointed fan of FC Hansa Rostock, his home club, and soccer is our small-talk, but I was not prepared for what he said next: "In two or three years we will have the same situation as in Poland and Hungary because we have exactly the same problems." I was fascinated but concerned for him. This was not the language of the uptight, buttoned-down GDR diplomat. Reemer's Polish-born wife shared my worry, for she returned the talk to generalities, and the couple soon drifted away.

If discipline is breached even in the Foreign Ministry, discontent must be rising faster and reaching further than we had thought. The GDR's untroubled calm, so praised by Honecker, is a mirage. We must probe more to get a fix on the reality.

JULY 18

Our small embassy operates informally, without hallmarks of the giant Washington bureaucracy. When we have ideas, we walk through an open door—even the ambassador's—and chat. For the meeting with Axen tomorrow, however, there has been a change in procedure. Bilateral relations and internal GDR politics are at a crossroads, and we hope to learn from the little man who is one of Honecker's oldest allies how the leadership means to reverse what is drift or worse. To prepare, Dick asked for briefing memos. Mine focused on three areas: the Washington climate, the President's foreign-policy initiatives, and bilateral ties.

Our best line to argue is probably that the new State Department team is interested in Eastern Europe and might be prepared to engage with the GDR if Axen and Ambassador Barkley come up with good ideas. Axen will probably share our cautious optimism about arms control. Given the chronic SED disposition to assume conspiracy, however, he will need reassurance about President Bush's visit to Poland and Hungary. The most difficult part of the conversation, nevertheless, will be the bilateral. Dick must say that he has no fresh proposals on the old triad—government claims, Jewish claims, and trade—but I urged him to parallel this tough message with hints of our ideas for marking new ground. We want to get Axen thinking about wrapping up negotiations for a cultural agreement and expanding environmental cooperation and exchanges of next-generation leaders.

JULY 19

Six weeks after Tienanmen Square, the GDR is still going out of its way to support how the Chinese answered the power question (*die Machtfrage*, as German Communists call it with reverence). Schabowski is in Beijing, where, *Neues Deutschland* reported, he found appreciation "for the GDR's solidarity with China's steps to put down the disorders, which had expanded to counterrevolutionary riots." The trip raises many questions. The Chinese Embassy says Schabowski substituted for Krenz, who was last month's point man on China. Does the Politburo want to identify both possible successors with an unpopular policy? Or has Honecker's health worsened? The Chinese believe the illness is "serious," and Krenz, formally Honecker's deputy in the state structure, was needed in Berlin.

Politburo appointments are special. They allow our ambassador to probe directly the mood and thinking of the twenty-three men who run the GDR. There is no doubt that power resides in the cavernous SED headquarters—a bank before the war—that stands modestly to the rear and side of, but far, far above the Council of State, the Parliament, and the Foreign Ministry with their grander addresses. But the Politburo is an unwieldy body, a number of whose members are posted in the provinces or are superannuated figureheads. The members who are also Central Committee secretaries constitute the inner circle. They set the agenda and cook decisions that the full Politburo makes in its weekly session.

Hermann Axen, whom the ambassador and I see this afternoon, is the Politburo's smallest man and one of its most powerful. Born into a Jewish family that was decimated in the gas chambers, Axen joined the Communist resistance and spent the war either in Soviet exile (the version of some Western scholars) or in Auschwitz and Buchenwald (his own account). He has never denied his Jewish heritage, though he is, of course, not religious; it disqualified him from a shot at the top, but he has worked closely with Honecker for forty years. Overweight and with eye problems at age 73, he is the undisputed boss of foreign policy. The vain, bright workaholic likes Western press references to "Honecker's Kissinger" and wants to be thought the architect of the GDR's advance to a position of respect in European diplomacy, a calculable, reliable factor, as he puts it, in the security structure.

The United States is a special challenge for Axen. Before his trip to Washington last year, he told us of his fascination with America and its culture. He admired Jefferson and Franklin Roosevelt, he said, but his real heroes came from films—Gary Cooper, for example. Reemer, who considers him a demanding, sometimes petty, master, says Axen constantly orders the Washington Embassy to send him new books. And yet, he does not really understand how to interact with Americans. His English is good, and he can charm, but often he comes across as everyone's preconception of a stiff, Germanic Communist ideologue. I have seen him bore Congressmen, and his Washington visit was a disaster. He lectured George Shultz, and then movers and shakers at the Institute for Contemporary German Studies, on Communist verities. By the time he loosened up and recounted his youthful journey of commitment, he had lost both audience and opportunity. If Axen's mission was to prepare the invitation Honecker covets, he and his one superior must know he flopped. He has the power but probably not the honesty and the imagination to make the lost chance good, and he has been more rigid than ever this year trying to prove he was always right.

Chairman Les Aspin is to bring the House Armed Services Committee in August. The Soviets have offered a tour of sites never before open to Westerners, and the idea is to stop first to talk with the forces here. It is not to be entirely a U.S.-Soviet show, however. Aspin also wants contact with East German military.

JULY 20

The Axen conversation was good-tempered, exhaustive, and disappointing. Nothing in the ninety-minute exchange—conducted informally over coffee in a comfortable alcove, rather than across a long table, as most of his colleagues favor—gave any indication the GDR will react imaginatively to its challenges.

Axen wanted to talk about the bilateral problem, once even saying "Not so fast" when Dick sought his reaction to a Gorbachev initiative. Ties were "stagnant" and "underdeveloped," with "both sides waiting for the other to make a move," but it was the Americans who should go first, he said. He was unmoved by the point, self-evident to us, that the GDR needed to help build a consensus in Washington that the time was ripe for moving forward. We know the GDR will not reform merely to establish a better bilateral climate, Dick argued, but at least it must resolve the old issues that have held us back virtually from the day embassies were opened. Axen merely shrugged off the suggestion that the GDR could help itself by participating more actively in exchanges. All that was fine, he said dismissively, but the central problem remained the package deal the United States abandoned last year. Difficulties holding up the cultural agreement, he said, were minor. With goodwill, experts could solve them quickly. He meant there would be no GDR will until we showed something of what they want.

Axen returned repeatedly to his theme of political dialogue. It had been progressing well, he believed. John Whitehead met three times with Honecker; then, he complained, something happened. The GDR had contributed in the tough days of the early 1980s, he recalled with pride, when superpower negotiations broke off, and it wanted to be part of the East-West conversation again. Only if we began speaking at an appropriate level, he asserted, could we make the progress for which the GDR was ready.

The Politburo is marking time, and it may be unfair to attribute this only to Honecker's illness and its own general sclerosis. If we would understand them at what is so obviously a difficult time, we need to ask what they believe and want. Axen gave a hint when he recounted meeting George Ball after the former deputy secretary of state had left office but before the GDR had broken its diplomatic isolation. The time for official contacts would come, Ball said. "And he was right," Axen noted proudly. "We were in no hurry then, and time proved we are a factor that must be dealt with." These old men believe that the world will come to them, that their policies will be proved correct, and that the United States will eventually have to deal on East German terms.

What the GDR wants from us is not only, or even primarily, trade concessions. It remains fixed on prestige and legitimacy to a degree that would be paranoid were it a normal state. The United States must decide, Axen said: "Is the GDR a reality? Will the GDR last, or does it have no substance? You have to have a concept of that. You know what I mean."

President Bush's talk about the Wall and reunification has stung. Renewal of senior political dialogue would be reassurance that the United States remains prepared to do the practical business with the GDR that, Axen carefully pointed out, the West Germans, the French, the British and the Japanese do. But it was hard for us to leave Axen's office with optimism. Though we shall keep trying because that is a diplomat's work, the ambiguity of their position can be resolved only by the East Germans themselves. Are there adequate grounds for Axen's confidence that time is on their side? Or is the underlying insecurity he betrayed more justified, as this summer's disquieting trends begin to suggest?

JULY 21

Solidarity is still ignored, but *Neues Deutschland* put Jaruzelski's election as Poland's president on the front page. SED contacts stress that the GDR realizes it must accept radical change in Poland. National interests dictate that its large neighbor is, with the Soviet Union and West Germany, one of the few countries with which it simply must seek a good relationship. More favorable, if highly selective, coverage is a sign of pragmatism, they say.

On a day when *Neues Deutschland*'s other regional headlines said such things as "Gorbachev on the situation in the strike areas" and "Tass on the situation in Abchasia" (ethnic strife), there was an almost audible sigh of relief to the line "Jaruzelski Elected President." As Honecker's congratulatory message put it, "We see in your selection . . . a guarantee that the close relations and extensive cooperation that have developed between the GDR and Poland in over forty years will develop and deepen further." It is the best guarantee available—but not, the SED well knows, a very strong one.

JULY 24

The Office of Central European Affairs, responsible for both German states and Berlin, has done yeoman work in engaging Washington's foreign policy machinery on the GDR. The unabashed goal, in the words of its director, Pierre Shostal, is to do some "open field running." Dick and J.D. asked me to coordinate comments. Everything is "Official-Informal," restricted to those working the topic directly. It must be formalized later, but this is a means to share candid views before anyone is on the record.

The recommendations are cautious, the major new element more environmental cooperation. Important as that subject is, it could be an "open sesame" only if we had money to clean the Elbe and put filters on all the smokestacks around Halle-Neustadt and Leipzig. Our colleagues propose nothing new on the core claims/trade deadlocks because many in Washington still believe either that tariff neutral trade would be a concession not justified by the GDR's human rights record or that this market is too small to make negotiation worthwhile.

The ideas are laudable, but they are a strategy for marking time, for keeping the GDR on the edge of Washington's radar—not the worst thing, since we are struggling to prevent minimal ties from unraveling further. It likely is a fair judgment of what is feasible and therefore what we should fight for. We have been asked for ideas, however, and I believe an embassy should be imaginative and let the State Department tailor the final product to Washington reality. I am suggesting a bolder strategy to tackle the hard issues—the Wall, claims, trade, and political dialogue—first and with a fresh approach.

The GDR will not take the Wall down soon for all the reasons we condemn but that seem vital to it. We should point out its incompatibility with CSCE principles but make clear that what we will hold them to as a test of sincerity is to continue, and accelerate, the process of making it more permeable—and, of course, avoid shooting. In the near term, the GDR must give generous claims commitments to us and to the Jewish organizations. At the same time, we must redefine the trade issue so that its benefits are a two-way street. The GDR should get limited tariff relief on selected items that it believes it can sell and that would not deprive American firms of profits, but our businessmen should get more opportunities through a trade-facilitation agreement to make money here.

Axen would say these benefits are heavily on the American side. The Wall and "claims" are our issues, and we would change trade from theirs into a wash. Political dialogue, however, is the GDR's issue. They want from it a little of what we have in adequate measure: prestige, legitimacy, a Big League franchise (the NFL, if the metaphor must be consistent). Even I would not propose to bring Honecker and Bush together, but there could be variants a step or two lower, such as an invitation to Krenz tied to major GDR concessions. The East Germans know such things do not come free. We would have to learn how much they would pay. Since we know they have a weakness, however, it seems only reasonable—if we want to be a player here—to exploit it.

JULY 25

Contacts with the GDR military are controversial, but for a change the United States has been prompt off the mark. Though legalists and skeptics are reconnoitering the ground, the Department supports us against the qualms of the West Berlin Mission (Berlin status) and the Bonn Embassy (the West Germans might not like our doing what they themselves have begun). Our point is that there is legitimate U.S. interest in exposing the Warsaw Pact's most important non-Soviet component to Glasnost. In any event, one important foreign policy principle is on view during this exercise: the Foreign Service can weigh issues or split hairs as much as we want, but when a political power like Les Aspin decides he wants to meet GDR troops, we set about making it happen. Sometimes it is good that Congress is a law unto itself even in "our" field.

JULY 26

Ständige Vertretung colleagues are increasingly worried about a new wave of sit-ins. The situation is particularly acute in Hungary, where hundreds of vacationing East Germans have slipped across into Austria. Unlike past practice, those stopped by the Hungarian police have not been returned to the GDR. If blocked at the border, they either try again or go to Budapest and become guests of the West German Embassy. Official reaction here has been muted. The GDR continues to pursue a relatively liberal travel policy. At current rates, 1.5 million working-age East Germans, up fifty-fold from three or four years ago, will pay private visits to the West by year's end; there will also be record legal emigration. On the other hand, indications are the GDR will be tough about embassy sit-ins, arguing that there is no reason to allow "line jumpers." And, of course, there is no sign the SED will launch reforms, which is a big reason for deteriorating domestic morale.

Late on a Saturday at a party given by our friends Helmut and Petra, Gaby and I met two young people whose stories illustrate important contradictions in GDR life near the end of the Honecker era.

Jürgen grew up in a house where religious values were pervasive; his father was a Protestant clergyman, his mother was one of five sisters who married clergymen. (We know one of those uncles; alternative society GDR is a small town.) Tall, handsome, self-possessed, and intelligent, Jürgen had excellent prospects for university and a profession, but at age sixteen, when he received his draft registration notice, he decided that his religious principles would not allow him to serve. He rejected the "halfway house" most conscientious objectors choose: the "Construction Troops," young men who do not carry arms but wear uniforms, take an oath, and may be required to work on military projects.

The state respected his decision, Jürgen said. It did not send a final order, which he would have rejected, and it never took legal action against him. Such tolerance is new; not many years ago, Jürgen would have been jailed. Nevertheless, his academic prospects were gone. Blocked from university, he moved from Schwerin in Mecklenburg to Potsdam, where he graduated with honors from a church school. He could have become a pastor, but he lacked the calling, he said. His interest was law and the diplomatic service, but those were impossible goals, so he applied to emigrate.

Jürgen has been told his application is "acute," that in two or three weeks he can leave "for the Western part of Germany, where I believe I can pursue the kind of life I want." But, he added, the hardest thing about the decision was that it was irreversible. There was much he loved in the GDR, Jürgen said—family and friends but also landscapes and some of the lifestyle. "Will Schleswig-Holstein be like Mecklenburg?" he wondered. He knew he could not return even to visit for years, so he was wandering about filling his memory banks and using up his emotional reserves in farewells. His girlfriend would not follow immediately, but she might apply when he was settled in his new life.

Renate, a friend of Jürgen's, works at the Academy of Fine Arts. Though Jürgen was introspective, sad, and a bit anxious, she bubbled with enthusiasm. For the past year, she has pursued part-time university studies in art theory. The program frees her to spend two days weekly at classes, and she does forty hours of homework on her own time. She expects to earn a degree in five years.

Almost everyone she used to know was disillusioned with the GDR, Renate acknowledged. Many had applied to emigrate or had dropped out, joining the internal emigration. She often wondered whether she would be the last person left on the GDR ship. This changed, she said, when she entered university and found other young people who asked the same questions as she and her friends, but optimistically. She met professors who opened her eyes to new intellectual vistas. "The things we talk about and the way we talk about them," Renate said, "are unknown in our newspapers. I didn't know there were people like this until I started my studies." She wants to run an art gallery, perhaps even open her own, once she has her degree, and she has gained confidence that the GDR will be a place where she and her new friends can feel comfortable.

To paraphrase an old television show, there are seventeen million stories in the country, and these have been two of them. I know there are many like Jürgen. I suspect there are many like Renate. Frustration with a rigid political culture links them. Circumstance as much as character or intellectual differences has set them on separate paths. The GDR's tragedy is that it loses so many Jürgens, who would gladly contribute if the state met them halfway. The GDR's hope is that it still has the Renates, who believe change is in the air and that their idealism will find meaningful outlets.

JULY 27

The major U.S. newspapers, which discovered Eastern Europe several months ago, are beginning to focus on the implications for Germany of the region's virtual revolution—only, a GDR contact joked, "They are not sure whether to write about the German Question or the German Problem." "The Europeans know," he said, "it is the German Problem." Officials here say that, like "socialism in the colors of the GDR" or not, everyone should value their state as a factor for stability. They count on European antipathy to a larger Germany and on naked Soviet power interests to block any precipitous attempt to upset the postwar balance. Poland, Hungary, and the Soviet Union are not in the throes of wrenching change because Bonn or Washington meddles, however. Their troubles have internal causes and need internal solutions. Addressing reform, and soon, is risky for East German leaders, but the only way to master challenges that will come in any event.

Washington Post journalists have highlighted the dilemma. Richard Cohen wrote that after a lifetime of commitment to a different communism, Honecker and his inner circle will not look at Gorbachev, "slap their foreheads and say, 'Boy, were we wrong!' " Still, "East Germany can't hold out indefinitely. It must either reform and face a loss of legitimacy, or stay the course and face a crisis. If the latter happens, the ultimate question is what the Soviet Union will do. . . . Will Russia, with its well-earned German phobia, countenance an unreliable or obstreperous East Germany? The thinking is that it will not. The troops will move." This, Cohen noted, is "precisely the . . . crisis both the West and reformers in the East want to avoid. . . . A crisis here could well spell the end of Glasnost and Perestroika—not to mention Mikhail Gorbachev. . . . Once again, the coming problem is Germany."

Marc Fisher wrote from Bonn that the U.S. President's motto of a "Europe whole and free" "has been accompanied, particularly for West German audiences, by calls for an end to the Berlin Wall. It implies that Europe, including East Germany, should be free, but does it imply that the two Germanies should be made whole again? That is left unsaid." He quoted Pierre Shostal to illustrate his thesis that the ambiguity is intentional: "We're moving in very uncharted waters. I think we're seeing the breakdown of an ideology, and any detailed prescription would be premature." But among West Germany's political elite, Fisher found uneasiness about American enthusiasm. "All this talk of reunification is crazy nonsense," the SPD's Egon Bahr told him. "Both sides know it's not in the cards. The United States is the only country that could live with a united Germany. . . . It is absolutely impossible for Gorbachev to give up East Germany."

The American emphasis, Fisher said an unnamed State Department official told him, was reform; "the West Germans put the emphasis on engaging the East Germans, increasing human contacts—things that will help stabilize the regime. Our policy and theirs are potentially in conflict." German politicians studiously avoided the tension between "ritual incantations" on the German Question and their consensus policy of inner-German cooperation, Fisher noted, while "the most impassioned calls for reunification come from the United States." Explained another unidentified State Department source: "We have taken a very large step forward now on Poland and Hungary, defining how we will encourage change there, but we haven't worked out how to treat the laggards, and especially East Germany. So American statements keep using the old rhetoric on the German Question." Fisher concluded by quoting Karl Kaiser, a Bonn insider: "You Americans have taken our reunification debate far more seriously than we have." There would be no political union because "that the Soviets could not allow."

The GDR is no longer the easily ignored stepchild of U.S. policy: The stakes here are high both for Gorbachev's experiment—and so superpower relations—and for the post–cold war power balance. We need a strategy that makes us an influential participant, not a bystander whose isolation is self-imposed. In our embassy's uphill struggle, the press interest can be a helpful new factor that we should discreetly encourage.

I found the *New York Times* article on the more prosaic question of Honecker's successor, with its sharp juxtaposition of Krenz the "hard-liner" and Schabowski the possible "reformer at heart," too simplistic. Neither has a more "archetypal Communist" background than Gorbachev, who was KGB Chief Andropov's protégé. Krenz represents a hard-line constituency—the security apparatus—but so did Honecker before he reached the top and in GDR terms proved surprisingly flexible. Schabowski has a different constituency and profiles himself accordingly.

That said, there has been little to suggest Krenz has inclination or intellect to break the mold if he gets to the top, but there are intriguing hints that Schabowski has unplumbed depths. I am not comfortable predicting how either would react in power, but Schabowski might pursue new solutions more consequentially once he realized that neither old ways nor quick fixes were promising. In other words, Schabowski may have more capacity to grow into a genuine reformer. I tried to sum it up recently by calling him a "might-be, would-be quasi-Gorbachev." But Krenz impressed me up close in April when he hosted nearly a dozen Congressmen, led by Dan Rostenkowski. He said nothing startling, but he handled himself well, mixing humor into his message in a way that led the visitors to call him a real politician—the compliment of professionals for a professional. We should not be too quick to typecast him.

It is unclear which man enjoys more Soviet favor, but Moscow's support is no longer necessarily decisive. For good or ill, the GDR is responsible now for most of its own decisions. That is something to remember when considering the SED's most intriguing prince, Hans Modrow, the SED leader in Dresden, who is believed to be sympathetic to Gorbachev-style reform. It goes too far to say he is popular, but he attracts interest in circles that ordinarily keep the SED at a distance, such as the new Catholic bishop in Dresden, Reinelt, who told us Modrow approaches problems without protocol and bureaucracy. Nevertheless, his chances are scant. Decisions will be made by the same people who have kept him from the Politburo.

JULY 28

Wolfgang Gerz of the Ständige Vertretung was in Conway, New Hampshire, last month for a conference on the GDR with East German, American, and West German academics. Over lunch he gave me a copy of his report. As the East Germans gained confidence, he said, they spoke more critically than ever before about a "democracy deficit," the Party's all-encompassing "leading role," and how the constant need to justify a second German state frustrated reformers. Our embassy should try to be there next year, Gerz said. Remember Sally Bowles's song in *Cabaret*, "Money, Money, Money," I replied lamely. Wolfgang's approach was a rebuttal of those who argue Bonn does not really want the United States more involved with the GDR, and I sent his report to Washington with the recommendation that someone from the Department attend in 1990.

JULY 31

Dick compressed my twenty-seven-paragraph analysis of the policy memo into eleven paragraphs, which was all to the good. Nothing loses senior officials more quickly than a long telegram. They may read the summary, and possibly the comment often appended as a last word, but realistically they frequently do not get beyond the title. Not all telegrams are meant for policy-makers, of course. Many are aimed at desk denizens, who need details to answer questions from State's Sixth Floor (the assistant Secretaries) or the Seventh Floor (the Secretary and senior advisers). Analysts in the State Department and other foreign affairs agencies with insatiable desire to know everything are further targets. One of the toughest tricks is to write for multiple audiences; often it takes multiple messages, the time for which, it seems to a Political Section that wants to get to the next matter, is always lacking. Dick's cuts also ensured that our telegram would be read more seriously as a reflection of his own thinking. Because they are too wise and lack time, ambassadors rarely write lengthy cables—George Kennan's famous "Long Telegram" from Moscow at the dawn of the cold war notwithstanding. By shortening the cable, Dick made it both more readable and more credible.

The substantive changes were, of course, more debatable. Dick endorsed the cautious strategy. He argued that we needed to gain leverage with the Soviets and on the German Question, but he pared away the concept of using Honecker's almost manic desire for high-level dialogue to force a claims/trade breakthrough. A Krenz visit remained, but keyed to getting to know the likely successor. He would pass other ideas on as they matured, Dick advised, but for now the important thing was to get the ball rolling. Amen.

A usually well-informed Eastern European insists that Schabowski told him three months ago he would be in Beijing in July and that after Tienanmen Square the Politburo decided it "would send the wrong signal" to cancel. He is sure Honecker's illness is not as serious as the Chinese suggest. Perhaps, but speculation will proliferate until he returns.

Not everything is high policy. An embassy is a team of diverse human beings, each drawn from familiar American surroundings by a sense of adventure and desire to explore foreign cultures, but with a wide variety of interests and abilities to survive often difficult conditions. East Berlin is a great European city with a world-class cultural life. Its deficits can be made up on the Western side of the Wall. For privileged diplomats, who possess an ID card honored instantly at Checkpoint Charlie, Berlin truly is a single metropolis. There are problems, however. The air is filthy, especially in winter, when heating is by foul brown coal, and low clouds press down the fumes from the environmentally abhorrent Trabies. Then the city is gray, outwardly depressing, undeniably unhealthy.

For Gaby and me, with our fluent German and my job that justifies virtually every contact with East Germans, there is no more exciting, satisfying, and enjoyable place to live and work. It is different for families in which neither spouse can communicate with neighbors. Single people are most disadvantaged. East Berlin is a "nonfraternization" post, and prudence dictates that those without job-related reasons to have social contacts respect the Stasi's potential for mischief. No one can be confident any conversation is truly private. The Stasi are certainly present electronically in our houses. The situation is not unique to the GDR, or even necessarily to Eastern Europe, but to work here the loss of privacy must be accepted. Not everyone can cope. I once accompanied a delegation to Wittenberg, Luther's city. When Friedrich Schorlemmer, a great voice of the democratic opposition, mentioned the Stasi might be listening to the lunch conversation, a Congresswoman hit the ceiling and never came down. She was too shocked to accept the credibility of the brave young people who spoke the truth about life in East Germany despite the third ear.

Today I lunched with J., a bright, capable secretary who has requested early departure. Transferred directly from Central America, single, and isolated by language and security precautions from the life of the country in which she lives, her tour has been a nightmare. Sadly, the job not infrequently fails to satisfy the expectations of Foreign Service secretaries, who have left the comfortable American milieu because they have an extra dose of intellectual curiosity and ambition. I wanted to remind her that she will always have friends who shared the GDR experience and not to become discouraged. We are not quite a family, especially at a post where the centrifugal force of West Berlin is so strong. But the loss is real when someone leaves like this, and so is the sense of guilt that perhaps each of us did not offer enough support.

AUGUST 1

I took Mike Mozur, Reno's successor, to lunch with Dave Pozorski, his West Berlin counterpart. There is little interaction with colleagues on the other side of the city, but I wanted to question Dave about Poland, where he served. Berlin is huge. Most of our business requires no coordination between the two posts, and Gaby and I consciously avoid being seduced by the comfortable, ghetto-like Allied communities in West Berlin. Of course, we have friends in the West, and Gaby's family, but except for unavoidable obligations we stay in the East. This is no hardship; there is more than enough culture and entertainment, and our purpose is to learn all we can about this society. A meal across the Wall is merely a pleasant dinner. Here, everything from the waiter's attitude through chance conversation teaches us about GDR life.

With his own Eastern experience, Dave neither scorns the GDR nor regards it primarily as a source of cheap opera tickets and Zeiss binoculars. I tried out thoughts I have been formulating since it became apparent weeks ago that this state faces a degree of discontent that has its closest parallel in the summer of 1961, when the Wall was built. West Germans are holding their breath, hoping no crisis will disrupt holidays and the comfortable web of cooperation they have spun here; Americans are mesmerized by more overt drama in Warsaw and Budapest. The great question is whether the GDR will react by turning toward repression or reform.

AUGUST 2

Neues Deutschland's long interview with Károly Grósz had no news for anyone with access to the *Herald Tribune*, but it was unusual for a press that has largely ignored Hungary. While Grósz explained that Communists expected to share power with new parties in Budapest, the larger message was undoubtedly meant to reassure the SED. Grósz is the most traditional of the Hungarian Big Four, with greatest credibility to say Hungary will not abandon the Warsaw Pact even while differing with the GDR on national roads to socialism. The average person will find more meaningful his upbeat remarks on tourism, since there is fear of a crackdown if too many use vacation travel to end run the Berlin Wall.

It may only be whistling in the dark to keep up SED spirits, but the tone is different from Joachim Herrmann's in June. The GDR wants to prevent a trickle of escapees from becoming a flood and not cut Hungary from the short list of countries open to its vacationers. Downplaying disagreement and saying tourism will grow counteracts "the door is closing" panic. Grósz's interview suggests the Hungarians are prepared to help on both counts.

AUGUST 3

Late this afternoon on the staircase, Dick congratulated me for the telegram I had put on his desk, the one whose theses I tested at lunch two days ago. "I wonder what they'll do when it hits Washington," he said. "At least it should set people thinking."

I called it the silent crisis. The last time so many East Germans renounced their homes to go West, a superpower confrontation and the Berlin Wall resulted. This summer, hardly anyone notices, but the capacity of a resource-poor GDR to absorb enormous losses is already strained. There must be a reaction soon. Given the changed international constellation, it is hard to conceive that it would produce the global tensions that marked the drama of that summer twenty-eight years ago. More likely is an internal political crisis that could hasten leadership change, and possibly the beginning of serious domestic reform.

We have become so used to the idea that the Berlin Wall holds East Germans inside their little country that the new figures will shock many. In May, more than 9,000 received permission to leave for the Federal Republic, in June more than 10,000. In this spring, West German diplomats estimated legal emigration might top the single-year record of 40,000; now they speak of 100,000. To legal emigrants must be added those who—also in record though much smaller numbers—seek to scale the Wall now that fear of shooting is diminished, and those who besiege West German diplomatic missions. Finally, a small fraction of 1.5 million working-age East Germans will not return home from family visits to the West this year.

The GDR will lose enough people in 1989 to populate one of its large cities. Mostly these are not pensioners, hardened criminals, or others who take rather than contribute to society; they include young couples with children, workers and artisans at least as often as intellectuals. This occurs in a country where shop windows in every street, and factory gate signs, advertise urgently for new employees. With a birth rate as low as in the prosperous West, the economy is slowing in part because there are not enough people to make it go. There is only one historical comparison: After Khrushchev's note set off a Berlin crisis, 150,000 crossed the then essentially open borders in 1959, and just under 200,000 crossed in 1960. This summer, in other words, at real economic cost, the GDR is allowing to leave about half as many people as the numbers whose illegal departures drove it to the desperate measure of erecting a barrier that has ever since blackened its name. We have to ask what it will produce this time.

The surge of emigrants shows that both little and much in Honecker's GDR is different. There have always been many who preferred the West, for whatever mixture of political idealism, economic self-interest, or family ties. Obviously there still are. But most who leave now have the authorities' consent. It is grudging to be sure, but it says something about change in East Germany. In 1961, the socialist state was scorned and isolated. It had little to lose by hunkering down behind its Wall. Today's GDR is increasingly enmeshed in international activities, particularly those with an origin in the inner-German relationship. That the SED has gone so far toward meeting the emigration pressure shows it knows it has something to lose this time if it does not seek at least a more liberal accommodation of its people's demands. The GDR is stamping "Exit Approved" on hundreds of applications daily to reduce both internal pressure and isolation in the CSCE process that is changing standards of expected Eastern European behavior.

Those considerations carry the day for now, but how long can it continue like this? Dick asked that of Wolfgang Vogel, who has abandoned his vacation to cope with the embassy sit-ins. "Ask me an easier question," Honecker's lawyer, said with a grimace.

Once before, in 1984, but on a smaller scale, the GDR opened the emigration doors relatively wide. The goal was a one-time housecleaning of malcontents, but the policy failed miserably. The numbers of would-be emigrants were quickly replenished. As human rights expectations rose in the second half of the decade with the beginning of Soviet reforms, the intensification of inner-German contacts, and the CSCE, applications multiplied into the hundreds of thousands (the exact number is a state secret). Those who seek emigration are not leftovers from prewar society. They are a cross section of the GDR's forty-year-old polity, and it stands to reason that their numbers will be constantly replenished, not only by the example of those who succeed, but also because others will become as disillusioned or dissatisfied unless life here changes.

That, of course, frames Honecker's dilemma. If he cuts back on emigration, travel, and the other inner-German contacts that are now recognized as fueling the discontent and contributing to draining his state's human resources, he risks isolating the GDR from Europe even more. He knows he can ill afford to put at stake the West German support that is increasingly important to his economy and his legitimacy. The big question is whether he can afford to come to terms with the gripes and systemic shortcomings that cause so many East Germans to turn their backs on the GDR.

Honecker's GDR began to liberalize human contacts in recent years, with the plausible expectation that a chance to visit the West would remove the greatest cause of domestic dissatisfaction. If it has become clear that personal exposure to West Germany breeds even more dissatisfaction, and that a return to isolation would be fraught with political and economic risk, might it be reasonable to expect the SED now to correct its domestic course? Possibly, but reform is a process with its own internal logic that the old leadership has resisted out of concern it might not be able to keep it under control.

No one can say in what time frame answers are needed. Vogel, however, told Dick that the reliable, personalized system he and a succession of West German go-betweens have for years used to resolve problem cases may be within weeks of breakdown simply because of the numbers and physical demands. The stubbornness with which East Germans in Budapest refuse to accept Vogel's assurances may be another sign that time is running out for the old way of handling things.

Honecker has long argued that the GDR's best course in a time of region-wide uncertainty is the status quo. As summer winds down and preparations begin in earnest for the May 1990 Party Congress, new uncertainties are developing. The harvest looks like a further burden on the laboring economy; for the first time, his own health is a topic of speculation. However, the hemorrhage of citizens, not over but through and around the Berlin Wall, just might become the catalyst for the fundamental reassessment Honecker has sought to avoid because the consequences are so unpredictable.

AUGUST 4

Conflicting stories are coming from Budapest, where a senior official has denied reports that the Németh government is about to break with the GDR and grant political asylum to fleeing East Germans. Meanwhile, the GDR continues to scorn reform. An article in a West Berlin paper that critiqued the economy unsparingly drew *Neues Deutschland*'s ire. Imre immediately dubbed the author—the otherwise unidentified Ute Reinhold—"Otto's sister." Born in Estonia and raised in Bavaria, Imre came to the Foreign Service from a twenty-year army career. He has a superb sense of humor—and an Eastern European appreciation of conspiracy. "Ute" is not likely related to the powerful Central Committee Otto Reinhold, but the name might be a pseudonym for an East German propagating heresy in the West.

Neues Deutschland said, however, "Only ignoramuses and professional mudslingers could overlook the development. . . . Socialism in the colors of the GDR is a thorn in the eye of all who want to reverse the wheel of history. That is why they talk up a crisis where there is none."

AUGUST 5

We spent two hours at the Distel rediscovering the political art form of cabaret. Almost unpracticed in the United States, cabaret flourishes in Central Europe and has a special status in Communist lands, where it enjoys semi-freedom to lampoon foibles and problems otherwise barred from public notice. Almost every major GDR city has its theater; the censors may have killed even more skits at Leipzig's Pfeffermühle than the Distel. The latest program, "delayed" six months, is one of the Berliners' best.

The third-floor walk-up across from the Friedrichstrasse train station is probably East Berlin's toughest ticket. Party and trade unions take up most seats at most theaters and distribute them according to favor and protocol, but determined fans can usually get something at the box office just before the curtain. Political cabaret, however, is always sold out; if you don't have connections and want to celebrate your wife's birthday, buy her dinner this year and apply for next year. (Embassies are privileged; the Foreign Ministry offers front-row seats, but few diplomats have the language skills to pick up the rapid-fire jokes, often in dialect, so they concentrate on opera.) Once inside the unpretentious auditorium, the audience is an important part of the show, with responses as interesting as what happens on stage. Where does it laugh or gasp and ask itself if the double entendre really meant ———? How do those who wear SED buttons respond?

The current program is the Distel's most consistently tough and critical since questions about political change began to be put openly. The staples of the troupe's humor were there, including complaints about consumer goods and boring media. A skit on inner-German military contacts did not quite degenerate into the soupy "We're for peace" paean inserted at least once into earlier shows, to satisfy the SED and cool audience temperature. The main themes, however, were travel, Party privilege, and lack of reform. The opening dialogue set the tone. Quips about visits to West German relatives have been common since the mid-1980s. Unexpected was open mention of a taboo variant: "You mean some of those who want to travel don't want to come back?" "Yes, that's what everyone is saying." The GDR's dilemma was also alluded to unmistakably in a skit with a clever reverse twist. A prosperous Western couple was driving to Berlin in their Mercedes on the transit autobahn through the GDR. Stopped by a cop, the woman told her husband to let her handle it. She lost track of her speed, she told the policeman, because she was so excited about the GDR. "Tell me," she gushed, "where can we register for immigration?" "What did he say?" asked her husband. "He said we have to take a Breathalyzer test," she replied as the curtain fell.

There was another gasp when the "Party Secretary" told an underling to visit his West German aunt next week and take 50,000 East Marks to exchange at 1:7 (the official rate is 1:1) and buy parts for which the factory had no hard currency. The practice is common, but not the acknowledgment. The wistful high point, however, came in the little skit called "Venice." The troupe's oldest member shocked his foreman by refusing to work a "voluntary" Saturday so the factory could meet another plan:

"I am going to stay home and read."
"Can't we persuade you?"
"Give me a passport to visit Venice, the Canals. . . ."
"That's too expensive, why not Czechoslovakia . . . or Leningrad, the Venice of the North?"
"No, I want to see the real thing before it sinks into the sea. I've worked hard for forty years. Isn't that enough?"
"No, forty years isn't enough in the GDR."
"Then I'll stay home and read about Paris."

The brief skit in which the "Minister's" driver told his boss to get out of the luxury car brought heartfelt reaction. "There is an unannounced ban on Volvos between Schönhauser Allee and Pankow [the relatively posh suburb where the Minister obviously lived]. You will have to take the single Trabant that is operating on a shuttle route—once every half hour." "Are you crazy, man?" complained the Minister. "New schedules, hours of delay, standing in the rain. Where do you think we are?" The answer: "Berlin, capital of the GDR, Sir."

The May elections, with their 98.7 percent approval, were lampooned in a bitter monologue titled "The Unemployed Representative." At the end of an office hour to which no constituent came, the actor groaned that democracy left him with nothing to do. Who were his voters? he asked plaintively. "You are, but you must have been the 1.3 percent. If we have democracy, why don't people take it seriously? They elect me and then ignore me. But I have my job for four years, and I predict you will elect me again the same way, and you will just sit there and nod and nod."

Lack of reform was a constant refrain. Periodically an actor would say a code word like "change," then cover his mouth in embarrassment while the audience guffawed. In one skit, "Herr Szabó" from Budapest had the best lines while the GDR "Economist" tried unsuccessfully to explain SED policy and find "a single price that makes sense." Three bakers discussed an order to discontinue their Russian bread. Odd, one said, the people liked its taste; it wasn't like the old stuff "Baker Lomontov, or was it Molotov," used to put out. "No," said the head baker. "It must go. We need good German bread now, in GDR colors." But can we not, another asked, rename it, perhaps Polish bread? "Too cheap," came the answer. Hungarian? "Too expensive." Rumanian? Incredulous stares and cries of "Stop joking!" Well, chimed in another baker, if we do have to use "the colors of the GDR," our flag's red-black-gold are not enough. We need more green, for our Environmental Ministry . . . and we need more Rosa . . . Luxemburg" (she fought Lenin over free speech, free press, and genuine elections).

The above can give no more than a faint flavor of a hot, sticky evening with a few hundred East Germans who followed every nuance intently. Nothing would make an American audience slap its sides, even if it did understand the words. Even more than most humor, political cabaret translates poorly and travels worse. It belongs to the idiom of language, time, and place. Nor is the Distel every East German's cup of tea. For every uptight apparatchik, there is a citizen like our friend Ute. The targets of the buffoonery, she explains, are real, and she gets "too angry to laugh."

The Distel is a special political barometer. Whether a storm is coming or the Party is merely releasing a little pressure, the show and its appreciative audience indicate that more is being discussed more openly, at least just off the main SED stage. "Wasn't it exciting to see hundreds of thousands of young people marching into the future at the *Pfingsttreffen*?" asked an actor. "Yes, but there was always an old man at the gate."

AUGUST 6

Last week *Neues Deutschland* carried a surprisingly positive critique of the theater season. The Party paper's assessments of GDR events are usually positive, of course, but it has more than once criticized drama trends this year. Most striking was the broadside it ran against *Farther, Farther, Farther,* which is part of a historical trilogy by Gorbachev-backer Shatrov that the SED's watchdogs considered ideologically suspect. It has not yet played here, but its companion piece, *The Dictatorship of Conscience,* opened immediately after the press attack and provided Gaby and me with the most exciting two hours we have ever spent in a theater.

The opening lines, spoken in a provincial Russian newspaper's city room, riveted the audience: Our press, complained an actor, is the world's dullest. Yes, a colleague agreed, I can no longer work within these oppressive walls. As the journalists called historical witnesses for a "trial" of Lenin, the proverbial pin drop could have been heard, except for the occasional gasp or spontaneous applause. Lenin was not convicted; in that sense the play was orthodox, but the actors condemned distortion of his ideals and violations of justice committed in socialism's name. In the climactic passage, an actress recited Rosa Luxemburg's prophetic warning to the Bolsheviks and German Communists: Without free speech, free press, and free elections, dictatorship of the proletariat inevitably degenerates into dictatorship of the apparatus. I asked one of the actors about that scene. It was not, he said, in the original script. The director inserted it because Rosa Luxemburg speaks with special force to German audiences. The SED was unhappy, but the theater fought and won.

Older plays never staged, or dropped after short runs, including Volker Braun's *Lenin's Death* and Heiner Müller's *The Wage Depressor,* also were hits. The latter is a devastating examination of worker attitudes on the eve of the 1953 revolt that, the author told GDR Radio, is shockingly up-to-date. There were also two bold new plays by Christoph Hein. Berlin's Gorki Theater was sold out for *The Transition Society,* an adaptation from Chekhov about the desire to break out of a decaying society and travel. Janice saw Hein's *Knights of the Roundtable* in Schwerin, which has the GDR's finest provincial theater. No one, she said, could miss contemporary allusions in its portrayal of old men at their isolated seat of power discussing reforms. A character laments having sacrificed his life to an ideal no one wants. East Berlin's theater magazine described the central scene—a discussion between King Arthur and his son—as showing that "the first precondition of the search for a new ideal can only be to disband the old Roundtable so that there can be 'air to breathe.' "

Of course, Stefan Heym was right to caution me that it is one thing to allow intellectuals their kicks by the hundreds in the theater, and another to put daring material in the press or on television. Still, a theater-goer must conclude that much is stirring just below the smooth surface the GDR's leaders and their propaganda organs display to the outer world.

AUGUST 7

When I first came to Berlin, it was unthinkable that a quorum of the House Armed Services Committee could spend a pleasant morning and lunch with the GDR Army (the NVA) and then drop in at Soviet Headquarters. That is what Les Aspin and his colleagues did today, however, before flying on to Moscow. Wolfgang Herger, who runs the Central Committee Security Department as Egon Krenz's right-hand man, hosted the first portion.

The GDR had not wanted to use the radio-relay regiment "Konrad Wolf," but it was conveniently located halfway between West Berlin and the Soviets. Nothing about the small caserne suggested a showpiece. Flowers had been planted and paths raked, but there was little fresh paint or just-out-of-the-box feel. It was not exactly homey, but it looked like the real GDR. Officers lived in apartment blocks resembling those dotted throughout the town that came up to the gate. Space was at a premium in barracks where conscripts slept mostly five—noncoms three—to a room. There were spartan common areas with television and books and a well-equipped sports complex. We saw off-duty soldiers playing Pacman or chess on GDR-made cassette-programmed computers, but a conscript complained of infrequent leave. The mess would make an East German feel he had wandered into a neighborhood restaurant: plain fare, two choices for enlisted men, three for noncoms and officers. The latter's privileges were upholstered chairs, a menu, and waiters.

By contrast, the Soviet motorized rifle division we saw after lunch had palace-guard functions. It protected headquarters, and the troops were, by Red Army standards, perhaps a bit pampered. An elite unit paraded past us. Soldiers fired weapons (defensive weapons, defensive tactics only, General Fursin, acting commander of all Soviet forces in the GDR, assured us) on a rutted, smoky range.

Wünsdorf is no typical Soviet base. A prewar German Army complex, its modernized, renovated, well-tended yellow stucco buildings benefit from a headquarters budget. Even so, to my civilian eyes, it has drawbacks. The barracks, where a dozen soldiers sleep in each open bay, offer not even the minimum privacy NVA conscripts enjoy. The recreation areas were an even greater contrast. The small reading room was dominated by propaganda: Lenin on one wall, Politburo on another. I saw three full Politburo displays on the grounds amid innumerable posters and heroic statues. Except for one or two "Be prepared to defend peace and socialism" signs, the NVA caserne, like GDR towns generally, was free of overt propaganda. The GDR soldier is given time to enjoy a private world, much as most East Germans can slip away evenings via Western television, and weekends into their small gardens. The Soviet base was itself a town, with shopping and other services for virtually every need. Soviet soldiers are expected to stay on their compound—where they enjoy an only slightly Germanized Soviet Union—and avoid fractious mixing with locals in downtown Zossen. It must be lonely.

The Congressmen were impressed by the sophistication with which the NVA pulled off this first Western visit. While the initial briefing was as stiff as nervous soldiers could make it, most of the morning was relaxed, even spontaneous. Unlike on the Soviet base, where the only conversation was with the general, there were dozens of chats with all ranks. Seating at lunch was loose (partly because neither the Foreign Ministry desk officer nor I could devise a protocol order on the fly), noncoms and conscripts mixed with officers and Congressmen. The soldiers replied easily to questions that ranged from personal to professional. One young man, who said he was a practicing Christian, told Imre conscripts selected for lunch were advised only by the posting of a normal duty roster. I suspect the GDR wants to put Westerners in contact with the formerly off-limits NVA in part because it is one of the best available examples of an institution that need not fear comparison with the other German state. At Wünsdorf, the pop of weaponry was memorable; at Ludwigsfelde, it was the quality of soldier.

In its first "official" notice of the sit-ins, the GDR warned Bonn against putting inner-German cooperation at risk. The line is hardening, and Vogel has told us that he may soon no longer be able to work his magic. Meanwhile, two hundred say they trust nothing the GDR offers and refuse to leave the Budapest Embassy.

AUGUST 8

The Ständige Vertretung has been closed to the public "until further notice." Bonn acted because "the facilities do not permit the stay of further persons under humane conditions." The spokesman added meaningfully: "The Federal Government again notes that a sit-in . . . is not an appropriate way to solve the emigration problem. The decision on emigration is entirely the GDR's." The situation worsened considerably over the weekend. By Monday, there were 130 sit-ins and simply no more room. Our colleagues confirmed to us that Vogel told Bonn his mandate has been cut. To induce desperate East Germans to leave, he can no longer promise preferential treatment, only that there will be no punishment.

The standoff may get much worse, though both parties seem still to want a pragmatic solution. While the Ständige Vertretung was never without "visitors," the numbers were bearable until recent weeks. With numbers came publicity, and then more sit-ins. It was only a matter of time before the GDR did something to make credible its insistence that a sit-in could not jump the line, but at the same time it signaled that it wants to protect its Bonn ties. Liberalized emigration procedures are not affected, and the controlled press predicts tourism to Hungary will reach a record 1.8 million this year. The West Germans held back from closing as long as they physically could. Their original guidance had been to shut down if sit-ins topped eighty-five.

What happens next? When the Ständige Vertretung excluded the public once before, in 1984, high-level bargaining quickly restored matters to normal. The GDR is probably willing to let current sit-ins go if it is assured the process will not just resume. The Federal Republic obviously cannot abandon Germans who seek its help, but Bonn is emphasizing that its ability to assist is limited. It will be harder to reach agreement this time, however, because the scope is larger, and the citizenry's fever, akin to fear that can run through a crowd leaving a theater that the door may slam shut, is greater.

We had a foretaste yesterday that people who can no longer get into the Ständige Vertretung may look to us. One woman left the embassy only after Vogel advised that her application had been approved, allegedly just before she came through our door. He asked us to hold the information closely. The implication was that if we got many cases, he would tell us—as he now tells the West Germans—he can no longer promise happy endings. Our new procedures to maintain access while screening out would-be sit-ins will almost surely be tested.

Under a Protocol signed this afternoon, West German and East German libraries will recover material displaced during the war. This is another fruit of the 1986 Cultural Agreement that West German diplomats tell us has been more successful than expected. Little attention would normally be paid, but the timing reminds everyone how far the two states have come and how much they have to lose if they do not find a way out of the escalating confrontation.

AUGUST 9

The United States knows too little about East German political and military leaders. It could not be otherwise, given our late start with diplomatic relations and the restrictions on contacts that the GDR places on our activities. That is one reason why the Aspin visit, which opened closed doors, was useful. A few notes on the personalities we met:

Wolfgang Herger. This fifty-four-year-old politician will probably make the Politburo if Krenz succeeds Honecker. The exposure was too short to learn his views, but he showed poise and political skill, including the wit to keep his pitch short and light. Unlike more pugnacious ideologues of the SED's founding era, he is at ease with Westerners and mixes humor with serious ideas. He performed like the former university philosophy major he is rather than a class warrior. I urged Dick to request an office call.

Major General Ernst Kusch. A deputy chief of staff, he was self-confident enough to tell "Wolfgang" Herger in a near-equal's tone when to move on. Most East Germans are reluctant to discuss personal details, but Kusch volunteered them, including that his father was in an American POW camp. "My father was on the wrong side," he said. "Not everyone can have an anti-Fascist background." Kusch spent six years at Soviet military academies and claimed personal ties with Marshal Akhromeyev. His wife was to help him learn English on their last holiday, "but you know what happens to holiday resolutions." The general joked mildly at his own and Soviet expense. At lunch, he was eager to talk substantively with me and sophisticated enough to argue that the danger of the West German far right was not a new Fascism but that it could imperil the Bonn consensus for pragmatic inner-German ties. I suggested that Gorbachev's ideas must be popular among conscripts. To a point, he admitted, but Soviet nationality and economic problems made East Germans cautious. Kusch is likely a comer. If the military-to-military project develops, perhaps we can keep contact.

Colonel Roland Rantzsch. The tall, powerful regimental commander with cropped blond hair could be cast for Waffen SS tanker or concentration-camp guard in a wartime potboiler. Soldiers called him a tough, by-the-book officer with high standards—not loved, but respected because he stands by his men. Rantzsch started as a conscript and worked his way up. He has stayed an unusual thirteen years with the regiment he built from scratch. Perhaps this indicates he is unlikely to advance further, but he probably represents the NVA average.

AUGUST 10

On a day with humidity like mid-summer Washington, I took time off to call on the Soccer Association, which had granted my request to meet its secretary-general, Spitzner, out of curiosity. Diplomats might talk with the Olympic Committee, Spitzner said, but none had ever visited him. After a half hour proving my fan credentials, I asked why GDR soccer teams, alone in the fabled sports empire, lost, and whether he was really introducing "reforms."

There were as many reasons for losing teams, Spitzner said, as "experts" in the country, which meant several million. One point was that it was difficult to identify youthful talent scientifically. Soccer defied categorization, he said, in indirect confirmation that the GDR "system" has difficulty with team sports that must coordinate many efforts and channel initiative. The Soccer Association, Spitzner said, was introducing "new arrangements." He would not call them "reforms," or agree that they derived from the Soviet Union. They were East German ideas to improve performance—for example, by allowing player and club to contract only for a specific period. Players would gain incentive, and clubs in smaller cities have less reason to complain that the Soccer Association was favoring Berlin. But, he insisted, the system was the GDR's own and differed fundamentally from the West German system by requiring that players be trained for a postfootball trade.

Before I left, satisfied that Spitzner would not use the "R" word, I was given a necktie with the Soccer Association monogram. It authorized me, Spitzner indicated, to enter any pub and answer the same questions I had been asking. I showed it proudly to my Embassy driver. "What were the answers?" he wanted to know. I cannot satisfy him or Reemer, but I will wear the tie and root, as I agreed with Spitzner, for a U.S.-GDR match in an early World Cup.

AUGUST 11

The sit-in standoff promises to be protracted. The Ständige Vertretung is overwhelmed by 131 "guests" and closed to the public; the Budapest embassy has 158, but remains barely open. The GDR blames everything on West German provocations and cold war propaganda. Wolfgang Vogel went public yesterday, unusual for a lawyer who has always stressed that to be effective he must work in the shadows. He urged the sit-ins to leave with only the assurance they would suffer no harm, underlining that the mandate Honecker gave him five years ago to settle such cases has indeed been revoked. His helplessness poses serious questions about his patron, who remains in convalescence. Has Honecker concurred in the new instructions? Is power slipping into the hands of others, who may be less concerned about preserving the inner-German cooperation Honecker considers one of his historical legacies? Who makes Politburo decisions this difficult summer?

The Hungarians, who say East German tourism is up 15 percent, are still trying to please everyone, to "leave the cabbage in the field and the goat full," as one of their diplomats here put it. They helped the GDR yesterday by telling reporters they would enforce border rules. The GDR hopes the message will cool emotions and persuade would-be emigrés to return to the long line.

The West Germans will never force the sit-ins out, but the Ständige Vertretung acknowledges it is trying to persuade them to go home. Privately the diplomats make no secret that they are aggrieved by the human misery and hold the GDR responsible for not creating more attractive conditions in this state. At the same time, they worry the sit-ins could imperil the legal emigration of tens of thousands, as well as the inner-German rapprochement patiently constructed over two decades. The West German press corps has seldom felt so torn by conflicting personal and professional emotions. For weeks it played down the story, despite home office pressure. Since the story broke, its reports from East Berlin have been more nuanced than those from Bonn, Budapest, and Vienna, some of which have created illusions about how easy the Hungarian route is.

What makes a solution so difficult is that there is a "right" on both sides, though of different quality and scope. The GDR's logic is flawless when it says it loses credibility if it yields to pressure. The West Germans are right in a more fundamental sense when they say the true source of difficulties is the GDR's internal situation, especially the opposition to reform that makes so many desperate. The operational crisis does not yet seem to have escalated into a crisis inside the SED, but it may yet if Honecker cannot soon demonstrate that he is master of the situation.

Writers have journalistic and political, as much as literary, functions in this society. They can speak on issues about which other institutions are quiet or untruthful, but they have not found their voice this summer. The exception is Stefan Heym, who used West German television this evening to call the emigration wave a "frightful phenomenon" that threatened "to destroy the entire GDR." It could still be stopped "almost at a single stroke," he asserted, if the leadership would simply say that it recognized the dissatisfaction and would make changes, but the GDR needed to give "controlled" freedoms and produce an attractive socialism. Heym is probably right about the effect the SED could achieve by restoring hope, but I am sure he shares my skepticism that an aging Politburo can reverse lifetime habits. Even then, a new policy would need new leaders to be credible. Honecker is not likely to see his dilemma this way. Those accustomed to power rarely conclude their best contribution is to yield gracefully to another generation.

AUGUST 12

The GDR's attempt to accommodate the heresies of its allies says much about the new staying power of Eastern European reform. Statements out of Budapest the past few days are regarded here as helping to calm fears and give citizens tempted to believe in a risk-free route west second thoughts. The Hungarian Embassy insists there is no tilt toward Berlin, that the objective is to straddle a spiky fence and avoid giving offense to either Germany. Hungary would not do that much, however, if the East Germans were making their job harder. The GDR called for armed suppression at earlier periods of tumult in the region, in 1956, 1968, and 1980. The onetime Savonarolas may not have changed that much, but the SED is pragmatic even as it is perplexed and more than a bit frightened. As long as it is Gorbachev's Soviet Union, there is nothing to be gained by offending apostates with whom, the East Germans recognize, they must get along. The sit-in dilemma is but the most dramatic example. There have been alliances of convenience with lesser rationales: pragmatic help for the Germans, protection of their flanks for the reformers.

AUGUST 13

This 28th Anniversary of the Berlin Wall has been a day for polemics, but there is need for serious thought before what has been achieved between the two German states—as well as much of the improvement the Gorbachev revolution has brought to East-West relations—is put at risk. About one thing, after all, GDR rhetoric is accurate: the inner-German border, inner-German ties, are the most sensitive aspect of postwar Europe. No one will benefit if crisis festers.

For most of this weekend, I put politics aside and enjoyed the visit of my school friend, Al, his wife, Johanna, and their three children, ages 11 to 14. We left the beaten path and stopped at the tiny *Schlosspark* in Biesdorf, one of the city's smaller districts, now largely given over to apartment projects. The "palace" has become a run-down library. The postage-stamp-size park with grand old trees is squeezed between the developments and a through highway. A few-score residents who had stayed in the city over the hot weekend were sampling a Sunday fair. Small bands alternated on a bare stage, while cheap beer, bockwurst, clothing odds and ends, and gardening tools were offered at a dozen stands, an example of GDR entertainment for the masses: embarrassingly plain, dated compared with the West, but moving in its simplicity. It was an eye-opener for our friends, though it was difficult to say whether they were more impressed at the state's efforts to subsidize a good time for those left behind by summer or depressed at the drabness.

When we crossed to the old church preserved on a traffic island around which the highway divides, politics intruded. Inside, a poster urged contributions to an environmental fund, and drawings depicted Secret Police evils. The fine print explained it was Somoza's Nicaragua, but no one will miss parallels close at home.

This evening we had twenty friends, mostly East German, for a cookout. "Never worse" was the somber consensus on the national mood. What impressed me, however, was the interaction between the American children and those of Gunnar and Gabi. The American boys introduced Henning to baseball; Mechthild and Catherine charmed the guests by bringing snacks. It hardly mattered that no one knew the other's language. They became friends and promised letters. How simple they made GDR-American relations.

AUGUST 14

Honecker reappeared to accept the first GDR-made thirty-two-bit microprocessor chip. (Wags call it the world's biggest microchip.) He was gaunt, and he read his remarks in a low voice, stumbling over words. Given his less than reassuring physical appearance, the decision to return now suggests political motives, but he merely praised GDR achievements and adapted a folk-saying to his purposes: "Neither ox nor donkey can halt the course of socialism." There was no hint of new policies.

The West German press claims Honecker has ignored a message from Kohl, indicating policy paralysis. Vogel, working day and night on the sit-ins, told Dick that Honecker has not yet heard from Kohl. He added that the GDR wants to compromise but believes its hands are tied. Of course, the West Germans also say their hands are tied, by both law and practical politics.

In the past, Honecker has been relatively flexible about protecting the rapprochement with Bonn, and his return may yet be a positive factor. Nevertheless, he is in close to a no-win situation. Magnanimity invites trouble with conservatives, who probably hold his gradual liberalization policies responsible for the disorder. Stonewalling imperils the German-German structure. The clearest sign of a new beginning that could disperse the storm clouds might be his own retirement. Is that imaginable for an old man whose life has been the struggle for power and who would have little assurance that his heritage would be more respected than what he has seen happen to János Kádár's? There are no easy answers to the problems of this leader who came back two weeks ahead of his seventy-seventh birthday while half his fellow citizens were still on holiday and a significant fraction of the second half was demanding a one-way ticket to the other Germany.

AUGUST 15

The GDR's allies continue to give public support to its hard line. *Neues Deutschland* reprinted *Pravda*'s boilerplate on the August 13 anniversary ("The Wall That Guards Peace") and reproduced an "Information of the GDR Embassy" in Budapest under a Hungarian news agency byline. Some East Germans are going to Hungary without a visa over "the green border" from Czechoslovakia, but the sympathetic Prague regime has reportedly agreed to patrol that border more carefully.

AUGUST 16

The Associated Press wrote Monday that, like the Ständige Vertretung, the U.S. Embassy is essentially closed: "GDR citizens have . . . at this time no access to the U.S. Embassy. . . . The Embassy's Marines would put every 'uninvited guest' out on the street." Most Western reporters accepted Jerry Verner's denial or stopped by to check. The Ständige Vertretung sent Wolfgang Gerz over to see with his own eyes. Now, two days late, *Neues Deutschland* is trying to use the story to persuade East Germans that the United States cooperates with the GDR's efforts to limit its citizens' rights. Dick protested, but we must walk a delicate line. It would help no one if we were to find ourselves in the Ständige Vertretung's situation. Nevertheless, we are still serving East Germans—with only tighter front-door screening procedures, to discourage those who want to stay. Mary Rose Brandt, the consul, or Steve Slick, the vice consul, passes personal details of the latter to the Ständige Vertretung, which then brings up the cases with the GDR. If East Germans refuse to leave, we shall have to hope Vogel can again make a deal. There is no question of turning anyone over to police and Stasi.

Mary Rose and Steve say the would-be emigrants tend to be in their twenties and thirties, frequently married with children. Many are skilled workers; few are intellectuals or professionals. They come mainly from small to mid-sized cities, particularly in the south, cite neither religious nor overtly political reasons for flight but want greater personal freedom and economic prosperity, and do not believe there will be change here soon. Boredom, drabness, the arbitrariness of the omnipresent bureaucracy that bounds their lives are the leitmotifs, not abstractions like democracy. They are the very people who should be the backbone of a genuinely socialist state, not classical malcontents or human rights idealists. They do not think in systemic terms, but say the GDR has not given them what they want, and they are unwilling to lose more years. The Stasi must sketch similar composites, but how much reaches the Politburo, and what conclusions will it draw about how to recapture this turned-off generation?

AUGUST 17

Kohl's letter left Honecker feeling he lacks maneuvering room, Vogel told Dick, but the lawyer did have some good news. Christian Gaudian, a twenty-year-old imprisoned for attempting to cross the Wall on February 5, when his companion was killed, will be allowed to go to the West. Resolving a case that the Allies protested vigorously is another signal the GDR wants to minimize damage. A new front of the bigger problem on which it remains dug in is opening in Prague, however, where there are forty sit-ins. Given the ease of East German access to Czechoslovakia, that figure could rise steeply.

I need to get a feel for what is being thought in the country, and Wittenberg is a good place to start. After the usual difficulties with the catastrophic phone system, I reached Friedrich Schorlemmer, who invited us to drive down next week. Friedrich lives in Martin Luther's house and preaches from his pulpit, and the great reformer's spirit is within him. Last year at a church synod, he offered a twenty-point program that amounted to a call for Glasnost and Perestroika. I have not seen him since July 4, when we talked about his eighteen-year-old daughter's efforts to find a theater job in Berlin.

At our dinner this evening, the Esches were readier than three months ago in Potsdam to make bitter jokes about SED paralysis. Fritz Klein, the historian who as a young man helped Honecker start the FDJ, shared their pessimism. Peter Pragal, the West German journalist, brought me a gift—a new novel, *Claus and Claudia*, by Erich Neutsch, a respected GDR writer though not one with a particularly critical reputation. Read it, Peter said. It describes a GDR diplomat who returns from abroad when his daughter attempts suicide. As he tries to understand her, the honorable socialist discovers the cynical careerism, the corrupting intellectual dishonesty of the

Nomenklatura that destroyed the belief and nearly the life of a young idealist. It is a parable for the GDR in 1989 that suggests distress extends far beyond traditional opposition circles deep into the thoughtful elements of the SED. Gaby and I know real-life Claus and Claudias; that their painful journeys of discovery are receiving such circulation is another sign that this society is ready for change. But why do the Neutsches keep silent about the contemporary crisis?

AUGUST 18

Bob McCartney of the *Washington Post* came by to compare notes. Was Honecker likely to step down or be pushed? he wondered. It was becoming possible, I surmised. His health was uncertain, but there was no hard evidence yet. If Honecker did fall, Bob speculated, would Modrow get his chance? I was skeptical. Many SED members wanted change, but it would be rash to say this disciplined Party was ripe for revolt. Honecker's successor would likely come from within the circle that had excluded Modrow. Bob said he would come from Bonn more often now that the GDR was a real story. I enjoy these exchanges and speak candidly. Journalists respect the proviso that they are on background—only the ambassador or his press counselor talk for the record.

A further 800 East Germans are camped near the West German Embassy in Budapest demanding permission to go west. No one knows how many others are trying to slip over the border. The numbers at the Prague Embassy are up to 50. Kohl told reporters that both he and Honecker desire "to continue a policy of good sense."

AUGUST 19

John Le Carré adapted a rhyme to the title of one of his novels, *Tinker, Tailor, Soldier, Spy*. If he follows GDR politics, he might add "reform politician" to cover the intriguing case of Markus Wolf. I have tried for months to see Wolf. He politely avoids us.

For thirty-six years, Wolf was an espionage master, second man in the Stasi, its legendary head of foreign intelligence. He was so secretive that there was only a single known photograph of him, a long-distance view of a trenchcoat-clad figure on a mysterious visit to Sweden. Two years ago, Wolf retired amid hints of a disagreement with his Stalinist boss, the eighty-year-old Mielke, and Honecker's opposition to Gorbachev's reforms. In this year of the GDR's troubles, Wolf, at age sixty-six, has become its most visible pensioner. His vehicle is a book written to fulfill a dying brother's last wish, the theme of which is coming to grips with history, including Stalin's show trials. His message is praise of Gorbachev and Glasnost; his goal, some believe, may be to position himself for an important role in a reformist (and more pro-Soviet) post-Honecker government.

Markus Wolf always seemed a bit odd for a Communist spy. Father Friedrich was a doctor, an early prochoice advocate of women's rights and one of the handful of prominent Jewish authors who chose the GDR as their postwar German state. Until his death in 1982, brother Konrad was an internationally admired film director, a champion of greater artistic freedom for the hard-pressed cultural elite. But rumors of Markus's differences with the leaders he served so well so long appeared fanciful.

His book *Troika* tells of three friends in the Moscow of the 1930s who were separated by terror, global war, and incipient cold war but came together again in the Berlin of 1945 at a brief moment of hope for a better world. Konrad returned to Germany with the victorious Red Army. George, son of Louis Fischer, the American journalist and Lenin biographer who gave his heart to the Soviet Revolution but broke with Stalin over the purges and the pact with Hitler, came to the Reich's destroyed capital in a U.S. Army uniform. Lothar was already there. He had returned with his mother in 1941, before Germany attacked the Soviet Union and after his father, a Communist who fought Hitler, was murdered by Stalin. Markus says Konrad's desire to bring the story to the screen was the subject of his last talk with his brother. He inherited the notebooks and the obsession. He could learn the medium of words quicker than film, and so a movie became a book.

Undoubtedly Markus had family motives for debuting as an author in his seventh decade. He and Konrad were close, and the *Troika*'s story—the idealism, horrors, and vagaries of fortune that shaped young Communists, and former Communists, of that generation—was also his. "*Troika*'s idea," he wrote, "contains the attempt to explain the history of our lives, linked with the fate of close friends of our youth, to indicate the sense of it with all its chaos and contradiction. It attempts to pick up almost lost threads, to tie them together between the romance and ideals of our youth and the experience and knowledge of age." Most observers, however, have concentrated on the political significance. The history Wolf describes, especially the dawning realization of the purges among Communists in prewar Moscow, is the stuff of current Soviet efforts to understand Stalin's legacy. The implications of historiography have been lost neither on Gorbachev's allies nor on the conservative SED. A year after Honecker banned the Soviet magazine *Sputnik* for likening the two dictators, it is surprising to see a former Stasi chief show understanding for a Louis Fischer, who "began openly to equate Stalin with Hitler."

Troika was published this spring in both Germanies. That is less uncommon these days, but Wolf's public access is intriguing. The GDR edition was unobtainable. Booksellers told me their few copies were reserved for months. This is not comparable, however, to the effort the SED organized last year to keep Gorbachev's book, *Perestroika*, in safe hands since Wolf's text is being serialized in the widely read weekly *Wochenpost*. At an introductory East Berlin reading covered by Western television, Wolf criticized the GDR's reluctance to look candidly at the Stalin period. Asked if the *Sputnik* ban was justifiable, he replied simply, "No." Gorbachev's reforms, he said, were "very important, very right, and necessary." Since then, Wolf has been continuously on the GDR lecture circuit or giving interviews to West Germans. The GDR, he says, needs more Glasnost, its citizens more "civil courage," to face up to history. Like Soviet intellectuals in Gorbachev's orbit and SED censors, Wolf regards history as a metaphor for tomorrow's politics.

The former Stasi chief as liberal reformer? Like most things in East Berlin these days, appearance half deceives; answers are more complex than questions. The apostate Communist Wolfgang Leonhard sketched the young Markus Wolf he knew in Moscow and at the GDR's birth in his classic *Child of the Revolution*. That Wolf was a subtle blend of intellectual and ambitious politician who warned Leonhard to tack with the winds from the East. A man of Wolf's intelligence and lifelong positive disposition toward the Soviets might well appreciate the poisons corroding the facade of Honecker's GDR and believe that the train to board is again a Soviet express, called Glasnost, and possibly Perestroika as well.

Could Wolf have a political future? Possibly. He resembles a slightly aged Paul Newman. Brains, charisma, and Soviet connections are not bad credentials. My reform-minded SED contacts view the phenomenon with satisfaction. Wolf has too much clout to be shut down, they say, and important Party people, perhaps even the Soviets, are using him to prepare the way for reforms. He has a platform that is inconceivable for the normal new author. The former spymaster probably cannot dream of doing an Andropov, but the idea that he could be prominent after the Honecker era ends is no longer implausible. He is at least playing in the political game being contested here with growing vigor for control of the GDR's future.

Some 900 East Germans used a "Pan-European Picnic" to cross the Hungarian-Austrian border today. The dramatic television coverage is certain to heighten emotions and complicate the search for a compromise. Media here featured a different event. *Neues Deutschland* called the Warsaw Pact's march into Prague twenty-one years ago "the only effective way" to "protect socialism and prevent a change in the political and military balance of forces to imperialism's advantage." East Germans will see another provocation and warning.

AUGUST 20

Gaby and I spent a troubling Saturday in Cottbus, the industrial city southeast of Berlin, between the Spreewald and Poland. Helmuth Gröpler, the pastor, invited us to meet a half dozen East Germans who had made church visits to the United States. All had been fascinated by America and mostly admiring of its freedoms, openness, and hospitality, but they were also troubled at the flashes of violence, poverty, and waste of human life. The intention had been for us to answer questions about our land, but the conversations, in Helmuth's apartment overlooking the medieval church and during a long walk in Branitz Park, returned inevitably to the GDR's agony.

"I should not be here," said Werner Krätschell, a senior Berlin churchman, as we circled the pyramid under which Prince Pückler is buried. "Our twenty-two-year-old son called last night from Austria to say he had crossed the border. My wife and other children are home crying," Werner said. "I decided after university to live here. It is my home. I want to make the 'church in socialism' work. This is where God has put us and our fellow man needs us. But how can I blame my son? He is idealistic, and he put so much of himself into the effort to raise social consciousness. After the election scandal, after the students were shot in China, he signed up to stand a vigil in church. Every slot had three times as many volunteers as needed. But the SED made clear it was going to change nothing, and his friends said, 'Let's go to Hungary.' My boy did not believe anything would happen here for years, and how can I say he isn't right? The old men just want to preserve their power, and they have lost all credit."

There was more of the same today when we visited Lutz and Heidi in their summer cottage on the Spree River, another couple with children wrestling with the meaning of events that highlight the contradictions and frustrations of life here. Something new must come out of this summer of discontent, but how can an American, no matter how sympathetic, offer solace and advice?

AUGUST 21

After a weekend of rumors, ADN ran a cryptic five-line report that Honecker was operated on "last week" for gallstones. While the illness that felled him in Bucharest could not have been hushed up, this unusual admission suggests his condition may be more serious than first thought. Coming as the SED faces the implications of a mass exodus and changes in the Communist world, it at least increases the perception that he is losing his grip.

AUGUST 22

The result of the policy review by the new team in the European Bureau was disappointing. We are authorized only to propose a date for routine political consultations. It did go better than a similar exercise last year, when one participant dismissed the GDR as simply "the Warsaw Pact's Doberman Pinschers." Still, there was skepticism about any effort to become a player here. "What will we have missed if we do not have substantial relations when change comes to the GDR?" asked one doubter. An obvious answer is that foreign policy is not only about geopolitics. Collecting monetary and moral debts owed for more than forty years and fair trade opportunities in themselves justify vigorous efforts.

Another experienced Germanist sounded like Honecker when he said the GDR's choice was between destabilization and Stalinism. That is not the Bush administration's assessment for Poland or the Soviet Union. Does the divided-nation aspect make the GDR so different that for it alone respect for human rights and a more effective economy would be destabilizing? Bonn, for whom stability has a high value, believes the GDR is heading for worse trouble unless it reforms.

The ultimate justification for the United States staying on the sidelines was to protect relations with West Germany. But even if one accepts that a superpower with major commitments in Berlin and Central Europe has no other interest, we risk damaging relations with Bonn more by remaining aloof. The GDR is already into the transition from Honecker. The summer has been a shock for old leadership and population alike. Change may come faster than anticipated, and it is important that we not be caught unprepared.

An East German has been shot by a Hungarian border guard. The tragedy may give some refugees pause, but it may also force Hungary off the fence. By trying to satisfy both German states, it can ultimately only anger both. Provided the Soviets stay neutral, Bonn can offer Budapest much more to come down on its side.

AUGUST 23

Dick seized on the Washington review's one positive element and called at the Foreign Ministry, where Kurt Nier was delighted with an invitation to consult. Even if the unimaginative Nier is not a policy-maker, the timing is good. Dick will not take the State Department on frontally, but he intends to make the point at home that the GDR is on the verge of major decisions. In Margot Honecker's phrase, it sees "counterrevolution" coming "from Moscow" while neighboring Communist Parties cede power; it sees its citizens by the scores of thousands opting for richer, freer West Germany; it sees its leader, Erich Honecker, wan, ill, in pain as he turns seventy-seven, all too obviously nearing the end of his career; it tacitly acknowledges that the economy is struggling and that as workers, managers, and specialists hemorrhage west it may stall. By the May Congress, the SED must decide whether to maintain the opening to the West and not whether but how to stimulate the economy, to live with radicalized allies, and to regain a modicum of popular consent. Above all, it must pick a leadership team.

The answers—we want to persuade the State Department—matter. The GDR is still the Soviets' strongest ally, it impinges directly on our strategic position in Europe, especially our Berlin commitment, and it is half the

Fig. 1. January 1989. Erich Honecker, *left center*, greets the author; Ambassador Barkley, *far left*, has just presented his credentials to the GDR leader; Jerry Verner, *center*.

Fig. 2. May Day 1989. The "check" on the float represents a clothing factory's pledge to exceed the plan in honor of the GDR's 40th Anniversary and its 17 million citizens. (Janice Weiner)

FIG. 3. Gaby's mushroom harvest on the island of Usedom. (Author)

FIG. 4. Wolgast, May 1989. ". . . Cultural riches nearly lost to poverty, neglect, and decay." (Gaby Greenwald)

FIG. 5. October 4, 1989. The prayer vigil for political prisoners at Gethsemane Church, Berlin-Prenzlauer Berg. (ULLSTEIN, Rolf Zöllner)

Fig. 6. October 6, 1989, the 40th Anniversary of the GDR. FDJ musicians march in the torchlight parade on Unter den Linden. (ULLSTEIN, ADN-Zentralbild)

Fig. 7. On the reviewing stand for the military parade marking the 40th Anniversary of the GDR, October 7, 1989, Erich Honecker, *right*, and a preoccupied Mikhail Gorbachev did not see eye-to-eye. (ULLSTEIN, Werek)

FIG. 8. October 7, 1989, 5:00 P.M. Young people begin the first demonstration in Berlin, Alexanderplatz. (ULLSTEIN, Poly-Press)

FIG. 9. Later on October 7, 1989, police move massively against the demonstrators along Schönhauser Allee in Berlin-Prenzlauer Berg. (ULLSTEIN, Kai Garfeld)

FIG. 10. October 15, 1989. Revolutions take many forms: unauthorized street dancing in front of Gethsemane Church. Francis Fukuyama (in windbreaker) is in the left foreground, Gaby is in the center with her back to the camera and partially hiding the author. (Steve Flanagan)

Fig. 11. The GDR's new leader, Egon Krenz, here harried by reporters, was unable to master either democratic politics or the revolt within his own Communist party. (Landesbildstelle Berlin)

Fig. 12. October 29, 1989, Berlin Town Meeting. A member of the audience (*at microphone, center*) makes a well-applauded point to Günter Schabowski in front of the City Hall. (German Information Center, K. Lehnartz)

German equation that increasingly preoccupies Europe. The United States cannot ensure that East Germans get the answers right, but this is the time to influence them, and consultations with a cautious bureaucrat will not carry us far. In the next six weeks, the United States needs to think hard to define interests and priorities, to increase its options and identify where it can engage the GDR more even before all big bilateral problems are solved. We shall feed in embassy ideas, and Dick will recommend a nongovernmental invitation again for Krenz, the likeliest heir.

The West Germans have closed their Prague Embassy, now host to more than 100 GDR citizens. At least 3,000 have reached Austria this month. How many of the hundreds of thousands of vacationers will come home from Hungary by next week, when school holidays end?

The latest dispute is about abandoned Trabies. The new West Germans who hiked into Austria want them back; the GDR is pressing Hungary to return them here, where they could reduce the waiting list of ten years or more for new cars. This is not a time for jokes, but one is so evocative that it bears repeating: One side of the ten-Mark bill shows a young woman at her workplace on the day she registered to buy a new Trabant; turn it over, and you see her on the day she gets the car. (The reverse side depicts Clara Zetkin, a septuagenarian early German Communist.) A serious point suggested by this contretemps is that as bad as the Trabi is, it is a remarkable mass flight when so many have their own cars to abandon. East Germans pressing for emigration tend to be, by most measurements, comfortably off. The stories of abandoned apartments make the same point. Except in the relative inner-German sense, it is not poverty that has produced this hemorrhage of GDR lifeblood. That these are people who have many accoutrements of the good life makes their willingness to risk much for a new start the more troubling to the SED.

AUGUST 24

We drove to Wittenberg yesterday to spend the afternoon in Martin Luther's rose garden. When we met Friedrich Schorlemmer two years ago, he described a struggle for the GDR's soul between those in the SED interested in problem-solving and those of the old apparatus, especially the Stasi, who held to Stalinist ways. A man of boundless energy, creativity, and wit, he was optimistic about an outcome he was determined to influence. "When I left high school as a pastor's son," he said, "the only higher education open to me was a church school. My daughter can go to university. If there is trouble about the education of children of religious families, we, the church, can usually appeal the case. That is progress."

A somber Friedrich received us yesterday, worried for his society and family. "It hurts me," he said, "to see so many leave. I said on Western television, and many people here looked at me disapprovingly, that most of them are not the ones who struggled and suffered trying to make a difference. They go primarily for economic reasons and because they are panicked that if they do not leave now, the West Germans may turn against refugees, even German refugees, and the door could be shut from both sides."

"I believe it is important for the GDR to succeed as a Socialist German alternative," Friedrich explained. "A year ago, when my circle drew up a Glasnost and Perestroika program for the synod, I had some hope that the Party would take notice. It did. The answer came in December when it shut the door to reforms. They have banned *Sputnik,* insulted our intelligence at the elections, and threatened us with China. I will keep working here. We have to concentrate for now on real fundamentals, single environmental issues, for example. There is no tolerance for broader issues. But the young people are attracted to our ideas. The other day, after I said on Western radio that the GDR needed a social democratic alternative because the SED was frozen into immobility, a plant manager who last year criticized me publicly came up in a restaurant and whispered, 'You are right.' But how can I tell my daughter she should stay? When she went to Berlin to work last month, she said she would never leave the GDR because she knew how much of myself I have put into the effort to change things. I told her with tears in my eyes that she had to be a free person and make her own choices. I cannot blame her if she doesn't stay in East Berlin."

Friedrich has been traveling, staying in touch with activists who share his concern and belief that society needs a democratic alternative. The Stasi, he indicated, were everywhere. Those who shadowed him in Dresden let him see the pistols under their windbreakers. (Friedrich has a practiced eye for Stasi. As he accompanied us from the garden, he unerringly pointed out the cars that would follow us to the city limits.) "The Party leadership can think of nothing except its own power," Friedrich concluded. "People are depressed, and a mood is growing like 1961, when the Wall went up. I don't know what is going to happen."

Early today, Hungary allowed the Budapest sit-ins to go West. The West German Embassy there is closed for cleanup and to prevent it from filling again. The fate of East Germans who overstay their holidays remains uncertain, however. While Hungary tilts toward Bonn, the Czechoslovaks again told East Germans in Prague to go home.

AUGUST 25

Erich Honecker celebrates a troubled seventy-seventh birthday today. His body has betrayed him twice this summer, but East Germany's body politic has embarrassed him more seriously. Its citizens have responded to political and economic stagnation and increased opportunity by leaving, or making clear their determination to leave, in record numbers. The threat to the GDR's reputation as Eastern Europe's most successful state, if not to its very existence, is growing. The contrast could scarcely be greater with two years ago, when Honecker celebrated his seventy-fifth birthday between Berlin's 750th Anniversary and his trip to West Germany. The convalescing leader's Politburo colleagues, who are circling the wagons to protect his—and their—power, will do their best to cheer him up. If I could join the circle, however, I would want to tell him of conversations Gaby and I have had in these hectic weeks. Despite the omnipresent Stasi, who are supposed to keep the politicians informed, there is a serious question how much reality finds its way into the golden Wandlitz enclave.

Can Honecker understand the agony of Schorlemmer or Krätschell, men of the church but also idealists of the left, who would gladly work with a responsive government to realize democratic socialism? Can he appreciate how much potential support has been lost, perhaps irretrievably, by refusing such cooperation, or what the apostasy of a diplomat like Reemer means? Would he write off the Esches as traitors or ask himself why they say "We are too old to start over, but this SED can no longer claim to be the leading force in society, only the ordering force"? If this old man who knew Hitler's prison for ten years can still remember the dreams of his youth, I would want him to hear Gunnar and Gabi, professionals with a fine apartment and attractive children, say, "When we came back from West Germany this month, we almost could not face it. The contrast was too much. This is our home, but should it be our children's? Can it change? Is it fair for us to make them face the same compromises, and for how much longer? We would never put them in danger. We won't try the Hungarian border. Only the legal way would be possible, but for the first time we are thinking about it. We don't know what is right."

And if he brushed all this aside as the complaints of intellectuals, churchgoers, and the middle class, what would Honecker say if he were with us at a street stand as workers—Saxons sent to build up the "capital"—spoke over beer and bockwurst? "Have you heard that Jochen has gone West?" "No, but they say Georg and Walter have. At home it seems everyone is applying, even the private craftsmen who make so much money." "I know. I'm too old, and I'm staying, but how many of us will be left?"

Last weekend Otto Reinhold framed the fundamental issue, even if he was not quite bold enough to speak "in clear text" about solutions: "The crucial issue is what can be called the GDR's socialist identity. Regarding this, there is obviously a fundamental difference between the GDR and other socialist countries. They all existed as states . . . prior to their socialist restructuring. Their statehood was not primarily dependent on the social system. The GDR was different. It is only conceivable as a socialist alternative to the FRG. What right to exist should a capitalist GDR have side by side with a capitalist Federal Republic? Naturally, none." That is the dilemma. The GDR cannot adopt many solutions of Eastern Europe's radical reformers lest it be left with only *Realpolitik* justification for a separate room in the European House. Between unadulterated Western capitalism and neo-Stalinism, the SED has only one choice.

I do not expect the GDR to collapse. It has many resources: a disciplined Party and world-class security apparatus, a population that may emigrate but does not organize politically, a reservoir of critical spirits still prepared to give socialism a chance if met halfway, and above all a standard of living that takes the rough edge off much unhappiness, and an insurance policy underwritten by Bonn, which fears instability. The risk—if the choice is framed so starkly—is rather that it will sink back into the isolation, this time self-imposed, from which it thought it had escaped in the 1970s. It may then become a poorer, meaner place, less able to take even marginal comfort from standard-of-living comparisons with Eastern Europe and less relevant to East-West changes. The choice, of course, is not that simplistic. For the very reasons Reinhold outlined, it is more important to the GDR than to other states that it make an arguably socialist system—not just any system— work and be attractive. The GDR badly needs to adopt and implement a formula for reform communism.

If Honecker's spies are half as candid as they are pervasive, he must be aware that things are going badly wrong. In past troubles, the instinct has been to rely on the bedrock support of the instruments of repression. The biological fact that old, ill, worn leaders are unlikely to summon the energy to do more than cling to power also argues for a temporary effort to retain the status quo. But there are those who are younger and more dynamic in the SED, one step below the top. Though many are more cynical than the founding generation, they must apply longer time frames when they calculate how to get and retain power. They must be increasingly uneasy as they watch a slide begin. Will they now apply pressure for change?

AUGUST 26

It can only have added to Honecker's birthday unease that the Hungarian prime minister and foreign minister spent four hours with Kohl and Genscher. The keys to the investments Hungary needs and the European club she wants to join are in Bonn, not Berlin. A fundamental reorientation is under way in Hungary. *Neues Deutschland* has no hint of unusual times, however. It headlines that dedicated farmers have again won the "harvest battle."

AUGUST 27

After work on Friday, we drove to Dresden and crossed the Czech border the next day, wondering how many East Germans around us were trying to make their way west. The government in power since the 1968 invasion has much to answer for, but it has invested large amounts of money, so it is fair to speak again of "Golden Prague." The central areas, the square before Hradčany Castle and narrow streets that wind down to the river, have been lovingly restored. No city so rewards a walker. Wonders from the Middle Ages and the Reformation are everywhere, and a café with superb beer at a price for the worker's pocketbook is always at hand. We sought a respite from the GDR, a carefree weekend at "The Three Ostriches," a 400-year-old inn at the foot of the Charles Bridge, and delighted in the small restaurants, state-owned but with verve and service rare in stolid Berlin. But the GDR was not far away. As we climbed to the castle, we came upon the elegant palace that houses the West German Embassy. Police observed carefully all who came near, and we heard the throng of suppliants in the garden. A restaurant had no time for us; it was cooking for the beleaguered embassy staff.

AUGUST 28

The Soviets rebuilt their embassy after the war on Unter den Linden where the Czars' embassy stood, a half block from the Wall's no-go zone, which bars access to the old American Embassy lot. Along with the larger-than-life Lenin bust in the front garden, it is Stalinist monumental architecture, an early contribution to the rebuilding of Berlin's government quarter, which begins east of the Brandenburg Gate. I enter it only when I accompany Dick or J.D. for calls—usually on the number two, Maximyschev, a great bear of a man and a shrewd German expert—formal occasions spent sipping tea from good china in an ornate sitting room off the grand staircase. I keep in touch with my counterpart at restaurant lunches. As familiarity has grown, our conversations have become more relaxed. The Soviet Embassy knows more about what happens here than any other. G., a good and cautious diplomat, says less than I want to hear, but his views are always worthwhile.

I want to speak with him, but he is away. He owes me an answer to a daily more urgent question. In spring, after a lunch at which he talked around my questions, we walked Unter den Linden. "What do *you* think about reform?" he suddenly asked. I replied that it was badly needed and, if attempted, had a chance to make a society to which citizens would feel real commitment. Only by risking it could the Politburo avoid even greater dangers, I said. It would not be easier a few years hence. Standing at the corner where our routes diverged, we continued speaking, perhaps more freely than ever before. (The Stasi would not shy at monitoring the Soviet "friends.") "It is not so easy for them. Perhaps you should tell them," G. said. "What do *you* think they must do?" I pressed. "Next time," he said, smiling, and we parted.

G. and Maximyschev understand the GDR too well not to give Moscow detailed reports on the social ferment and political paralysis that have since gripped this land. If Gorbachev visits in October, he will find a situation unlike anything he has met before. It would be good to know what our colleagues recommend.

AUGUST 29

We left for Bad Salzungen yesterday to meet the local Party secretary and the author of the best-seller. Weimar, once home to Goethe and Schiller, was our first evening's goal. The drive was a nightmare. Rain, fog, and repairs that narrowed the autobahn beyond Leipzig to a single lane doubled the budgeted two-and-a-half hours, and we awakened to a chilly morning with an unmistakable smell in the air. Brown coal is virtually the GDR's only natural resource. Poor in energy and high in pollutants, its pungent odor is more evocative of the East than even the diesel residue of Trabi engines. This gray morning it must have signaled a dispiriting return to daily drudgery to East Germans for whom summer has been more shock than relaxation. Vacations are again a year off; a political opening seems even further away.

After a stroll through the city center, we drove southwest, pausing once at the garden show outside Erfurt. By noon, as we passed through Eisenach, glimpsed the Wartburg above us, where Luther found refuge from the Pope, and entered the deep Thuringian Forest, summer's heat and blue skies were back, but I paid little attention to scenery. As Gaby drove, I thumbed through *Der Erste*, the slender volume that is the closest thing to a look behind the curtain of secrecy the Party draws over the private lives and much public activity of its leaders. It is controversial in SED quarters, but the author, Landolf Scherzer, enjoys a popularity equal to Markus Wolf's on the lecture circuit.

What makes it special? County Council Chairman Eberhard Stumpf is quoted as saying it demythologizes senior officials and shows them to be "damned dull, normal people," but it also explores themes from the viewpoint of a man who is one of the GDR's hundred or so local princes. Hans-Dieter Fritschler ("HDF" in the book), the Party secretary, is shown wrestling over what to do about a senior SED man whose daughter has been arrested trying to escape to the West; he fires him, though there is a hint the decision comes from above. "Flight from the Republic," of course, is still a public taboo. In the book's climactic scene, Fritschler must accept defeat and enforce Party discipline when Berlin refuses to shift resources to build apartments in Bad Salzungen. Stumpf grumbles that not every county resident without a dry roof over his head is thrilled because the capital's Nikolaiviertel has been completed on time utilizing resources "contributed" by Bad Salzungen.

Scherzer describes how Fritschler, expecting to talk with eighteen families on a "Day of Mass Political Action," found that only a single police husband-wife couple had been invited. After recounting its minor complaints about garbage cans, the author reprints the SED paper's article on extensive "enthusiastic discussions." "Our damned punch-your-ticket formalism!" Fritschler explodes. After a frustrating day, HDF asks whether the Party is not to blame that nothing happens unless the First Secretary sees to it. Must we really take responsibility for everything? he wonders. Should not more initiative be left to government and individuals? How can this be changed? Fritschler says a first secretary is used up and should retire by the age of sixty. It is a passage no one can read without reflecting that this state is run by men well over seventy. Finally, he is brusque with a functionary who complains about early Soviet Glasnost (the book takes place in 1986). "Tell it as it is," he responds.

At three o'clock, we descended into a pretty valley and saw a sign, "Welcome to Bad Salzungen." Two men at a parking lay-by waved frantically to stop our car. We walked back. "Herr Stumpf sent me," said the protocol man. "HDF is waiting."

AUGUST 30

We returned to Berlin with so many more questions. What did it mean, for example, that bumper stickers in a factory parking lot proclaimed loyalty to the nearest big-time soccer club, Bayern Munich, the West German champion? Only that Bad Salzungen has no GDR League team? Not many years ago, the Stasi would have been after anyone who displayed such a Western preference.

The highlight, however, was three hours around a table with Scherzer, Stumpf, and the 47-year-old Fritschler, child of a broken working-class family who did Army time in a unit that built the Berlin Wall and rose through Krenz's FDJ before returning to Thuringia. The county has beauty only occasionally marred by potassium mines that spill sludge into the Werra River. Neat villages and spas suggest comfort and reasonable prosperity not unlike Franconia with which, despite the border scar, they share the Rhön plateau. But appearances can deceive. Scherzer wrote that Bad Salzungen is "30 kilometers from Bavaria by line of flight, otherwise, much, much farther." We found a microcosm of today's troubled GDR: a society that works, but not well enough; worried officials at least open to discussing existential questions that until this summer's crisis were ignored; Party discipline but also almost furtive hints that pressure for change is building within the establishment.

We drank the distinctively bitter Rhön beer, and then yet more beer, and unlike every other session I have had with local officials, the East Germans did not want to cite statistics of apartments built or milk produced. They were willing—to an extent eager—to reflect on the bigger themes broached by the book and lately highlighted by the drama at West German embassies and the Hungarian border. Stumpf, during walks around the town as at the table the most predictable, mostly repeated *Neues Deutschland* clichés, but Scherzer and Fritschler were more nuanced. The latter spoke sparingly, but the nods, smiles, and other body language he contributed suggested sympathy with at least some of our provocative questions, even if he felt it inopportune to say so.

Fritschler surprised us by asking what we believed the GDR should do. The informal atmosphere, or perhaps awareness of how dangerously wrong things can go here, caused me to put aside the questioner's role. Gaby and I recently saw a film about young workers, *Berlin Around the Corner*, I said. Shot during the 1965–66 cultural thaw but then banned, it is only now occasionally shown in the Babylon, East Berlin's "art" theater. In one scene, an old Communist who had probably marched in 1919 with Rosa and Karl demanded that the police be brought in to investigate slogans scribbled on the factory wall. When the plant's young Party secretary demurred and showed some sympathy for the workers, the old Communist exploded: "Don't you realize how easily we can lose all this?" That, I said, was the point. Could it be lost that easily, or had the SED built better than it dared believe? If the situation was precarious, must resort always be to the "organs of control," as they are euphemistically called? The question the GDR had to answer at its October jubilee, I argued, was whether to treat its citizenry as a forty-year-old child to whom everything had to be prescribed, or at last as an adult. The metaphor intrigued Fritschler. It recurred throughout the conversation.

Fritschler smiled when we called *Neues Deutschland* inane, and inquired how we would give youth a sense of purpose. Allow initiative in the market, we replied, and open politics up for discussion. A football fan and jogger, Fritschler agreed with Scherzer, who carried the forty-year-old child motif into sports: athletic success was once a reasonable policy to build pride and gain international recognition, but a mature society must use its resources for more than just winning Olympic medals.

Scherzer argued that Honecker's generation had achieved an apartment for everyone, stable prices, full employment, and social security. These were reasonable goals if one understood the 1930s when it was young, he said, but a new generation had other priorities and needed different policies. Fritschler gestured approvingly. Neither disagreed with us that there is a dangerous chasm between leaders and citizens, who are bitter when Honecker compares their bounty to "the Kaiser's time."

Scherzer's book is another hint that away from the front lines where the Politburo gerontocracy keeps watch, there is establishment support for at least early Glasnost. Neither the book nor our conversations were radical, except by GDR norms. At its core, *Der Erste* is system-supportive, portraying Party representatives who are close to the people and working for their well-being. Fritschler is probably at least representative, however, of many relatively young officials who are disturbed by the drift and want to modernize the operation but are infused with the iron discipline that makes grassroots revolt improbable.

When change does come at the top—and the conversation left me certain that the possibility this may occur by spring is growing—many questions will be open. How much do the forty-year-old Fritschlers have in common with the second row of the Politburo, those around sixty, who may be almost as isolated from popular expectations and frustrations as Honecker? And does either group understand that meaningful change must be more than public-relations Glasnost, a little tinkering? The generally positive impression of Fritschler I gained came as much from how he acted and what he did not say as from what he put into words. That three SED figures were this open was progress; that they trimmed comments and watched each other (and the Stasi's omnipresent third ear?) as much as they did was an even greater sign of how pervasive caution still is within this hierarchical Party.

The last word should go to the author. As we broke up, Scherzer pulled me aside to say: "I was glad you came this week. Next week I go to live in a village on the Volga and write a book on Perestroika in which I will talk about all those serious things we have to change that I could not mention in this room."

AUGUST 31

Western journalists are writing that Honecker is gravely ill. Fritschler, who was probably already aware of the cancer rumors we heard on the drive home, volunteered that he expected to serve under Honecker for "several more years" but that there was procedure and precedent for the Party to act if necessary. HDF is not senior enough to have real inside information, but he may have ties to Krenz, and it was the first time I heard an SED official admit there may be early change. Honecker's illness, of course, could not have come at a worse time. His policy of opening to the West while rejecting reform and holding Gorbachev at arm's length is being declared bankrupt by the thousands seeking to reach West Germany. He has appeared helpless since the crisis began. Unless he shows soon he is in charge, the Politburo's second row will be under great pressure to end the drift.

3

The Fall of Honecker September 1989 — October 17, 1989

SEPTEMBER 1

Unless the East Germans make a reasonable dollar offer to settle claims, we will not get far into our bilateral agenda, so I gave Dick and J.D. today a modest idea for revitalizing that negotiation. The GDR's bid last year of fourteen cents on the dollar of our $78 million principal may seem less unreasonable to them than it is, because their claims agreements have never exceeded 25 percent of principal. I recommended we hint how far they must come to get into the ballpark by giving them a "nonpaper" on our negotiations with other socialist countries. This classical diplomatic device, which has no formal status and can be disowned, would explain that the United States has normally received a percentage of principal—between 35 and 65 percent—without interest. The GDR knows this, but it would be implicit that while we could not regard 14 percent as a valid opener we would consider a proposal that was compatible with what Congress had ratified from similar countries. If we continue to say we expect $300 million—four times principal—the GDR will believe that we are not ready to negotiate and thus refrain from making a meaningful new offer.

SEPTEMBER 3

I fly home today on family business. Max Kampelman's lecture, part of a series my parents endow, will highlight the time in Wilkes-Barre. I worked for Max at the Madrid CSCE conference in 1980–81. His arms negotiation duties in Geneva have prevented him from coming sooner. Even now, he is sacrificing time and money to do a deed of friendship and kindness, and I have promised to introduce him. I know, however, that the GDR will preoccupy me.

Honecker missed the opening of the Leipzig Fair, another sign his convalescence is difficult. Willi Stoph, the seventy-five-year-old erstwhile rival who has served quietly as prime minister for thirteen years, substituted. Stoph has a politician's way with people. At least he has impressed me by remembering note-takers and including them in eye contact at the table. But this aging chain-smoker, who falls asleep at state occasions, will not be acceptable if a new leader is needed. Not much has been seen lately of Krenz or Schabowski. Are they lying low, waiting for a chance—or are the elders closing ranks around Honecker?

More important than the fair is this weekend's meeting of GDR Protestant bishops. Imre expects a public call for Honecker at last to talk honestly and heed demands for more freedom. The bishops will be reluctant to assume an exposed position as go-between for a despairing population and an SED paralyzed by fears and hierarchical principles, but they are the most likely candidate. Writers still heed the ambiguous advice Stephan Hermlin, the independent-minded Communist and Honecker contemporary, gave last year: to remember that "patience is one of the revolutionary's virtues." With economic and social collapse imminent possibilities, and Politburo proponents of a harder line saying they are prepared to use Chinese methods to maintain order and their own power, however, I doubt that waiting still serves those who want reform.

I encouraged Imre to assess whether conditions are ripe for a GDR "civil society." The term refers to citizens' readiness to construct areas of freedom across the full spectrum of life, from press through workplace, independent of state and Party control. The process has been influential in Poland and Hungary for a decade, and Washington asks whether it will take off in the GDR. There are some components here. I am impressed by Stefan Bickhardt's friends, who will not request permission to hold their art shows. The "niche society" Günter Gaus identified—the withdrawal into weekend circles from which the demands of public life are excluded—also tends toward civil society, but one tolerated precisely because it is unpolitical. Free areas within church walls have carefully circumscribed political significance, but the Stasi intervenes if activists leave sanctuary to carry a cause to the wider public.

In recent years, the state has less frequently and blatantly put to activists the choice given the pastor, Rainer Eppelmann, at the height of the independent peace movement: S-Bahn to exile in West Berlin, or train to Bautzen Prison. (The church saved him from either ride.) Nevertheless, energy that in Poland or Hungary goes into institution-building is diverted by the ever-present example of the other Germany across the Wall. Actual emigration is usually preceded by years of "inner emigration," a psychological withdrawal. Those who have entered it are little inclined to involve themselves in making something better in the part of Germany they inhabit only physically and provisionally. It is impossible to know how many are fully infected by this peculiarly GDR condition, but virtually the entire country lives in West Germany during prime television hours. Ironically, while the more successful West German society adds greatly to dissatisfaction, its nearness makes East Germans less inclined to take risks.

Police efficiency and public passivity argue against emergence of an essentially anti-(Communist)state organization like Solidarity. However, while most who have broken with the regime focus on emigration, there remain many critical spirits who out of conviction or pragmatism are prepared to work with (or within) the SED for a more democratic, productive socialism. They have about given up on Honecker and his geriatric inner circle, but would support a genuine attempt at reform. You pay your money and take your choice, but I do not foresee revolution or even direct competition for power between activists and SED. Serious reform is more likely if the Party can bring itself to meet halfway the frustrated idealists sheltering within church walls, and even in its own ranks, who want to stay and make the GDR a better place. The activists provide a vital impetus, but the looming struggle is within the SED, which must choose between reform and repression.

SEPTEMBER 9

Max Kampelman was superb. I was delighted to "work for him again," as I said in my introduction and appreciative of the pleasure he brought my parents. It was instructive how small an impression what preoccupies Berlin has made at home. Max spoke mostly about the Soviet Union, and the questions were on arms control and Israel. Germany has yet to seize the awareness of even a sophisticated American audience.

As good as it is to be home, trying to keep up with German developments is frustrating. Tens of thousands of East Germans who had been on vacation in Hungary during August are insisting on going west. The Hungarians must act soon, and there is little doubt they will decide for the West Germans—provided the Soviets stay on the sidelines. After six weeks, however, the sit-ins left the Ständige Vertretung yesterday only with promises they would not be prosecuted and could pursue emigration from home. On the surface, the GDR won a point. The Ständige Vertretung remains closed as Bonn tries to avoid another full house.

And that is the dilemma, because nothing has been done to lance the boil of discontent. For the first time, protests against the rigged elections reached downtown Berlin. The eighty arrested two days ago were quickly released, but no senior politician has spoken up for new policies. I catch the evening flight from Philadelphia more than curious at what I shall find in Berlin.

SEPTEMBER 10

Gaby met me at Tegel Airport, and we crossed into East Berlin. Unlike Allied soldiers in West Berlin or other non-Germans, diplomats accredited to the GDR are not restricted to Checkpoint Charlie and Friedrichstrasse Train Station. We also use special lines at Invalidenstrasse (downtown) and Bornholmer Strasse (north of the center, where Prenzlauer Berg becomes Pankow) and other German crossing-points. In Berlin terms, this ability to move instantly between worlds by showing a plastic ID, the *Ausweis*, is the greatest of privileges. Like everything in the divided city, that card has a history of confrontation and accommodation. We do not use passports to enter what we consider the Soviet Sector, lest this imply an international border. We only "identify" ourselves to the police (actually officers of the GDR's specially trustworthy border force). Like the decision to put the embassy in East Berlin near the government with which it must do business, the procedure balances principle and pragmatism. All Berlin remains a Four Power responsibility, legally part of neither German state. However, except for insistence on certain forms, the United States conducts day-to-day relations essentially as if East Berlin were as much GDR territory as Potsdam or Dresden.

We wonder what sort of people the Checkpoint guards, who briefly hold the *Ausweis* to compare photo with face politely and impersonally, really are. If those with whom we come in contact are not themselves likely shooters—riflemen patrol between the double Wall, and other soldiers are in observation towers—they have been known to tackle East Germans making a dash for the West. They rarely show a personality. There are only a handful of women, but one attractive Charlie guard, "Legs," always smiles pleasantly. One of her male colleagues surprised me last year, shortly after the election, by asking about George Bush. It never happened again, and I believe he was in his way apologizing for being rude on a rainy afternoon with traffic backing up when I gave him incorrect forms for my parents. The Bornholmer Strasse team is more relaxed. Gaby speaks of "a charm offensive" since one boyish guard has begun to call her "Gnädige Frau" ("honored lady," a gallantry expected from the Austro-Hungarian Army, not the Red Prussian). His colleagues chat about cars and tell me whether Gaby has been through. Signs of détente or embarrassment at a despised job? It is odd to joke with a man who may shoot a friend of mine for trying to exercise a human right without the proper document.

By crossing at Bornholmer Strasse, we missed the Unter den Linden traffic jam produced by the annual "Memorial Day for Victims of the Fascist Terror and Day of Struggle Against Fascism and War." The old men swore to stay the course. Hermann Axen claimed defiantly: "A dirty wave of hate and great lies is breaking over the GDR. . . . Don't fool yourselves, Gentlemen. As often in the past forty years, your speculation is condemned to failure."

Imre greeted me with news that an open letter was read from every Lutheran pulpit this morning. In some of the plainest speaking the church has ever done, the bishops noted "with unease and concern" the rising numbers seeking to leave. They admitted they could offer "no short-term solution," but found "an important cause . . . in the fact that the long overdue changes in society . . . are being refused." The churchmen renewed "urgent" proposals for candid public discussion about "the discontent and deformed development in our society, . . . realistic media reporting that does not contradict what the citizen experiences every day," and freer travel. Even then, solving the problems will be a "long and difficult process" requiring help, particularly from West Germany: "To reduce tension and the gap between the two economies requires new thinking and new concepts."

But there was also a restatement of church policy on emigration, which the state should have welcomed: "We ask that you . . . not leave the GDR. . . . Our country will be poorer if people withdraw and emigrate. . . . The participation of precisely those who suffer under our society's deficits and seek changes is also needed. We must ask some of those who want to emigrate what standards they use to measure the conditions and expectations of their lives. We warn against the illusion that greater economic well-being brings automatic fulfillment. In view of the unmistakable gaps already torn in health services, the economy, and other areas, we must recall that every person bears responsibility not only for his own life but also for the society in which he has been placed."

The church is the one institution that may have the stature to bring together a people and a Party marching in opposite directions. But is either recipient of its appeal in a mood to listen?

SEPTEMBER 11

At midnight, East Germans in Hungary became free to depart for their country of choice, and thousands are streaming into Austria. West Germany has won the struggle for the Hungarian soul, and the GDR has been humiliated. Not all reasons for restraint with its military ally and economic partner are removed, and a senior Hungarian Party official, Mária Ormos, comes to Berlin Thursday, but public excoriation of Budapest foreshadows a major rift. I am invited to what promises to be a lively talk by Mrs. Ormos at the Hungarian Cultural Center.

There are indications that the Politburo is urgently debating a new travel policy with options ranging from further restrictions to escape forward by liberalizing. Most contacts expect a crackdown. The policy review is surely linked to Honecker's physical and political health. New rumors allege that he lost the will to recover when he learned the magnitude of the disaster. Others more moderately claim that his recovery from gall bladder, kidney, and liver complaints is unlikely to be complete, but his life is not in danger. The handful of power brokers must be distressed that his once adroit balancing act has become paralysis. Though their immediate reaction has been to close ranks, they must soon show that the ship of state is moving through troubled waters with an active helmsman and a clear course. I would not write Honecker off yet, but he and his policies are in serious trouble.

SEPTEMBER 12

Events are coming almost too fast to order. East Germans seeking emigration have met in Leipzig's Nikolai Church every Monday evening this year for a service and discussion. Yesterday several hundred went into the street, and fifty were arrested. With open confrontation now threatened at home, the GDR is engaged in polemics with Hungary, charging it accepted Bonn's "thirty pieces of silver." The regime's one half-glimmer of hope comes from Prague, where Wolfgang Vogel talked 250 of 460 sit-ins out of the embassy.

The Soviet attitude is the most important external determinant of SED policy, and Gorbachev is giving Honecker first aid. His Foreign Ministry spokesman called the Hungarian action "unusual and unexpected," and Tass criticized a campaign against "an inseparable element of the Warsaw Pact, our true friend and ally." More important will be the message Yigor Ligachev brings to Berlin today. Since he is the Politburo's leading conservative, most observers take his visit as a sign that the Kremlin wants to buck up shaken Comrades and remind Bonn and other capitals that its tolerance still has some power-politics limits.

West German television news opened yesterday with the claim that "the Opposition in the GDR is beginning to organize." Skeptical, I sent Imre and Heather to sample their contacts, and they returned with two sheets of onion paper containing a declaration, "Awakening 89—Neues Forum." Its authors are careful not to suggest they mean to fight the SED for power. They say they seek "democratic dialogue" and to offer "a political platform for the whole GDR that should enable people from all professions, trades, social circles, parties, and groups to discuss and work out society's vital problems." Neues Forum (the name means "New Forum") says it will try to register as a legal association, but the SED has never tolerated an independent political force. Western publicity may deflect prosecution, but it would be remarkable if the regime granted official status.

Except for dislike of the SED, activists here have always been fragmented, and the thirty signers of this appeal admit their policy disagreements. There is also a very important question of how representative they are. Several names are familiar. The painter Bärbel Bohley, exiled in 1988, this summer became the first dissident to return to the GDR; the church protects her, but considers her as difficult as she is principled. Katja Havemann is the widow of the dissident Communist, Robert Havemann, Honecker's fellow prisoner in the Nazi period, who spent his last years under house arrest. Rolf Henrich was banned from practicing law this spring for writing a critical book. Many are unknown, but at least those from Berlin, Leipzig, and Dresden have long activist credentials. That the founders do come from a variety of professions and from across the country indicates that advance organization, not just courage, was behind their step. They are intellectuals, but the presence of both apostate Communists and a handful of pastors suggests they may be able to bridge the gap that has hampered cooperation between church-basement activists and reform-minded nonbelievers. Only time will show whether they can also tap the deep pool of discontented citizens who have hitherto opted out in favor of internal or actual emigration.

SEPTEMBER 13

A suddenly concerned Washington is asking what will happen next and what it means, above all for East-West relations. The silent crisis has been brought into the open by two events that were only barely perceivable when I tried to call attention to it six weeks ago: Honecker's illness, which is more debilitating than first believed, and the refugee flood. Honecker is almost surely not now in effective control, though he means to return. The odds increase, perhaps to probability, that by spring he will be replaced and his policies will be seriously reevaluated. Less certain is the direction in which the GDR will move.

The East Germans rushing across the Hungarian border to life in the other Germany are only a fraction of those for whom the GDR has authorized emigration this year, but the television images dramatize the scope of the political, moral, and economic catastrophe. After two decades of a more civilized paternalism that produced Eastern Europe's highest living standard and a semblance of normal human contacts between Germany's two halves, Honecker's GDR is little better able to retain its people's toleration, much less active loyalty, than was Ulbricht's Stalinist structure. That realization is bitter enough for any politician to make plausible rumors that Honecker is in deep depression.

Vogel told Dick that it was Honecker's personal decision to allow travel to Hungary this summer. The result shocked the old man and cannot have left unaffected the faith others have in him. Nevertheless, the lawyer said two days ago, Honecker is not as ill as portrayed. He means to hold on, and no one can yet challenge him. Vogel foresees the GDR entering a "Brezhnev phase," during which the old leader retains formal power and others cannot broker a succession. In the Soviet Union, it was called "the period of stagnation." My guess is the time frame will be telescoped even if Honecker's health does not deteriorate further. SED leaders are out of touch, as every halfway objective observer agrees, but the problems of morale and substance are too obvious to ignore entirely. Even conservative Communists can learn from experience, and no one now thinks the Soviets eased their problems by allowing Brezhnev to be propped up for years. Moreover, Honecker may have trapped himself. Advancing the Party Congress to May forces decisions that might otherwise have drifted a bit longer. He may not have cancer, but he certainly has bad luck.

But if Honecker cannot bounce back, and the Party will not accept lengthy stagnation, what leader and policies might benefit? Here one is obviously deep in the speculative thicket, but a few points can be suggested. Where no successor is certain—and I suspect Honecker balanced contenders to protect himself—a new general secretary will have to respond to his electorate, at least initially, rather than set a personalized course. The SED is the relevant electorate, not Gorbachev. More especially, in this most disciplined and hierarchical Party, it is the Politburo, not the grassroots or even second-level princelings, that truly counts. Traditions and instincts have schooled that self-selected body to fear instability above all and to rely on repression when in doubt. This Politburo is unlikely to conclude Honecker went wrong by being too tough. More probably, his key policies—including a dynamic inner-German relationship, expanded travel, and generally though not universally improved human rights and more civilized church-state relations—will be reassessed to determine to what extent they should, and can, be tightened.

Many expect a "hard-liner" to emerge, and the reaction to the last days backs up the view that a bunker mentality is the short-term prescription. But the Politburo's maneuvering room would not be great. It is not so economically unschooled and politically insensitive to believe it can cut ties to Bonn and the non-Germanic world and return to harsh 1960s isolation without being presented with unpayable bills. It is more likely to shade things, not make an abrupt rear turn, albeit in ways that Honecker would consider rejection of much he has done and that most East Germans would oppose.

There is a brighter scenario, perhaps over a slightly longer period. The SED grassroots, the population as a whole, and intellectuals (despite efforts of a handful of activists) have basically remained quiet, apparently willing to wait for the tracks to be repositioned from above. The drift worries them, however, and in varying degrees they want at least a more honest approach: Glasnost if not necessarily Perestroika. The preconditions for broad consensus on a new beginning are in place. SED leaders are politicians, not merely ideologues. They are not congenitally incapable of concluding that immediate costs and long-term dangers of a hard line outweigh risk of losing control of a process that would enlist popular support. If Ulbricht was a milder Stalin and Honecker a bureaucratic compromiser, serious reform (not necessarily the unproven Soviet model) remains the one policy not yet found wanting in unhappy GDR history. Honecker's Politburo may not be less capable of authorizing a real attack on problems than Brezhnev's became, either at the old leader's demise or after an unhappy interlude with a traditional successor.

What are U.S. interests? Suddenly, the GDR is no longer either stable, dull, or predictable. The only certainty is that it has begun to move from the Honecker era to something much different. Now that concurrent crises of health and confidence have shaken it, the pace will increase, and no one knows the end. Nor should anyone underestimate this Politburo's limitations or the resources of the state and the ingenuity of its people to make a German try, given half a chance, at producing a socialism that works better. Even the West Germans, with their commitment of treasure and passion, have limited ability to channel the outcome. Nevertheless, our own security concerns should dictate greater U.S. engagement with the Warsaw Pact state most important to West Germany, the Soviet Union, and Berlin.

SEPTEMBER 14

Honecker rumors are Berlin's hottest item. A Latin American ambassador told Dick he had learned from his Cuban colleague that Castro asked the GDR and was advised that Honecker has cancer but could survive "months" or "years," depending on response to treatment. But a *Neues Deutschland* editorial poked fun at the claim he is dead or dying, noting it ran in a West German tabloid next to a confession: "I became pregnant from petting." The editorial was signed "E.H.," initials not known to belong to a regular staff member and that in the past have indicated a personal Honecker contribution.

In Washington and Bonn, the shocking realization that fundamental issues are up for review is striking home. There is no longer doubt that, as the phrase goes, the German Question is back on Europe's agenda, and not for the twenty-first century. While I was away, Vernon Walters, U.S. Ambassador in Bonn, was asked whether he could "foresee a united Germany in the near future." He answered, "Yes. It is not normal with two Germanies." The interviewer observed: "It marked the first time a senior Allied diplomat has spoken of the possibility of German reunification in the short term—rather than the distant future."

Walters was rebuked for what seems both an improbable and imprudent personal remark. How stable the imposing facade of the East German state, with powerful army and efficient secret police but a grave problem of popular legitimacy, really is, however, is suddenly a topic for a conference at some think tank in a pleasant location each week. A wag once denigrated such affairs as providing for "the leisure of the theoried class," but they give politicians and academics the chance to talk through issues whose contours can otherwise be lost in the rush of operational decisions. At one such conference Egon Bahr, formulator of the small-steps policy that has become a West German consensus approach to the GDR, worried that instability in the East was only hours away. Deputy Secretary of State Larry Eagleburger said the United States was the only major power that would be fully relaxed about unification.

The distinguished conservative daily *Frankfurter Allgemeine* yesterday urged a reexamination of Western priorities. It argued that the far-reaching changes in the Soviet Union made it overly modest to seek merely to ease Germany's division. The thesis was that policy should be reoriented toward unification within a much shorter time than hitherto believed realistic, and that debate should be joined in the 1990 Bundestag election. As attractive as achievement of the fundamental national goal must seem to most West Germans, however, realism about residual GDR strengths and international complications gives pause. They know that if they stress early unification, reevaluations of all aspects of postwar relations and institutions—to include the European Community, NATO, and the CSCE—will begin in every European capital. There undoubtedly are politicians who are tempted to seize the opportunity to push the GDR toward collapse, but this still looks unrealistic. I doubt many will want to risk Bonn's interests in Europe, East and West, by acting as if unification were just around the corner.

As history accelerates, this embassy struggles to get the United States off the sidelines and positioned to represent its own interests in the GDR. We have few helpers. Harry Gilmore, head of the West Berlin Mission, professes concern for Berlin status. With regard to even the modest proposals the European Bureau is considering, he cautions that "once we embark on these steps, we will be traversing a very slippery slope." Although Deputy Secretary of State John Whitehead met Honecker three times, he argues that military-to-military contacts and policy-level visits should be allowed only when the GDR is more positive toward U.S. Berlin positions. Cautions come also from Embassy Bonn, which agrees the Federal Republic would not object were we to improve minimal relations with the East Germans. Nevertheless, our colleagues argue, the United States has no significant interests here, and the most effective way to influence inner-German relations is merely to consult with Bonn. They also ask whether it is appropriate to deepen the relationship while Honecker is still in power. There will be chances for initiatives, they say, when and if new leaders merit U.S. approval.

A suspicious mind could conclude that "clientitis" is behind this passivity, but it cannot easily be rebutted. There is no constituency in the United States willing to support an effort to do anything with the GDR. This situation is different from that of other Eastern European countries, each of which has an ethnic community that potentially could back an activist policy. If another example of how hard it will be to overcome the alliance of vested interest and plausible prudence were needed, it is in the State Department's response to my idea for a "nonpaper" on claims settlements. It was shot down because it might imply readiness to compromise with the GDR. We are to continue to insist on payment exceeding by a factor of four the best deal we have ever achieved in Eastern Europe.

The promising news from Washington, however, is that the Secretary's policy-planning staff believes that if the old patterns in Germany break up fast the United States may need a bolder policy that will assist the GDR into the reform process without igniting instability or dangerously unrealistic talk of imminent reunification. It accepts that Bonn has tried to foster economic relations and human contacts with the GDR, not sudden and risky political change. Nevertheless, Bonn's priorities could shift if there were upheaval here. It would be costly if our ally believed we wanted merely to freeze inner-German relations. Consequently, the "policy planners" want to find a way to avoid stirring up controversy over future German unity while not leaving the field entirely to the West Germans. Their objective is to promote self-determination prudently, without risking European stability, especially the German commitment to NATO. They want to begin dialogue with a GDR that is in transition and to talk with the Europeans about the implications. In other words, they at least have an open mind toward an activist policy now, not at an indefinite future time, in order to develop American leverage in both East Berlin and Bonn. They may be our best hope in a less-than-friendly bureaucracy.

Larry Eagleburger is also a factor. He believes the GDR situation is "explosive." I think this is slightly overdrawn. The Politburo retains too many tools of repression, and apparently the will to use them, to make likely an outright revolution that would pose for Gorbachev the stark question whether to intervene to save the most important element of his position in Central Europe. But an enormous political challenge with vast implications for East-West relations is under way, and we need to address the deputy secretary's worry more in our reporting.

SEPTEMBER 15

Over lunch, my Hungarian contact said the Ormos visit failed to solve anything. Nevertheless, the GDR did not threaten trade reprisals, he claimed. Mrs. Ormos was tight-lipped about her meeting with Kurt Hager, the Politburo's seventy-seven-year-old ideological and cultural czar, but the press made it easy to divine the chilly atmosphere, and the gap between East German and Hungarian thinking was also apparent at the lecture I attended. No ground rules were set, but neither Ormos nor her mixed-generation standing-room-only audience of 350 referred directly to the bilateral problem on everyone's mind. Her prepared remarks were a straightforward review of Hungarian politics, but the questions and answers got closer to the heart of the matter. A sample:

> YOUNG EAST GERMAN: How can the Hungarian Party bring itself to have real dialogue with dissidents and social interest groups, not just small gardeners and animal breeders? [A reference to the

"expanded" local councils here that brought snickers.] Did the old leaders have to be removed first? [More laughter.]

ORMOS: They are our children. The opposition leaders are young people whom we Communists raised and then drove out because we called those who thought differently "heretics." We have to get back in touch with the creative forces these people offer.

Not everyone liked what they heard. A pensioner appeared genuinely troubled when he asked whether there was any difference between the Hungarian Party's program and bourgeois liberalism. What would remain of even socialism's remnant when the Communists negotiated a coalition? he wanted to know. Most were open-minded. Idealistic socialists (and the GDR has more than might be suspected) are troubled by the gap between rich and poor in Hungary, and there is wide distaste for the inflation. Nevertheless, there is substantial sympathy for Budapest's reforms, and particularly its border decision. The Hungarian ambassador says he has received many flowers in the past few days.

One exchange puzzled me. A young man asked whether the Hungarians could be confident they would not be routed in elections like the Polish Party. Mrs. Ormos replied obliquely that police and military methods could only make problems worse. Was she reacting to the advice she sensed in the air, even if it was unlikely to have been given explicitly, when she discussed reform dynamics in Kurt Hager's lair? It was odd, but then so are the times.

Afterward, I complimented Dr. Dietzel—an editor of *Berliner Zeitung*, the SED's Berlin daily—on a Romania series that was more critical than usual. He grimaced and said he had to include a few negatives to get credibility. His readers knew how bad things were, but there was high-level interest in praising Ceaucescu. That was why he had been sent to Bucharest, not Budapest.

Because senior Social Democrats, like other West German politicians, have become strongly critical of the GDR, Parliament President Horst Sindermann today revoked an invitation to SPD legislators. It is another sign that the fronts are hardening. When he wants to, Sindermann has a common touch that transcends ideology. In small circles, he likes to reminisce about his youth as an accomplished soccer player. Stefan Heym's memoirs describe how he carried an ill prisoner on his back when he broke out of a Nazi concentration camp. And yet, Heym points out, in old age he has become as insensitive as the others who live cut off from GDR reality in the compound at Wandlitz. Is he even the same man who once risked his life for ideals and friends?

Honecker's one item of welcome news was in Ligachev's message. The Soviet assured a television interviewer that the GDR was an inseparable member of the Warsaw Pact and said Gorbachev will attend the 40th Anniversary celebrations next month. A boycott would have been a blow; a "captive" Gorbachev on the reviewing stand can make the point that the Soviet security guarantee is unaffected by disagreements about reform. Still, it will be a difficult assignment for Gorbachev, who cannot welcome too close an association with a leadership that has an image very different from the one he himself is at pains to present.

SEPTEMBER 17

Even more than usual, politics overshadowed theology at the church synod. Bishop Leich of the host Thuringian Church appealed for "clear signs" at last of social, political, and economic reform. "We want our citizens to stay," he said. "We are convinced the GDR's stability, which our neighboring states also desire, is maintained by change but endangered by delay of change." Imre believes the most significant development may have come in the corridors. Four second-level CDU members circulated a "Letter from Weimar," a self-critical statement of co-responsibility for the crisis and a call for intraparty democracy, a larger CDU role in government, and honest media. It is the first sign that the Bloc Parties, never more than SED handmaidens, may respond to the challenge with some independent thinking.

SEPTEMBER 18

Two SPD Bundestag members were turned back at an East Berlin checkpoint today as "undesired," and other Social Democrats were disinvited by SED hosts in Rostock. It is time to ask whether inner-German relations are becoming a major casualty.

A chill in relations is likely, but I think both sides still judge that their practical interests are served by not allowing ties to unravel. There remains room for the irrational in the politics of a divided country. Romantic nationalism may lie just below the cool exterior of many West German politicians; blood that runs faster at the strains of the "Internationale" is in sclerotic Politburo veins. Nevertheless, the pragmatic calculation that two decades ago put the two German states on a cooperative path has been less affected by events of the past month than might be thought. The currencies the West Germans pay in are hard cash, and the prestige and legitimacy of the special political partnership they offer. The East German units of account are human rights concessions, visits, and titillation. Both get what they want. The GDR has become economically more dependent and incalculably more open to Western influences; a largely common culture has been maintained, and the vision of a single national state someday has gained semblance of reality. In turn, the GDR has economic wherewithal and political entrée. It is a reasonable bargain that neither has the leverage to convert to unilateral advantage.

Were the West Germans to push the GDR much harder, the effect would probably be counterproductive. This Politburo would not be shy about patching the cracks in the Berlin Wall, rolling itself into a ball, and putting up its prickly bristles. It is a porcupine with very big, very good, very reliable security services. Are there politicians on the Rhine willing to risk reversing the greater ease with which Germans East and West from every walk of life have been renewing personal and professional acquaintances in recent years? If so, there are hard men in the SED who would be happy to oblige: those who have always feared that the West Germans have the sums right, that their small, weak, insecure, and unpopular state cannot indefinitely experience extensive exposure to its large, rich, confident, and dynamic neighbor without changing fundamentally.

Review of obviously failed Honecker policies is likely to produce temporary tightening here in any case. Provided West Germans do not make the reunification premise behind their policies much more explicit than it has been for two decades, however—if they do not make the mistake of believing the GDR's current severe problems are terminal—the Politburo will find its room for maneuvering limited. It will not want to wall itself off again, because—unlike 1961, when it had no viable option—it cannot afford the economic and morale costs. All bets should be hedged, particularly in Eastern Europe these days and when they involve family feuds, but odds are both capitals will do their best to keep the real stuff of relations protected from this patch of rough weather. Once the winds die down, their interdependence will fairly approximate what all have become used to. And the GDR will be left to grapple with the heart of the matter: not whether it is to survive into the twenty-first century, but what kind of state it will become, a militant recluse or an open, moderately successful and more democratic but still socialist version of Germany.

Pete Ito is on his first orientation visit since assuming the GDR Desk at the State Department this summer. The increase of interest in the GDR is exponential, he said. Our reporting goes directly to Larry Eagleburger. Everyone asks whether the SED will crack down or reform, whether the West Germans will push for reunification, whether the Soviets will intervene. Meanwhile, the European Bureau has been told to write a new paper on Germany's future in a fast-changing Europe.

Bob McCartney was back, asking about the Opposition, particularly Neues Forum, which today tried to register with the Interior Ministry in Berlin and in eleven of the GDR's fifteen districts. The latter point suggests it is attracting adherents around the country. Would it become the East German version of Polish Solidarity, Bob wondered, and did it have a Lech Walesa? As customary in our talks, I played the skeptic. Neues Forum seems to consist primarily of intellectuals long critical of the SED. There is little evidence yet that they can win over the average citizen, even if the Stasi keeps hands off. But, I acknowledged, we also want to get to know them better. I explained that the focus of the Monday demonstrations in Leipzig has been on emigration—the chant in the street last week was "We want out." We were watching for two keys: Were those who previously stayed on the sidelines joining, and were they calling for reform?

SEPTEMBER 19

The West German Embassy in Warsaw has been closed, and Prague sit-ins are increasing again. Several thousand East Germans chanting for emigration went into Leipzig's streets yesterday. The police arrested more than a hundred. Church and state are responding in radically different ways to the challenge. The Eisenach Synod ended with a blunt call for far-reaching reforms so young people would again see "a future for themselves and our country." By contrast, *Neues Deutschland* gave a full page to a polemic that caused several of my SED contacts to shake their heads in despair.

A senior policy-planning delegation will be here on October 13 to discuss its memo with us, but also to meet experts from GDR think tanks. We will include an "official" meeting at the Foreign Ministry to give the former protection. While our institute contacts are often more open, it does them no good if Washington visitors seek out only them. Most talk should be in-house, however, since that gives us a chance to "play" in Washington's policy evaluation.

SEPTEMBER 20

The Political Section's most thankless daily task is to read not only *Neues Deutschland* but also the Bloc Party papers. At least the former gives an authoritative, if aggravating, insight into SED thought processes. *Der Morgen* (the Liberals, LDPD) and *Neue Zeit* (CDU) are generally pale reflections. We go through them—as well as *Junge Welt* (the youth organization, FDJ), *Tribüne* (the labor organization, FDGB), and periodicals of the other small parties and special groups, such as the army—like a prospector panning for specks of gold: the hint of disagreement or a nuance that may signal policy change. Last year I used end-of-year funds to subscribe to SED dailies in Leipzig, Dresden, and Rostock, in the hopes we might spot early signs of reform, or at least debate.

There has been little reward except the good training for junior officers, but this morning Janice Weiner struck pay dirt. *Neues Deutschland*'s summary of a speech by Manfred Gerlach, the LDPD chairman, was pap. Janice, however, thrust *Der Morgen*'s full text before me. Cautiously but unmistakably, Gerlach had broken new ground. Even LDPD members are leaving the GDR, he acknowledged: "We must ask why they lost faith; they are mostly children of the Revolution, raised and politically educated here." It is necessary "not to blockade the new but rather to search it out and put it into motion." He declared himself a fan of Gorbachev and Perestroika.

Gerlach is the most intelligent and dynamic Bloc Party chief. His break with conformity is more significant than the "Letter from Weimar" of junior CDU rebels and gives prospect of a serious effort, perhaps the first in GDR history, to take an initiative opposed by the SED. Gerlach probably recognizes how disastrous the Politburo line is; that he is speaking out indicates he either believes the situation is extraordinarily grave or has an alliance with a prince prepared to challenge Honecker. Either way, it is a major new factor.

SEPTEMBER 21

More regime tough talk: the Interior Ministry told Neues Forum to shut down, because it filled no "social need." ADN claimed that the "goals and purposes of the would-be organization . . . constitute a platform hostile to the State."

Neues Forum, which promised a court fight, is the only group to seek registration, but others are announcing themselves through the Western media. Stefan Bickhardt is among twelve signers of the appeal by a group called "Democracy Now" (Demokratie Jetzt) for "an alliance of Christians and Critical Marxists," a conference of grassroots groups from all over the GDR to draft a platform for "democratic transformation," and free Parliamentary elections. Another member is Konrad Weiss, a film director who frequents embassy cultural evenings. Friedrich Schorlemmer is a key figure in a third group, "Democratic Awakening" (Demokratischer Aufbruch), as is Wolfgang Schnur, the prominent human rights lawyer and a man with close ties to the church. The willingness of such groups to step into the street, literally or figuratively, adds to the authorities' nervousness. What is not yet clear is whether they can draw into their risky endeavor many more than what Imre calls the "same half-dozen kids and two dogs" who have met in church basements since independent peace movement days early in the decade.

The official GDR, that interlocking net of SED/government/media, shows no readiness to accommodate the stirrings in the country. *Neues Deutschland* warned the church against siding with counterrevolutionaries and defiantly editorialized: "What the enemies of the Socialist German State were unable to achieve in four decades despite great efforts, . . . removal of Socialism, . . . is now to be made up for with '. . . reforms.' . . . Of course, nothing will come of this." As if that were not enough to discourage any who still hoped that this SED and its people could find their way to the dialogue the church is ready to broker, the paper offered the following alleged personal experience under the headline "I have experienced how FRG citizens are being made":

> QUESTION: How and where did you wake up?
> ANSWER: In a tour bus, still fairly foggy. My "tour guide" from Budapest sat next to me, slapped me on the shoulder, and answered where we were: in freedom, on the way to the FRG.
> QUESTION: How do you explain, then, that you lost consciousness in the Budapest apartment?
> ANSWER: Obviously they gave me a drug, . . . a preferred method of Western secret services and their helpers. . . . I consider myself a victim of kidnappers, of criminals. . . .

"How dumb do they think we are!" an SED member exploded to me this afternoon. I don't know, but if the Party's search for answers goes no deeper than West German revanchists and drugged menthol cigarettes, things can only get much worse.

SEPTEMBER 22

After some days on the sidelines while Prague and Warsaw sit-ins swelled beyond 1,000, Wolfgang Vogel has gone to Bonn, reportedly with a message from Honecker for Kohl. This embassy's special reason to hope a satisfactory solution is found quickly is that we remain concerned we could soon become a sit-in target ourselves. Thus far, we have had only a single case; a young man stayed several days. Vogel told us the authorities knew him well and had no objection to his emigration. His real demand was for recognition as a novelist. Before he finally walked out with his parents, we and the Ständige Vertretung explored the possibility of getting psychiatric help for him. It has remained an isolated instance, but this could change, particularly if the GDR stops travel to Eastern Europe. That psychologically devastating step would evoke memories of the decision to put up the Wall. It sounds incredible, but there is talk of it if Vogel fails.

Political Section priority this week is to assess whether the groups springing up all around the country can be catalysts for real change. After an hour with a key figure, Heather is convinced that Neues Forum will at least not be scared off. As best we can judge, most of its initial adherents have extensive activist backgrounds and want to work within the system for a more attractive socialism. Jens Reich, the doctor and microbiologist with whom Heather spoke, has been involved with the Sophien Church, one of Berlin's most socially engaged congregations. Heather found Reich uncomfortable with his prominence but determined. He told her that nearly 2,000 persons, including SED members, have contacted Neues Forum in ten days. The SED claim bears especially close watching.

The decision to launch Neues Forum was made the weekend of September 2–3, Reich said, by twenty-five people who met to discuss the emigration crisis. They came from all around the GDR and had widely differing views. Their shared consensus was that state and society had become dangerously alienated and that new structures were urgently needed so problems could be discussed openly. The plan was to book events in neighborhood halls to appeal to a broad spectrum. Now, reluctantly, he said, Neues Forum like others before it would probably have to seek church protection.

The long-term goal, Reich explained, was to build a better socialism. He agreed with Otto Reinhold that this was the only way the GDR could justify its existence, but Neues Forum wanted to explore alternatives between Honecker's "real existing socialism" and the West German system. His own ideal GDR would be socialist, taking the best from the past but with room for much change, Reich said. More private economic initiative was needed, but the GDR should not become a "sharp-elbows society" like West Germany. More consumer goods were required, but social and environmental costs must be carefully balanced. Genuine communication between state and people was essential, Reich said. Neues Forum's hope was that the summer had both motivated those who previously were satisfied with escape to private niches, and persuaded the SED that its policies were producing the very instability it so fears.

Reich said Neues Forum was reluctant to seek church support because that would inhibit many, including idealistic SED members and citizens wary of being branded dissidents. Moreover, the church itself would be reluctant to associate closely with an overtly political group, even though Neues Forum did not want to become a party. That, he said, would require it to target a limited part of the population and develop specific positions. Neues Forum should help people come together to find their own solutions, he said, not prescribe answers.

Neither in composition nor in objectives does Neues Forum seem to be an incipient East German version of Polish Solidarity. The founders do not want to overthrow the system. Their moderate goal is to work from within to create a more attractive and more democratic but socialist GDR. Had the regime permitted Neues Forum to hold public meetings, it would have legitimized a mechanism for change that would have been difficult to control. But refusal has signaled an intransigence that could precipitate a radical reaction. The Politburo's conclusion predictably has been that dialogue would be a fatal sign of weakness, but its dilemma can only grow more acute. The SED's sharp language this week was probably calculated to warn its own members and others to stay away from the fledgling groups. If that is not enough to keep them isolated, the Party may soon have to employ more forceful suasion.

Imre and Janice obtained Democracy Now's "Call for Involvement in Our Own Affair," including two closely typed pages of "Theses for a Democratic Transformation." Like Neues Forum, the group wants a better socialism, but unlike Neues Forum it has begun to formulate a program: separation of powers, U.N.-supervised elections, independent trade unions with the right to strike, free travel, workplace democracy, an end to the planned "command" economy, more private enterprise, and environmental laws with teeth.

For the first time, influential persons are associating with the activists. The Berlin branch of the Writers Association passed a resolution the press has ignored: "It is unbearable the way responsibility is pushed [onto others] although the causes lie within our own country. . . . The exodus is only a sign for dammed-up fundamental problems in all areas of society. . . . We demand that democratic dialogue begin immediately on all levels." More bluntly, in another resolution ignored by the local media, forty-four rock musicians objected to the "unbearable ignorance of the State and Party leadership that . . . holds to a blind course. . . . We have taken note of Neues Forum's declaration and find much that we think ourselves and still more that is worthy of discussion. . . . We want to live in this country, and it makes us ill to have to watch helplessly as attempts are made either to criminalize or ignore efforts at democratization." The signers' names, except for Tamara Danz, mean little to me but much to young people in the GDR. Heather and Janice were right to say this spring that rock music was a protest idiom. Is it one the old men can ever understand?

Finally, and in its way most remarkably, there are these cautious words: "[We need] to think about what circumstances produce in this person or that the wish to leave the country. . . . [We should] speak openly, . . . we need dialogue everywhere . . . ; we need to be open to suggestions." Mild compared with what writers and rock musicians have started to say, their force comes from two facts: they were spoken by Deputy Minister of Culture Klaus Höpcke and were printed in yesterday's *Junge Welt*, the FDJ daily that has the largest circulation in the country.

The ice is breaking. "Perhaps," Gaby said, "you were right to stay another year. Maybe something big is going to happen."

SEPTEMBER 23

Can the GDR reform? Can it become acceptably democratic and prosperous? Can it even survive on any basis other than sheer, repressive power? Is it heading for chaos and violence that will endanger Gorbachev's revolution and East-West accommodations? High drama can sway any observer's objectivity, but I would sketch a few probabilities, with the caveat, of course, that in Eastern Europe's unprecedented swirl I could be proven wrong tomorrow.

It is difficult to see how Honecker can long survive his twin failures of policies and health. The GDR is in an extended, severe political crisis that will force it to face up to hitherto eschewed decisions. Nevertheless, I think it has reasonable prospects to consolidate, and perhaps eventually emerge with greater legitimacy. More problematic are the conceivable variations of answers to the German Question, which the summer's events have returned to Europe's political consciousness.

Every commentator is susceptible to hyperbole. I have spoken recently of the GDR as no longer either "stable, dull, or predictable." No one can dispute the last two adjectives, but "stable" is more subjective and sensitive. We shall have to take the pulse daily of the disaffected, within and without the establishment, but I foresee neither uncontrollable riot nor Lech Walesa's German cousin jumping a factory fence. The GDR still has too many control mechanisms, the world-class security apparatus by no means least. Its society also retains too many alternatives for diffusing tension, including the option of emigration and an economy that creaks and groans but has not seized up and continues to take the sharper edges off much dissatisfaction. And then there is German discipline and sense of order. True, there is a boiling point. Workers here were first to challenge the post-Stalin order in the streets. There have been other interludes—1848 and the peasants of the 1520s—but it is not the dominant national gene.

By "no longer stable" I mean the GDR is moving rapidly from virtual immobility to a stage during which policy and personnel will be much in flux. New and often unstructured influences will be felt from youth, the church, intellectuals, and possibly hitherto compliant Bloc Parties—certainly from tumultuous events within the Warsaw Pact. But look for a strong dose of politics, not incipient revolution.

The crisis is much deeper even than suggested by the numbers who have reached West Germany. The Honecker program—that mix of virtually absolute social security guarantees but mediocre consumerism, of an opening to the world and improved travel opportunities but an overwhelming, overweening Party/state apparatus that, to put it kindly, insists "Father knows best"—is discredited. The old leader had a long run, and most give him grudging credit for being fairer and more effective than his Stalinist predecessor. But he and his policies are badly ailing, and sooner rather than later will be set aside.

Their removal, however, is not equivalent, or likely preliminary, to the state's collapse. Those turning their backs on the GDR are a fair cross section of its forty-year-old body politic, not an easily disposable remnant of vestigial classes but its lifeblood. The drama has changed the political calculus and will drive the policy debate in new directions. Nevertheless, "Last one out turn off the lights" is black humor, not political or demographic reality. By summer's end, 1.8 million East Germans had visited Hungary. Just over 1 percent now carry West German passports. Three of every four East Germans still along the Danube when the Hungarian foreign minister said the border was temporarily open drove their Trabies home. They had many reasons to return—occasionally idealism, more often attachments to family, friends, jobs. They were rarely enthusiastic about their choice, but they lacked overwhelming personal dissatisfaction. It was hardly a vote of confidence, but they and others with less golden opportunities have in effect given the GDR another chance.

Nor does the profile of those who made the break support fully the idea that this state is unviable. A West German poll found that 37 percent would not have left if the GDR had instituted reforms similar to those in Poland, Hungary, or the Soviet Union; 89 percent considered German reunification "desirable" but only 26 percent thought it "possible"; more than 61 percent preferred the CDU/CSU; less than 2 percent preferred the SPD. Clearly, few were suffering in the classical economic sense. Many were GDR Yuppies, with car, a new apartment, and a secure, relatively good job.

That is a damning indictment of life under Honeckerism. On the other hand, many who cited "political" reasons meant primarily the right to travel or, more generally, to have a greater say in everyday decisions without bureaucratic harassment. Party preferences were atypical. Kohl may well have obtained a bonus in the first flush of gratitude for championing their cause, but by all indications East Germans who stayed behind lean to the Social Democrats (certainly those tending toward activism). The inference is that GDR citizens most inclined to some optimism about internal reform in Eastern Europe and the possibility of finding partners within the establishment have not lost all hope of domestic change. In some ways, the poll's most remarkable finding was that even these respondents split almost evenly on whether their ideal German state would be a mix of West and East: 52 percent favored the Bonn system, 42 percent wanted to retain GDR elements. Such results should encourage open minds as to whether a reformist SED could legitimize its rule by tapping into the large pool of citizens who do not think reunification feasible, who want more personal liberty, and who want especially no longer to be treated as children by Father State, but are neither fully enamored of West Germany nor prepared to reject everything GDR out of hand.

SED ideologue Otto Reinhold's dictum that a GDR that aped the Federal Republic would have no rationale for existence is often cited. Reinhold is too intelligent, however, not to recognize that the GDR, with socialism as raison d'être, is the Eastern European state that most needs a reform communism that works. The summer exodus may convince even the more dogmatic of the dangers of standing pat on a losing hand. East Germans I know, well into middle levels of the Party, are increasingly critical of the policy of drift. There is broad consensus on need for Glasnost, a new way of treating citizens as adults, honesty about problems, and flexibility about solutions, if not necessarily radical, systemic reform.

The hierarchical SED is not yet quite ready to launch reforms, though internal pressure is growing. Its leaders have more than their share of human foibles, including reluctance to admit how wrong most of what they have been doing has been, a tendency to hope that if they keep their eyes closed whatever is out there will go away, and of course fear of the unknown. Their inclination is to waffle a while longer or even retrench harshly. Nor can I say that if a new leadership does attempt serious change it will get the mix right. There would surely be reluctance to try radical Perestroika for fear of losing control. For all Moscow's worry about what could happen if the East Germans get it wrong, however, I suspect Gorbachev would count himself fortunate if he could trade his hand for one with their potential advantages:

the people's understanding of what is at stake, their competence, and the disciplined readiness of many to meet the state halfway.

The longer leadership transition and policy uncertainty continue, the more speculation on the future of the two Germanies will intensify. Nevertheless, policy implications, for Americans as well as Germans, are likely more prosaic than they may seem in the emotions of the moment. They revolve around degrees of influence, not an imminent, fundamental shift of East-West gravity. Grand history is being made, but its time frame is still extended and its ultimate shape less sharply resolved than the television pictures of the last days. Our embassy's challenge is to engage the debate and help define U.S. interests.

The German Question was submerged in a polar sea for four decades. The warming East-West climate allowed its peaks to appear, and the summer's drama reinforced the feeling that almost anything is suddenly conceivable. This has lent stridency to many comments. There are, apparently, Bonn politicians who sense the moment has come to push the GDR down the road to dissolution. There will be temptation to speak more about "Germany" as the 1990 election season begins, which will cause the GDR to play on European fears by talking up the risks of "revanchism." I expect that, on second thought, mainstream West German parties will conclude that pushing the GDR hard in any direction, much less toward dissolution, will not work. The GDR will try to build fire walls around the rhetoric to protect its economic stake in inner-German cooperation. As one SED contact argued to me, once the "euphoria in the West" fades, the realistic options for both states will be not very unlike the small steps, dialogue, and pragmatic cooperation based on calculation of mutual interest and agreement to disagree on ultimate objectives that have marked relations for two decades.

It has become legitimate, even modish, to discuss the German Question again, but its contours remain too blurred to permit confident conclusions. A few examples of the uncertainties:

- Is it true that every reform brings the GDR closer to collapse? That is what both SED mastodons and some of those quickest to draw radical conclusions from what has been going on since summer conclude. Might it not be as likely that if a new leadership enlists popular support with new policies, the GDR will, over time, become more stable, more accepted by its citizens? Or, if reform really does produce chaos and instability, that the response of those who hold power here (and in Moscow) will be to use force to control the situation at whatever cost?

- How would West Germans react to a reformist GDR? No one is attracted by Honecker's "real existing socialism," but what would the response of those susceptible to "Gorby mania" be to a German innovator? As the one-fifth rump of the nation, the GDR can never compete equally for the German soul, but for the first time not all influence might necessarily flow West to East. Would West Germans (and Europe) be willing to change their structures and institutions if this were the price for uniting Germany?
- How willing are Germans to sacrifice for reunification? They may be more responsive to pollsters at moments of high drama than during gray everydays stretching into the next century, which is likely the relevant time frame. Preoccupation with reunification is greatest in East Germany, and its intensity is probably in inverse proportion to tolerableness of daily existence.
- That freedom is more important than unity meant, in 1949, the Federal Republic opted for full integration into the West at the expense of reunification. What might that same formula, broadly subscribed to in both halves of Germany, mean in future? Is it conceivable that unity might seem less important as a goal to the extent East Germans become freer within their own state and artificial barriers between the Germanies are removed? Would reservations most Europeans still have about a united Germany then be dropped—or would the Germans be more willing to accept a definitive settlement of their problem that acknowledged those reservations?

I do not have answers, or even confident guesses. The point is that uncertainty—a form of instability, to be sure—will be with us a long time before Germans, East and West, definitively exercise their right of self-determination. In the meantime, if the GDR were a person, a life insurance company would probably demand a risk premium but write a policy. And the United States will need to engage with it if it wants to protect its high stake in the liberalization, economic well-being, and security of Central Europe.

Now I have to discuss these thoughts with Dick and J.D. and find out if they are willing to send them to the State Department.

SEPTEMBER 24

The embassy finished runners-up to the mission and ahead of Embassy Warsaw at today's softball tournament. The Barkleys' seven-week-old daughter, Katie, made the day's biggest hit.

SEPTEMBER 25

Most days, I drive to the embassy down my favorite street, Schönhauser Allee, with its cobbled pavement, small shops, and overhead train tracks evocative of 1920s Berlin, then past Alexanderplatz and into the government center along Unter den Linden. Near the embassy this morning, preparations were under way for a major 40th Anniversary event: the FDJ's torchlight procession. The reviewing stand for Honecker and Gorbachev was going up near the Neue Wache, the small Greek Classical building designed by Schinkel early in the nineteenth century, which houses the eternal flame for victims of Fascism. Across the broad avenue, television lights were being tested. The eventful summer is over, but the problems it brought to the fore are not solved. The city's mood could not be less festive.

Wolfgang Vogel called Dick before lunch. He returns to Prague today to negotiate a quick and "generous" end to the sit-in. The single requirement is that the East Germans go home until their emigration applications are processed. This lends substance to press reports that Bonn expects the confrontation will be largely resolved this week. It is tempting to see Vogel's reactivation as a sign that Honecker, who is just back at work, is trying to reassert himself and clear up a large blotch on the GDR's image before its birthday party. The Poles and Czechoslovaks may also have given him incentive to cut losses before he is again humiliated by an irresolute ally. Fundamental questions remain, not least how to prevent the sit-in cycle from resuming, but there may now be a brief respite.

Examples that much still goes smoothly in inner-German relations: The joint Border Commission has doubled the area in Mecklenburg Bay from which West Germans can fish; the motorist organization ADAC is expanding its breakdown service on GDR autobahns; another city partnership has been ratified. There are too many stakes in cooperation at too many levels for politicians in either state to reverse course easily. The new interdependence mixes economics, human contacts, and psychology; the balance favors West Germany in virtually every area, but it limits the freedom of both sides more than would have been conceivable not long ago.

After the new independent groups met in Leipzig yesterday and sent a letter to the Interior Ministry supporting Neues Forum, Bärbel Bohley vehemently denied they had formed a united opposition. It is hard to judge whether it is more significant that the activists talked with one another or that they were unwilling to submerge differences in a single organization.

Modrow, the Dresden Party chief suspected of reform sympathies, broke Party discipline to say the SED must talk openly about the causes of the crisis. It will not help him with Honecker, but it further marks him as the rare official with some credibility.

Imre was denied a hotel room in Leipzig, where another demonstration is expected tonight, and reporters are being kept out of the city. As a diplomat, Imre needs no authorization to go; if hotels in nearby Halle are also "full," he will sleep in his car.

Maram Stern, the World Jewish Congress representative, came by last week to drop off Belgian chocolates and talk. He had been at the Foreign Ministry on Jewish claims and wanted to tell us the unpromising state of play. The optimism with which Israel Singer left Berlin in July broke down in early September, Stern said, about when it became obvious Honecker's illness was serious. The Foreign Ministry now held out little hope Fischer would offer Bronfman anything in New York this month. Stern said he was "thinking out loud" about suggesting that Bronfman invite a "senior" State Department official to sit in. I told him that until the GDR is ready to move, busy people would not help it preserve a facade of progress.

Deane Wylie has asked me to write an article for the *Los Angeles Times* Sunday commentary section he edits. I did one on Hungary three years ago, and last fall he tracked me down to request another on Eastern Europe. Since the assistant secretary, Roz Ridgway, felt it inappropriate for a Foreign Service officer to publish personal views on sensitive policy issues, the European Bureau asked me to withdraw it. I told Wylie I was not optimistic about being able to send anything on the GDR but would query the new Washington team.

My view, like Frank Meehan's and Dick Barkley's, is that it is good for diplomats to do these things. Our profession is too anonymous—one reason it enjoys little prestige and support when it comes to participation in policy decisions or share in senior appointments. It is wasteful of a national resource and harmful to the country's security that every President puts more political appointees in senior foreign affairs jobs at the expense of the career corps. The public would not tolerate this with the military because it knows the relationship of expertise and professional morale to national strength, but it has little understanding of this in diplomacy. The Foreign Service misses an opportunity to build a constituency, as well as contribute to understanding of issues, if it unduly confines its activity to the bureaucracy where its tasks and perspectives remain obscure to a larger citizenry.

SEPTEMBER 26

Vogel failed. He guaranteed 1,100 East Germans in Prague that they could emigrate within six months if they went home. Fewer than 200 did so, and their places were taken by some of the thousands who have journeyed to the Czechoslovak capital in the last days. The Turkish ambassador told Dick that Honecker looked tired but in fair health when he presented credentials to him yesterday. He had good color and was alert and in command of facts, but their conversation was superficial. Honecker touched on the emigration crisis only in passing, claiming relations with Hungary were better than Western papers indicate. How much of the tide the old Politburo can hold back, and for how long, depends vitally on Honecker's ability to give the appearance of being in charge. He has passed a first test, but all eyes, literally, will be on him when he presides over the fortieth birthday party and hosts Gorbachev in ten days.

Any new administration wants to define its themes, but senior State Department officials are trying to come to grips with a world order that is changing at an unprecedented pace. Gerd Basler asked me for two items. The first is an Eagleburger lecture at Georgetown that the *Herald Tribune* labeled "bizarre nostalgia for the cold war." I do find the deputy secretary too skeptical about Gorbachev and our interest in his success. Watching change accelerate almost daily from ground zero in Eastern Europe, however, I applaud his effort to shift the public's mind to new grooves. What will have especially attracted Basler is the observation that "the process of reform in the Soviet bloc and the relaxation of Soviet control over Eastern Europe are . . . putting the German Question back on the international agenda." Gerd wonders what that agenda item means operationally for the Bush-Baker team.

The second article, by Francis Fukuyama, carries its intellectually stimulating if overstated thesis in the eye-catching title "The End of History." Fukuyama cleverly uses definition (history in the Hegelian sense as a struggle of competing concepts of liberty) to attract attention. He is now number two for policy planning at the State Department, a major player in devising new approaches to German matters, and leads the delegation to Berlin next month. I think Gerd is intrigued with the idea of a Hegel scholar at State.

The latest memo on Germany is meant to go to Secretary Baker this week, so we must get our comments in quickly. It rightly notes that the promise—fear, for many Europeans—of reunification has become a preoccupation for the first time in two generations. The speed with which the German Question will need to be answered, however, depends mainly on events in the GDR, particularly whether Honecker or a successor, by reform or repression, can restore domestic tranquillity.

When Dick, J.D., and I discussed it, my inclination, as usual, was to take the central points head on. Policy, I argued, should be agnostic about the inevitability of reunification. We should not postulate that the Soviets have no options between intervention and accepting that the GDR will become essentially an incorporated province of the Federal Republic. Especially if more flexible leadership than Honecker is found, the Soviets may use their extensive assets to influence events politically, most likely to encourage efforts at careful reform with a view to stabilizing and legitimizing this state. I want us to question the assumption of SED hard-liners, which finds some acceptance in Washington, that reform is tantamount to suicide. It is risky, but a bunker mentality and neo-Stalinist policies would be more surely fatal. A serious effort to enlist popular support in creating a more open, democratic, socialist German alternative not fully emulating the Federal Republic is an unproved proposition but the GDR's best hope for survival. Significantly, most of our church contacts, as well as opposition groups, say they want to improve socialism, not simply copy West Germany. Not all that is tactical caution.

Similarly, I argued, we should neither speak nor act as if self-determination was inevitably equivalent to the GDR's absorption into a single, larger Federal Republic. The West Germans themselves do not go this far. When the United States refers to self-determination, at least a minor key should be that our commitment is to free exercise of popular will, not any particular outcome. This would complement more credibly our advice to the GDR that reform is the only realistic option for achieving legitimacy. Unless we hold open the prospect that the GDR can reform and survive, we play into the hands of SED cement-heads (*Betonköpfe*), isolate ourselves from Bonn, and give the Politburo no reason to meet our bilateral agenda or accede to our exercising influence on their policies.

I found Washington too pessimistic about whether the GDR would reform. Honecker will not, and his immediate successor might well be a transitional figure following a conservative line. It seems a fair probability, however, that the Honecker generation will be out by May and that a status quo, much less reactionary, policy cannot be sustained. Consensus within society and parts of the SED on need for a different approach is broad enough that it is plausible a moderate reformer will be in power next year or shortly thereafter. The paper should acknowledge there are reasonable prospects the GDR will soon begin at least Glasnost, I suggested, and then sketch implications for U.S. policies. Unattractive as it is, the GDR is a central concern for our closest friends and potential adversaries. We need to increase options and leverage and thereby gain ability to affect developments in a sensitive place over a longer time frame than we usually feel comfortable with and before the contours of the ultimate outcome are clear.

Merely expanding contacts cautiously, as the State Department is prepared to envision, would not make us a real player. We should explore more actively GDR willingness to pay a price to achieve improved trade and greater political legitimacy. We should work hard now at resolving old problems, such as claims, not least so that we will be positioned to enter on a more extensive relationship with the new leadership that must soon be in place.

Dick and J.D. are more skeptical that the GDR will become reformist, but their suggestions were tactical: our message should be less hortatory and more supportive. The point is we can get our ideas across best with specific line-in line-out recommendations that shade the meanings, and that is how I tried to write it.

Yesterday's Leipzig demonstration brought 5,000 to 8,000 into the streets. Police were everywhere but detained only about a dozen. Most interesting, Imre reported, was the shift in focus. The "We want out" chants were slightly outnumbered by those for reform and Neues Forum. Bob McCartney asks if real revolution is now brewing in the streets. Most people are still holding back, I cautioned. A handful of activists are bolder, not yet the average man. The protests do not yet have critical mass. Honecker must soon move decisively if he is not to lose at least his own power, but his preoccupation is probably to get through the "celebrations" next week without too much embarrassment.

SEPTEMBER 27

Stephan Hermlin is losing the revolutionary's patience with the Honecker line. He told West German Radio that "in distinction to some senior comrades" he had "no anxiety about the word 'reform' " and wanted to see "the Party, individual Party members, enter into a confidential, considered, sensible dialogue." The poet acknowledged he did not know whether the SED was ready. "The Party leadership is not accustomed to telling me its conclusions. But I can hardly imagine it will hold itself aloof forever. If I am mistaken, I would be very sad."

The health minister criticized the emigration of doctors and nurses as "an inexcusable violation of professional ethic and elementary humanity. . . . A good doctor does not leave his patients in the lurch." His remarks were the frankest acknowledgment yet of the extent to which health care has been affected. There are reports, hard to confirm in detail but plausible in tendency, of hospitals no longer able to maintain anything like normal services.

G. accepted lunch tomorrow at the Domklause. I reserved a table with my favorite view, over the Spree to the massive cathedral. I want the Soviet perspective on Gorbachev's visit.

SEPTEMBER 28

Leadership and people continue to move apart. Erich Mielke, the eighty-year-old Stasi chief, publicly attacked "the so-called Neues Forum" and claimed that the old bogeyman—Bonn elements who "seek to establish an anti-Socialist opposition in order to undermine the . . . foundations of our Socialist State"—is responsible for the trouble. He makes it understandable why the sit-ins ignore Vogel and more than 2,000 are camped in the Prague Embassy despite "catastrophic" conditions. Each day, hundreds if not thousands of East Germans enter Czechoslovakia, aiming for the West.

Signs of discontent in the establishment are increasing, however. Markus Wolf, the retired spy chief, last night again used a book-reading to campaign for Glasnost. *Der Morgen's* coverage was at least the third flicker of independence from the LDPD in a week. But the heresy pales in comparison with the problems.

Early next week, I will write a "scene-setter" cable for the 40th Anniversary. J.D. wants it to focus on these questions: Will there be protests? Can they be controlled? What will Gorbachev do—and, in particular, will he demand reforms?

Franz Bertele, head of the Ständige Vertretung, told J.D. of a remarkable talk with a senior GDR diplomat. Bertele said he had emphasized that Bonn could not solve the GDR's problems and was not responsible for the mess. The East German surprisingly responded that the Politburo was incapable of decisive action and that not everyone agreed with the official line. His own family, he noted, had lived in Berlin for hundreds of years. He did not approve of all aspects of the system, but it had been imposed by a superior power (the Soviet Union). To achieve a decent life, he said, he did what many ambitious East Germans have done—make a separate peace. Now there was no one at the top to give directions, and they were forced to reassess their positions in light of the obvious failure of GDR policies. What, he demanded to know, was Bonn's concept for Germany? What did it want to do with people like himself in a reunited Germany? Bertele, who must have been as astonished as I would have been, fell back on what is becoming a standard cry of despair: Events are moving so fast that concepts cannot be developed rapidly enough for governments to control them.

SEPTEMBER 29

Gorbachev must tread carefully if he comes next week, G. agreed at lunch, but his priority will probably be to reassure the shaken old men. The Soviet Embassy expects him for two days, but since events at home are unpredictable, abridgment, or even cancellation, is possible. G. left no doubt the Soviets are concerned about the drift here, but they are, as he put it, "without any good advice." It appears the objective is to shore things up, not least with a harder line against reunification, while hoping the SED gains enough confidence to attack its problems.

G. was notably less willing than usual to defend Honecker. He agreed the emigration crisis revealed serious internal problems and asked repeatedly whether the United States was considering a new Germany initiative. His most frequently expressed concern, however, was for the Bonn reunification debate. By talking "this reunification nonsense" (*Quatsch*), he suggested, the West Germans paralyzed the GDR. Under attack, East German leaders retreated to polemics, blaming everything on the West rather than examining what they should do. The more the Politburo believed itself and the state's foundations threatened, G. said, the greater the Soviet requirement to give verbal support. This was what Ligachev in Berlin, Tass, even Shevardnadze at the United Nations were doing. While G. could not reveal much about what Gorbachev would say in Berlin, he clearly anticipated that he would give the Old Guard a psychological boost.

Some of the argumentation that Western talk about "Germany" holds the GDR back from reform may be self-serving. G. seemed honestly perplexed, however, when he spoke about policy prescriptions. "Can anyone guarantee that if the GDR were to open its borders and pursue Glasnost people would no longer want to leave?" he asked. More Soviets seek to leave since Glasnost and Perestroika, he noted.

If Gorbachev stays home, it would be a major disappointment for Honecker, who has reason to be confident that his security apparatus can minimize unwelcome demonstrations. The Politburo is fanning out around the country to show it is in control and nothing has changed. But Gorbachev's reiteration of the security guarantee is vital to the short-term strategy.

Church circles report that eleven arrested in Leipzig received jail sentences of up to six months for "unlawful assembly." Others were fined heavily.

Pierre Shostal called to say our comments have been worked into the memo for the secretary of state. Pierre is coming to West Berlin and suggests Gaby and I reserve the first November weekend for a trip to Leipzig or Dresden. The Bureau is open-minded about my writing on East Germany for the *Los Angeles Times*; send a draft for review, Pierre said. I shall write after next weekend's birthday extravaganza, which looks increasingly like a watershed.

We went to dinner this evening with Gerhard Kunze and his wife. A senior official in the West Berlin government with more than twenty years experience at sensitive GDR negotiations and the embodiment of the best Prussian civil servant—dedicated to duty, scrupulously fair—Gerhard is in fact a Saxon, much of whose family is still in Dresden. The talk was of the GDR's agony. The Kunzes recently visited Gerhard's brother, a master baker, in the old Saxon capital. There is much more anger, they noted, in the south than in privileged East Berlin. Dresden, one of the few areas where geography prevents "inner emigration" via Western television, is especially disaffected. It should give pause to hard-liners who believe Glasnost would simply make people unhappier that attempts to leave the GDR are most frequent from places the broadcasting signal does not reach. Leipzig, the other great Saxon center, is in range of Western transmitters but resents keenly that it is shortchanged by the "Red Prussian Capital."

SEPTEMBER 30

This extraordinary day began with a newspaper sensation, once more in *Der Morgen*, not *Neues Deutschland*. The latter had another of those symbolism-laden front pages that make most East Germans groan: a seven-column-wide picture of the mighty, Honecker frail but stiffly erect in the middle, at a celebration of China's 40th Anniversary. The headline: "In the struggles of our time, the GDR and China stand side by side." Manfred Gerlach, the LDPD chairman, however, called for "the clash of critical ideas that aims at unity but need not in every case end in a single voice." In the circumstances, his implicit endorsement of Neues Forum's declared objective was perhaps both brave and inadequate. If made by a senior SED man, it would have signaled that the Party was at last showing some understanding of the forces beginning to spill into the streets. Coming from the nearly powerless and hitherto loyal LDPD chief, the motivation is probably opportunism or despair.

The real news, however, was the climax of the sit-in drama. Rumors flew throughout the day. Finally, in the evening, from the balcony of the Prague Embassy, Genscher told thousands crowded into the courtyard that special trains would carry them west across the GDR. "The most moving moment of my political career," said Genscher, himself once a GDR refugee, who seemed as exultant and drained as those who had risked so much to force their emigration.

But what next? The West Germans acknowledge that 25,000 refugees have already come from Hungary this month. Will the fever now break? The GDR hopes this dramatic concession, attributed to Honecker personally, will win it a breathing space and that Bonn will cooperate by keeping the embassies shut, as it has done in Berlin. If the bolt holes are closed without addressing the discontent that started the cycle, however, will Honecker gain even the peace and quiet he so badly wants for next weekend, when it is this troubled state's turn to celebrate a fortieth birthday?

OCTOBER 1

Political storms threaten to tear this society apart, but it has been a long and beautiful summer. Though a gray sky and more seasonal temperatures have come in with October, the chestnut trees in front of our house in the village-like Wilhelmsruh section of Pankow are blooming a second time. We have followed on television the progress of the trains carrying refugees to the West. ADN editorialized fiercely that those allowed to go "stomped on moral values by their behavior and excluded themselves from our society. One should shed no tears for them." That will be received bitterly by those still here who hope the Politburo will finally be shocked into reforms.

Examples of new readiness to criticize and even organize politically are coming to light. The Berliner Ensemble, the theater Brecht founded, issued a warning: "You do not strengthen socialism by spreading half- or quarter-truths. You produce more anger and dissatisfaction." The troupe has posted its statement in the theater foyer and encourages audiences to stay on for discussion. Similar activity is under way at other Berlin theaters.

A few days ago a small group of activists and radical pastors boldly called for the founding of a Social Democratic Party. They began: "It cannot go on like this! Many are waiting for something to change. But that is not enough! We want to do our part." They urged those who sought "an ecologically oriented social democracy, a state of laws and a division of powers, parliamentary democracy and party pluralism" to organize. Because the potential is substantial, the Stasi can be expected to intervene with special rigor against any effort to revoke the unequal alliance the Communists forced on the SPD in 1946. Most critical East Germans may prefer a more limited risk with Neues Forum, which says it is not a party and professes to seek a purified socialism.

A critical open letter from twenty workers claiming to represent union members at the Bergmann-Borsig factory here in Pankow presents special difficulties for us. The AFL-CIO objects to any embassy contact with union officials in Eastern Europe as legitimizing undemocratic organizations. Why this should be more so in the labor field than with other institutions of dictatorial government is unclear, but the State Department acquiesces. Because Hungary was seen as different, even then, I could have "a cup of coffee" with union officials on neutral ground when I served in Budapest. Janice cannot do even that here where unions are egregious exponents of Lenin's "transmission belt" concept—organizations to control, not represent, workers by passing on Party dictates. We must report entirely from published materials. Our effort to learn what may now be building thus starts far behind.

OCTOBER 2

Even Gerd Basler was subdued at Dick's lunch for Bob Hutchings of the National Security Council staff today. Honecker's weekend concession already is going wrong. The Prague Embassy is filling again, and the emigration crisis looms over the big birthday party, straining relations with West Germans and Warsaw Pact allies alike. Yesterday, two of Imre's friends watched one of the special trains pass through. The people along the track, even some policemen, waved. "Ten years ago, I would be gone too," a skilled worker said to him over supper. The son, an army conscript, added, "I don't think our political officer believes what he prattles to us. We don't." The three mid-level SED men who lunched with Hutchings agreed that Honecker must do more than allow Bonn to clear out its embassies again if he is to save himself.

Neues Deutschland printed the weekend schedule, starting with: "FDJ torchlight parade: Friday, October 6, 7:00 P.M., at the historic Unter den Linden sites. Youth demonstrates its love and trust in the Party of the working class and our Socialist Fatherland, its readiness to struggle to strengthen Socialism and assure peace. Between Brandenburg Gate and Marx-Engels-Platz, Berliners and their guests greet the FDJ . . . from all districts of our Republic."

Shortly after I came to the GDR, Basler recommended I read *Junge Welt*, the FDJ daily, because "it is a hundred times better than the FDJ." How strong a criticism of the FDJ that was I appreciated only after I began to scan the paper. Directed to youth, it is livelier than the starchy *Neues Deutschland*, but with few exceptions it is no more likely to address readers' real concerns. I was the more intrigued, therefore, when Heather showed me today's edition with an interview of a rock musician who said Neues Forum members were "normal citizens aware of their responsibilities, not oppositionalists." This could be a more important crack in the media monopoly than the heresies of *Der Morgen*, which reaches but a tenth of the youth paper's audience.

Heather spoke today with another Neues Forum founder, Sebastian Pflugbeil, a middle-aged energy expert from the Academy of Sciences, who said membership has passed 6,000. If true, his claim that half are SED is a telling sign of how brittle Party discipline is. Neues Forum already has an identity crisis, however, Pflugbeil said. Its moderate goal of working within the system for a better socialism attracts many who do not want to risk overtly oppositionist associations, but the state's hostile response suggests there may be no middle ground. The founders have been preoccupied with managing growth, he said. They must soon develop a long-term agenda and effective organization.

Pflugbeil was sober about the immediate future, Heather found. He believed there were no reformers in the Politburo. Honecker and his lieutenants were old and out of touch, and the likely successors were self-serving bureaucrats even less likely to endanger their positions. Why, she asked, was he with Neues Forum if reform prospects were so poor? "It is better than resignation," Pflugbeil replied with a shrug. At least Neues Forum had become too prominent for the SED to use strong-arm tactics, he said. There would be an outcry if the Stasi arrested its leaders, and with discontent so widespread, Honecker wanted to avoid this.

Even if he is right about Stasi restraint, the new groups will not be effective if they atomize. Press accounts that Neues Forum wanted to become an opposition umbrella organization were "untrue," Pflugbeil said, and had angered other movements. This sensitivity to Neues Forum leadership suggests that divide and marginalize, if not conquer, may be a promising Stasi tactic.

Pflugbeil gave us a copy of the latest position paper, agreed in Berlin yesterday. It says Neues Forum is for those who want to make the GDR a better place, and it asks that "those who are of another mind [not] misuse our efforts to achieve quicker emigration." The paper continues: "For us, 'reunification' is not a theme since we proceed from the two-state character of Germany and seek no Capitalistic social system. We want changes in the GDR. . . . We admit we never expected this storm of interest. Neither organization structures, full-time workers, nor offices exist. . . . Our goal is to build a legal political platform and start the urgently needed social dialogue. No one should be excluded, whether he or she is now a member of the SED or another organization. . . . Let's start the work!"

OCTOBER 3

The situation we have dreaded—a sit-in by desperate East Germans—has begun, and my decision allowed it to happen.

I was nearing the end of my talk with visitors from the Atlantic Council when a Marine motioned urgently from the doorway. Several children were in the embassy, he said; another dozen adults and children were outside the front door demanding entrance. Once the receptionist realized what was happening, he told the Marine to lock the door. What should they do now? he asked. With Dick and J.D. at lunch, I was senior officer.

I excused myself and went with the Marine to find frightened children inside, their parents and several other young families outside. The two Vopos posted in front of the embassy were not intervening, but passersby had taken notice. Through the door, the adults promised that, if admitted, they would not cause any trouble but would not leave until they could go to the Federal Republic. They were near hysteria, and I told the Marines to open the door and allow them into the foyer. There was no alternative. It would have been inconceivable to force the children out. Had I not permitted the others to enter, they would have remained as suppliants on the sidewalk, attracting ever more attention until the police took them away. By then, and certainly by such an action, our dilemma would have been made worse, both in fact (we would have been responsible for the children) and in public relations. I knew what I had to do before I reached the door.

With Mary Rose's help, I settled our visitors where they would not be overly visible. We hoped to resolve the situation before the press noticed, so the chances of a run on the embassy would be minimized. Mindful of Vogel's cautions, we believed the GDR would be more ready to make a concession away from the glare of publicity. Once our visitors told their story, however, I realized the situation was serious indeed. They came from towns north of Berlin and had not previously known each other. Some had filed for emigration, some had not, but all had been trying to reach the West German Embassy in Prague when their train was turned back. They decided during the return ride to come to us because they feared arrest at home and were convinced the GDR was closing the border in order to crack down. It was now or never, they said.

Official word of the border closing arrived at mid-afternoon. Vogel promised Dick to do what he could, but with no guarantees. The embassy's young mothers are collecting food and blankets for our guests. If we get into the overflow situation of West German diplomatic missions, they may be in for a long stay since we have nothing approaching Bonn's leverage. Dick wants to keep the Embassy open to the public, however, and Washington agrees.

The decision to close off Czechoslovakia "temporarily" is a sign of desperation. Honecker's standing with the public, and probably the Politburo as well, has been further reduced. A serious struggle over position and policy is increasingly likely, but the regime's immediate priority is to pull through this weekend without further severe embarrassment in front of Gorbachev.

Almost as many are in the Prague Embassy as before the weekend exodus, with no end in sight. The sit-ins we acquired bear witness to the reaction sweeping the GDR: they saw the tumultuous scenes on the weekend and decided to go as much from fear the chance would not come again as from distress about their immediate situation.

Pressure for reform is also increasing. Last night's demonstration in Leipzig attracted 10,000. The chants were for legalization of Neues Forum, and for Gorbachev, who arrives in Berlin on Friday. The police were restrained, though there were a few clashes and seven arrests. Berlin, where security is heavy, has had no equivalent demonstration, but two dozen began a vigil in sympathy for the Leipzig detainees at Gethsemane Church last night. I saw many police near the church as I drove by this morning.

The travel ban is bound to increase the anger not only of would-be refugees but also of millions for whom Czechoslovakia has been the single land they could reliably visit. It is the last birthday present the regime could have wished to give its people. For Honecker, it is a declaration of bankruptcy. While the GDR hunkers down behind a wall to the East as well as the West, I assume its leaders are prepared to use the force necessary to prevent disruption of the weekend's events. The unforeseen, accidental, or irrational cannot be excluded, but probably most East Germans are sufficiently persuaded of the old men's resolve not to mount a major frontal challenge. The real struggle for power and policy is likely to begin next week. Even before the border shock, SED contacts were saying openly that Honecker would likely go and major reforms would come within months. Significant attitudinal changes are occurring rapidly: among the people, who are becoming more surly and assertive, and within the SED, where many with the most stake in the GDR are beginning to conclude that the greatest risks are in standing pat (or going backward).

Rainer Eppelmann, pastor of the Church of the Samaritan in the heart of Berlin, says Democratic Awakening wants to work for reform, not destruction, of socialism. The new group is "deeply persuaded that the further development of the GDR to the end of the century and beyond is not conceivable without the SED. . . . If we can make clear this is about sharing, not taking, power, the number of those in establishment organizations who participate in this dialogue will grow greatly." The contrast was the television image of Honecker this evening presenting awards to "activists of the First Hours," veterans who laid the GDR's foundations and are perhaps the only component of the body politic older on average than the Politburo. Nothing there gave hope that Eppelmann will soon find a partner.

OCTOBER 4

The sense of foreboding, of large, potentially tragic events, is tangible. Berlin has the highest ratio of police of any city in Europe, but even by its standard what I saw along my route this morning was excessive. In the Neustädtische Kirchstrasse, small knots of people watched the embassy from across the street and were watched in turn by the reinforced Vopos.

Prospects for getting our overnight visitors safely to the Federal Republic look better since the GDR told the West Germans last night that the Prague Embassy could again be cleared. Vogel handles our problem as a sideline of the main show, and it should be only a matter of time until he can win the confidence of the frightened and determined handful to whom I opened our door yesterday. As the day wore on, however, the trains from Prague were delayed, and rumors of trouble inside the GDR spread. The mystery and tension heightened with each hour, inside the embassy, where Imre and I monitored the radio and vainly called contacts, but also in the streets. When I left for lunch, there were dozens across the road—an hour later, hundreds—and Vopos were drawn up facing them. The crowd stared silently at the large building that was built as a department store for the Kaiser's navy and was taken over by the United States in 1974 from the Craftsmen's Guild. (Dick Barkley, then negotiating the start of diplomatic relations, talked the GDR into making it available. "Impossible," was the first reaction. "The GDR is only Socialist, not Communist; not everything belongs to the government," he was told. "Let us help you build communism," Dick said, and a week later we learned that the Guild would move and that we could have the building.)

None of that history was on anyone's mind today. The crowd knew East Germans were inside. The road to Czechoslovakia was barred, and it feared the government meant to get tougher after the weekend. For many, it must have seemed that the only way to a new life they dreamed of, or away from a familiar life that had become intolerable, was through our front door. As the throng grew, the tension was oppressive. My only comparable experience has been the onset of a thunderstorm, when the air was heavy enough to feel.

We would not ask Vopos to clear people away because we did not want to discourage free assembly or offer the regime a pretext for limiting future access, but we wanted to avoid a storming of the embassy that could endanger lives, make it harder to help those inside, and create a situation in which it would be impossible to carry on operations. Dick ordered the library and consular section kept closed after lunch, to reduce risk that the crowd would rush the entrance. But that is what it came to in the late afternoon. Several youths crossed the street, rang the buzzer, and politely said they had urgent consular business. Steve Slick came out to ask them to return in the morning. Seeing the door ajar, the crowd surged forward to force its way through the police line. Scores of Vopos emerged from trucks parked on side streets.

I watched, shocked, at my window. There was much shoving but no real violence. The crowd wanted to get past the police but not do injury. The Vopos formed a wedge and shoved back, but used neither clubs nor other weapons. Within minutes, the crowd realized it could not break through and allowed itself to be pushed across the street. Once back to their starting point, most lost heart and left. Hours later, however, Western television showed some demonstrators being put into paddy wagons around the corner. There was a heartrending scene of a distraught mother being taken away with her young children. Dick immediately obtained Vogel's promise to help. If the GDR valued American public opinion, he said, it should release the detainees and permit them to go to the West at once. The same messages will be given officially to the Foreign Ministry, but experience has shown that Honecker's trusted lawyer is the key channel.

We were all shaken, perhaps our Marines most of all. They would not have removed desperate East Germans from the embassy, but for a few moments they had faced the possibility of having to defend the upper floors, where classified material is kept, and conceivably even the physical safety of embassy personnel, from a mob. These young men, in their teens or early twenties, have an embassy's most thankless job: Forbidden social contacts in the host Communist country for security reasons, they are accustomed to standing lonely watches to protect against intrusion by Stasi, the KGB, or terrorists, but not by ordinary East Germans, many not much older than they. None of us was prepared for a siege from those whose demands are for fundamental human rights. In those few terrible minutes, we knew firsthand the panic and desperation sweeping the GDR. Many seem no longer to care for the risks in confronting security forces. There was still some restraint today, but not much, and I am considerably more worried about what could happen this weekend than I was when I came to work this morning.

Despite the emotion and tension, it is necessary to step back and assess where the GDR is forty-eight hours before Gorbachev arrives. Honecker's first public comment since he left his sickbed admitted no crisis and blamed all problems on the devil in Bonn. His prime minister, Willi Stoph, pledged that next spring's Congress would bring continuity, not the major changes almost everyone wants. The gap between old leaders and political reality is still growing.

None of the alarming rumors attributing late arrival of the Reichsbahn trains in Prague to a Politburo split or tracks blocked by angry citizens is confirmed. Their appearance is symptomatic of the uncertainty, however, and they gain plausibility from the distress the curb on travel to Czechoslovakia has produced. At a Foreign Ministry reception after that news came through, Jerry Verner told me, SED members openly called the decision "dangerous." The official media, which ask "loyal" citizens for understanding, reveal none of this, of course, but today Neues Forum urged its followers to refrain from provocative public actions this weekend, and the experience of our friend Gunnar illustrates that a powerful mix of caution and prudence still overlies the frustration of most East Germans. He and his Charité Hospital colleagues drafted a letter to their union, demanding reforms. It produced vigorous debate even from "One Hundred Percenters" (the term applied to SED true believers), but in the end, concern for consequences and doubt about whether the moment was ripe caused most to hold back. Gunnar himself is uncertain whether to sign. It is a closer call every day, but the situation still seems better characterized as politically pregnant than physically explosive.

OCTOBER 5

The trains with another 10,000 aboard came through the GDR last night. With travel to Czechoslovakia now cut, there are not likely to be many more such refugees, but a last extraordinary scene was played out in the south.

The GDR's legalistic insistence that the trains cross its territory rather than proceed directly to the West German frontier led to the first serious clash between demonstrators and police, at the main station in Dresden.

Jeff Biron, a young American who married a Berliner and works as an embassy driver, phoned us an eyewitness account. Thousands gathered on the narrow square opposite the Hotel Neva, where he was staying with his family, he said. When they tried to force their way into the station, there were pitched battles with police, who used heavy nightsticks. The unorganized crowd, which wanted to board the trains as they came through, hurled rocks. There were injuries on both sides, and many broken windows.

The violence is further disturbing proof that the situation is reaching a flash point. As word spreads, it will contribute mightily to the gloom forming around the weekend. The mood is apparently particularly bitter in Dresden. Jeff has gone on to Czechoslovakia, but on Friday the Economic Section secretary, Mary Agnes McAleenan, will be at the Neva and promises to call in.

The latest sign that the GDR is in a state of nervous alert is the announcement that Western visitors are barred from East Berlin until Sunday. This will not affect U.S. networks and newspapers, which have permission to cover what they expect will be more than a "GDR turns 40" story, but hundreds of West Berliners were stopped at the checkpoints today. Brave Politburo talk notwithstanding, security authorities know how dry the tinder is.

Counterdemonstrations are planned this weekend. Peter Claussen, who is Jerry Verner's deputy and has good contacts in the cultural scene, and Heather have picked up specific information that young people will gather in Alexanderplatz. They intend to avoid attention by making their way individually into the city center Saturday afternoon. At 5:00 P.M. they will come together and hope their chants attract the large crowd that will be in the square for the holiday fair. They expect prompt, possibly brutal, police intervention but say they do not care.

I desperately hope events take another course. Honecker and Gorbachev will be just down the street at a gala dinner, the weekend's last major event. Security will be extraordinarily heavy, and I fear a tragedy. Last spring I discounted Otto Reinhold's preoccupation with a "Tbilisi in Rostock." Amid the jangled nerves and foreboding atmosphere of fall, I am less confident. Friedrich Schorlemmer, a brave man, is speaking about the "Chinese anxiety in the belly" of those who stand up now. That anxiety is encouraged by Stasi and Politburo. Is it only bluff? I do not want to find out. We will have officers in Alexanderplatz Saturday, however, to observe if anything does begin.

I am trading notes with our Bonn Embassy about the impact on inner-German relations. Western politicians speculated last month that the old policy of cooperation on "small steps" had been discredited. Now more sober views are taking over. No one wants to be seen working with the GDR while popular opinion is dominated by refugee images. Our colleagues believe, however, that behind the scenes the Bonn parties have reestablished their consensus. They back reforms, hope the GDR remains stable, and consider that there is no practical alternative to cooperation once the crisis ends. Kohl reportedly has offered the SPD a moratorium on partisan politicking because he and the Opposition are basically of one mind. Of course, the key variable is "once the crisis ends."

OCTOBER 6 (Morning)

Mikhail Gorbachev's plane touches down at 10:30 A.M., and the GDR's 40th birthday party begins. The omens could not be more different from what Honecker would have wished. A generation of youth has left in the glare of world publicity. The citizenry is sullen and shocked; a largish minority, those who feel they may literally have missed the last train, is desperate enough to be, possibly, only a spark away from violence. The generation that has ruled the GDR for two decades faces the fight of its life for political survival. It may still make it, but the odds are lengthening.

The uncertainties begin with the Soviet leader. Will he push Honecker toward retirement? Will his presence, wittingly or not, set off demonstrations? Gorbachev is often good for a surprise, but my bet is he will try to avoid the unexpected this time. He sent his old expert on German affairs, Valentin Falin, to titillate Bonn with hints of new Soviet thinking about the Wall and German unity, but the Soviet Embassy believes he will put his reformer image on hold and buck up his ally. If he mingles with crowds, they are likely to be largely preselected by his hosts. The GDR leadership expects and badly needs such help, but it will not get a blank check. The Soviet Embassy hints that Gorbachev is aware of Honecker's failure but that he will go easy on criticism or advice, even in private, in belief that the badly shaken Politburo here will take corrective measures more readily if not pushed further into a corner.

There is a body politic odor of nervousness, uncertainty, even fear. The desperation of those whose flights over Eastern European way stations have dominated world attention finds reflection in the bitterness of those who now believe that their chance is gone with the closing of the Czechoslovak border. These are the people who were ready to force their way aboard the trains that moved west across the GDR and produced the ugly confrontation in Dresden. No one will exclude the possibility of more serious trouble, and not necessarily in Berlin. Incidents and arrests are almost inevitable, and in the current climate what might otherwise be easy to isolate could start a chain reaction. But on balance, I still think extreme scenarios are unlikely.

The security services are prepared, efficient, and numerous enough to cover all likely and most even conceivable trouble spots. The GDR has probably the world's densest concentration of police, regular and secret. The *Betriebskampfgruppen*—paunchy but tough factory militias established, coddled, and coached since June 1953 to prevent or put down a repeat of the single occasion when East Germans took to the streets—are on alert, as is the non-Soviet Warsaw Pact's best army. We hear that reserves have been called up, perhaps as much to keep young men in barracks as to add muscle. The most turned-off East German knows he can trust his government on one point: to do what is necessary to survive. A major reason for the embrace of China has been to convey the message that this regime too will use force if its back is to the wall. A pastor friend said yesterday (and the church is repeating this widely in private) that he has been given a "China" warning. I doubt many East Germans are prepared to "run onto the open knife." Church and Opposition groups are spreading the word: Keep cool, neither provoke nor be provoked.

Honecker will be under intense scrutiny. If he flags while escorting Gorbachev through two receptions and two parades, speculation that he is very sick—not just as frail as a seventy-seven-year-old coming off surgery has a right to be—will escalate exponentially. His major speech will be scrutinized for policy directions. Vogel hints that something fairly dramatic on travel and emigration is in the works, but weeks hence or, vaguer yet, when the situation has stabilized. Indications are that the inner circle believes the slightest sign of reflection over the earthquake shaking its world would be viewed as fatal weakness. Last evening's news could not have been more symbolic: three times within the first six minutes the Old Guard was seen standing rigidly at attention for the national anthem.

This "celebration" has become a trauma the Politburo seeks to get through with minimum damage, but the crisis will not end Sunday. Even without new shocks, the problems will still be festering. Honecker is unlikely ever to achieve that moment of calm when, possibly, he may make concessions, and if he does he probably has lost so much standing that they would win him minimal credit. The old men search for a formula that would offer breathing space, if not peace, keep reasonably intact the GDR's web of special relations East and West (particularly with that old devil Federal Republic), and, above all, enable them to hang on to power. Their hands are on the classical levers, and they may carry it off a little longer, but increasingly attention will be on a new politics. Independent activism is growing. One hundred came to the politicized services in Gethsemane Church at the beginning of the week, 800 came on Wednesday, and 1,500 came last night. The march in Leipzig gains adherents every Monday, and its focus has become change within the GDR, not emigration. The Opposition, trying to reach an extensive grassroots base beyond the church and to start dialogue with the state, believes it is finding more resonance. For the first time, slavishly loyal "Bloc Parties" are restive.

The SED itself, however, remains the most probable catalyst—if catalyst there is to be—for at least the initial stage of any serious effort to solve the GDR's problems. One-on-one, we hear more criticism, and admission that reforms can succeed only if there is also change at the top of the Party. Symptomatically, Hermann Kant, author, cultural bureaucrat, and Central Committee member, last month refused to sign a protest letter. He now publicly confesses that the SED needs to examine where it has gone wrong.

Will ferment crystallize into a consensus that new policies and leaders are required? The prognosis is likely to be uncertain for months. But our calculations can be changed by the unexpected in the next two days.

Vogel has come through again. The young families I admitted Tuesday can emigrate.

There are two new Neues Forum statements. The first, a letter to Gorbachev signed by Jens Reich, was accepted at the Soviet Embassy—itself a novel development. "We need," it says in play on a Gorbachev phrase, "dialogue, democracy, like air to breathe." The second statement is a "call to all SED members. . . . It is SED passivity that endangers socialism on German soil. . . . You claim the leading role—well, use it! . . . Grassroots [SED] groups have sent many resolutions to the Central Committee. Do Central Committee members at least know their number and substance? . . . The discussion the SED itself must conduct is a vital part of the overall social discussion our country needs." As Eppelmann and now Neues Forum recognize, dissatisfaction in SED ranks is nearly as great as in the country as a whole. The key question is whether the Party can be won for reforms. The opposition is appealing to it over the heads of the Politburo.

OCTOBER 6 (Late Evening)

The end is nowhere in sight, but the crisis did not visibly worsen today. All my officers were about the city trying to sense the mood at both official galas and Opposition counterevents. I collated their reports in my office, but was able also to form firsthand impressions from television. Then, in early evening, as the FDJ assembled, I went into the streets with Gaby.

The skies were somber at Gorbachev's mid-morning arrival. Respectable crowds and polite applause greeted him as he drove through town, but his schedule was not publicized, thus reducing numbers and spontaneity. Imre and Janice joined about 2,000 along Unter den Linden. A few shouts of "Gorby, Gorby" went up as the motorcade arrived, and as he shook hands in the crowd there were cries of "We'll stay," a counterpoint to the emigré slogan. Imre was close enough to hear his answer to a man who called out "Gorby, help us!" "Don't panic," Gorbachev said. The GDR's problems were minor compared to the Soviets', and "the dangers are only for those who do not react to life in time." That last was surely a polite message for his hosts.

We do not know what Honecker and Gorbachev said at lunch, but it was a smiling, chipper East German who spoke later in the Palace of the Republic. His face showed the strain of his operation, but his voice was strong as he delivered an uncompromising message. Nor did Gorbachev spring surprises. GDR-Soviet solidarity had accomplished much, and the SED would solve its problems, he said. Every country had the right to choose its own form of government; in an alliance, pluralism was strength. As cameras panned to a smiling Honecker, he appeared to reply to those (like Ronald Reagan) who have appealed to him to remove the Wall. GDR questions were decided in Berlin by a sovereign GDR, Gorbachev said.

It may have been imagination, but I believe Honecker sighed with relief when Gorbachev finished, and sang the "Internationale" with real gusto.

The key passage—GDR decisions are made here, not in the Kremlin—has a certain ambiguity. It is consistent, after all, with Gorbachev's many assertions that the Brezhnev Doctrine, pursuant to which the Soviet Union has propped up Communist regimes, is buried. The spontaneous smile suggested, however, that Honecker worries more that Gorbachev will remove him than that he will lose control if Soviet troops stay in their barracks.

As Honecker and Gorbachev repaired to the grandstand to review "more than 100,000" FDJ members brought to Berlin from all corners of the GDR, I joined Gaby. Political processions with burning torches have a long history in Germany. Just such a parade along an Unter den Linden still showing heavy war damage was held when the GDR was proclaimed in 1949. The desire to repeat that moment of pride and optimism was surely a Honecker motive for this spectacle. He, as the FDJ's first leader, and wife Margot, one of the prettiest girls in a blue shirt, are prominent in those old photos. But it was a psychological blunder, what Germans on soccer fields call a self-goal—a kick of the ball into your own net.

It was not just that many, especially non-Germans, had to recall that Unter den Linden also knew the flickering torches, the stamp of boots, the chanted slogans in the 1930s. There was a more ancient origin for the chill that went down our backs as we moved in the semi-darkness, acrid smoke contributing a physical element to the pall over Berlin, shadows of young people and the ever-present Stasi coming out of the mists. There is something atavistic about such a ceremony, something that speaks of tribes and forests and a tradition that predates civilization. There may be legitimate times and places for those symbols and emotions, but not now, not when this society is desperate for rational, humane discussion, the coming together of different political and ethical viewpoints to explore a common way out of peril.

The FDJ gathered in streets near the American Embassy. The Stasi watched only for those who looked like they might join the procession with unauthorized banners, and we made our way easily among the young people, who mostly stood quietly in small groups, awaiting their turn to swing onto Unter den Linden. It was hard to tell whether their dominant mood was sullen or a resigned do-your-duty, perhaps even tinged by the near dread Gaby and I began to feel for what might be ahead. Certainly there was little enthusiasm. Spectators were sparse, but security kept us away from the VIPs. We pulled ourselves up to the ledge of a high ground-floor window of the state library and scanned the sea of torches. The young people marched well enough—this is, after all, Germany—but the lack of spontaneity even compared with May Day was unmistakable. There was almost no live singing, though loudspeakers played the FDJ's anthem repeatedly. Gorbachev's name drew cheers. Honecker's name and the GDR anthem attracted light applause and a few derisive whistles.

As the FDJ formed along Unter den Linden, 1,000 filled Gethsemane Church. The mood was serious—Janice reported in—and the audience was attentive. The pastor called for individual courage, not explicitly for collective political action, but the time for silence has ended, he said. The 400-year-old hymn editorialized "Wake up, wake up, you German land! You have slept too long."

Across town at the packed Church of the Redeemer, the Lutheran youth ministry put on an alternative workshop entitled "How will you proceed now, GDR?" The message 3,000 heard was reform, not emigration. After a ninety-minute concert of political songs, members of the major groups, including Neues Forum, spoke of improving GDR socialism. The audience enthusiastically applauded the speaker who said: "It's not the system that's at fault, it's the leadership." Another speaker, Heather said, reported on three consecutive evenings of demonstrations in Dresden. Most of the 2,000 who were driven back from the station by firehoses the first night, he noted, were would-be refugees pulled from trains after the border was closed. The next night, 10,000 protested the rough handling.

Mary Agnes called from Dresden a short while ago. She estimated that 500 to 600 were again in front of the station chanting "Freedom, freedom" and singing and jeering. Riot police were sealing off the street, and there had been at least fourteen detentions but, so far, no violence. We cannot confirm reports that a silent march was broken up in Magdeburg this evening. It would be significant if disturbances spread out of the south, but I would expect Eberlein to deal sharply with disorder in his fiefdom.

OCTOBER 7 (10:00 P.M.)

The GDR came through its two-day "celebration" with a minimum of trouble—and no new hope of an early way out of its crisis. By appearances, Gorbachev correctly supported a shaken ally. Imre and I failed to catch up with a small demonstration in Berlin that police, operating before Western cameras, handled smoothly. Other protests in Dresden, Leipzig, and Potsdam produced some arrests, but the security services seem never to have been close to losing control. Honecker looked fitter after a grueling forty-eight hours than anyone imagined he could, but he showed no policy flexibility.

The mid-morning military parade went off with Prussian precision. The crowd was thin, Gorbachev looked bored, Honecker looked chipper and pleased. It was followed by the customary county fair activities, especially at centrally located Alexanderplatz but also at locations throughout the city. I spent several hours in Alexanderplatz, along with dozens of Western television crews, watching for something out of the ordinary that did not come. It was easy to spot the muscular Stasi in gray windbreakers. But all any of us saw during daylight were game booths, food stands, and band concerts. The children had a good time; the adults were subdued. "Let's drink to the Anniversary," Imre heard one Berliner propose at a stand selling the fatty, tasty bockwurst he and I make our almost daily lunch. "I already did," said his friend, "in the spring." He meant the Federal Republic's 40th.

Gorbachev and Honecker skipped the fair to spend two hours together. Afterward, Gerasimov, the Soviet spokesman, dodged questions on the GDR and told a press conference Gorbachev had described the necessity for Perestroika—in the Soviet Union.

Mary Agnes called again from Dresden to say that the Friday protest, the fourth in as many evenings, grew to 2,000. After bottles were thrown, police used their nightsticks. We hear that 350 of 500 in yesterday's Magdeburg demonstration were arrested and that about 4,000 assembled in Leipzig on Friday. Police broke them up roughly, and the inner city was off-limits today.

As we had been tipped off, Berlin's first trouble started at Alexanderplatz, on the fair's fringe, at 5:00 P.M. Heather and Anne Bodine (an administrative specialist but a fluent German speaker and, by good chance, the duty officer) witnessed 400 young people begin to shout "Gorbachev!" "Freedom!" and "Freedom for the imprisoned!" In spite of a massive police presence, the crowd around them quickly tripled and surged toward the Palace of the Republic, where the VIPs were holding their final reception. With Western crews filming, the police funneled the crowd smoothly into side streets, where it largely dispersed. Heather called me from a street phone a little later, however, to say several hundred demonstrators were moving into Prenzlauer Berg, a half step ahead of police. At 7:00 P.M. Imre and I left the embassy to see if anything was still going on at Alexanderplatz. It was not easy to get there. Security forces, in uniform and out, manned checkpoints well before the Palace of the Republic, where police stood shoulder to shoulder. We had to show our diplomatic ID repeatedly and insist on our right to proceed. At the main checkpoint, across the bridge that spans the Spree and divides Unter den Linden from Karl-Liebknecht-Strasse, our cards were examined by a nervous and excited Stasi officer who looked no more than twenty-one. He consulted a superior, who waved us through.

We crisscrossed spacious Marx-Engels Forum and the square itself without finding protestors. We did encounter a dozen groups holding animated talks at the edges of Alexanderplatz, however, as police hung back. Young people argued that the government restricted freedom and lied; others, mostly older, replied that they began with nothing and that the government should get some credit, or, simply, "We don't want to be unemployed" (presumably in capitalism). Some older SED defenders sounded committed; younger ones had phrases that tripped off the tongue so glibly we assumed they came from a crib sheet. Still, if they were sent to debate, the Party may yet respond to youth dissatisfaction with a little more sophistication than Honecker's platitudes indicated.

Honecker, foreign dignitaries, and ambassadors shared a three-hour social interspersed with food, classical music, and an act from *Fledermaus* before the two-day party closed. Dick said Honecker worked his table, which included the Czechoslovak leader Jakes, the PLO's Arafat, China's Yao Yilin, and, until he left early for the airport, Gorbachev, of course. Daniel Ortega stopped for a long chat. Dick's impression was that the two days strained Honecker, who looked much older than three months ago, but that he performed well. Dick spoke briefly with one Politburo member, Joachim Herrmann. The man responsible for the media policy even SED stalwarts condemn insisted that he had been pleased by FDJ "enthusiasm" and that things were going well. Reluctantly, but with more candor than *Neues Deutschland*, he admitted they could certainly be better.

On balance, it might have gone much worse for Honecker. Gorbachev did not press him, embarrassing demonstrations were controlled with limited force, and, above all, he himself showed unexpected physical vitality. The Politburo is surely relieved, but the morning after is only hours away, and nothing Honecker said or did in his remarkable personal show indicated he has any recipe for the hangover except the same failed policies and attitudes.

OCTOBER 8 (3:00 A.M.)

At 11:00 last night, I gave our final cables to the communicators and telephoned Gaby I was on my way home. She said our dinner guests would wait and a plate had been saved. Long before we knew the holiday weekend would climax the GDR's severest crisis, we had invited West Berlin friends. Since it would have taken months to reassemble them, we did not cancel when it became obvious I would have to work all Saturday evening. Gaby ferried them across Bornholmer Strasse or they would have been kept out by the travel ban.

Unter den Linden remained closed, so I detoured to Schönhauser Allee via Friedrichstrasse and was surprised to see that trucks loaded with paramilitary police were posted across from the Ständige Vertretung. I guessed they were meant to prevent an attempt by would-be emigrants to rush the West German offices, but a few blocks later it became apparent they were in reserve to deal with an active and different disturbance. The sparks of the evening's earlier demonstration had ignited in Prenzlauer Berg, home to many activists and cultural free-thinkers. Side streets were full of squad cars and paddy wagons. As I moved up Schönhauser Allee, knots of police and pedestrians forced me to slow even more than its cobblestones normally require. Below the Colosseum Theater, a block west of Gethsemane Church, police could keep only a single lane open. Hundreds of excited youths were seeking the nearness of the church, which has become a protest center.

From home, I called J.D., who had already informed the State Department that more serious protests were in progress, and we agreed to meet early Sunday. At midnight, I apologized to our friends and sat down to eat. We knew each other well and spoke our minds. It was good that a few had at last gone into the streets, said Jörn, a schoolteacher and physical giant of a man, but why not many more? Why were they so timid? Most of our dinner party had been part of the '68 Generation, when the Free University in West Berlin was Germany's most radical, Jörn recalled. They faced tough cops in their time. What could the "pigs" do if as many protestors turned out here as there had been in West Berlin when the Shah of Iran visited? I nearly lost my temper at the end of the long day. That was easy talk from West Berlin,

I said, but you do not know the situation here (not fair, because Jörn regularly visits the GDR). "These police are not like those you played against as students. There is a chance for real change here, but if the old men feel their state's existence and their own power is at stake, there could be a bloodbath."

I escorted our guests back at 3:00 A.M. Unusual numbers of border troops openly carrying rifles were around the checkpoint, clearly on high alert, and the usually chatty Bornholmer Strasse guards—their faces expressionless, their demeanor correct, but nervous as they peered at my card—had no small talk. The radio reported the demonstrations over, but as I turned onto Schönhauser Allee I saw the route through Prenzlauer Berg was blocked by police officers standing stiffly in the middle of the street, hands folded behind backs, nightsticks at the ready. There was no sound except my car, and almost no movement, only the line of police, ghostly in the yellow pools of light cast by streetlamps. They paid me no heed. Their eyes looked the other way, trying to catch the first glimpse of marchers who might yet come out of the darkness toward the Wall.

OCTOBER 8 (5:00 P.M.)

Schönhauser Allee showed few signs of the demonstrations this morning. The police were gone, and I had no trouble reaching Gethsemane Church. Four or five police officers observed from across the street, but they made no effort to hinder worshipers arriving for Sunday services or those tending the flame that has burned all week for Leipzig and Dresden detainees. This surface normality was repeated around town, including Unter den Linden, where the traffic controls were gone. I was at the embassy by 10:00 A.M. The first task was to get a better feel for what happened during the night, then make plans for the day. I asked Imre to go to Dresden today and proceed to Leipzig for the Monday evening demonstration. Heather, Janice, and Anne will contact the church and the Opposition. A key unknown: will there be more street actions tonight?

Heather, who had the most complete picture of last evening's events, had followed instructions and pulled back when it looked as though the hard core from the original Alexanderplatz demonstration was being maneuvered into a dead end in Prenzlauer Berg's narrow streets, where paddy wagons waited. However, as the scattered protestors moved before the police through the old workers' district that has become an East Berlin Left Bank, she explained, they collected reinforcements, and by late evening a fairly coherent group ranging again into the several thousands was moving toward Gethsemane Church. After police used nightsticks to block the path and arrested many, Bishop Forck intervened. He negotiated safe passage and convinced the young people to go home. About 300 were detained overnight, though most will probably be released quickly if the Dresden/Leipzig pattern holds.

Details are still sparse about other protests across much of the country. The largest—several thousand participants each—appear to have been in Leipzig and Jena. Potsdam, outside Berlin, and Plauen, in the far south, turned out hundreds. We know nothing further about Dresden since Mary Agnes and her family have gone on to Czechoslovakia.

Heather reached Pflugbeil, who told her most Neues Forum members stayed home last night. He did not expect direct reprisals against the organization. Moreover, he has heard that a sympathetic senior official in the Culture Ministry, as well as young SED members, have written Honecker to call for a new attitude. He was cautiously hopeful that these breaks in Party discipline and the events of the last two nights would give the Politburo pause.

In the early afternoon I stopped at Alexanderplatz, where the fair was ending. Crowds were sparse, and police presence was heavy and obvious. Back inside Gethsemane Church, a dozen fasters sat quietly while scores of the engaged, interested, or curious wandered the aisles, talked among themselves, and examined the petitions, open letters, and Neues Forum information on side tables. Japanese television interviewed the pastor. I saw tearful reunions of overnight detainees who came to the church after release seeking family or asking about friends from whom they had been separated.

I compared notes with Helmut and Petra, our Ständige Vertretung friends, who were listening quietly to the stories, and then went into the sunshine to join the shifting, spontaneous discussions around the courtyard. Honecker defenders were hard-pressed. I monitored one lively debate with a middle-aged man who said he was an LDPD member and was proud that Gerlach's speeches were available inside. True, Gerlach should have spoken out sooner, the man said, but he was doing it now, and it was vital to start dialogue. Much in the GDR needed improvement, he agreed, but there was also much to preserve. Citizens should not put everything at risk. Had the Stasi sent him? someone asked. Of course not, the man replied. His name was not important. What mattered was to agree not to tear the state apart, to stay off the streets . . .

Most at the church were young, but I was struck by the middle-aged couples. They were quieter, as if slightly frightened and surprised to be there, but concerned about what was happening and listening to the activists for the first time. Several claimed they had returned union membership cards or had colleagues who had resigned from the SED.

The West German press I began to read on what was left of Sunday afternoon reported that on Saturday several dozen East Germans met in Schwante, north of Berlin, to found the "Social Democratic Party in the GDR," with historian Ibrahim Böhme as provisional head. The first tasks of the would-be party—called "SDP" lest it be thought simply an adjunct of the West German SPD—are to show it can organize itself and draft a program. The founders will notify the Interior Ministry tomorrow. It is doubtful the authorities' response will be as legalistic.

What to make of it all? While the scope and spontaneity of the first demonstrations the GDR has known since June 1953 will dismay Honecker, he probably is reassured by other weekend developments: The numbers that turned out, notably including Berlin, were not particularly large, and the state's massive security forces were in no danger of losing control; Gorbachev gave the GDR a pat on the back, not a kick in the pants; and, above all, his health held. Gorbachev let drop just enough ambiguity to show he is aware of the root problem, but Honecker conceded nothing. ADN said he told Gorbachev that "hopes of . . . reforms in the direction of bourgeois democracy to the point of capitalism are built on sand." Until Honecker admits the deep unhappiness the weekend pomp and circumstance failed to conceal, the crisis must worsen. The real politicking, within SED and the Opposition and, possibly increasingly, on the streets, is just beginning.

OCTOBER 9

Street protests resumed last night. Only the presence of a few more uniformed police shows this is not a routine Monday morning, but just below the surface is heightened nervousness about what the growing youth assertiveness means.

The most tense scenes Saturday had occurred around Gethsemane Church, and last night police cordoned off the grounds to separate the 2,000 inside from another 2,000 in the street who were chanting "We want reforms" and "Gorbachev, Gorbachev." Worshipers could leave only in small groups, a police tactic to prevent the two crowds from feeding on each other. Anne, who remained well past midnight, said Schönhauser Allee was fairly calm, until an officer ordered the street cleared of the remaining hard core of 200 with the aid of German Shepherds. Though the dogs were not unleashed, the protestors ran, and helmeted riot police pursued them up the avenue. Some were detained, some escaped into side streets, but others joined as the demonstration was pushed north block by block. The protestors, who never grew back above a few hundred, remained peaceful, Anne said, but they were beaten with truncheons. There was great concern among onlookers. Many residents placed candles in windows; others, of all ages, came down to the street to watch but mostly did not join in. One woman in her early forties remarked hesitantly that it looked as if the young people had done no wrong. She was obviously watching such a scene for the first time and seemed deeply affected. Many made similar comments.

We do not have a good fix on the weekend arrests. The reunion scenes I witnessed at Gethsemane Church on Sunday morning confirmed that many of those arrested the first evening were released within hours, but the state apparently intends to prosecute "ringleaders." Some reportedly have already been given quick trials and jail sentences of up to six months. Neutral observers agree Berlin demonstrators have been peaceful. We know of no serious injuries, but those bloodied and bruised toward the end of both evenings are conservatively estimated at over 100. While police were in the forefront, the workers' militia assisted on both evenings, and church officials confirm that elite army paratroops were nearby. The visibility of militia and crack troops was probably meant as a warning, but it signals regime nervousness as much as resolve.

Günther Krusche, the second-highest figure in the Berlin-Brandenburg church, called the demonstrations counterproductive. He said he knew his words would be unpopular with many young people but that street disturbances were unlikely to make this regime more willing to talk. What was required was calm and mutual willingness to engage in dialogue about necessary changes.

On Sunday evening, Imre called to report remarkable events in Dresden, where he found 2,000 young people filing through downtown and 1,000 riot police deployed near the station that had been the scene of protests every evening since October 3. When the police marched at double time to split them, the protesters simply sat down. They sang the "Internationale," repeating over and over its refrain "Fight for human rights," called for free travel and nonviolence, and chanted "We're staying here—we want reforms" (in German it rhymes: "Wir bleiben hier—Reformen wollen wir").

After ten minutes "on the ground," Imre reported, a young man suggested that he and ten others negotiate with the police. Several minutes later, they returned and announced the astonishing news that Mayor Berghofer would receive a delegation of twenty this morning. Results are to be announced tonight in churches. Even some police applauded, Imre marveled. Their shields came down and cigarettes appeared. An officer broke ranks to engage young people in serious talk. Bishop Hempel, present all evening, helped mediate. Perhaps, Imre said before ringing off and driving to Leipzig, it is the beginning of something important.

Nationally, however, the regime keeps to its hard line. The "ringleaders" who disturbed the fair have been arrested, ADN said without elaboration yesterday. Today's *Neues Deutschland* devoted virtually all sixteen pages to a glowing account of the 40th Anniversary and dismissed the Berlin troubles in a dozen lines of an editorial: "Influential FRG forces sought to put aside the results of the Second World War and of the postwar development by a coup," but rioters had learned that "no one can shake the foundations of our Socialist State." The "rioters," *Junge Welt* claimed, were neither good young people from next door nor workers. The latter were in the militia from whom marchers ran. Don't those involved, it asked, "know that all attacks against Communism begin with the demagogic cry for 'more democracy'?"

There is little doubt that the regime has the resources and the will to maintain power. The tougher questions are whether growing frustration and bitterness can find a constructive political channel and how they will affect the SED. We know those attitudes find some reflection within the Party. The fear that moved Krusche to criticize both sides for street troubles is historically founded. The church remembers that it was escalation to real violence that saved Ulbricht when he was about to fall in June 1953. But after another night of trouble, all one knows is that the GDR will not be the same as it was, not yet what it is becoming.

OCTOBER 10

The marches following Monday evening services in Leipzig's Nikolai Church have grown steadily, reaching 10,000 last week. The outlook yesterday, church leaders told us, was for serious trouble. Imre, who drove over from Dresden, called to say police had moved massively into the center of town, and workplaces were closed early. Later, one pastor deeply involved with the protest movement told Imre that what turned matters around was a letter that arrived just in time to be read from pulpits. It was signed by three members of Leipzig's SED hierarchy (but not the first secretary or his deputy) and cultural figures including Kurt Masur, director of the Leipzig Orchestra. They pledged to work for change and called for nonviolence. The letter was also read over local radio.

Nikolai Church was packed, Imre said, the overflow absorbed by three nearby churches, while those outside chanted reform slogans. When the congregations filed out, they marched past the railroad station in Karl-Marx-Strasse, clapping rhythmically and urging drivers to honk horns or join in. Before services, riot police and militia were out in force. During the march, they kept to the sidewalks, traffic cops predominated, and all kept their heads. The young people tried to talk with the police. The marchers—40,000 by Imre's estimate—wanted only a say in things, a girl explained. "You know that having a say is not very well tolerated here," the officer replied.

There was positive news also from Dresden, to which Imre returned this morning. Following up on their agreement, city officials sat down in an unprecedented meeting with representatives of those who had demonstrated in the city center for six consecutive nights. Mayor Berghofer promised to pass on to Berlin demands for travel and registration of independent organizations that exceeded his powers and vowed to keep talking. In the evening, what is being called the Group of 20 reported at four packed churches. It faced accusations that the state was buying time to split the opposition, but for the first night in a week there were no protests downtown.

Dick, with a Dresden commitment long booked for Monday, called on the Catholic and Lutheran prelates, who told him they were moderately optimistic. The young Catholic bishop, Reinelt—a man I know takes a very reserved view of the SED—was the more skeptical, warning that Berghofer may only be putting a local nuance on a hard national line. The mayor, of course, is not a major player, not even a Central Committee member, but at age forty-six and in office only three years, he may be more flexible than many older functionaries. It is tempting to draw a line from City Hall to Dresden SED headquarters, but we do not yet have evidence of an independent policy by Party black sheep and rumored reformer Hans Modrow, who last month told Dick he would skip the birthday party for a health "Kur." Saxon church leaders have two worries. The Group of 20 is an ad hoc body formed in a half-hour Sunday. In contrast to Neues Forum, blue-collar workers predominate. The Protestant church, we were told in confidence, is considering how to help save the Group from being overwhelmed by its interlocutors. What is more dangerous, if the state is indeed only waiting for the moment to crack down, there could be an explosion.

In response to church and Opposition pleas, there were no demonstrations in Berlin on Monday, but 2,000 mostly young people crowded into the evening service at Gethsemane Church while another 1,000 maintained a vigil outside. Police made no attempt to interfere, though we saw strong reserves nearby. Inside the emphasis was on avoiding violence. Bishop Forck pleaded for citizens to stay off the street but to speak out fearlessly, and for politicians to start dialogue. A member of the slowly stirring LDPD offered the youth club hall he manages to those who wished to talk, provided the press was excluded.

Hermann Kant, a good novelist who has served the SED loyally, last month opposed Berlin writers who appealed for reforms. Yesterday he wrote his own outspoken letter. The best thing about the GDR, he wrote, "is that it exists"; the worst thing is "that it exists as it has until now." The second sensation, beyond the fact that a Central Committee member wrote it, was that the FDJ paper *Junge Welt* printed it.

The weekly cultural paper *Sonntag* and, again, *Der Morgen* carried other hints of establishment disaffection. Perhaps most striking, however, was one little quote attributed to a nineteen-year-old girl who came to Berlin with her FDJ group for Friday's torchlight parade: "I can't really celebrate because some people aren't here, many of my age who have left our country. They believe, unlike me, that they have no perspectives here. That makes me sad and thoughtful." It appeared almost secretively in the middle of a column of polemic in the SED's *Berliner Zeitung*.

But there are no new tones from Honecker, who still acts as if he does not see what is happening. Meeting with his Chinese Politburo visitor, he spoke of "further perfecting" GDR socialism and added, "Every attempt of Imperialism to destabilize . . . Socialism . . . is and will be nothing but the fruitless tilting of Don Quixote against a windmill." *Neues Deutschland* remains ice-cold and granite-tough, its "news stories" and commentaries backed by letters, allegedly from average citizens, that express outrage over the rioters and support for the police. It did give relatively hard figures for unrest in cities we could not observe firsthand: Magdeburg, 93 arrests; Karl-Marx-Stadt, 4,000 demonstrators, of whom 600 were "hard core" and 26 were arrested; Luckenwalde, 12 arrests, in a small city where no protests had been reported by Western media; Arnstadt, the first indication of trouble in the small southern city. The most detail was from Potsdam, the former royal residence, where local officials said 103 arrests resulted in 10 jail sentences, 40 fines, 44 releases after warnings, and 9 ongoing investigations.

I cannot fully reconcile the conflicting signs of rigidity and flexibility, old thinking, and self-criticism, so apparent now in the establishment, but in the absence of direction from above, local and second-level officials are showing some imagination. Imre told me that church leaders and average citizens alike, with whom he talked in Leipzig on Monday, were convinced that the police had been authorized to use firearms before someone made a last-minute decision and prevented tragedy. None of the flexibility shown there or in Dresden is yet evident at the top, but the Politburo met today, and a definitive reaction to the watershed events of the past days may soon be apparent. Everyone else is drawing a deep breath, but the pause is likely to be brief.

Our embassy has made an embarrassing blunder that the GDR will not believe was accidental. Governments routinely send each other anniversary congratulations. The GDR publicizes such messages excessively, out of its chronic insecurity and longing for international legitimacy. Late last month we received Washington's message for the 40th Anniversary. It could scarcely have been more formal, but it would have been prominently displayed by *Neues Deutschland* as proof that the world accepts the GDR. I prepared a diplomatic transmittal note, and the documents should have gone to the Foreign Ministry last week. In the rush, I did not notice our "congratulations" was missing from the press. I found it buried in a secretary's in-box today, and we sent it on with the notation that it had been received September 29 and that the embassy regretted a technical delay. In the paranoid world the GDR leadership inhabits, it will probably conclude we withheld this message as part of a campaign to embarrass, if not destabilize, the state. But there is such a thing as a genuinely fortuitous botch-up.

OCTOBER 11

Rolf Reissig is one of the SED establishment's few certifiable liberals, a man who was slapped down in recent months for outspokenness but who retains an important position in the Central Committee apparatus. The Politburo must act immediately to regain the initiative, he said over lunch, if the GDR is not to face real danger. He was guardedly optimistic because the alternatives were so clear, but only if Honecker left soon. For now, everyone "looks to Berlin and waits for a sign." During our meal in the new "Peking," East Berlin's only true Chinese restaurant, he was alternately deeply worried, cautiously hopeful, and dead tired. Just back from Denmark, he leaves tomorrow for Moscow, where he and Reinhold hold "routine" talks with Soviet counterparts about the theoretical constructs for a more democratic socialism.

Two or three years ago, Reissig argued, when Honecker's prestige was high, the Politburo could have gradually liberalized society and economy, but it ignored recommendations from his institute and others. Now it was almost too late. The situation had deteriorated so much that it was impossible to wait until May to address fundamental questions. There was a little time left, he said, only because good sense had prevailed in Leipzig, Dresden, and Berlin, where protests had either ceased or the police had backed off. However, the half-year time frame our contacts cited last week was unrealistic. Without a new approach now, initiative would pass out of the SED's hands with unpredictable consequences.

Important Party people long silent were at last raising their voices, Reissig said—for example, Kant and the three Leipzig secretaries—but local officials could only take emergency action. Reinhold, he said, was comfortable advocating cautious reforms, but many people "were expecting more of him." All eyes were on the Politburo, which was even then meeting. Though the old men could continue to waffle or even crack down, he believed it slightly more probable that they would realize they had to act and that going forward was the lesser risk. What might be the first sign of meaningful liberalization? I asked. His answer, which parallels what many within the Opposition and the church are saying, was twofold: change in the disastrous media policy, and an offer of genuine dialogue to all elements of society. The latter point, Reissig cautioned, did not necessarily mean legalizing Neues Forum. Like his "friend" Manfred Stolpe, the senior lay churchman, he said, he preferred to put real life into existing institutions, including the Bloc Parties. But Neues Forum had to take part in decision-making. The rub, Reissig acknowledged, was that a fresh start required Honecker's discredited team to step aside—and promptly.

The past twenty-four hours have produced much news but no consistent pattern: 500 people arrested during Dresden demonstrations were released, but 10 remain in custody; the Leipzig press reported seventy-five convictions (four weeks to one year) for participation in earlier protests, but no one was arrested during Monday's giant march; the fifteen Neues Forum members detained around the country over the weekend are free; *Junge Welt* continued the tentative opening of its columns to unusual viewpoints, carrying a surprisingly sympathetic account of Leipzig's Monday evening; Stephan Hermlin urged acceptance of Neues Forum. This is the eye of the hurricane, a period of relative calm during which, as Reissig said, the SED may still be able to give some direction to the churning political forces if it acts quickly, decisively, and intelligently.

A word about the restaurant where Reissig and I dined may seem frivolous, but the Peking illustrates how far the GDR has traveled in my twenty-seven months here. Shortly after I came, S. of the Chinese Embassy told me about tough negotiations to establish a genuine Chinese restaurant. Good chefs insisted on West Mark salaries, and the GDR balked at arrangements that would require huge subsidies or, in effect, make the restaurant an off-limits hard-currency oasis. At each lunch, S. would recount the latest twist, and we would joke about future meals at the Peking with a "next year in Jerusalem" air. A few months ago, an exotic Friedrichstrasse restaurant accessible to all GDR citizens (though at, for them, shocking prices) seemed a sign of openness to new forms of economic cooperation reminiscent of Hungary's decision to have such a restaurant five years ago, a symbolic step into the larger world. Now we can eat Chinese dishes, but the GDR is rocked by storms that raise more basic questions; the China tie has ominous undertones, and S. and I can no longer meet, because "social contact" with Chinese diplomats is undesirable so soon after Tienanmen Square.

OCTOBER 12

Just in time for last evening's news, the Politburo issued a declaration acknowledging need to consider important policy changes. I heard this as I drove home, and I saw lights still burning at SED Headquarters, a clue that extraordinary activity continues. Normally the old men are back in their Wandlitz retreat well before the dinner hour.

The document has much old rhetoric, but the tone is not the self-congratulatory one used until now to reject reform. It identifies as key areas the media, travel, environment, wages, consumer supplies, and citizen involvement in decision-making, and it admits the emigration wave revealed serious problems that require SED self-examination and "dialogue" with the people. For now at least, the Politburo has responded to unrest with willingness to consider concessions rather than with more repression. As important, however, there are no specifics. It is a holding action while Honecker assesses how little he must give to retain power. Church leaders welcomed it as a step in the right direction. A prominent opposition figure belittled it as "formalism." Both are probably right. The question is what follows and how fast. Suspicion of the Politburo is so widespread that yesterday's action by itself cannot buy much time.

Even before the Politburo's statement, church circles were cautiously upbeat about the new willingness of officials to talk rather than bash heads. At Gethsemane Church, Bishop Forck reported a promise by East Berlin Mayor Krack that police would stay away from the church if the crowds remained peaceful. Major political changes were being considered, the mayor said. Jail sentences for demonstrators would be reviewed, and police brutality complaints studied. He could not meet with Neues Forum representatives as such, Krack added, but he would talk with them if they were in a church delegation. The bishop accepted the offer.

Meanwhile, with *Neues Deutschland* the most prominent exception, the press shows flashes of what Stefan Heym is calling "embryo Glasnost." Provincial and Bloc Party papers are finally rewarding our diligence. They run articles on demonstrations or reprint critical letters. *Junge Welt* reported a protest at Berlin's Humboldt University that has not yet been mentioned in the West. The SED daily in Dresden cited a young Christian who resented media claims that she and other protesters were rowdies and complained that nothing she said would be printed. It has become common for actors and theater-goers to stay on after the curtain to debate. There are also more reports of worker activism, though nothing credible on Polish-style independent unions.

More reflections: Perhaps three paragraphs of the five-column Politburo declaration contained "new thinking." The rest was defensive and self-justifying. That dichotomy probably fairly portrays the struggle within the SED. It will be hard for Honecker to persuade a critical mass, even of Party members, that his team can be trusted to carry out new policies. The challenge is illustrated by Kurt Hager's effort to put himself near the front of those calling for change in an interview carried by GDR Radio yesterday. The memory of his one-line dismissal of Gorbachev's reforms—"You don't change your wallpaper just because your neighbor does"—sits too deep.

I discussed this at lunch with Jörg von Studnitz, the Ständige Vertretung's political counselor. His short list of those who must go if the Politburo is to have a chance to win a modicum of credibility is Mielke, Herrmann, and Hager. What about Honecker? I asked. The SED might still need him, Jörg said; he is respected for his efforts to preserve arms control and inner-German contacts in the early 1980s. Possibly Jörg is right, but it is hard to believe Honecker can survive. He must be tempted to save himself by jettisoning allies, but their records also burden him. If the ice cracks, he will be sitting on a rapidly dwindling floe.

The October 11 declaration cannot end the crisis. It must be either too little too late, or merely the first sign of much more massive changes to follow. If the old leadership can still muster a majority for only minor course corrections, the atmosphere could quickly deteriorate again. The declaration's conclusion that socialism cannot be questioned is already read by many as a sign the Party does not yet grasp that it must step back from its absolute domination of every aspect of public life.

Despite efforts to put a positive gloss on events, church leaders are worried. Stolpe, the most savvy, told us privately he believed that Honecker had blocked the dialogue Leipzig officials offered protesters Monday. The Politburo may well believe it can buy time by crafting a more congenial bureaucratic style, but if it fails to address the fundamental issues, there will be ugly turmoil, he said. Others are more optimistic that the declaration is the first crack. The top aide to Klaus Höpcke, the progressive deputy cultural minister, told Jerry Verner the dam would break within two weeks and there would be far-reaching policy and personnel changes. The point to watch may be whether alarmed Central Committee members can force an extraordinary Plenum. If they are kept out of the game until their next regular session, in December, it will indicate Honecker is hanging on. If the Plenum is advanced, it will be an equally strong sign of a power shift. The Soviets believe that decision has already been made, but if it is not to miss the chance, the SED probably must move before the next Leipzig march.

OCTOBER 13

On direct order from the secretary of state, who ruled that it was too sensitive to talk with representatives of a regime whose police a few days ago were beating peaceful demonstrators, the policy-planning delegation met no East Germans. Neither Francis Fukuyama nor we were pleased. There has been a turn for the better, and a case can be made for talking more, not less, with this government now that it may at last be starting to face the need for major change. There is no lobby for building influence in the GDR, however—and just possibly political risk in being thought soft on the builders of the Berlin Wall.

Some of our ideas were worked into the "Future of Germany" paper. Fukuyama's people accept that dramatic events could unfold quickly, up to and including collapse of the regime, massive uprisings, a swing back to hard repression, or a major new Soviet gambit on Germany. They tend, accordingly, toward our activist view: No one wants to prop up a discredited regime, but since we should not leave protection of our interests in Central Europe solely to Bonn, we need to get involved with GDR reform. After this week, many better appreciate the urgency.

This was a routine day on the way to Glasnost—without sensations, just more proto-candor breaking out in the media and discussions between local functionaries and citizen delegations, usually church-dominated. Heated debate continued at the highest levels as the SED tries to determine whether it can channel the new forces that are remaking the political landscape almost hourly. Most rumors centered about Honecker, who is clearly weakened by the need to reverse rhetoric nearly 180 degrees, but the only power-brokers visible were Hager and Tisch, pillars of his regime, who implausibly are trying to establish reform credentials with calls for dialogue and new policies.

Organizationally the strongest Bloc Party, the CDU is hampered in any effort to gain credibility by its longtime, sycophantic chairman. Gerald Götting is trying to change his image with a call for—what else?—dialogue, as well as praise for the very "Letter from Weimar" he attacked last month. One reason the CDU wants to get on the Glasnost bandwagon is to save its newspaper from being struck. The same plant prints the church paper and the CDU daily. Imre heard that workers threatened to stop the presses unless *Neue Zeit* put some real life into its pages. More significant is that Manfred Gerlach, the one Bloc Party leader with a slightly independent profile, took a direct swipe at the Politburo declaration, asking, "What good does it do to further perfect the inadequate?" The SED, he indicated, must share power.

The Academy of Arts and the Culture League were the latest to try to catch up to their memberships. Their statements were published this morning by the SED flagship, *Neues Deutschland*, which for the first time began to reflect some of the liveliness spreading through the press. Included was this neatly formulated sentence: "The citizen's daily experiences determine public opinion in the country, which often is the opposite of the published opinion." Television news—hitherto the other main redoubt of agitprop—broadcast interviews with workers who spoke fairly openly about problems, including that the press "doesn't write about everything." *Junge Welt*'s now daily eye-opener was a letter by rock singers and pop musicians who complained that the paper had distorted their views last week. They said they had not joined Neues Forum but supported its right to organize, and they claimed their initial resolution was backed by 3,000 colleagues, many of whom were being punished for signing.

More and more groups, institutions, media organs, even politicians, are testing the new limits. While the Hagers, Tisches, and Göttings are doing it for tactical reasons, the experience seems increasingly normal and agreeable to many others. Their thirst is not likely to be satisfied easily. It is not yet impossible, but with each day's experience it becomes harder—or at least more costly—for the Politburo to put the cork back in the bottle. For the moment, its intention is rather to ration the drink carefully.

OCTOBER 14

We do not need to report this Saturday, unless something beyond the simply extraordinary occurs, so I spent much of the day in the office reading and talking. J.D. brought up the draft assessment of the GDR's future (whether a life insurance company "would write a policy") that I showed him several weeks and half a world ago. "Dick has considerable doubts the system in the GDR is reformable, some of which I share," he said, but my view is valid, and I should consider sending it as a "Dissent Channel" message. "Dissent" is a poor word for such a message, J.D. said; it would be an "additional" comment, something the State Department encourages when officers feel strongly that alternative thinking is needed. I thanked him, but I will pass. The situation is moving so fast it would be difficult to refocus the piece. I would still write a policy on the GDR, but I would set the premium higher and warn the client it could soon be uninsurable if it did not move boldly on reforms. It is more important for us right now, however, to concentrate on daily reports that can be used as building blocks for another broad assessment when we gain a clearer perspective.

J.D. also related a worrisome hint of the uncertainty at the top of the SED. Basler told him the Leipzig SED secretaries called Berlin "at the highest level" when violence had appeared imminent Monday. They received "some" but, Gerd emphasized, not unanimous support for compromise. An even bigger test of nerve and common sense comes in Leipzig within forty-eight hours. Bloodletting is still possible.

Imre passed on another conversation he has had with his Soviet colleague, who said CDU contacts were telling him bluntly that Honecker should go, followed by Götting. The Soviet also described Gorbachev's two Berlin meetings. At the first, he had only a personal assistant and Falin, his Germany expert, with him, while Honecker had Mittag, and it lasted nearly double the scheduled hour. Gorbachev did press on reform, but Honecker and Mittag replied with a litany of GDR achievements, especially computers. In effect, they talked past each other, and the Soviet emerged depressed. The session with the full Politburo and heads of key Central Committee departments went better; at least Gorbachev left smiling. The Soviets liked Modrow, Imre's contact said, but he was too junior to take over now. There could be a transitional solution, however.

The Soviet Embassy also had East German "visitors" who were "persuaded" to leave last week, the diplomat said. It is a remarkable indication of Gorbachev's standing that desperate people would believe a sit-in at the Soviet Embassy was a route to reach West Germany instead of Bautzen Prison.

The Soviet tipped us off that another Politburo member, Lev Zaikov, arrives unexpectedly on Wednesday. He is Boris Yeltsin's successor as boss of

Moscow, and thus Schabowski's counterpart. Possibly the Soviets want to sound out one of the contenders, but his primary task is probably to inform Gorbachev about the Politburo's emergency deliberations. Of course, he may also bring a message, or his presence might be welcome to Honecker as manifestation of Kremlin support. The bottom line is that we do not know why a visit was arranged on short notice. The Soviets are not saying, but it is intriguing that they tell us as much as they do. They show more interest in sharing information since the crisis began. That both positive and vaguely troubling development suggests how deeply they worry that the situation could get out of hand. It is almost as if, after years of insisting the GDR is fully sovereign, they are gingerly dusting off old Four Power concepts. Gorbachev referred to Soviet responsibilities as a World War II victor in his speech last week. I thought he was reminding us that the Soviets guaranteed the postwar order, but as so often, he was ambiguous. He may have been laying the groundwork for Quadripartite cooperation should events require, not just reserving unilateral rights.

Neues Forum's latest statement "welcomed" the Politburo declaration as "a first sign of grappling with the deep-seated problems." However, it added, real dialogue would be possible only when political prisoners were released, when grassroots citizen groups had been accepted, and when there was freedom of press and assembly.

Many consider Gerald Ford's signing of the Helsinki Final Act and his missteps on the CSCE process in debate with Jimmy Carter major factors in his loss of the 1976 election. Ford writes in the *Washington Post*: "The encouraging changes in Poland, Hungary, East Germany . . . make me prouder than ever to have signed the Helsinki accords. I did not symbolize an America abandoning the hopes and aspirations of the captive nations, as many pundits and some former governors charged at the time. Rather, I acted for 200 million Americans by countersigning the East Europeans' own initial and cautious declarations of independence, with formal Soviet concurrence." Partisanship aside, he has a point many may only now realize.

OCTOBER 15

Gaby and I took the Fukuyama delegation for lunch to Friedrichshagen. That little community on the Müggelsee, Berlin's largest lake, is home to the Friedrichshof, which doubles as disco and cabaret and is owned by a nuclear physicist who preferred to get rich (in GDR Marks) by working twelve hours a day to produce the best meals we have had in the country. The restaurant exemplifies the diversity and entrepreneurial spirit that exist in nooks and crannies here. Since it was full, however, we settled for its neighbor, the Spindel, with quainter atmosphere and nearly as solid a kitchen. This was its monthly "Asian Day," when the menu is quasi-Chinese. S. would have been critical, but we enjoyed it. Though many restaurants make such efforts to satisfy the craving to partake of the outside world, culinary tastes are conservative. Were the "Bulgarian specialties" genuine? I once asked in an establishment on Wilhelm-Pieck-Strasse. "Not really," the waitress admitted. "We put red peppers on top to make 'Sofia Beefsteak' look exotic, but our customers want familiar food."

Amid high rises outside Erfurt, Janice once found what *Neue Zeit* called the GDR's first Vietnamese restaurant, but the closest to an Asian dish it offered was curried *Eisbein*, a pig's knuckle Berliners claim as their specialty. The manager said he had a Vietnamese cook, but "we have to go slowly with our public." Restaurants like the Spindel or the new Italian (a genuine first) in Köpenick, do offer quality to a receptive audience, but in this, as much else, Gaby says the GDR reminds her of 1950s West Germany, a provincial, more old-fashioned, ingrown society, yet to discover much of the non-German world.

Colorful wind-surfers were enjoying perhaps the year's last Sunday sunshine on the lake, but we moved on after lunch to Gethsemane Church. It was much as last Sunday, a mix of young activists, the curious, and those (often middle-aged couples) who were sampling the reading table. Outside, however, the police had pulled back. There were no obvious Stasi, but also no political debates and no SED defenders, spontaneous or delegated. The few police on the corner and 100 bystanders watched benignly as young people danced to rock music. A circling squad car was reassured by the patrolmen. Our visitors may have been disappointed not to see more drama, but revolutions take many forms. Two weeks ago the police would never have tolerated unlicensed street-dancing.

OCTOBER 16

In an effort to lower temperatures and make its "dialogue" line more plausible, the regime has released all but eleven of those arrested over the

40th Anniversary weekend. The amnesty's scope is actually broader than officially acknowledged and includes people detained last month in Leipzig as well as several Berliners held since June when they protested the Chinese crackdown. We hear, however, that Honecker is still fighting in the Politburo against major changes. After a quiet weekend, everyone asks how large the Leipzig demonstration will be this evening.

Meanwhile, Glasnost is breaking out everywhere. Particularly the youth paper, the provincial dailies, and the Bloc Party journals are becoming challenging and rewarding to read instead of a gray bore. *Neues Deutschland* and the evening news show "Aktuelle Kamera" are showing signs of life. Most Politburo members are out telling citizens—especially factory workers—that they want to "talk openly." There are clear indications, however, that the SED is trying to limit the openness even as it proclaims the process its idea. Nine-tenths of *Neues Deutschland*'s letters, like nine-tenths of the Politburo declaration to which they supposedly responded, were "old-think." Significantly, the leadership openly opposes the extraordinary Plenum that would-be Party reformers (or pragmatists) see as the SED's only hope to regain the initiative. Its argument that time is needed to develop new policies suggests a classic formula of delay in the hope pressures will relax until they can be co-opted into familiar channels.

Three signs of the times: The Writers Association resolved that "what is now necessary is revolutionary reform; reform is not to be feared but rather the fear of reform." Fall school holidays began Saturday, and by Sunday 1,500 had used vacation visas to cross the Hungarian border to Austria, three times the "norm" of past weeks. A pro-reform demonstration attracted 20,000 in Plauen, a city of 77,000, a remarkable commentary on attitudes throughout the industrial south. The church urges caution in Leipzig this evening and may try to keep young people inside in order not to endanger the tender shoot of dialogue. Stolpe hints this, and the Leipzig SED press reports that talks about channeling the demonstrations into new forms are being held. Both the church and those within the SED who question the Politburo's perception of reality fear the consequences of an incident.

Heather and Janice came back from a day of talking with the new groups to tell me about last night's concert in Salvation Church. Rock musicians, who last month were virtually the first to speak out, performed original songs full of biting allusions to politicians who are unable to understand what has driven young people into the refugee camps of the Federal Republic or the streets of the GDR. Their music was interspersed with personal experiences, such as that of a teacher fired after joining Neues Forum. There was talk about organizing a new student association, and actors from the Deutsches Theater urged support for a freedom-of-the-press demonstration on November 4. At the end, everyone sang John Lennon's "All We Are Saying Is Give Peace a Chance."

OCTOBER 17

Leipzig has again made history. While Honecker doles out small changes and resists a Plenum, 100,000 marched for reform and new leaders. Police merely rerouted traffic. The protests, Imre pointed out when he called, are growing geometrically. Yesterday's was double last week's. By mid-afternoon, loudspeakers were broadcasting calls by an SED secretary, a worker, and a pastor for people to stay off the streets and pursue instead a church-state dialogue. Leaflets signed by the University rector and two professors were distributed on street corners with the message "Your call has been heard. The time for demonstrations is past." Obviously, the appeals had no effect.

The crowd in front of the Opera was predominantly young, but with a good sprinkling of other ages. As the "Join us" chants began, Imre saw an elderly couple out for a stroll exchange sheepish looks and close ranks. Others followed. There were many more signs, mostly for free media, travel, and ecology, but also "free elections." There were derisive whistles at Workers' Militia blocking off the Old Town, but no trouble. The crowd circled the Ringstrasse and disbanded back at the Opera. Members of the Western press were still barred, but as part of the new Glasnost, GDR reporters were there. Television showed no pictures but praised both sides' restraint. Imre too was impressed by the crowd's discipline. He saw a few beer-quaffing Skinheads at one point and thought an incident was likely, but peer pressure prevailed.

Dresden's dialogue continued into late evening Monday. At one point, 10,000 impatient citizens gathered in front of the town hall, chanting "Here and now!" After some hesitation, the mayor and the Group of 20 appeared together and urged them to disband. But Imre's church contacts remain worried about the mood in that city where the worst troubles occurred earlier in the month.

Leipzig's massive happening and Dresden's brittle mood are poles of the new reality within which the Politburo, expanded by district first secretaries, is again meeting. No one knows whether it will resolve its fight over "how much" and "how fast" today, but Janice spotted a claim in the Leipzig SED paper that the Central Committee will convene in "four weeks," a month early. At the same time, Vogel tells Dick, Honecker acts shockingly out of touch.

I had asked Heather to introduce me to Neues Forum leaders, and Monday evening she took Gaby and me to Jens Reich and his wife, who live in a comfortable, high-ceilinged, book-stuffed apartment in the Koloniestrasse, off the Pankow market square five minutes from our house. Their summer dacha, we learned, is down the road from that of our friends where in August we had discussed the growing crisis. The world of GDR intellectuals is small and ingrown, and almost everyone is at least an acquaintance of an acquaintance. That helps explain why Neues Forum can rapidly form chapters throughout the country despite almost complete lack of modern communications technology.

The Reichs are warm, hospitable people, somewhat overwhelmed by the sudden change in their lives (who would not be?). Telephone and door bell rang constantly, and visitors streamed in. Mrs. Reich tried to cook a hot meal between our talk and the West German journalist who had been promised a few minutes. About that prospect at least, neither Reich was optimistic. As the first reports from Leipzig came in, I asked whether the SED could recover. "The classical approach would be to change leadership," Jens Reich answered. New leaders might just be able to persuade people to give them a chance, but the Honecker team was too discredited. This, he hastened to add, was not Neues Forum's platform; it was the SED's decision. Neues Forum was still primarily interested in stimulating multiple views.

Interest was great, Professor Reich said as his wife went off to answer the door again, and official attitudes were less hostile. Neues Forum was no longer called "treasonous," but "only superfluous." He expected it to exist in an undefined gray area for some time, neither formally acknowledged nor forbidden, but legal ambiguity was not retarding growth. Inquiries were pouring in, and every type of club wanted speakers. Those with official ties put a fig leaf on the invitation by describing it as for the individual only. A priority now that Neues Forum had name recognition and membership, Reich indicated, was to improve its structure and, inevitably, become more programmatic. It had drawn up a "catalog" of political, social, economic, and environmental problems, he said, and eventually a consensus national platform proposing some solutions could emerge from grassroots meetings.

Reich emphasized his belief that it was desirable to reform and legitimize GDR socialism, not reopen the German National Question. He was sanguine, he said, about what the groups could accomplish, unconcerned about fragmentation, but he cautioned us not to double-count. Many activists belonged to several groups, he noted. For example, all members of the new Social Democratic Party (SDP) were also in Neues Forum. There was no inconsistency, Reich said. One was a political party, the other a mass intellectual movement.

Has Gorbachev decided to apply more direct pressure for reform than during his carefully balanced visit just ten days ago? I doubt he will violate his "noninterference" principle. He has reason to believe the SED is moving his way without heavy-handed interference that, whatever the motive, could damage him in the West. The bottom line of his Berlin sojourn was that the Soviets are vitally interested, will try to exercise influence, but will no longer play Deus ex machina. Honecker paid anxious court for two days, but I recall his smile when Gorbachev said decisions were "made in Berlin, not Moscow." That gave Honecker freedom but left him responsible for the tough choices. Most East Germans shouting his name see the Soviet reformer more as inspiration than savior. We went to the theater in Potsdam on Saturday. Ulrich Plenzdorf, a GDR dramatist, had adapted a Soviet Glasnost novel for the stage, and "Perestroika" was scrawled in bold letters across the back wall of the set. The politicized audience applauded frequently. The biggest response was to "We must organize to help ourselves."

SED intellectuals are flirting with Neues Forum. An example is Claus Montag, doyen of America studies. After the war, he finished school in West Berlin (his grandmother lived on Gaby's street) and chose the GDR from commitment. He now helps Neues Forum–Potsdam because he sees a last chance to make socialism work.

Bilateral consultations are still on next week, despite Secretary Baker's concern that we not get too close to the tottering Honecker. Because Dick flies to Washington tomorrow, I gave him my thoughts about where the GDR is and what we should be doing. The embassy had anticipated, I recalled, more repression for the rest of the Honecker era and perhaps the start of his successor's time, but within two days of the 40th Anniversary celebrations the regime had turned to dialogue. This was almost surely a tactic to reduce tensions and keep power with minimal change, but the choice to play the reform game rather than get tough was important.

The gambit, I told Dick, was unlikely to work. Everything was breaking against Honecker: Hitherto passive constituencies were developing a taste for action; the hemorrhage of young people west continued; the independent movements were winning support; and above all, street politics showed that a spark could ignite fully unpredictable consequences. The question was not whether Honecker would get away with it—he almost surely would not for long—but whether SED pragmatists could convince him and his circle to step aside. Only newer faces would have any chance to master the situation, and the time for decision was ever shorter. In early summer, Party moderates accepted that the old men would hold on at least until the May 1990 Congress and probably a year or two longer; after the emigration flood began, they shortened their time frame to three to six months: Now the key issue is whether the Plenum will be moved up from December.

Beyond that, I confessed, the waters were uncharted. The track record of the SED suggested it would never bring itself to do more than too little, too late. Public appetites would grow, especially as new groups gained stature and citizens became accustomed to open politics. What seemed daring and possibly adequate a few months back would probably be inadequate by the time a compromised version was acceptable to the traditional power brokers. There was, however, just a chance that the SED could start serious reform. There was societal consensus on much, most obviously, more open media and mature interaction between bureaucrats and citizens, generally speaking, on Glasnost. Without getting into Perestroika, bold leadership could probably improve public morale quickly. Such an SED might meet halfway groups that almost unanimously said they wanted only to reform socialism. While there was surely a tactical element to those statements, many activists were sincere. Conceivably the GDR could gain a breathing space with significant reforms that did not call its socialist identity into question. That would provide time and a quieter atmosphere in which to address more fundamental issues. I thought the GDR had intensified politics in its future: new groups outside the establishment, newly demanding bodies within it, and a no longer so hierarchical, conservative, all-powerful SED. But the probability, I said to Dick, was still politics, not outright revolution.

All this must increase West German involvement with the GDR. It would attract high-level Soviet attention, and probably efforts to influence a moderate reform course. The United States would inevitably be drawn into the wake of its two most important fellow actors in Europe, but, returning to old themes, I said we lacked leverage of our own, and thus real options, though GDR events were bound to affect our security. As soon as politically feasible, we should pursue greater engagement along mutually reinforcing tracks: with the Opposition, which would become increasingly important, but also with the power elite.

Finally, I argued again, we would hurt ourselves with the Opposition as well as with the SED if our reunification rhetoric outpaced Bonn's. The activists either wanted to make the GDR viable or considered it tactically foolish to question its existence. The United States should stand for self-determination, therefore, but not express itself on what form of state or states this would ultimately produce. It need say only that reform was required by the CSCE's human rights charter and gave the GDR its sole chance to legitimize its existence.

Pierre Shostal's preference for our November weekend trip is Dresden. His main purpose in calling, however, was to congratulate me on promotion into the Senior Foreign Service. I gave Gaby the news but said I would be home late. I first had to visit Sebastian Pflugbeil, whom I found winningly modest and determined but pessimistic, skeptical of SED claims, and half anticipating a crackdown. Nevertheless, he was encouraged at the landslide response to Neues Forum and committed to continue as the only honorable course. The Reichs had said that they became involved because they could not face their children if they did not try to make a difference. Both Jens Reich and Pflugbeil are scientists with good research positions. Their suspect views kept them out of the "travel cadre"—they were not allowed to attend conferences abroad—so they have been at a disadvantage. Their material existence is reasonably comfortable, however, and I can believe that they put themselves in exposed positions from idealism, not from a sense of personal persecution. Whatever their fate, they are impressive.

I stood in the street outside Pflugbeil's apartment afterward and talked with Heather. Like all of us, she has worked nonstop since late summer, but she feels bad about starting a brief holiday in England tomorrow and leaving us shorthanded. "Enjoy it," I told her. "You've earned it. The story will still be here when you get back. Even the GDR does not change that much in a week."

Gaby stayed up, and champagne was cold when I reached home just before midnight after another fifteen-hour day.

4

The Peaceful Revolution
October 18, 1989—
November 12, 1989

OCTOBER 18 (Noon)

The Central Committee has convened to discuss "organizational matters"—code for personnel changes. The Soviet Embassy alerted Tass and *Pravda* to "stand by." We have nothing concrete, but in two talks since the weekend Wolfgang Vogel gave Dick a sense of events, and Dick passed me his notes before flying off this morning. In the first conversation, the lawyer said Honecker was determined to hang on and keep his full Politburo. He argued that because any successor would come in too burdened with expectations and problems, the Old Guard should pass the baton only when the slate was clean. Last night, however, Vogel indicated Honecker had been forced to reassess. He would stay indefinitely, but some older people on whom he has relied would be retired, and fresh blood brought in.

There will also be new policies, Vogel indicated. The media have been changing for a week, though *Neues Deutschland* and television news lag, and he expects major travel liberalization. It is less certain the SED can accommodate new politics, but the more sweeping the retreat from discredited leaders, the more chance it will have to recover the initiative. The situation remains fluid, however. Vogel characterized the atmosphere in the Politburo as—not to beat around the bush—"shitty" (*beschissen*). Some remain ready to use force, he warned. If there were an incident during a protest, the consequences would be grim. In effect, he confirmed what Basler told us: the argument about whether to crack down is not settled.

Vogel, whom Dick had never seen so depressed, said Honecker was divorced from reality. He claimed this was why he himself had appealed publicly last week for release of all East Germans jailed for trying to flee the country. When Honecker asked for advice, Vogel said he urged him to order the bureaucracy to stop intimidating emigration applicants. After checking, Honecker called back to say the officials were polite and to ask what the problem was. He could not comprehend, Vogel said, that the Interior Ministry had become more impossible and that people were increasingly cynical about legal forms. The Honecker era thus seems to be nearing its end, but what follows is unclear. That is probably why Zaikov has come.

OCTOBER 18 (6:00 P.M.)

I kept a 12:30 lunch at the Domklause. Heinz Kosin, an older Central Committee researcher rumored to have intelligence ties but one of my best discussion partners, has always portrayed himself as a reform Communist willing to talk with relative frankness and not hide his belief that only a more democratic socialism can justify the GDR's existence. He bases his hope for the SED on West German Social Democratic influence and Gorbachev. Today he was by turn optimistic and worried. Honecker's fate was up in the air, Kosin said, but we should know within hours. As he started to the restaurant, he was told Schabowski would brief Party "activists" this afternoon. Most of the SED would be sympathetic to a German variant of Glasnost and Perestroika, and the institutes were working on bold concepts, he said. Papers could be pulled quickly out of drawers if new leaders truly wanted a fresh start. He did not know whether Dresden and Leipzig officials had talked with protestors on their own, he admitted. Politburo splits may have given them leeway. Berghofer, however, was Modrow's man. Like Gorbachev, Modrow had sought out those who shared his views to fill key jobs, Kosin claimed. "The difference is that it is much easier to find such people in the GDR than in the Soviet Union."

I turned on the radio when I reached my car, parked semi-legally by the footbridge to the Museum Island. It was 2:15 P.M., and the announcer was reading the laconic ADN bulletin that Honecker had been removed from all Party and state positions at his own wish, that Krenz had replaced him, and that an extraordinary Plenum would be held next month. The next twenty minutes were agonizing. For a half hour every Wednesday, Unter den Linden is blocked while goose-stepping soldiers relieve the watch at the Neue Wache. That pompous and chilling tourist spectacle forced me to circle the inner city on car-choked Spandauer and then Leipziger Strasse, as precious minutes ticked by. Finally at the embassy, I raced up three flights of stairs to find Imre, reliable as ever, on his way to dispatch the news. J.D. had telephoned the State Department's Operations Center to alert Secretary Baker and advise that our analysis would follow. I went to my typewriter, and we were on the wire within two hours.

That done, I sat back to sort out my thoughts. Those ADN lines signaled the end of an eighteen-year reign during which Honecker brought the GDR nearly full circle—from international outlaw, through member of the United Nations and the CSCE, to new isolation as Eastern Europe's most prominent reform holdout. The seventy-seven-year-old opened his country with an inner-German policy that gave millions the chance to visit the Federal Republic, but contradictions between their experiences in the liberal West and the stagnant neo-Stalinism they found at home increased discontent. At least until yesterday, Honecker believed he could hold on by sacrificing aides. What finally toppled him was the convergence this summer and fall of three factors: his failing health, mass flight of East Germans through the holes to the rear of the Berlin Wall, and finally the civic boldness that began to demand change in the streets. The Leipzig marchers, following protests over the 40th Anniversary weekend, apparently persuaded the last establishment doubters.

Egon Krenz, at age fifty-two the youngest in the Politburo, starts with great problems, not least a reputation as one of that body's toughest, but not brightest. He climbed the same ladder as Honecker, from youth organization leader to the Politburo, where like his patron previously he was responsible for security, including the Stasi. Many young people told me that if Krenz got the top job they would leave, because he is even less flexible than the Old Guard. That is not necessarily the final judgment. Honecker himself, though at the end badly out of phase with the Gorbachev era, was more moderate than his reputation as builder of the Wall led observers to expect. Krenz has handled the top-cop portfolio; now he must satisfy other constituencies. Whenever I have been up close to him, his politician's traits and presence have impressed me.

Krenz is credible to leadership elements that supported Honecker as long as they could, and at best a question mark for all who are now stirring GDR politics. Until he disproves it, he will be seen as the conservatives' answer to the dilemma of how to change minimally while dissipating popular pressures, restraining them by force if necessary, and ultimately absorbing them. But possibly there is more to both man and moment. He is now his own boss, not just a faithful reflection of elderly mentors. Pragmatic instinct may cause him to trim course better to the winds blowing through this land. Even then, Krenz is unlikely to seek radical reform models in Moscow, much less Budapest or Warsaw. He might, however, give leeway to would-be reformers within and without the SED who want to develop a GDR socialism that would build on what remains the region's strongest (though inadequate) economy while enlisting popular support through genuine dialogue. The challenge—to which he comes with many doubters, except within the Politburo's circled wagons—is to act boldly enough to catch up to a still accelerating crisis.

In late afternoon, ADN announced that two of Honecker's closest and most controversial aides have been dismissed: Joachim Herrmann, custodian of the discredited media policy, and Günter Mittag, sickly boss of the stagnating economy. Krenz is to speak on television at 8:00 P.M. Reaching out on his first day is a welcome change from secretive government by press release. I will eat a *Wurst* and watch with J.D. and Imre so we can give the State Department a quick reaction.

It is noon in Washington, and there will be questions at the daily press briefing. Dick is over the Atlantic, but J.D. spoke to Pierre Shostal. We cannot prejudge whether Krenz will pursue the cautious opening of the past week or jump backward, he noted. This argues for the United States to be carefully noncommittal, along these lines: We are watching closely; it is an internal affair, but it is in everyone's interest for the new leader to heed the people.

OCTOBER 18 (11:00 P.M.)

Krenz damned Honecker with faint praise, but there were no bold departures. With only flashes of personality, he read mostly familiar lines from neatly stacked sheets of paper. Mistakes had been made, but they had now been aired, he said. The Plenum should have met sooner, but it would reconvene once working groups had formulated concrete proposals. The new leader reaffirmed the Party's old leading role, saying that without the SED there was no GDR, and he engaged in some Bonn-bashing. Above all, he held out no hand to the Opposition. There should be more debate, he agreed, but there were enough forums. There was no gesture, no plea for time to find better answers. Much like last week's Politburo declaration, too little was new to persuade many that the SED has a concept for mastering the crisis. Krenz muffed a chance to rally the country. He may not have many more.

OCTOBER 19

Krenz has used his first twenty-four hours to establish an image of vigor appropriate to what he admits is a crisis. Thus far, however, he has done most to burnish credentials where he is relatively strong—with the Party leadership—and least where he is highly suspect, with the new political forces. Even before last night's disappointing speech, the new man had smiled an interview into a camera and received the heads of the Bloc Parties and mass organizations. He started Thursday at a factory pressing the flesh and talking to workers. Mostly, this will reassure old-line power brokers that he is what they want to ensure only enough change to keep the GDR fundamentally the same. It is unlikely to impress those with whom, to be generous, he has a credibility problem.

That is not to say Krenz is an inveterate hard-liner following a hard line. The latter would be inaccurate, at least for now. The regime put the billy clubs away two days after the 40th Anniversary weekend. Dialogue and promise of undefined reform is the line the Politburo set down last week, and Krenz elaborated on slightly yesterday. If he proves to be only a transitional figure, as many journalists predict, it will be because he has failed, not because his Party opted for a "Chernenko" waffle. He is fifty-two years old, not without health problems, but vigorous in appearance and a full-blooded politician who intends to make his own running. At this point, however, he is the Old Guard's vehicle. The departures of Mittag and Herrmann actually increased the Politburo's average age. There is no fresh blood yet, and the clockwork Plenum suggests the gerontocracy is keeping the lid on even intra-Party democracy.

If only to fortify his position, Krenz must put his own people into key positions and move out fossilized holdovers. It matters how fast this happens and who benefits. He needs a competent Mittag successor to put substance behind his pledge to begin to remake the economy at next month's Plenum. Whether moderates like Modrow and Lorenz are promoted and brought to Berlin will give a better idea how genuine Krenz's "dialogue" is. Until then, it is not only activists who will suspect he is just pursuing a tactic, and too cautiously to have a chance of putting things back together.

A second set of questions revolves around programs. Until ten days ago, Honecker was saying the GDR would pursue "continuity and renewal," but everyone knew all emphasis was on the first noun. Now Krenz balances that formula a bit. There are a few points of convergence between the emerging SED program and the embryo Neues Forum platform Jens Reich gave us, such as a more open press and a meaningful wage system. Obviously, there are many more differences. Nothing Krenz has said suggests he could tolerate the Opposition's call for "separation of powers and effective public control of all defense and security organs by the people's representatives, . . . above all, reformed voting procedures."

The first test of whether Krenz can channel popular dissatisfaction may come at next month's Plenum. If his working groups formulate specific proposals that take account of demands being raised outside the Party, Krenz may gain standing. If he fobs off the Plenum as a simple consultation, the suspicion that he is playing for time will become a certainty. Even before then, Krenz will almost surely be confronted with more and larger street protests of the kind that led to Honecker's fall.

Heinz Kosin insists that a majority of SED members share Neues Forum's views, but there remain big hurdles to cooperation. Party seniors are convinced Neues Forum leaders are sworn enemies of a socialist GDR, not the reformers they claim. SED discipline shows cracks as the Politburo plays Nero in a Germanic Rome, but it remains strong. Without a green light, communication between Party members and the new groups is circumscribed.

The widely respected Stephan Hermlin said at the beginning of the week that he disagreed with the Opposition but it should be listened to: "If one wants a real dialogue and not another monologue dressed up as a dialogue—what we have been masters at—then one must bravely tackle the question of whether specific individuals fit into your scheme of things and whether views that perhaps the Communists do not entirely like are aired in public." On the Politburo slogan "Continuity and Renewal," he added: "In the present situation, I am in favor, for a while at any rate, of doing without . . . 'continuity.' " If Krenz cannot catch up to a lifelong Communist like Hermlin, who two years ago publicly preached "patience," he has no chance of making the official policy of greater openness work. But before his odds can truly be assessed, we are in for an autumn of more intense politicking than the GDR has yet known, with high stakes, few rules to guide either participants or observers, and jokers throughout the deck.

Pete Ito greeted Dick at the airport with a straight-faced query: "Mr. Ambassador, what do you think of the Krenz government?" Dick recovered quickly and is much in demand at State today.

Speaking two days before Honecker fell, on the "historic opportunity" to achieve in cooperation with Moscow a "Europe whole and free," Secretary Baker included this important passage:

> Both we and the Soviet Union are challenged to deal with change in the countries behind the now rusting Iron Curtain. . . . These nations, however, cannot be treated as a single case. . . . In East Germany, the people themselves are taking bold steps. As I said last week, it is time for Perestroika and Glasnost to come to East Germany. The status quo is as unacceptable to the people of that nation as it is to the peoples of Poland and Hungary. The people of East Germany cannot be forever denied at home the better life that they now seek by fleeing to the West. Of course the United States and our NATO partners have long supported the reconciliation of the German People. Their legitimate rights must some day be met. But let me be clear—reconciliation through self-determination can only be achieved in peace and freedom. Normalization must occur on the basis of Western values with the end result being a people integrated into the Community of Democratic Nations.

Was it from respect for what Gorbachev can accept that Baker referred to "reconciliation" not "reunification"? There was a further statement: "It is not our purpose to exploit the movement toward freedom . . . to harm the security of the Soviet Union." But "normalization" only "on the basis of

Western values" sounds as if there is concern Gorbachev may soon repackage Stalin's proposal for a neutral Germany.

J.D. confirmed my four-week home leave beginning November 13. I have promised my parents, and the State Department mandates that such leave be taken to keep officers in touch with the United States. Nevertheless, I am concerned about missing history. Go home, J.D. said. The story will still be here when you get back. He is right, of course—but I remember telling Heather two days and one general secretary ago that she would not miss much if she left for a week.

OCTOBER 20

Two weeks ago, the GDR was Eastern Europe's conservative bastion. In Day Two of the Krenz era, it is embarked on reforms, both officially sanctioned and spontaneous. It is Glasnost, or to use the "in" slogans, the "Renewal" or "Turn" (*Wende*), but not yet really Perestroika. How consequential and permanent the changes are, how much the new leader's doing and to his liking, no one knows, but Krenz's GDR is rapidly distancing itself from Honecker's.

At a Berlin factory on Thursday, Krenz apologized that the Party has ignored workers. Television carried long segments of spontaneous debate that revealed a politician who believes he need not shy from unstructured interaction, as Honecker did. A worker told him many fled because their problems were covered up. This has begun to change, hasn't it? Krenz asked. To Krenz's plea that surely workers and Politburo had common interests came the answer that no one in Wandlitz knew what it was like to search for spare automobile parts after work. Another worker told Krenz to his face that his first speech was superficial. He replied, "I'll try to do better next time, but some things can't be answered concretely today. We don't have a magic wand to solve everything at once."

More surprising was that talking with the church was next on Krenz's agenda. This seemed to say that the SED, which had frozen discourse for two years, now wanted the bishops to help it communicate with the disaffected. He apparently recognizes that he must go beyond his own narrow base.

Imre's contacts told him the church had been promised an appointment with Honecker last week. It had expected cancellation when he was removed, but Krenz kept the date. (This tidbit says much about Honecker, who was maneuvering to save himself only days before he was dropped.) The seventy-five-minute session at a hunting lodge near Berlin produced few specifics, but Krenz went out of his way to sound forthcoming. Bishop Leich said he was a better communicator in a small circle than wooden appearances on television indicated—exactly my experience. Leich and Stolpe stressed the need for the state to talk with the new groups. Discussion of platforms in government-provided facilities would reduce pressure for street protests. Krenz was noncommittal, but he did claim he went to Leipzig last week to prevent violence. Every citizen should have a passport, the church leaders said, and the GDR needed new electoral procedures, a real parliament, and separation of Party from government. Krenz made notes, we heard, but no promises. Imre's sources, however, believe he is considering increasing the legislature's power and easing travel. Leich and Stolpe do not tend toward euphoria, Imre points out, but for the moment the church will give Krenz the benefit of the doubt.

In his speech Wednesday, Krenz signaled that "even *Neues Deutschland*" had to become worth reading, and the Party daily is complying. It revealed that despite the "unanimous" decision to retire Honecker, the Plenum had a brief dispute. Modrow called unsuccessfully for real debate. "Truth," he said, in a line that could have come from a Neues Forum manifesto, "must be searched for in dialogue and not proclaimed from above." Krenz's putative rival, Schabowski, moved to close the session but claimed he favored early resumption. Intriguingly, for what it suggests about his potential support in the Central Committee if not Politburo, Modrow also proposed that Krenz's speech include more self-criticism. ADN, but not *Neues Deutschland*, reported that this amendment was adopted. *Neues Deutschland*'s scarcely veiled editorial attack on Honecker also sought to underline change: "The Party is . . . initiating a turn (*Wende*). . . . Our Party is showing the courage to face truth. It is making an end to optimistic whitewash and braggadocio."

Television had a "first" last night, a call-in talk show during which politicians sounded new notes on the opposition, price subsidies, and travel. Those on the hot seat included Otto Reinhold and Dresden's Berghofer. Schnitzler, for decades a notorious polemicist, said scarcely a word. The evening belonged to those with a chance to be believed. Reinhold set the tone by apologizing for the times he had been ordered to defend wrong policies. He made headlines by indicating that the new travel law may guarantee everyone a passport. Berghofer, handsome, self-possessed, and comfortable on camera, said Dresden could not afford to improve living conditions unless rents were raised. At Aspen in May, Reinhold had brushed off a similar idea; last night he supported it. Though no panelist went so far, the moderator said callers favored legalizing "the Opposition." He apologized for the program's disorder. It was a first try, he explained, but it would become a regular feature.

Activism has reached the universities, hitherto an oasis of careerism. On Tuesday, 6,000 Humboldt students spilled over into nine auditoriums. A teacher and a student from an environmental group told Janice that the heated, inconclusive argument was over whether an independent organization should replace the FDJ on campus.

On a different front, the Theater Association has applied for a permit to demonstrate in Berlin on November 19 for freedom of the press. (The law requires a permit application thirty days in advance.) Journalists, especially at *Der Morgen*, are agitating for their association to join. The chance of the demonstration being approved has gone up, now that a more open press is official policy. Some activists are trying to take the media issue into their own hands, however. The Environmental Library, a group that operates out of a church basement and played a major role in confrontations with the Stasi nearly two years ago, has published several issues of *Telegraph*, a newsletter. A ten-page edition put to bed at midnight on October 18 combined skeptical reaction to Krenz with articles on the student meetings, the new Social Democratic Party, and small wildcat strikes. Pflugbeil told me Neues Forum will try to publish ten pages every two months. Even this modest goal is problematical, however, since Neues Forum has no reproduction equipment. This illustrates the practical difficulties all the groups face. The regime retains a virtual technology monopoly.

First word has come of protests in the hitherto quiet north, at Neubrandenburg and Greifswald.

OCTOBER 21

Most of this Saturday was spent in the office, but I joined Gaby in late afternoon to shop. As I carried the bags into our house, however, the telephone rang. Tom Quinzio, the embassy's budget officer, had seen police in Alexanderplatz and reinforcements moving down Prenzlauer Allee. When I arrived, Alexanderplatz was back almost to normal, but passersby described a demonstration against police brutality. Schabowski had come, and so had television cameras, they said; turn on the news.

The scenes were repeated all evening, for the first time with little difference in broadcasts West and East. Wearing an open-neck shirt, Schabowski spoke freely in broad Berlin dialect with a youthful, not overly respectful, crowd of 1,000 to 2,000. He implied the demonstration law might be liberalized, but warned against inadvertent violence should the streets remain the focus of politics. He was conciliatory about the police-brutality charges and said a travel law had top priority. In an exchange typical for what it showed of protestor suspicion and the sudden candor breaking through Politburo clichés, one young man said it was good Schabowski had come to talk, but if the travel law "was again a trick, that would be very bad." Schabowski's response: "We are going to have to live for some time with the idea that everything we do will be thought a possible trick. . . . The Party, the Central Committee, and our general secretary, Egon Krenz, are serious."

OCTOBER 23

Krenz spoke with Gorbachev on the telephone Saturday. As if reciting a mantra to banish Honecker's spirit, he reportedly acknowledged that "the experiences of Soviet Communists with Perestroika in their land are also meaningful for the GDR," and he accepted an invitation to visit Moscow "in the near future" to receive a personal blessing. In one of the better passages of his mostly "old-thinking" inaugural address last week, Krenz paraphrased Gorbachev's Berlin comment about the need for timely reforms. Now he is identifying himself not only with the Soviet Union—Honecker always did that to show the GDR had an important ally—but also with the spirit of Gorbachev's policies. To drive the symbolism home, the Post Office announced it will again permit import of the Soviet magazine *Sputnik*. The ban on that reform publication last year was probably the act that contributed most to the alienation of SED members, whether activists for whom Moscow was always the model or would-be reformers. A series that undermined the SED's anti-Nazi legitimacy by asking whether "Hitler would have been possible without Stalin" had been too much for Honecker. At the time, the loyal Krenz denied to Frank Meehan and me that the GDR and the Soviets were at loggerheads about history. Krenz now acts differently, but this is just one of many instances where he must overcome his own history if he is to get control of the speeding train.

The more we can learn about how Krenz toppled Honecker, the better we can judge his own survival chances. The following is the most plausible, though not necessarily fully objective, account Imre and I have pieced together, mainly from Eastern Europeans:

- Krenz decided to try for power just before October 7 when he realized how out of touch Honecker was. When it was apparent by mid-afternoon on October 9 that the evening's protest in Leipzig would be too large to repress without high casualties, Krenz held the security forces back. He then pushed unsuccessfully for leadership change in the Politburo the next day. That session was able to agree only that a Plenum could not be delayed beyond October 18, and personnel changes would have to be made before then lest the Plenum become uncontrollable and use its statutory authority to impose even more radical solutions. At that point, Honecker believed he could survive by sacrificing colleagues and was still maneuvering—witness his plan to meet church leaders.

- The October 16 Leipzig march must have been a sobering warning, and the next day Honecker gave a report so clearly divorced from reality that the last Politburo doubters were convinced. A Hungarian said it actually provoked disbelieving laughter. Reportedly only Mittag and Herrmann voted to keep him. An SED source claimed Honecker then proposed his close friend Mittag as successor, but this "Chernenko" option had no backing. The way was then clear for Krenz's unanimous selection, word of which was put about as a no-argument decision when the Plenum began to assemble the following morning.

- According to Eastern diplomats, the Politburo recognized that the seven other members over the age of seventy also must go, but because they provided key votes they would get honorable retirements. Their departures could be staggered through the May Congress. Younger Politburo members are perhaps equally guilty of incompetence—cadre boss Dohlus, for example—but may benefit from what Helmut Kohl once called the "grace of late birth."

Our interlocutors believe Krenz must tap Modrow to give his team stature, but it seems to me that how fast he moves is as vital. Working groups are to ready a program by next month. If Krenz is not strong enough to get his own people to run that process now, he is unlikely to have time to build his base in the ordinary way. From one end of the spectrum, an activist Janice met in a Dresden café said, "We'll give Krenz four weeks." Asked about a 100-day honeymoon, he replied, "I don't know if he has that long." From the other end of the spectrum, the Plenum may assert itself as early as next week. Even the limited debate at last week's coronation showed its concern that Krenz was starting too slowly.

Over the weekend, word of demonstrations in Rostock (extreme north) and Zittau (extreme southeast) came. The pattern was familiar: thousands in the streets, no police interference, then the beginning of talk with local officials. *Neues Deutschland* (yes, *Neues Deutschland!*) described a 20,000-strong protest in the deep south, in Plauen again. In Leipzig, the SED, cultural figures, and the Opposition set up a Sunday Hyde Park Corner in Symphony Hall hosted by Kurt Masur, to siphon off street frustration. *Neues Deutschland* broke new ground by quoting Neues Forum spokesmen, though it appended Masur's comment: "You Neues Forum people worry me because you begin by preaching." The one decision was to meet every week so that, in best German fashion, "we proceed from positions to concepts and actions to business-like work."

Signs of discontent in existing institutions proliferate. A potentially significant one involves a report that workers at the Wilhelm Pieck Tool & Regulator Factory in a Berlin suburb have left the FDGB and started an independent union, "Reform." They claimed to be circulating a political and social program to other factories. Janice is getting on it.

Dry tinder is everywhere, but the German sense of order was still evident in Berlin on Saturday. GDR and West Berlin media both noted approvingly that demonstrators used the underground passageway to reach the other side of Alexanderplatz rather than disrupt traffic. Which tendency wins out, radical or structured, remains uncertain, but not that change is picking up momentum.

OCTOBER 24

The people have been in the streets in greater numbers and with more far-reaching demands than ever before. Leipzig and Dresden again set the pace, but Berliners were also marching. Imre called from Leipzig late yesterday. Some may have thought last week's 100,000 was all that could be collected, he said. They needed to think again. By 3:00 P.M., the premarch prayer services were filled, and by 5:00 P.M. the throng had reached unprecedented numbers. Once in motion, it filled the entire Ringstrasse that circles the downtown, three miles in length. Official media reported 150,000, a Protestant pastor spoke of 300,000. Imre stopped counting at a quarter-million.

The chants had become more radical, Imre said: "The Wall must go," "Put the Stasi to useful work," "Forty years are enough." Placards jeered at Krenz: "You have no honeymoon with us." He would probably have been least amused by a large sign across an overpass demanding "Modrow instead of Krenz." There were loud cheers for Kurt Masur when the march passed Symphony Hall, where restaurant waiters waved from the windows. Despite its demands, the crowd was orderly and police were virtually absent. Stasi Headquarters, strongly guarded last week, had but a half dozen cops on its doorstep. Neues Forum members formed a protective chain and allowed only those placing candles within its perimeter.

Clearly the beginning of structured discussion in Leipzig on Sunday has not reduced street pressure. A pastor told Imre that those who cannot otherwise make their voices heard must still march. The terms of dialogue, he argued, cannot be defined by those who now act as if they were always closet reformers. On Sunday, Masur himself thanked "those who demonstrated and who will demonstrate." Imre said his church contacts remain concerned, however, that things could turn nasty if the state is only buying time. Return to old ways is no longer possible, but tragic miscalculation is. Meanwhile, dissatisfaction has reached the guardians of power. Some members of the Workers' Militia reportedly refused to go into Leipzig on October 9 when violent repression was contemplated.

Jerry Verner was also in Leipzig yesterday, and still excited when he told me about it. He and American visitors came out of their hotel, just off the Ring, as the march began, and the protestors called to them, "Join us! Join us!" Self-conscious as virtually the only nonmarchers, but not considering it proper to take part in a political demonstration, they moved diagonally through the crowd to cross the street. It was hard to see, Jerry said, how Krenz could win over these people—not with what they were beginning to demand, not ask for.

J.D. talked with Klaus Höpcke, who was in Leipzig to build bridges to that large part of his cultural constituency that has been in the streets. His presence, the deputy minister said, was meant to help drain the pool from which the Monday protests were drawing. The SED did not expect protests to end soon but hoped they would lose their focus as it became apparent that there were other channels in which to send a message, he said.

Berliners were in the streets for the second time in three days, though again in smaller numbers than in the Saxon south. More than 2,500 packed Gethsemane Church; hundreds talked in knots in front of the church. Janice said the mood was exhilarated but skeptical, especially about Krenz. Police kept their distance, though I saw more on Schönhauser Allee than for weeks. While Stasi were certainly outside the church, it was striking, Janice reported, that the once innate caution about speaking to strangers was virtually absent. There was anger at Krenz's uncontested election scheduled in Parliament, and interest in rumors of an independent union. Inside the church an open letter urging a contested election was read. A speaker proposed that it be delivered to the Council of State, and the congregation took this literally. It moved in orderly fashion with candles and letter toward Marx-Engels Platz two miles away, keeping to one side of the road so traffic could flow. I came upon it as I was driving from the embassy, and I counted nine truckloads of police in reserve several blocks away, but officers merely escorted the column. As the crowd passed a bakery, it called "Bake reform bread!" (Had everyone been in the Distel last summer?) Passengers left a tram to join. Candles were placed in front of the council, and after an official accepted the letter the protestors went home chanting, "We'll be back!" *Neues Deutschland* reported accurately this morning.

In Schwerin, the picturesque northern city built around ten lakes, the SED organized a demonstration of 40,000 in front of the Ducal Palace. Television showed citizens complaining about shortages, and officials announcing panels to discuss everything "without taboos." *Neues Deutschland* added that thousands held their own march parallel to the official affair. In the GDR's autumn of discontent, Bismarck's celebrated gap between backward Mecklenburg and the rest of the world is down to two weeks, perhaps spurred by incidents like those one resident described to Imre. Leaving a Dresden office, he found his car smeared with slogans: "Do something, Northerners!" (We hear of Berliners refused gas in the South because of Saxon anger at cautious Prussians.)

Krenz's election was a foregone conclusion, but speculation was threefold: Would there be debate? Would the vote be unanimous? What would he say?

The Parliament president, Horst Sindermann of the Politburo Old Guard, answered the first question, explaining it would be "normal" only to vote for the highest office in the land. Applications to speak would be taken up next month. Though there was no alternative, Krenz's election did spark resistance. Sindermann carefully twice counted twenty-six nay votes and twenty-six abstentions. His comment, "I don't want to falsify the result," reminded many (unintentionally?) of the charge the SED, under Krenz's direction, did just that in May. Krenz's acceptance speech was conciliatory but general. His most important pledge, if he meant it, was to use only "political means to deal with political problems."

Those in the streets, most say, are engaged in antigovernment demonstrations. *Neues Deutschland* claims they are "demonstrating for socialism." The assessments may not be as contradictory as they appear. There is strong opposition to the Honecker regime and a new leader who has yet to break with his past. Many activists still say with apparent sincerity, however, that they want a different socialism. Many SED members are flirting with Neues Forum. They say this may be the SED's last chance, that the demands of those who want to stay and make the GDR a different kind of place are an opportunity. But the people we talk with around the country are not impressed by Sauls who have become Pauls—like Hager, who on Monday continued to distance himself from his record by criticizing a "certain cult of the personality" under Honecker. The SED has a chance to reconcile the contradiction only if Krenz moves beyond his improving rhetoric to tangible deeds—and fast. Today he missed another of his few opportunities.

OCTOBER 25

In a break with the past reminiscent of early Gorbachev Glasnost, the press was allowed to report on Tuesday's Politburo session. Hitherto, even the agenda has been secret. The biggest revelation was that the Plenum will meet for an unusual three days, November 8–10. It must make vital personnel and policy decisions, and it will be indicative for the relationship between Central Committee and Politburo. Many SED members argue that the former must become more important because it better represents at least grassroots SED views. If so, it will have to meet more often than twice a year and have debates that are not play scenarios. Will Krenz be strong enough in two weeks either to restrain such a development or ride it bareback to where he wants to go?

The ADN court report on the Politburo meeting said the draft travel law, on which much hope for a breathing space rests, will be public next month and in force by year's end. Still unclear is whether financial/administrative restrictions will hollow out its promise of a passport for everyone. I squeezed in lunch with Dr. Dietzel of the *Berliner Zeitung*, who shrugged off the ambiguities. "The border is open, the Wall breached," he concluded. Like it or not, Hungary and Poland had made the Berlin Wall meaningless. The country could not endure losing so many of its best people, Dietzel said, but it could no longer prevent this, and it could ill afford being "the boo-man of Europe" by trying.

Dietzel's prescription was to make virtue of necessity, to jump boldly into water of uncertain depth with a law giving travel rights while working out transitional financial arrangements as well as possible. But he admitted that the issue remains controversial inside the SED. "By itself, of course," Dietzel cautioned, "travel will not be enough. The political system will have to have much more democracy, and the economy a new balance between the big *Kombinate*, self-initiative of small and mid-sized firms, and the productivity principle." Travel, however, if generous enough—if it largely heralds removal of the Berlin Wall as a meaningful barrier—could win time for concepts to be worked out, and time, Dietzel and others agree, is what Krenz lacks.

Dietzel also offered insights on the coming Politburo shake-up. The reluctance to turn key portfolios over to "outsiders," he said, made it unlikely that real experts or truly new personalities would be tapped. For example, it reduced chances that Mittag's old job would be filled by a "successful *Kombinat* manager." The only person who fit traditional criteria and had credentials, he claimed, was Siegfried Lorenz, the moderate Party chief in Karl-Marx-Stadt. While Lorenz would be widely acceptable, he said, a simple reshuffling of seats would be received poorly by the SED grassroots, which, like the people generally, wanted wholesale replacement of old Pols.

A moral test Krenz must pass is to provide a fair accounting of police brutality during the early October protests. Bishops Forck in Berlin and Hempel in Saxony have seized the issue, and establishment intellectuals are also speaking up. The topic is particularly sensitive because it goes close to the heart of the repressive structure, and Krenz was ultimately responsible as Central Committee secretary for security. It recalls the election dispute, but with higher stakes. How consequent Krenz will be is uncertain, but he is making, by GDR standards, novel gestures to show that he does not reject demands out of hand. Wolfgang Herger, his man, has put out a report that claims police were provoked and that there was reason to fear an assault on the Wall, but that also admits individual wrongdoing and promises further investigation.

We do not have a full picture of all that happened in those chaotic nights, though I have seen the church's documentation. The police were not much rougher on the streets than, say, West Berlin cops during some protests in 1968, but the worst abuses were in the lockups, where psychoterror and humiliation (though not torture) were widespread. The regime tried intimidation. It says much for young people's courage that this failed, and for the society's maturity that the reaction has been anger and demands that, fourteen years after the Helsinki Final Act, such behavior not be tolerated.

The young Americans running a U.S. Information Agency book exhibit fortuitously opened at Humboldt University described the campus ferment and gave us a copy of a widely circulated student appeal that demands a "nonpolitical," independent association because the "systematically discredited" FDJ represents only the SED. It is harder, however, to pursue reports of independent unions. A senior FDGB man at the plant where the union "Reform" was started claimed that only 12 of his 7,236 members resigned. We are handicapped in measuring the fire beneath this smokescreen because the State Department still does not permit us to contact the FDGB directly, alone of all regime representatives. Janice is trying to telephone the worker reportedly behind "Reform," however.

Berlin's largest demonstration (for the first time West and East agreed on a figure, 12,000) was pure anti-Krenz. A call went out in churches and via leaflets, and protesters gathered Tuesday evening at the base of the television tower near Alexanderplatz. They circled Parliament, where Krenz had been elected hours earlier, whistled at police, and chanted rhythmically, "Egon Krenz, wir sind die Konkurrenz!" (Egon Krenz, we are the competition!) The demonstration grew as it wound through downtown, and for the first time there were many banners, including "Egon, your election doesn't count because the people didn't elect you" and "Down with the SED's dictatorial, autocratic claims to power." Police rerouted traffic and provided an escort for three and a half hours. Janice, who trudged along, felt the crowd was self-consciously flexing its muscles. A bystander told her: "They should have chosen someone else, anyone who doesn't carry his political baggage. The leadership must first dismantle the distrust. Those here are just a few who had the courage to come out on the street."

Dietzel, the SED editor, told me he subscribed to the Leipzig chant "Krenz, no honeymoon," but he professed to be a bit shocked by his experiences mixing last night with the Berlin protest. Critical of much that has happened in the GDR in recent years, he believes the country needs radical change but that the SED should still govern. He warned, as Krenz now hints, that conservatives could use a street incident as an excuse to clamp down. Perhaps sobered by his glimpse of street politics, he was curious about the leaders of Neues Forum. He admitted that, until now, he has had almost no contact with such people, but he hoped the weekly open meetings that Leipzig originated Sunday and Berlin is to copy next weekend will bring SED liberals and such reform forces together. He will attend the inaugural effort, he said, as a private citizen.

Where this all is going is anyone's guess, but it is time to consign to the archives the cry of a character in a play that was popular just after Honecker came to power: "The GDR is the dullest country in the world." *Neues Deutschland* carried the new slogan today. Reporting a meeting at the State Opera about "long pent-up unhappiness over covered-up problems," it quoted Director Ruth Berghaus: "Damn it, I can get excited about my country again!"

I hastily scribbled these lines for Dick, who returns today:

> You requested a "Welcome Home" note. A "Welcome" note might be more appropriate. You will be able to recognize some things: The traffic patterns have not changed much, except when there is a demonstration downtown. You are returning to a different GDR, however. The proximate cause, of course, is the retirement of Honecker and the ascension of Krenz. It is not that Krenz is so inherently different a type, but that the event marked the cracking of the eggshell. It is a red German eaglet that is emerging, but what kind of hybrid it is remains too early to tell. Groups want to feed it many different formulas—and there are many more politically relevant groups, in the SED and the rest of the establishment, and outside, in nontraditional circles. Tracking the new politics will be our most difficult challenge. It will be more open than before, but much more diffuse and unpredictable. . . .

Appointments may be difficult to get, I concluded, but I urged Dick to pursue Hager, Axen, Gerlach, Herger, Klaus Gysi, and Reinhold.

OCTOBER 26

Dick said the consultations went well. No problems were solved, but Kurt Nier is going through his own *Claus and Claudia* transformation ("Who was that masked man?" Dick joked), and there was "dialogue" about need for new policies. The State Department and Congress were suddenly very interested in talking with a representative of the liveliest member of the Warsaw Pact. Dick thanked me for the "welcome" note, but he does not want to see the Axens and the Hagers, at least not as a priority; he needs the assessments of Opposition leaders, he said. And of course he is right. My note was a product of "old thinking," a phenomenon to which diplomats are as susceptible as SED functionaries.

Krenz and senior lieutenants took further steps yesterday to substantiate their claim that the October of its forty-first year marks a new era for a reformist GDR. Asked whether he would permit an Opposition, Krenz said, "We should drop this term 'Opposition.' Let's say that in the GDR there are citizens who think about how this land can go forward. And we are interested in every thought. No one is excluded from the exchange of views." Schabowski, the other regime heavyweight, claimed, "Talk with people who feel close to such Opposition groups . . . is already well in process." He meets today with Reich and Pflugbeil of Neues Forum, two of the most thoughtful new leaders. No topics are excluded, Schabowski said, provided "Socialist foundations" are accepted. Schabowski noted he is also in contact with Stolpe.

It is news even in the revolutionary GDR when a television roundtable brings together former espionage chief Markus Wolf; critical, often blacklisted authors, such as Stefan Heym and Christoph Hein; Neues Forum leaders Bärbel Bohley and Jens Reich; and government representatives. The discussion began Tuesday evening and ended early Wednesday. The theme was adapted from Martin Luther King: What dream did each have for the GDR? Wolf said his GDR would preserve socialism's ideals and be a place where all—from schoolchildren to Politburo—spoke their minds. Hein envisaged a socialist GDR that people would not want to leave. Bohley, accused of treason and expelled twenty months ago, said her dream had been realized because "I can sit here and say how I imagine the GDR to be instead of looking and thinking about it from afar." To her dream belonged also, however, that those in the Leipzig streets called out "We are the people!" The often-heated debate centered on how genuine the changes have been. Much trust had been lost, Wolf said, especially when many unscrupulously jumped on the reform train. "Were only three people in the entire GDR responsible for the mess?" Heym asked bitingly. A member of the audience noted that in the past her suggestions had been blocked by the very people who were now posing as leaders of change. Unlike the old days—say, a month ago—the program ended without definitive answers or unanimity.

The people do not agree that the time for protests is past. They feel the street is both their control on the SED and the motor driving reforms. There was only one procession in Berlin on Wednesday. I came across it in late evening, 200 candle-carrying marchers, most scarcely older than teenagers, escorted by two dozen police who rerouted traffic. However, about a quarter of Neubrandenburg's 80,000 residents were in the streets. Berlin papers list politicians, including Schabowski, and cultural figures, such as Hermann Kant, who will take part in an inaugural town meeting here Sunday. The authorities seem slowly to be recognizing that the street habit will not be given up easily. Police approval has been given for a demonstration in downtown Berlin on November 4 with Neues Forum as co-sponsor.

Stolpe, the canniest church politician, told J.D.: "There is such pervasive dissatisfaction in the CDU with its leadership's timidity that in a few days there will be a palace revolution."

I took Steve Larrabee, Eastern Europe specialist in the Jimmy Carter White House, and Ron Asmus of Rand to Gerd Basler's institute for a roundtable discussion. Our hosts' enthusiasm was summed up by the young man who said, "At last we are on the same wave length as the SU [Soviet Union]. Now we just have to do Glasnost and Perestroika better!"

West German courtship began as Wolfgang Mischnick, Bundestag caucus chief of the FDP, Kohl's junior coalition partner, visited. In the new style, Krenz shared the spotlight with Gerlach, whose suddenly assertive LDPD claims to be the FDP's counterpart. Heather has not learned much because Mischnick did not give the Ständige Vertretung a readout. She did hear that

Krenz also talked with Kohl by telephone. The Ständige Vertretung believes there can be no return to old ways, and Bonn is encouraged by the decision to broaden travel, to show restraint with the Opposition, and to start dialogue, but it is not certain Krenz can hold the reform impetus within the system. Reading between lines, Heather concluded that Kohl has strong doubts about Krenz's survival but wants to keep the relationship on a positive track.

At the Distel last night, the walls were covered with resolutions demanding reform, registration of Neues Forum, and an accounting of sins against artistic freedom. The performance mostly repeated what we saw in the summer, but with updates. An actor read a new poem about "go-alongs" (*Trittbrettfahrer*), those who board every train and ride as willingly toward reform as reaction "without apologizing." The sarcasm, anger, and skepticism that skit encapsulated is evident at every demonstration and in virtually every conversation with exhilarated and slightly puzzled East Germans. It is at the core of Krenz's political problems.

OCTOBER 27

The GDR has amnestied those imprisoned for trying to go to the West or participating in protests. This will virtually empty jails of political prisoners and meet a major church and Opposition demand. How different from my first week here, in 1987, when a major amnesty fine-tuned the climate for Honecker's Bonn visit!

Krenz's call for an end to demonstrations and veiled threats in the provinces have failed. There were 5,000 in Gera's streets, 15,000 in Erfurt, and 25,000 in Rostock; in Dresden, 100,000 demanded elections and an end to the SED power monopoly. Modrow was applauded when he said the process was irreversible and would produce a "revolutionary change of direction." Meanwhile, there are charges that local SED leaders infiltrated soldiers to give the recent Schwerin demonstration a more positive tone. I witnessed how counterproductive the chicanery is when I took Larrabee and Asmus to meet with Reissig. At the elevator, a young man approached our escort and, ignoring the foreigners, complained of the "outrageous" manipulation in Schwerin. Such arrogance simply could not be tolerated, he said, and his colleague agreed. The vignette brought home how bold SED cadres have become.

Institute academicians of reform inclination, like Reissig, are among the most excited people in the GDR. Long limited to nibbling at the margins of texts in hope of exerting slight influence, their time has come to present new ideas about which the Politburo claims to have an open mind. Reissig was slightly more optimistic, though more tired, than two weeks ago. It could all still easily go wrong, he indicated, not least because the SED might not move fast enough. Nevertheless, Krenz, though not Reissig's first choice, had seen the need for major change and pushed Honecker out. Reissig believed the Plenum would be decisive. Before then, he would work at full stretch, especially on a radical rewrite of the "Socialist Democracy in the '90's" paper he gave at Aspen. Regrettably, Reissig continued, the Plenum would probably not be ready to decide many specifics, but Krenz had said he would outline his program. The trick was to get as much into that speech as possible.

The new leader was still groping for a concept—thus academicians' chance for influence—but it was certain, Reissig noted, that the Central Committee would demand a more powerful role. It was a divided body, but more reformist than the Politburo. If Krenz could not persuade Honecker's lieutenants to leave, he should fight in the Plenum; if he was determined enough, that body would help him win, Reissig indicated. Citizens would never again passively tolerate absolutist SED rule, he said, any more than SED members would again accept dictation from above. The new maturity could not be revoked, and the LDPD must become more genuinely liberal democratic, the CDU more Christian democratic, and above all, the SED more democratic. And the Opposition? we asked. Krenz had decided it would be neither criminalized nor excluded from debate, Reissig responded. What remained controversial was how to fit it into the political process.

Larrabee and Asmus also saw Wolfgang Heinrichs, who runs the Central Economics Institute. A year ago, Asmus told me Heinrichs had confided that he was protecting his young staff, which was drafting reform proposals to cope with the economic crisis just over the horizon that he could only put in his desk. This time, Asmus reported, Heinrichs said he had emptied the drawer. The "radical" ideas were with the Central Committee.

Stolpe told J.D. that the SED worries most about worker attitudes. The protests have focused on civil rights. Should economic demands be added, there would be a real strike threat, he said. The church and most Opposition intellectuals want an independent GDR that is anti-Fascist (no anachronism, since Stolpe estimates Reactionary Right potential at 20 percent), democratic, and socialist. At the grassroots, he claimed, there also is no overwhelming reunification sentiment. Only a major crisis, such as might arise if protests turned violent, could produce that, he said. The Opposition does not want Krenz to succeed, however, Stolpe continued. It seeks to unseat the SED and to go immediately to Hungarian or Polish models. A reformist Party is not to its liking. On the other hand, he added, Schabowski told him powerful conservative forces remain, notably within the security apparatus and in Berlin. Krenz, not Modrow, can move fast, he believed, because he knows the security business, and the conservatives consider him one of them. The church hopes Krenz will take a leap forward, Stolpe explained, but nobody in the SED leadership, he stressed, is in a mood to share power.

The church, Stolpe explained, is in a difficult situation. Many church members want more activism; Krenz hopes its calming influence can halt protests, but this is not in the cards, Stolpe felt. He told J.D. he receives many calls from towns where Party officials are asking pastors for advice. Stolpe considered street pressure necessary, but no one should believe the SED would not defend itself violently if that were its only option. That could lead, he feared, to chaos, and ultimately to *Anschluss* (annexation) by West Germany.

Krenz's weakness, Stolpe said, is his burden of past sins. This preoccupies many in the church, who insist on his confession to the election scandal and police excesses before they will cooperate. The usually soft-spoken Bishop Forck told Imre with vehemence that he had personally turned over documentation on vote-rigging to the government months ago and still awaited a reply. Krenz's freedom of action is circumscribed. He loses credibility if he ignores a problem that does not go away. He loses face if he admits his role. On this, he can expect little Christian charity.

OCTOBER 28

GDR attorneys joined the call for sweeping reforms, charging that rights are vaguely formulated, laws are often circumvented, and judicial independence routinely curtailed. I will query Gregor Gysi, the Bar chairman, or his deputy, Lothar de Maizière, next week. Last year, I explored with Gysi the possibility that legal reform would be a field where the GDR might throw off its political straitjacket, and I want a better idea of what the lawyers intend.

Vojtech Mastny, a Boston University professor who is visiting us, exclaimed with wonder; "This is revolution here. There is no way the Communists can hold the GDR together. Why do the Four Powers not convene a conference on Germany while they can still manage events?" You may be right in principle, I replied, but politics is not so neat. It would be impossible to get agreement even to talk through the German Question. Regional issues are on the agenda of U.S.-Soviet summits, I noted, with one exception: Eastern Europe. Fear of a "Second Yalta" charge was too great to discuss a cooperative approach to the region aimed at ensuring democratic evolution, military disengagement, and reduced risk of explosion. (Indeed, this was what the European Bureau had not wanted me to write about for the press last year.) The United States would follow behind what developed on the ground, I argued, and hope Gorbachev meant it when he said GDR decisions would not be made in Moscow. It would be best for everyone, however, if Krenz won a breathing space—not by force, of course, but by genuine reforms—so outside powers could use that time to get accustomed to the implications, whatever they were. But Four Power crisis management was not realistic.

OCTOBER 29

On our way to the town meeting, we picked up the Bindenagels' house guest, Jim McAdams, a Princeton professor who has written extensively on "the other Germany." Our goal was City Hall, the "Red *Rathaus*" (as its brick facade caused it to be known long before the color had an ideological connotation and Berlin was divided). As we passed the Palace of the Republic, in the narrow Werderstrasse, a dozen muscular young men with short haircuts came toward us, each wearing a sports training suit. "Who are they?" Jim asked. "A soccer team?" "No," Gaby explained. "Those are Stasi bully-boys [*Schlägertruppen*]." That they were leaving was good, but the glimpse was a reminder that the SED can still play rough.

At mid-morning, when the town meeting was to begin, so many were waiting that proceedings were moved outside. Schabowski and other top-echelon political and cultural figures stood on the steps. Microphones were spotted randomly about the crowd. We worked our way forward to the right of the speakers' platform. By the time we withdrew for lunch, three hours later, the throng had filled in the front half of the Marx-Engels Forum behind us. Television reported more than 20,000—if anything an underestimate—and they stayed for nearly two more hours until Schabowski adjourned them with a promise that these "Sunday talks" would become a regular event.

The inaugural featured tough exchanges on the range of reform demands. Schabowski, taking most questions himself, improved his standing as one of the few in Krenz's Politburo with a chance to be credible with the new political forces. He promised that all complaints would be looked at and that "demos" would become "part of the political culture," but he also defended the SED's constitutionally fixed leading role. Almost everyone with patience to await a turn was able to put a question or make a statement. By GDR norms, the lack of structure was astonishing, but proceedings were orderly, crowd temper a blend of pent-up frustration, anger, and exhilaration.

The common themes were dissatisfaction—the populace's—and catch-up ball. The latter is the leadership's game, and few play it with Schabowski's verve and skill. He benefits from looking and sounding like a Berlin proletarian, not a fluent-in-four-languages intellectual, and the crowd had more respect for him than other officials. The police president, who apologized for the violence his men inflicted on October 7 and 8, was whistled down. An old Communist who claimed the SED was democratic but "could perhaps do better" was heckled. A woman movingly described how the Stasi had ruined her life, and demanded that it be abolished. Schabowski and the mayor promised that every question, including those addressed to "state bodies not present here today" (derisive cries were heard), would be reviewed.

Establishment figures took what a few weeks ago would have been daring positions. Hermann Kant apologized for his role in expulsions from the Writers Association in the 1970s and declaimed, "The People's Police does not exist to beat up the People." Dr. Fink of Humboldt University, whom I embarrassed five months ago with my remarks about the CDU Party Chairman, described being hit by police truncheons that fateful 40th Anniversary evening. The beating hospitalized and radicalized him and shocked many of his colleagues. Schabowski never touched the hottest potato: the call for the SED to share power. He would go no further than to say the GDR already had many forums, "and undoubtedly there will be some new ones." He hinted, however, at Politburo divisions and stressed the importance of the Plenum now eight days away. Indeed, Schabowski was only occasionally able to give direct answers. More common was his plaintive "Everything is on the agenda, but we cannot resolve a thousand questions at once."

Larrabee and Asmus concluded that they have talked with many in Eastern Europe who claimed to be reforming a ruling party. Most were going through the motions, or trying to give themselves courage. The difference here was that SED interlocutors seemed to believe their words. Perhaps they kidded themselves, Larrabee added, but if it was possible anywhere, then probably in the GDR.

OCTOBER 30

Dick, with McAdams, spent an hour with Schabowski. He later told me Schabowski admitted the Politburo was just starting to realize the size of its challenge. Opportunity for democratic change, he said, was wide open, with two big caveats: socialism and SED primacy must not be challenged. Schabowski was still pumped up from yesterday's no-holds-barred marathon, which he felt had gone well, and launched into a monologue on the need for far-reaching reforms. He concentrated on economic improvements, especially workplace incentives, but conceded distrust of the SED was at a record high. Unless this was reversed, there was no hope for overhauling governmental mechanisms. On reflection, he agreed that SED institutions must be changed, but the priority had to be advancing people with proper political "character." Indeed, Dick noted, Schabowski returned repeatedly to the character theme, implying that the situation called for men of his populist bent. The party structure in the National Front was adequate to encompass nonsocialist views, Schabowski claimed, though he recognized the initial decision to ban Neues Forum was wrong. That "club for concerned citizens," he said, represented legitimate aspirations.

The walk down the long corridor to the elevator and across the cavernous reception hall to the car is an SED Headquarters ritual, a time for vacation small-talk with the escort. This day it was different, Dick said. Schabowski's assistant began talking politics at once. The Politburo had not scratched the surface of problems, he said. His most bitter commentary was on "old Communists who had not had a new idea in thirty years," but his own boss too, he implied, was behind the curve on the need for drastic reform. Only because institutes had been working the problems ("We have cabinets full of unread studies"), he said, could Krenz give an initial appearance of energy and resolution. But if bold decisions were not soon forthcoming, he warned, the honeymoon would be short.

The articulate, even garrulous, Schabowski enjoys his new status as the Politburo's most effective spokesman, Dick said, but he may be more at home with debate than ideas. A man near Gaby in the crowd at City Hall on Sunday remarked, "Schabowski sure can talk." Dick posed the question: How well does he listen?

Though Schabowski was explicit that the SED's leading role remained a red line, that is just what *Der Morgen* criticized, calling GDR socialism a shell that no longer reflects the people's will. Coincidentally, Imre got another hint of revolt in the CDU. A prominent member, a Leipzig lawyer, told him almost matter-of-factly that its Congress would be moved up to February or March, "but we'll have new leaders before then anyway."

Janice squeezed into the Church of the Redeemer on Saturday for a program honoring "victims of the state's abuses of its power," especially young people brutalized on October 7 and 8. Socialists admitted discomfort at being in a church but proclaimed solidarity. Christoph Hein gave the best speech. It was time to get to work to change the structures with which each person had personal familiarity, the novelist said. His example was the lawyers' demand for legal reform. He also made this nice point: "It amazes me . . . that people speak such poor Russian in a country where everyone studies that language for five to ten years. Those chickens come home to roost. Glasnost is translated 'dialogue,' and Perestroika as 'credibility.' If I were a teacher, I would write: 'The student is making an effort, but his achievements are still defective.' "

Hein also spoke to the resignation of the conservative seventy-two-year-old president of the GDR Section of the PEN Club: "I also want to speak of a man with whom I do not have much in common, Heinz Kamnitzer. I had tried . . . to force his resignation. I failed. Now I had been awaiting anxiously a letter from PEN that would contain a fine delegation of guilt and a fine history of reform spirit, signed by him. Something different came, a PEN declaration with which I fully agree, and his resignation. I take my hat off to him. This man is not my man; his principles are not my principles. But this is a man with principles, and so he is again a person with whom to hold a dialogue. . . . He has set an example, by which I do not mean they all must resign. But those who do not resign should justify this, and give us good reasons."

Hein was addressing an urgent problem known as that of the *Wendehals*, a bird called the "wryneck" in English. The German is more vivid, with play on the name Krenz has given his policy: *Wende*, "Turn." The image is of an establishment that, by a twist of its collective neck, faces happily in the opposite direction and presents itself as reformist. There are people, even many, who honestly sought major change before October 18. But how is one to distinguish them from the *Wendehals*, who loads all blame on Honecker, Mittag, and Herrmann so as to go on as before? If the accounting Hein pleads for cannot be made, reform will either be destroyed from within by "old thinkers" (not necessarily identical to the old men around Honecker) or must fail because it is deprived of the services of honorable Communists and others in the establishment whose contributions the people will reject because they know no other way to rid themselves of opportunists.

Heather is arranging a talk with the Opposition over drinks at the ambassador's residence. She spends much time knocking on apartment doors to reach individuals who lack telephones and secretaries.

Janice's calls to the founder of "Reform" have yielded chats only with his child and father-in-law. The man himself is in Sofia. Perhaps the bosses have gotten rid of him for a week. It does suggest he is more than a simple worker. The main stage for union activism now, however, is the FDGB, whose reform effort is as difficult as the Party's. Harry Tisch says he will resign unless a special Presidium supports him. Krenz, sensitive to worker unrest, might welcome a new boss at the discredited official union.

Events since Honecker's fall say much about style, which is not insignificant, but little about programs and the political personalities needed to implement them. Though most of the challenges are still ahead, however, I must agree with the newscaster who smiled—television is now that revolutionary—at the end of Sunday's broadcast and said, "Politically it is spring, but meteorologically, look for autumn storms and falling temperatures."

OCTOBER 31

Signals about the strength and direction of winds tossing the GDR's ship of state were again mixed. A massive march in Leipzig last evening proved street pressure is unabated, but the FDGB revolt against Harry Tisch was put on hold, a sign that the internal SED power struggle is unresolved. The rebels hope the broom expected to sweep away Honecker holdovers at the Plenum will do the job for them, but the union's claim to independence was further eroded.

Krenz goes to Moscow in search of coattails. He has started faster than expected, but he lacks one thing Gorbachev has in abundance: the admiration of East Germans. Before leaving, he gave a speech. By Honecker standards, he was radical, but for late October he was conservative, repeating that the SED means to liberalize and revitalize the GDR, not negotiate its own departure from the stage.

That the SED these days is far from being the only political force, however, was abundantly displayed in Leipzig. Imre again estimated the crowd at a quarter million. It was the same disciplined, not mean-spirited show he has seen all fall: a fair representation of the population, though especially young people, striding along the Ringstrasse that girds the Old Town. Posters and banners appeared furtively two weeks ago, were prominent last week, and proliferated this Monday. Imre's sidewalk analysis identified two main themes: free elections and deep distrust of instant reformers like Krenz, Tisch, and Hager. But there were new nuances. Women in work smocks protested consumer shortages; there were calls for independent unions and political parties, for the resignation of Margot Honecker, and for market principles and effective managers ("Specialists, not Communists") in the economy. Poignantly, a simple banner stated: "Church, we thank you."

Mayor Berghofer has formally recognized the "Group of 20" and given it office space. It is careful not to call itself an "Opposition," but institutionalization (in Dresden this local-origin body is more important than Neues Forum) is a GDR first.

The "National Front" is cracking. An LDPD editor told Imre more letters are arriving than its Leipzig daily can answer. They demand specific improvements, and patience is thin. He stressed that the Liberals are—for now—committed to the SED alliance but no longer refer to that Party's "leading role." Symptomatically, when Imre telephoned to see LDPD leaders, he did not get the standard response "Go through the Foreign Ministry." Instead, there was a pause, then a promise to call back. Minutes later he had an appointment. A similar request to the CDU is still at the "We'll get back to you" stage, but Imre did see one of that party's original "Letter from Weimar" rebels. The Bloc Parties, with political structures already in place, were a better bet than Neues Forum, she said, but for the CDU to win trust, the present leadership would have to go. She gave Götting fourteen days.

Democratic Awakening has narrowly elected Wolfgang Schnur, the human rights lawyer, its chairman over Schorlemmer. It is moving away from a reformed socialism orientation as it seeks less to influence the SED than to compete against it, but the "Preliminary Declaration of Principles" still states: "The critical attitude of Democratic Awakening . . . does not mean rejection of the vision of a Socialist society. We are taking part in the dispute over the concept of Socialism." The platform also attaches a "high value" to the special relationship with West Germany, "grounded in the unity of German history and culture," but "on the basis of the existence of two German states."

My secretary, Kirsten, spent Sunday with a Neues Forum family from her church. The husband, an engineer, expects little to change but wants his voice heard. She asked the son ("almost eleven") if he ever disagreed in civics class. "I wouldn't speak against Marx. He had good ideas. Our teacher told us his Manifesto says that if the people don't like the government, it must change. When I heard that," the precocious child said, "I thought it was what's happening here." Had he told his teacher? Kirsten asked. "No way. I don't want the police at my parents' door," the boy replied.

During the kind of almost no-holds-barred talk commonplace in post-Honecker Berlin, Gerd Basler admitted to me that no one knew who had Krenz's ear. The Bloc Parties and the new groups had programs while the SED, "with all our resources, institutes, and experts," floundered, able to say only that it had begun to listen to complaints. Probably, Basler said, Krenz relied on a small group from his FDJ days or on Honecker holdovers. Neither prospect was encouraging. He needed to open up to new ideas and tap new people to take over thirty powerful Central Committee departments. Meanwhile, Basler said, it was good that citizens kept pressure on by marching. He himself planned to join the November 4 demonstration that SED members were now free to attend, he said. He expected it to bring greater numbers into Berlin's streets than May Day and to send a powerful message.

I agree that protestors show realism by not relaxing demands. It is street pressure that forces the Politburo to confront tough choices. If so inclined,

Krenz can use it and Gorbachev's support to argue for bold change at the Plenum. However, the FDGB hedge is a reminder that not everyone is certain, even within the establishment, of his intentions and power. But for the moment, it is a pleasure only those who have lived here can appreciate to experience a media that banishes a Schnitzler and interviews (as *Neues Deutschland* just did) Wolf and Wolf—novelist Christa and former spy, now reform politician, Markus.

NOVEMBER 1

Tisch's reprieve lasted twenty-four hours. He fell to grassroots union protest and, probably, a Krenz push. Krenz himself is still in Moscow trying for vicarious credibility. Television showed him speaking Russian to Gorbachev's intimate, Alexander Yakovlev, on arrival. "Obviously he needs no translator" was the reporter's symbolism-laden comment. Krenz will return via Warsaw. "Solidarity" is no longer a nonword here. The new man wants to show that he can face unpleasant facts abroad as well as at home and reach a pragmatic accommodation with an important neighbor, regardless of its ideological complexion.

Margot Honecker's political demise is imminent. Imre hears she is cleaning out her desk and is to "be resigned"—passive voice. Meanwhile, *Neues Deutschland* announced that a celebrated injustice is being righted. Four students dismissed in 1988 from an elite Berlin high school for protesting military parades can resume studies. It was rumored last year that the students were dismissed at the insistence of Krenz, whose son attends the school. The church was unable to help, which strengthened suspicion that the affair went far beyond the competence of school officials.

Tipping winners and losers in the coming shakeup is a major preoccupation of the diplomatic corps. The new favorite for Mittag's economic job is Alexander Schalck-Golodkowski. While the jump from state secretary for foreign trade looks great, he is the insider's insider, who negotiated a giant Bonn credit a few years back and directs GDR efforts to obtain hard currency. Markus Wolf is obviously back in the game (if he ever left). His growing prominence as a reform spokesman causes some to envision him as Mielke's successor at the Stasi, or even in Krenz's old Politburo job as supervisor of all security forces. But the bets change daily while we await a clearer signal of power relations and policy direction at the top.

Wolfgang Heyl, deputy head of the CDU, is the most senior GDR politician to call for legalizing Neues Forum. The signs are that it will soon be permitted to register as an organization, but not as a political party. That would meet a major demand without requiring the SED to acknowledge a formal political Opposition.

Heather found Pflugbeil pleased at the turnabout, which he attributed to public support. He hoped small advances would not lull East Germans into complacency, but he was enthusiastic about his meeting with Schabowski, whom he believed he and Reich had convinced that Neues Forum was reasonable. Neues Forum is not without problems, however, Pflugbeil noted. It is mistrusted by other groups that do not yet benefit from the new official attitude, and it is racked by divisions as it tries to decide what it wants to be. The membership, he said, covers a wide spectrum, and there are difficulties with workers, who are uncomfortable with consensus politics. These are the problems of an organization that has grown from nothing in two months, Pflugbeil explained. They are not insurmountable.

Pflugbeil is by nature a pessimist, but he described himself this time as optimistic. He does not trust Krenz or rule out a hard-line resurgence, but he believes the lawyers' call for legal change and the apparent emergence of the Bloc Parties as real forces are important developments. Eventually, he hopes, the SED will be forced to accept a reduced role. Though he confesses he cannot imagine the GDR with a non-Communist head of state, he envisions a greatly strengthened Parliament.

To learn of his talk with Markus Wolf, I walked with McAdams up busy Unter den Linden, across Marx-Engels-Forum, and into the small streets behind City Hall. Jim was heading for an appointment, but I could believe he had fallen under the influence of the spymaster's old milieu. In a nutshell, he found Wolf both encouraged at prospects for a liberalized socialism and worried about the situation's explosiveness.

Wolf in person, Jim said, was even more striking than on television—affable, interested in his interlocutor, highly intelligent, totally self-confident. He acted like one who knew what he wanted and was untouchable. Wolf made no secret that he is a dedicated Communist, Jim said, but he also came across as an idealist who sounded sincere when he insisted a secondary motive for his book was to say that friendship, cooperation, and decency could span chasms between individuals and nations. His primary concern, however, was to persuade East Germans that socialism should be a system where everyone felt free to speak out, and where the SED became more democratic and listened to the people. It was, he admitted, a socialism that had little in common with the Honecker era's deformations, much less the worse disfigurement he recognized (late) in Stalin's Soviet Union. Can it be done? Wolf professed optimism about the regenerative capacities of the socialist idea, but also worry that an incident could set the house ablaze.

Wolf sketched a divided Politburo initially inclined to use force. The decisive day was October 9. He gave Krenz credit for turning matters around when it was recognized that the Leipzig protest could be repressed only by spilling blood. Now, he claimed, a signed order forbids security organs from using deadly force even if their own safety is imperiled. Nevertheless, Wolf cautioned, the situation could go tragically wrong. His scenario sounded eerily like Budapest 1956: loss of discipline by a few in a crowd, a charge on a Stasi building, and pitched battle between desperate Secret Police and angry citizens. Wolf seemed to be describing a besieged mind-set that he knew existed within the security apparatus, and probably the Politburo as well, Jim said.

In contrast to many SED spokesmen who say the people should quit the streets, however, Wolf found common ground with Neues Forum. He recognized that citizens would not stop demonstrating, and that reforms would not be secure, unless change was institutionalized. This required new structures and laws, not just a few concessions, a different style, and promises. This was a point, Jim observed, at which Wolf differed from Schabowski. The populist Berlin boss would tinker with the machine that Wolf, apparently, would rebuild. Unfortunately, Wolf said little to fix Krenz in this spectrum.

Wolf also acknowledged that, if reforms were to have a chance, the GDR needed closer relations with West Germany. Increased exposure to Western lifestyles would mean more pressure to create attractive conditions at home. While he accepted that challenge as unavoidable, Wolf worried about a growth of neo-Fascism in the Federal Republic. What set his comments off from standard propaganda, Jim said, was that he feared equally neo-Fascism in the GDR. The susceptibility, Wolf indicated, could be traced in part to the Stalinist predilections still prevalent in some SED circles.

The intriguing spymaster was silent about his own future, but the SED has few with his mix of intellect, knowledge of the security apparatus, ties to

Moscow—and at least a modicum of standing with some of those demanding change in the streets.

An American journalist with whom I had talked earlier called to share an example of how fast the stodgy GDR is changing. She had asked a photographer at the Grand Hotel pool why he was taking so many shots of an "essentially naked" young lady. A *Playboy* spread on the girls of East Germany was the reason. That set me to pondering subjective aspects of revolution and politics. It is true that every politician needs luck, but how much will Krenz have? The GDR had almost no chance to qualify for the 1990 Soccer World Cup; then two late goals brought improbable victory over the Soviet Union. Last week, Austria as improbably lost to Turkey. Now, if the GDR can win in Vienna on November 15, it will qualify against all odds for the championship round. Most likely it is meaningless in the larger picture, but no one who witnessed the Miracle Mets win a hopeless New York election for John Lindsay can be certain.

More important than the jockeying for Plenum advantage is whether the SED can bring itself to renounce its absolute power monopoly. Krenz has not wanted to touch this. Opposition figures, including the many who say they want only a better socialism, and realistic mid-level Party officials agree that the old formula is hopelessly outdated. It cannot be enough for the SED only to listen better but still make all the decisions. Can structures be devised to regulate and reapportion power? No one knows what the Politburo has in mind when it announces it discussed "questions of interpretation of the leading role of the Party of the Working Class in a society renewing itself on the way to a better Socialism." It is probably mostly words, while the leaders concentrate on style, portfolios, and quick fixes. As Schabowski's aide indicated, the Politburo has comprehended only the iceberg's tip. The learning curve needs to be much steeper.

NOVEMBER 2

Visa-free travel to Czechoslovakia resumed yesterday, and hundreds went immediately to the West German Embassy, a reminder that fundamental problems have not been resolved. Meanwhile, Krenz's remarks to the

Moscow press about the SED's leading role and the Berlin Wall are likely to hurt him as much as Gorbachev's coattails may help.

Neues Deutschland's headline was old-style: "Total Agreement at the Mikhail Gorbachev–Egon Krenz Meeting." At least they did not talk past each other, as Honecker and Gorbachev had last month. Imre, who watched television, said Krenz was confident and voluble with the press. If his delivery was still a little wooden, he showed skill at dodging tough questions. Despite bows to reform, however, he was frequently conventional. The Party's leading role was anchored in the constitution, he said, and there was no need to reassess the invasion of Czechoslovakia. Travel would be eased, but the Berlin Wall protected the state, and reunification was not on the agenda. An East German with whom Imre shared a beer quipped, "The Wall, the SED's leading role, 1968—there goes another small town" into the emigration.

Gorbachev was sensitive to his ally's difficulties. His remark that he was a fan of thorough analysis and long-term political orientation, not rapid decisions, may have been a bonus, but perhaps not one relevant to the fast-changing GDR situation.

Surprisingly, while Krenz defended Honecker's most prominent building project, a Central Committee member, the first secretary of Neubrandenburg District, Johannes Chemnitzer, was admitting that the opening of borders in other socialist states has made the Wall an illusion. The final decision on its fate, however, must await a government and Parliament decision, he said. Chemnitzer, age sixty, has been little noticed during his twenty years in the north, but a native of that region touted him last week to Jerry Verner as perhaps the district chief closest to Modrow's thinking and style.

The Wall's growing irrelevance is being demonstrated again in Prague, of course. The outflow is a fact Krenz must live with. When the new travel law is on the books, even more will move west. One perceptive contact argues that emigration will increase even further if the GDR adopts Perestroika. Many would then leave to escape unsettled, even if potentially improving, conditions.

With protests now almost routine in many cities, the focus this Saturday will be on Berlin's officially sanctioned mass demonstration. A half million are anticipated, and police will be aided by 600 marshals from the sponsoring theater association. Colleagues at the U.S. Mission in West Berlin are nervous, and Pete Ito will be at his desk in the State Department with an open line to us. I expect no trouble. Still, the nearness of the Wall and the Brandenburg Gate lends special sensitivity should any protestors stray from the approved area.

"Chairman of Industrial Union Resigns over Corruption Charges" reads like a Western headline, Janice noted this morning. Only a day earlier the *Berliner Zeitung* had revealed questionable practices the IG-Metall boss used to build himself a house. Thoughtful East Germans note that more is required than cleaning up the present mess. Mechanisms are needed to guard against repetition once enthusiasm—or expediency—wanes. The IG-Metall case is a first instance here of the press exercising the control function Gorbachev had in mind when he designed Glasnost. In a related matter, *Neues Deutschland* announced that journalists and filmmakers are drafting a new media law. Gerlach says the LDPD will make its own suggestions. Of course, "media freedom" is also a demand of Saturday's demonstration. While the union embarrassment is ad hoc progress, time will tell whether the legislative exercise seeks to institutionalize freedom or censorship.

The FDJ's reform efforts are ambiguous at best. A few non-SED youths were promoted to senior positions this week, but consider *Neues Deutschland*'s editorial. After claiming that a young person's political or social preference no longer mattered, it added that the new FDJ "intends to be an autonomous organization that, proceeding from the SED's decisions, recognizes and undertakes its duties."

For the first time, an SED official has admitted that the real results in last May's election were less than the announced 98.87 percent positive. Before high school students, Magdeburg's Mayor Herzig attributed this to fatigue, a confession the local paper called "embarrassing." Herzig had not sounded worried when he said archly to Dick and me just before that vote "If I am reelected," but next time could be different.

Vogel, who retains the new regime's mandate, believes Krenz must at least put the SED's power monopoly and the Berlin Wall up for review. That seems right. Krenz faces many other challenges, perhaps even more immediately building his team and program at next week's Plenum. But the deep unrest signified by street protestors and, again, Prague refugees shows that he cannot long postpone those two questions. He has done a lot quickly, but he has not yet much affected the odds against him.

NOVEMBER 3

My lunch with Gregor Gysi today was at one of Berlin's fun restaurants, Zur Letzten Instanz, in the Waisenstrasse. It dates back 450 years and is the city's oldest; indeed, it is built into a part of the original city wall. A true *Kneipe* (pub), it offers little more to eat than *Eisbein*, but there is always draft beer and atmosphere, especially if, as today, it is possible to squeeze into the front bar. On my first visit, a voluble waiter described how Gorbachev had once eaten two (!) *Eisbeine* but, true to principles, cut the fat with fruit juice, not vodka. "We get the best customers here," he told me, "from the courts down the street, the church on the side, and the cemetery." I have not yet seen the latter, but the two former categories are regulars, as well as those who want to talk soccer or drink after the cabaret in the nearby "House of Young Talent." The name means "The Last Resort," because for centuries it has been the preferred appeal bar of judges and litigants, and it was the courts' proximity that brought us today. Gysi's office is a three-minute walk, and these days saving time is important for the outspoken establishment reformer.

I knew about Gregor long before I met him, especially from contacts in the Jewish community. One-quarter Jewish on his father's side, he participates in its "youth group." His father, Klaus, was then still in the Cabinet, and he himself had gained a reputation by defending "political" clients like Bohley. Our first talk was on legal reform, as I explored the hypothesis that while the Politburo resisted grand changes, creeping liberalization was under way in government and society. I spoke also with law professors, judges, supreme court justices, and a state prosecutor, and drove to Rostock for an afternoon with Wolfgang Schnur, who now leads Democratic Awakening. Gregor, however, gave the most detailed description of what it was like to struggle within a system that was skewed against defendants but that, he argued, provided some possibilities if the lawyer fought hard enough. The picture he painted was in lighter colors than Schnur's, but he made it clear that he was impatient for change on the Gorbachev model.

It has been easier for Gysi, with impeccable socialist background and connections, to be a "courageous" lawyer, but I have no reason to doubt his sincerity, and I enjoy his self-deprecating humor. As we once walked along the Wilhelminian corridors of the High Court, I told him I had not known what to do with my own legal training. It was the same with him, he said, but the GDR offered only three possibilities. "I could not be a judge since I cannot make up my mind, and I could never be a prosecutor because I could not put people in jail," he said. "That left only defense lawyer."

FIG. 13. This bitter cartoon depiction of the *Wendehals*, the establishment bird that could present itself as a reformer by a twist of the neck, appeared on the Wall shortly after it was opened in November 1989. (Janice Weiner)

FIG. 14. November 4, 1989. On the way to Alexanderplatz in Berlin: Banners demand "An End to the SED Dictatorship" and "Free Elections." (Landesbildstelle Berlin)

FIG. 15. November 4, 1989. View of the giant demonstration that filled Alexanderplatz. One banner demands that the "Stasi be put to work in factories." (Landesbildstelle Berlin)

FIG. 16. Another view of the Alexanderplatz demonstration, November 4, 1989, with one banner urging citizens, "Stay in the Street and Don't Ease Up!" (Landesbildstelle Berlin)

FIG. 17. November 11–12, 1989. The open Wall: Trabies and pedestrians stream through the Bornholmer Strasse checkpoint in both directions. (Bundesbildstelle Bonn)

FIG. 18. November 11–12, 1989. After the Wall opened, the Kurfürstendamm, the heart of West Berlin's shopping district, became a pedestrian zone—one vast mall, its six lanes and median strip given over to strollers. (Bundesbildstelle Bonn)

Fig. 19. Marches in Leipzig, Dresden, and other large cities changed character in November–December 1989. Banners demanded "We want *one* new Germany," no longer a reformed GDR. (German Information Center, © IN-Press/AP)

Fig. 20. Gregor Gysi, a lawyer who defended dissidents, tried to reform and preserve the Communist (SED) party after Krenz's fall. (Landesbildstelle Berlin)

Fig. 21. Ibrahim Böhme helped found the opposition Social Democratic party in October 1989 and was its unsuccessful candidate for prime minister in March 1990 before charges of a Stasi connection destroyed his political career. (Landesbildstelle Berlin)

FIG. 22. Lothar de Maizière, a lawyer and close associate of Gysi, led the Christian Democrats (CDU) out of their alliance with the Communists and negotiated unification as the GDR's first democratically elected prime minister. (Landesbildstelle Berlin)

FIG. 23. Free elections in the GDR, March 1990. Party posters in Berlin. (Janice Weiner)

FIG. 24. East Germans holding West German flags and signs that say "yes" to unification cheer Helmut Kohl at an election rally in Magdeburg, March 6, 1990. (German Information Center, K. Lehnartz)

Gysi-son and Gysi-father are proof that long before Honecker's fall there was dissatisfaction within the SED elite, but the old man may be more calculating and realistic. Last summer, shortly after he was encouraged to retire, he described bitterly over whiskeys to Ambassador Meehan how bad the rot was. "Gregor said to me, 'Father, you must go to Erich and tell him this.' I asked if he thought I was crazy. I am not going to commit suicide."

Gregor arrived fifteen minutes late today, still stuffing papers into his oversized case. As we hurriedly ate *Eisbein* and drank beer, our conversation was interrupted by other patrons, who asked Gregor to greet his father and praised his recent statements. Was he becoming a politician? I asked. Serious people had no other choice these days, he indicated.

Where did Krenz stand on our old topic, the rule of law? I wanted to know. Protestors demand that the GDR no longer be ruled arbitrarily by the SED, and there is much talk of placing controls on state power to ensure that there are never again "aberrations," as all now admit occurred on the police side over the 40th Anniversary weekend. The justice minister, a member of the increasingly assertive LDPD, told the press yesterday that thirty new laws were urgently required, especially to improve human rights "in the sense of the CSCE negotiations," not least what he euphemistically titled the "special part" of the criminal code. Gysi noted with pride that much of what the justice minister was saying had been called for by the lawyers. Parts deleted from their document by the press, he indicated as he gave me his annotated copy, went even further in demanding that laws "which can be interpreted according to wish" be repealed, and "law be freed from the influence of daily politics."

In fact, Gysi said, he was late because he had been telling the justice minister that drafts worked on for years and that the minister had promised would go to Parliament this fall must be thoroughly redone. The cautious, small steps that he and I had discussed last year were now inadequate, Gysi said. Too many of those in power believed that a few quick fixes would let them return to business as usual. Fundamental reform, including creation of new structures, was essential so that the GDR did not revert to the disastrous practices that had produced the crisis. Gysi admitted he did not know whether Krenz supported more than superficial change. Under Honecker, his portfolio included law matters, and he had helped with such measures as abolishing the death penalty and initiating a limited administrative court review. The issues now, however, Gysi said, went much deeper. The SED had to give up some power. It must recognize the distinction between retaining "the leading role" and insisting on its "sole representation right."

Gysi, who had just reviewed the draft travel law with the justice minister and made minor suggestions, described it in detail. It should be released for discussion Monday, Gysi said, but it gives a citizen the right to a passport and an exit visa. The state could prohibit travel on only four grounds: national security (e.g., for someone in the military); possession of secrets; reason to suspect travel would be misused to engage in criminal activity, especially blackmarketeering; and pending criminal charges. It also provided, he noted, that every citizen could apply for emigration and strongly implied this should be approved. On the key point of how travel would be financed, Gysi explained, there was no decision yet. The dispute was between those who recognized a political need and the economists. As Gysi described it, the draft is a substantial advance, at least if the "rubber paragraphs" that left so much room for administrative arbitrariness have indeed been dropped. The emigration terms seem to reflect the new reality created by events in Prague, Warsaw, and Budapest, but they will still be a gamble on the popular mood.

Gysi excused himself before coffee. He had to consider what to say at tomorrow's demonstration, he explained. As he shoved the papers he had spread over the table into his case, he called this a time of opportunity. Almost everything needed to be reformed, "but we must also be careful not to throw the baby out with the bath."

The Turk who haunts football training camps at roster-cut time checked into the Grand Hotel last night and whetted his sword. He warmed up for the Plenum by removing two Bloc Party Chairmen—Götting of the CDU and Homann of the NDPD—ratifying Tisch's departure from the FDGB, and giving SED bosses in two southern districts (Gera and Suhl) pink slips. The new people, in a foretaste of the Plenum where Krenz will pick his team to play the championship game, are younger and, superficially at least, more in tune with the times. The day's most startling news, however, was an LDPD proposal that Parliament convene in emergency session, that the government resign (Willi Stoph's cabinet, not Krenz), and that its own chairman, Gerlach, become Parliament president. Some believe it caught the SED by surprise.

Krenz, however, was drinking toasts this afternoon with the Diplomatic Corps. Dick, called over for a polite word, found him more gaunt than he seems on television. The man-killing pace now imposed on political leaders tests Krenz's uncertain health and reminds the gerontocracy that, politics and reputations aside, it cannot meet the standards necessary to confront the GDR's problems.

Jörg von Studnitz passed Dick a disturbing further clue that Krenz's understanding limps behind reality. Jörg was back from Dresden, where Berghofer told him the leadership simply did not grasp that power-sharing was the key issue. The mayor predicts disaster if Krenz will not compromise.

It is not just the people in the street who demand that the SED rethink the most fundamental of its assumptions, though they, of course, apply the strongest pressure. The Bloc Parties, especially the LDPD, have ears to the ground and are becoming more restive daily with Communist insistence on retaining control, even a more enlightened control, of all that matters. The Parliamentary initiative is apparently the LDPD's boldest step yet, but Imre notes suspicions that Krenz and Gerlach formed an alliance in summer when it became clear Honecker's political health was failing. If so, some of Gerlach's early criticism may have been tactical, and he may now be claiming a payoff. Gysi argued at lunch today, however, that the LDPD liked its taste of independence, and *Neues Deutschland*'s scanty coverage of the new demands showed that the SED did not know how to react.

On television, the new men in the south look like model forties-generation officials eager to put new life and style into the SED. Time will tell. They have "picture book" apparatchik biographies, and their predecessors were as young when they were first tapped for large things, albeit in very different circumstances.

Word is just in that Leipzig's governing mayor, Bernd Seidel, has resigned. At age forty, he was not of the Old Guard, but he reacted more slowly to protests than Berghofer did in Dresden. He talked to demonstrators this Monday, but it did not save him.

The new union leader is fifty-five-year-old Annelise Kimmel, a member of the SED Secretariat in Berlin and for ten years the city's FDGB chief. Until her union was first to call for Tisch's head and then protested loudest when the FDGB Presidium tried to put the question off, she had not distinguished herself from the gray apparatchiks. Many will doubt she is more prepared than Tisch was to stand up for workers rather than pass down the Party's commands.

Günther Jahn, the SED chief in Potsdam, and Kurt Hager, have backed off from talks with Dick, pleading work, but Otto Reinhold came to his lunch today. Krenz's broom, he said, may also sweep away Horst Dohlus, the unpopular cadre czar. Schabowski is to take Herrmann's agitprop responsibilities. The job will not get a name that is more attractive to Western ears, like "public relations," and it will remain important. The former *Neues Deutschland* editor may appreciate the need to turn the media into a Glasnost watchdog against Government-Party arbitrariness.

Most interesting was Reinhold's comment that, though the country's mood was very bad, "the mood within the Party is almost as bad." There was more dissatisfaction than he could ever remember, and little willingness to give the new leader the benefit of the doubt. Krenz faced almost as much trouble persuading Comrades as street protestors, he said. Sometimes they were the same people.

Complementary accounts cast new light on Honecker's final day. Wolfgang Vogel repeated to Dick last night that he had expected to stay until the May Congress. At the decisive October 17 session, however, he was attacked by several "nervous colleagues." According to his longtime friend, Honecker finally resigned, saying he was fed up and would take it no longer. Reinhold fingered the "nervous colleagues" as Stoph, Hager, and, surprisingly, Stasi chief Mielke. Stoph's intervention pushed Honecker past his limit.

The stakes in Berlin tomorrow are enormous. If it goes well, a giant step will have been taken to making legal "demos," as Schabowski put it, "part of the GDR's political culture." There is no reason to think it will not go well, but when so many do something still so novel so close to the Wall, there is a collective intake of breath. The speakers will say less than the people can by their presence and demeanor.

NOVEMBER 4

I drove early to the embassy before the inner city was shut to traffic. At 8:00 A.M., Alexanderplatz was empty, but police and army were deploying in side streets on the Unter den Linden side of the Spree, near the Neue Wache, to "protect" the Brandenburg Gate if marchers crossed the Schlossbrücke. All was still quiet, I told Pete, at his desk at 3:00 A.M. Washington time. As Pierre Shostal and I walked back across the bridge, demonstrators were disembarking from trains at Alexanderplatz or marching down Schönhauser

Allee. From the square, they made a circuit, Leipzig style, first on Karl-Liebknecht-Strasse, then, at the Lustgarten, taking a left past the Palace of the Republic, where Parliament meets, to the Council of State, where Krenz has his office, and across Marx-Engels Forum or along Mühlendamm back into Alexanderplatz. As we met them at the Palace of the Republic, we realized their numbers were enormous.

Wardens wearing green armbands with the legend "No Violence" were active. The mood was cheerful, buoyant, almost exalted. Hundreds mounted the stairs of the Palace of the Republic to drape banners from the Parliament balcony. Others detoured to place homemade signs, or simply candles, against the walls of the Council of State. Many sought out the police with a deliberate kindness, as if to emphasize the grotesqueness of the violence that marred the October 7 weekend. I saw cruisers with windows covered by flowers while bemused officers looked on from the curb. Only once did we think there might be trouble. The march had passed the Palace of the Republic, and the wardens with it, when several hundred black-leather-clad Skinheads appeared. They were not part of the main demonstration; some had been drinking, and their hard mood was what I associate with the fringe of a soccer crowd, not the disciplined protests that have shaken the GDR this fall. Would they turn left and join the tail of the march filing into Alexanderplatz, or would they continue toward the Brandenburg Gate? A thin police line stretched across the bridge, but I had seen the massive reinforcements nearby. We breathed out slowly as, cursing, the Skinheads swung left and were absorbed into the peaceful mass.

Crude signs and banners were everywhere, some requiring a half-dozen bearers, most single pieces of cardboard on a stick. They employed a biting humor dependent on often untranslatable rhymes or puns and showing deep distrust of Krenz and the SED:

> "Stay in the street and don't ease up!"
>
> "Suggestion for May 1: The leaders march past the people."
>
> "First you make a mess of it, then we trust you?"
>
> "Stasi, show your face!"
>
> "Plebiscite on the SED's leadership claim!"
>
> "Passports for everyone—a pink slip for the SED!"
>
> "We are the People—and there are millions of us!"

"We demand free elections!" [Propped against the Parliament entrance]

"Pluralism instead of Party monarchy!" [Affixed to the outer wall of the Council of State]

"We don't trust you, Mr. Krenz. You are still hiding the truth about May 7, 1989."

"Grandmother, what big teeth you have." (Under a caricature of Krenz as the bonneted Little Red Riding Hood wolf)

"Bye-bye [*Tschüss*] SED."

"A turn [*Wende*] of 360 degrees?"

"Further, further, further, and don't forget!"

To anyone who has seen the carefully prepared sanctioned slogans carried on May Days past that claimed to represent public opinion, the imagination today was astounding—but with all the variety, I saw only a single small sign borne by an elderly man that touched on one theme: "My name is Hans Schmidt, Florastrasse, Berlin-Pankow, Germany." No one paid him heed. On this day, and with this massive crowd, either reunification was of no interest or the instinctive consensus was that it was too sensitive to broach.

Pierre and I merged with the marchers for a half circuit into Alexanderplatz, where we tried without success to estimate size. I could accept the half million most media cited. The one million others claimed defies comprehension but is no more astonishing than the realization that washed over me as the speakers came to the microphone and we made our way back toward the embassy: It was exactly four weeks since Imre and I had talked our way through police barricades to reach Alexanderplatz in search of the first protests on the GDR's fortieth birthday. "These people will not be satisfied with cosmetic changes," Pierre said, "and I don't see how the SED can control the situation, not with what those posters demand." We told Pete to go home and sleep but that the GDR would never be the same after this day. This is revolution, without violence or fixed goals, but revolution nonetheless. The people call the music, not the politicians—and the people know their power.

We left before the speeches, not only to phone Washington but also to pick up Gaby and drive to Dresden to see the Semper Opera and pay a Sunday morning call on Superintendent Ziemer, the Protestant church leader who helped get the negotiations between the Group of 20 and Berghofer going. Would GDR Radio carry the speeches? Pierre asked. Doubtful, I said, but I was wrong. We heard speaker after speaker try in five or ten minutes to come to grips with the essence of this historic day.

- Gregor Gysi was received well, except when defending Krenz. He called for political structures to ensure democracy, new economic thinking, and reform of the criminal code. He skirted the tolerance level when he said, "I am—and I know I disagree here with many—for the Party's leading role but not its power monopoly." But the SED, he said, must reform thoroughly and quickly. He delivered one of the day's best lines, typical cynical Gysi wit: "If I tried to join demands for a better service sector and rule of law into one sentence, I would say every household should have a telephone, and the comment 'I would rather not say this on the telephone' should be consigned to history."

- Markus Wolf had less success. He heard whistles, boos, jeers, even calls of "Stop! stop!" A Stasi reformer is more than most of those in the streets are prepared to accept. His viability as a major player was at least wounded on Alexanderplatz.

- Jens Reich's call for recognition of the Opposition groups was cheered, but he cautioned, "Dialogue is not the main meal, only the appetizer." Peaceful struggle had to continue in every branch of society: "We have to use our rights not only here, at the demo, but in front of the boss, with colleagues, before teacher and bureaucrats, everywhere, and we have to stand beside the person who exercises his rights, not wait to see whether he breaks his neck."

- Gerlach gave a campaign speech for his LDPD, which "pushed open the door." He is, as Imre points out, running for Parliament president. His biggest cheers came when he demanded that the Stoph Cabinet resign and rejected the SED's truth monopoly, but the crowd did not welcome being reminded that after this fall's emotional high a long slog would be needed to turn the economy around. Was it only because it resembled old SED calls to sacrifice for an always receding future? If patience is indeed so thin, Krenz has even more trouble than assumed. The gap between East German and West German living standards must take years to narrow.

- Schabowski's talk was the most dramatic. The contrast to his city hall appearance last Sunday could hardly have been greater. Then he was the People's Tribune, heard respectfully by an audience impressed that an SED chief would answer its questions. This time he had difficulty making himself heard over derisive whistles. He is a fighter, and he put down his text to speak freely, again in Berlin jargon. "Bitter things have been said here, and they go to our address, also to mine," he admitted. He claimed: "The SED subscribes to reform. That came late, damn late [shouts: "Too late!"], but it is irreversible. We are determined to learn to live with contradictions, with pepper and salt." But the moderator had to plead with the throng to listen, and much of his conclusion came across as old-fashioned and out of touch. Schabowski got some applause and probably won some respect, but the jeers showed that in six days the demonstrators' self-confidence and expectations have grown exponentially. On Monday, Dick found Schabowski on a high from his first "bath in the masses." He will be sober this evening.

- Stefan Heym's voice betrayed excitement and wonder as he said, "We are learning how to walk upright—and that, friends, in Germany, where until now all revolutions went wrong, and the people clicked their heels, under the Kaiser, the Nazis, and later also. But to speak freely, to walk upright is not enough. Let us also learn to rule. Power belongs not in the hands of one man or a few, not in the hands of a bureaucracy or one Party." It was his great moment, and he earned some of the strongest applause of the day.

- Christoph Hein eloquently warned against euphoria: "We haven't done it yet. The cow isn't yet off the ice, and there are enough forces that want no change, that fear a new society, and that have reason to fear it." Just as he had last week in church, he had the grace to spare a moment for the political bankrupts. He recalled Honecker, a man "who had a dream and was prepared to go to prison for this dream." The GDR has been characterized by "demagoguery, spying, abuse of power, denial of its citizens' maturity, and also crimes, . . . and I believe that also for this old man our society can in no way be the fulfillment of his dreams." In the end, he said, even Honecker was nearly helpless against the structures he had built and allowed to grow cancerously. Hein spoke of Honecker "only to warn that we do not also create structures that one day we find ourselves helpless against." The need was to "create a democratic society on the basis of laws that can be appealed against, a socialism that does not caricature the word."

- Another sign of how fast things are moving: Schorlemmer was virtually the most moderate speaker. Not that he did not demand change—"Democracy, now or never" was his call. But Friedrich was also true to his pulpit: "Let us not tolerate anywhere voices and moods of revenge." And, more surprising: "I want to say to those of us from the new democratic movement, let us not replace old intolerance with new intolerance. Let us be tolerant and honorable with old and new political rivals, also with a changing SED. Let us recall what fears the new First Man produced in us and what new movement has already started with him. I mean that we do not want to and we cannot now build our land up without the SED—only it must not lead us." His peroration reminded me of my first visit to him in Wittenberg. As we walked side streets and saw piles of lung-poisoning brown coal before crumbling houses, he said he was willing to accept a decline in the GDR's modest living standard as the price for environmental responsibility and freedom. Today he said: "We shall still go through a valley; we shall not distinguish ourselves by special prosperity, but perhaps by more friendliness and warmth. Coming from Wittenberg, I recall to the ruled and rulers— that is, to all of us—a word of Martin Luther's: Allow the spirits to struggle with each other, but keep fists still."

- And finally, the last of nearly thirty speakers, there was Steffi Spira, an actress as old as Heym, one of those idealistic socialists with a biography that reminds us of the hopes many in an earlier generation had for this "other" German state. She went alone, she recalled, into a foreign land in 1933, carrying nothing except what was in her head, including a Brecht verse:

> So as it is, it will not remain.
> Who lives, never says never.
> Who has recognized his situation,
> How should he be held back?
> And from never there will yet be today!

Let us, she concluded, "make Wandlitz an old people's home. Those over sixty . . . can stay when they do as I do now—get off the stage!"

It ended shortly after 2:00 P.M., and as we continued through the gathering darkness, we listened to news reports. The first gave the size accurately but described the demonstration only as for "renewal." Each successive account was more candid. As we pulled up before our hotel, the announcers were telling whatever small part of the GDR did not already know that "a half million citizens demonstrated in Berlin today for far-reaching reform in our country, including free elections and an end to the SED's leading role in the state." Indeed, a peaceful revolution.

The Semper Oper is an architectural marvel of opera's classical age, a cultural treasure of Europe, and a slightly controversial glory of the GDR. Some resent the money devoted to rebuilding it from the ruin the 1945 bombing left, and especially that for a "normal GDR mortal" a ticket is more than hard to get. On this evening, the main event came after Gluck's *Orpheus and Eurydice*, when the tenor stepped forward to speak. Theater people were proud to have stimulated the demand for free speech and democracy, he said, but further struggles were ahead. We sat, diplomatically correct, with folded hands, observers not participants, but the audience responded enthusiastically. More than half were West Germans on hard-currency cultural tours.

NOVEMBER 5

Dresden looked no different from previous visits as we strolled the Baroque complex of the Zwinger Museum this morning. Away from the immediate vicinity of the political happenings that have shaken this state to its core, buses and trams run on schedule; there is no physical disruption, much less damage. People go about routines, at least until evening or the weekend. A factory hour has rarely been lost. A half hour after the speeches on Saturday afternoon, Imre said, Alexanderplatz was empty. Scarcely a sausage wrapper littered the square. At one corner, demonstrators had neatly stacked their signs and banners in response to the organizers' desire to collect them for historical exhibition.

Surface routine deceives, of course, as we relearn daily, but outsiders are also misled. Pete Ito might not be ordered in at 3:00 A.M. if Washington appreciated the extraordinary discipline of East Germans. There is fear at home for the slide into violence, bloody repression, and civil strife that is the stuff of gaming scenarios for outbreak of world war. I do not discount mischance, but this society is united by a consensus that should keep the nightmare away. Its ordered sense of purpose reassures and inspires. Pierre observed yesterday that the revolution will go further than he had anticipated, but also that the risks of it spinning out of control are less than they seemed from Washington.

We spent an hour with a quiet hero before departing from Dresden. Church Superintendent Ziemer channeled ugly-tempered and at times violent protests into peaceful dialogue that has set a national example. Over coffee at home, he called it a "near thing." He had been roused from bed to keep peace more than once. However, Dresden has come furthest toward institutionalizing a role for new political forces. The Group of 20, Ziemer said, has found novel ways to legitimize its mandate. It asked citizens to pay one Mark each into a special account. The authorities grudgingly allowed the procedure, which is meant less to defer expenses than to document backing. The account holds more than 70,000 Marks.

Halfway to Berlin, we inspected mushrooms at makeshift roadside stands. One had *Steinpilze*, the noblest variety found in German forests. Though the price was high and in West Marks, it was a microcosm of the economic energy a reform policy can hope to unleash. But the fixation on making the effort only for hard currency, not the GDR's own weak Mark, shows how tough it will be to devise incentives without a truly radical overhaul of the economy.

NOVEMBER 6

Egon Krenz has had only nineteen days in power, but this week may decide his fate. I began it by reviewing the televised speech he made Friday evening, on two-hour notice. Verbally, he had sided with far-reaching reform. Because he talked only of a more enlightened SED, however, most reaction in the last sixty hours has been negative.

Reforms "may not come fast enough for some, and for some they may not go far enough," Krenz said, but there was no turning back. The Politburo had approved the action program he would lay before the Plenum: creation of a constitutional court; administrative reform; reduction of Party and government privileges; an alternative to the military draft; an attack on "many consumer shortages" and "a thorough change of economic policy tied to extensive economic reform"; education reform; and SED democratization, including term limits. Change at the top was required, Krenz admitted, and five of Honecker's Old Guard—including Axen, Hager, and Mielke—had "volunteered" to resign.

Though this Krenz was vastly different from the traditional SED man who spoke three weeks ago, it is fair to say that the GDR has made much progress and he little. He is only scratching the surface of objective problems and subjective distrust that have accumulated for forty years, but he demonstrates too much adaptability to be written off yet.

The draft travel law published this morning is much as Gysi previewed Friday. The headline is "Citizens of the GDR Have the Right to Travel Abroad," but restrictions on duration of travel and the need to meet application deadlines will dampen joy for the suspicious, and the vital currency question is still not resolved.

This draft is close to a total break with a fundamental feature of the repressive society and may soon call the Berlin Wall's continued existence into question. Immediately, it tests whether Krenz can get credit with a distrustful, impatient citizenry. It is a very good thing with some regressive elements. Given the mood, it could be another example of too little, too late. However, it is not the final version. Krenz wants the law in force for Christmas. Parliament will have its first chance to exercise that meaningful review he says he expects and the Bloc Parties are demanding. Citizens may send comments to a special postal address, "Keyword Travel Law." Old thinking can still be worked out.

Six weeks and a political age ago, GDR leaders, including many now born-again reformers, blamed "certain circles" in the Federal Republic as refugees fled through Hungary and the Prague Embassy filled. *Neues Deutschland* told of a loyal cook who smoked a drugged menthol cigarette and woke up on his way to Vienna in the care of a West German "tour guide." That exposé became a metaphor for the infantile media style and the silence of the political class. On Friday, *Neues Deutschland* apologized for the story. Imre points out that this blossoming of journalistic ethics comes late. Leipzig papers acted last month. It is the new pattern: Saxony sets the pace, a week or so later Berlin kicks in, and the north lags a fortnight behind.

I joined Dick for drinks with key figures from three Opposition groups this evening. I already knew Reich and Pflugbeil of Neues Forum and Stefan Bickhardt of Democracy Now, of course. We were most curious about Ibrahim Böhme and the bearded young men with him. It was our first opportunity for real talk with their SDP, the month-old GDR version of the West German Social Democrats.

The talk flowed freely between Americans and Germans and, not infrequently, between the Germans themselves. The latter know each other well. Almost without exception they share Berlin-based, intellectual roots. Attitudinal and policy lines of division are fuzzy. SDP "party politicians" were at least as interested in philosophy and as vague about programs as their colleagues from the "movements." Indeed, "colleagues" is the appropriate term. They consider each other allies against the SED and Krenz (whom none trust), not competitors. An outsider could easily transpose, say, Democracy Now and Neues Forum spokesmen, and I eavesdropped as Böhme offered Stefan leadership of an SDP policy committee.

I do not want to judge the new politicians harshly. They are understandably startled at how far they have come. The Social Democrats are just beginning to believe that jail does not lie before them and to ponder the details of building a national party. In much of the country, their organization is no more than a few sympathizers. Neues Forum is larger but not much further along with putting muscle on its frame. All suffer from near total lack of equipment, beginning with phones and copiers. Stefan showed me Democracy Now's one-page paper, published irregularly, apparently by stencil, giving a "contact address" but no telephone number. The others are as far from real time communications.

They cannot have been at ease in the American Ambassador's living room, though Dick tried to relax them by introducing three-month-old Katie. Böhme sought escape from nervousness in constant talk. A historian and an SED member in a naive youth before the violent end of the Prague Spring, as he explained, he ranged over Bismarck's Reich, the Counterreformation, and classical Greece. But he was less confident than he pretended, and unable to direct the debate. Jens Reich was more composed, if less loquacious, and Dick was particularly impressed with "the good head" on young Stefan's shoulders. Nevertheless, I came away feeling that the Opposition is not yet ready to control events. Its leaders may have potential, but the rare natural talent has not been found. Ironically, they share a challenge with Krenz: to master tasks their experiences could scarcely have prepared them for.

NOVEMBER 7

The Plenum, where the SED tries to get its down-but-not-necessarily-out act together, is where the action is for the next three days. It is worth recalling, however, that it is scarcely a month since Honecker's world of illusions broke down when the sounds of citizens striding across the borders and into the streets of Berlin, Leipzig, and Dresden drowned out the lockstep march of the 40th Anniversary celebrations. The GDR is playing in the Soviet-Hungarian-Polish League. It may not have gone as far toward Western concepts; many here insist they seek a German Third Way. But basic assumptions and behavior patterns are being replaced at a pace no other country approaches. Gorbachev broke in with a splash but has moved in relatively careful fashion. Hungary compromised for years before achieving take-off speed. Even Poland was only a maverick until Lech Walesa jumped over the Gdansk Shipyard fence. The GDR seemed to sleep for decades, yet within a month we can barely stifle a yawn when television reports, as yesterday, that Leipzig had its biggest march, perhaps approximating the half million Berlin turned out on the weekend.

Because a broad consensus already existed, the GDR could move so fast, with little disorder, toward a culture of peaceful political strife, a more open press, liberal travel, and serious discussion of new structures to provide legal security and economic well-being. That consensus had formed almost unnoticed over recent years in this society, much of the SED included. The end of that breathtaking but relatively easy phase is approaching, however. There is no second consensus on how to implement the general goals—for example, what kind of freer press and economic reform, how much more democracy—much less on how to resolve power-sharing and inevitably, though further down the road, the German Question. The issue now is whether some political group can achieve the balance of organization, concept, and popular trust required to carry through that more difficult program.

There are four powers in this land: the street crowds, the Opposition, the Bloc Parties, and the SED. All have weaknesses. The people know what they detest: a Honecker-style all-power-to-the-SED state. They have shown they can exercise a remarkable control function and stimulate the SED to more energy and honesty than it would otherwise wish or dare. If a driving November rain did not dampen enthusiasm in Leipzig on Monday, demonstrations will be with us all winter. Even disciplined, politically sophisticated German crowds, however, cannot formulate detailed policies. The odds on an ugly incident are low, but something else is already apparent. The longer the people march, the more radical their demands are. Unless more traditional political actors gain their trust, these could escalate to where a peaceful resolution becomes improbable.

The Opposition enjoys trust, but more on faith than for its personalities or platforms. Indeed, the amorphous groups have little of either. Bob McCartney of the *Washington Post* and Serge Schmemann of the *New York Times* told me of watching Neues Forum "leaders" smoking cigarettes and debating theory in a Berlin coffeehouse on Saturday while the half million focused pent-up anger on the SED. They may not come out of the coffeehouse in time to meet their rendezvous with history, Bob said. That may be prematurely dismissive, but little common-sense organizational skill and problem-solving was evident at Dick's cocktail party. The Opposition has a great chance to play a major and perhaps ultimately decisive role, but it is too green, fragmented, theoretical, and intellectual to shape events yet. It is beginning to talk of roundtables and similar devices for confronting the Communist establishment with programmatic demands, but it is quite simply not ready.

Other political forces are emerging, especially the suddenly assertive Bloc Parties, with the Liberals (LDPD) and their impressive Chairman, Manfred Gerlach, in the forefront. They have national organizations and a press. None, however, has escaped the taint of subservience to the SED. For the near term at least, they can be more active at the margin, trying to anticipate requirements and move the SED to where it is not sure it wants to go, but they lack muscle and standing to control developments.

That leaves the SED, with its giant handicaps, front and center for now. Not only is it blamed for the mess, it really is responsible. There is no reason to believe it can win broad support or be more effective if the people who made wrong decisions or carried them out poorly retain power. Can the Party regenerate itself and earn control of the political activism in the country, even if only temporarily? The areas to watch start at the top.

Can Krenz survive? He almost surely will last the Plenum, but he needs to put his stamp on it and emerge with a bright new team. He shows more speed of foot than most believed he possessed. In words and style he has made some correct moves, including putting himself close to Gorbachev and trying to respond to demands on the media for an amnesty and a travel law. Krenz has made little dent, however, in the massive mistrust that derives from his record under Honecker. His first speech was 90 percent old, 10 percent new. The proportions were almost reversed when he went on the air last week, but for most East Germans the amount of the old, not the degree of the change, is decisive. As one church leader told us, "I believe in mercy and will urge it be extended to Krenz—but only when he repents." If Krenz counts on the mercy of forgetfulness, he misjudges the depth of antipathy.

The second set of questions is about Krenz's team. He can replace at least half the Politburo, and a key point is whether the few certifiable SED reformers, especially Modrow, are promoted. The economic portfolio is special. The choice to replace Mittag may tell much of Krenz's predilections. The security job is another sensitive one. Markus Wolf might have some standing with those for whom police and Stasi are anathema, but the maverick spymaster may enjoy less support within the SED than longtime Krenz aide Herger, a virtual unknown to the public. Schabowski, more than anyone else in an elderly, isolated Politburo, has a style that gives him a chance to make himself heard (though just barely as Saturday showed) when he argues, "Give us another chance." He is so bright, ambitious, and active that he might normally threaten Krenz, but the SED cannot afford to do without him. He is one of its few conceivable pinch hitters if Krenz strikes out.

Krenz has largely previewed his program, but in the present climate of distrust, it can have psychological impact only if it is made specific. That will not be easy, because the economic problems are complex. Still, it would be disastrous for the Plenum to postpone decisions.

Legally, the Central Committee is the SED's highest organ, but it has always done the Politburo's bidding. Since the crisis began in late summer, however, the Central Committee has pressed to become engaged, and the Politburo has held it off. The 160-odd members are a step closer to the Party grassroots, whose dissatisfaction, as Otto Reinhold confessed, is currently not all that different from the broader population's. They are thus more activist (and for the moment that is essentially equivalent to reformist) than the Politburo. The Plenum will not allow itself to be muzzled as it was three weeks ago when it could only anoint Krenz. It will almost surely force a more candid discussion than the SED is accustomed to, and it may not accept all Krenz's nominations. If he waffles on his promise to pay more heed to it, or the Plenum feels its general secretary still has not grasped the extent of the Party's crisis, outright revolt is conceivable.

Closely related is a larger question of Party democracy. Krenz is not the first general secretary to profess commitment to the concept, but he faces real internal trouble if he does not give it more substance than his predecessors. Markus Wolf used his Alexanderplatz platform to call for a Party conference to take emergency action without waiting for the May Congress. SED members at the Political Science and Law Academy in Potsdam are making a more radical demand, that a full Congress convene before year's end. Both argue that the Central Committee is also responsible for the mess and must pay the price if the SED is to be regenerated. In other words, the Plenum feels hot breath on its neck.

Dominating the situation is the most fundamental question of all: Will the SED stick to its claim, anchored in Article 1 of the Constitution, to be not only the leading party but also the sole repository of authority, as Krenz swore to do in his inaugural address? He soft-pedals this now, agreeing that the leading role must be "earned" daily, but he still insists real power belongs only to the SED. The banners in Berlin on Saturday and in Leipzig yesterday showed this is bottom-line unacceptable. A Parliamentary committee today symptomatically first rejected the draft travel law and then debated the SED's constitutional claim. No one believes the Party is in a mood to withdraw from the GDR's political future, but is it prepared to redefine its core philosophy and explore compromise areas between leading role and exclusive power?

Its best thinkers recognize the need. Rolf Reissig, still close to Reinhold, told J.D. and me on Monday that the SED should abide by competitive elections at every level of government. He has gotten some advanced ideas, though nothing that radical, into *Neues Deutschland*. Many more senior officials, however, are still on the Krenz line. Modrow's protégé in Dresden—Berghofer—and others with more immediate experience than the Berlin leadership of the street mood predict disaster if Krenz is obdurate.

Of course, at the current pace, potential disaster never seems far away. That realization, brought home most dramatically by hundreds of thousands of protestors and tens of thousands of refugees, has already pushed Krenz, the improbable reformer, and the hidebound SED leadership fairly far. Both show a knack for improving just enough to stay behind but not out of sight of rising demands. They will probably do about that well again. If so, both will survive to face the next challenge, but it is just conceivable the Plenum will be more radical than that. The times demand it, and so do many bright people within SED ranks. If that happens, the Party's chance to make the reform process its own for a time should not be discounted. But we shall all be wiser in seventy-two hours.

NOVEMBER 8 (Noon)

As scene-setters for the Plenum that opened hours ago, both the government and the Politburo resigned last evening. The Cabinet will remain as caretaker until Parliament confirms a successor. The Politburo surprise allows Krenz to replace even more than the half that has resigned or been declared lame duck since Honecker's fall. However, the Central Committee is angry and under pressure. A small possibility exists that it could turn on Krenz, who also submitted a resignation. In another important event of the last twenty-four hours, the Parliament's Constitution and Law Committee rejected the travel law for having too many restrictions, too much bureaucracy, and too little about financing. This is a first sign that the consultative procedure is to be taken seriously. A new draft is certain to be more liberal. Plenum deliberations are closed, but Imre, Janice, and Heather will stake out the Press Center. Schabowski is to give a briefing at 6:00 P.M. It will be a long day.

NOVEMBER 8 (6:00 P.M.)

At mid-afternoon, Imre raced back with the new Politburo roster, which we immediately analyzed for Washington. Krenz was reelected general secretary. His Politburo, however, contains only ten others—half what Honecker worked with; counting Krenz, seven are holdovers. Hans-Joachim Böhme, the conservative Halle boss, received a bare majority, and three from Krenz's original list were rejected: Dohlus and Günther Kleiber of the old Politburo, and Gerhard Müller, a hard-liner from Erfurt. Modrow succeeds Stoph as prime minister. On balance, although some portfolios remain to be clarified, and there are anomalies (including Eberlein), the new team appears more streamlined, younger, and better-suited for reform politics than its predecessor. By choosing many Honecker regime colleagues, however, Krenz did not break cleanly with the past.

The most important move brought the sixty-one-year-old Modrow into the inner circle. He had languished in Dresden for sixteen years while he acquired a reputation as a Soviet favorite and the senior SED official most open to Gorbachev-style reform. It would be wrong to say he is widely popular, but he is respected enough to be given a chance. Booed and jeered when he spoke to an early Dresden demonstration, he and his young mayor made a major contribution by being the first to engage protestors in dialogue. Klaus Höpcke, who picked up Hager's culture portfolio, is a bit of an insider's reform hero. As deputy minister, it was believed he did what he could to protect writers; he nearly was fired this spring when he defended a GDR PEN Club resolution on behalf of Vaclav Havel, and he was one of the few establishment figures to be cheered at the Berlin town hall ten days ago. Wolfgang Herger takes over security. Werner Rauchfuss, 58, and in the Cabinet (minister for materials management) for fifteen years, was a surprise Politburo choice. He made a fast rise early and then hit a wall in the 1970s.

In some cases (Modrow's, for example) that has meant someone was too open-minded for Honecker's taste, but that is speculation. Chemnitzer, 60, the Neubrandenburg boss who questions the Berlin Wall, won an intriguing promotion to the Secretariat.

Just after the selections were announced, however, 5,000 who identified themselves as grassroots SED demonstrated in front of Party headquarters and forced an obviously uncomfortable Schabowski and Krenz to leave the Plenum to address them. Their chant was "We are the Party," an eery echo of the Monday evening calls from Leipzig. A banner demanded an end to "one-party dictatorship," another asked "Who can trust a Party run by the apparatus?" They called for free elections and a Congress to choose a totally new Politburo and Central Committee. If the SED lost a vote, they said, it should give up power. Janice mingled among them to sample their anger, and there was live television coverage. Krenz has a two-front fight.

NOVEMBER 8 (Midnight)

We are getting details of Krenz's speech to the Plenum. He said the origins of the crisis were inside the SED, and he had stinging criticism for Honecker and Mittag, but he minimized his own culpability and self-servingly stressed his role in forcing Honecker out. He was strongly for intra-Party democracy and said the SED's leading role should not be confused with running every bit of the government administratively. He implied that there would be major economic changes, but gave few specifics. The citizens' groups, Krenz said, had an important role in a more-democratic GDR. Nevertheless, he avoided power-sharing and free elections. In short, while he was fairly candid about mistakes, he offered no blueprint and may have missed another chance to put the SED into the fight for the political initiative. Schabowski was a little better at his press conference, a Plenum innovation. He hinted at new readiness to risk elections and sit down with the opposition for a roundtable discussion, and confirmed that the Party has lost tens of thousands of members this year through protest or expulsion.

The Big Three are clearly Krenz, Schabowski, and Modrow, with the latter two enjoying more, though limited, public toleration. The Central Committee proved itself not entirely subservient by turning down three nominees, and the protests showed the possibility of grassroots revolt is serious. The Plenum debate that begins tomorrow will tell us more about whether the SED has made a genuine turn or is still going down a dead-end street.

NOVEMBER 9 (10:00 A.M.)

The text of Krenz's address, which became available this morning, gives a slightly fuller idea of the program he wants Modrow to implement. On the political side, he largely repeated what he announced Friday, but he did go gingerly onto new ground to support "free, democratic, general, and secret elections" conducted under public control. This is the closest he has come to acknowledging the linked demands that the SED submit to a genuine election and be prepared to yield at least some power. He defended the Party's leading role, however, and made it clear he does not envisage the SED going into opposition.

Mike Mozur says he had thought of Krenz in terms of pre–October 18 orthodoxy that may not do the practical politician full justice. He found the references to a market orientation in the economic section of the speech an indication of surprising flexibility. Mike believes it may herald an effort to join the mainstream of Eastern European reform. But Krenz put people on notice that hard times lie ahead. Repeated references to "stabilization" suggest that shortcomings in consumer goods and finances can no longer be covered up by misleading statistics, but he was careful to stake out a position as the champion of lower-income groups. He made it clear where the GDR's real interest lies: West German firms dominate each area he identified for new cooperation.

Demands are coming in, most recently from the FDGB, for Parliament to convene on the weekend so that Modrow can make a quick start. I suspect the general reaction will be that Krenz is moving—faster than before and in the right direction, but still inadequately to accommodate rising expectations. He will certainly need to make more precise whether his concept of an adjusted SED role and free elections is within the same ballpark as what the people in the street mean when they insist that the Party share power and submit to a democratic test.

NOVEMBER 9 (Noon)

The *Neue Zeit* and *Der Morgen* have opened their pages to Neues Forum, the former calling for a democratic vote to decide the SED's leadership claim. *Neues Deutschland* concentrated on the Plenum, but in belated domestic election news it reported the resignation of Magdeburg Mayor Herzig, who spoke disingenuously to us before last May's rigged vote—and listed continuing after-work demonstrations: in Neubrandenburg, more than 25,000; in Wismar, a smallish northern coastal city, 50,000; in Nordhausen, 35,000 to 40,000; and in Meiningen, in the far southwest, "around 20,000."

NOVEMBER 9 (3:00 P.M.)

Frank Teutschbein, the U.S. specialist in the Central Committee apparatus, is among the best of the new breed: bright, sophisticated, and disaffected or self-confident enough to be relatively candid even before October 18. At lunch, he told J.D. the new Politburo would not last. There was too much pressure to restructure the Party radically since, as constituted, the SED could not lead a democratic GDR. Early replacement of Krenz was possible, he said. The failed draft travel law, which had not even been shown to the Bloc Parties before *Neues Deutschland* printed it, revealed how much old thinking the SED had to overcome, and he feared the election bill would be approached the same way. The SED would self-destruct unless it made fundamental changes, Frank said. In any event, emigration would continue until 300,000 of the 750,000 with applications on file in summer had left. They were already lost; reforms could not be effective quickly enough.

J.D. raised another subject with me. Before President Bush meets Gorbachev on Malta on December 2, he said, the embassy should assess the reform process and identify possible U.S. initiatives. I promised to put ideas quickly on paper. I have my own deadline. Despite misgivings, Gaby and I have tickets to depart Monday for four weeks of home leave.

NOVEMBER 9 (5:00 P.M.)

A reluctant Plenum judged the Krenz regime could not afford another charge of insensitivity to the grassroots and has convened an extraordinary conference for December 15–17. The conference is both risk and opportunity. Few Central Committee seats are safe, and Krenz's own position will be at risk. A democratic delegate election process would be a referendum on the team selected only yesterday and on its program of action, and a fraudulent election would have grave consequences. All this adds greatly to pressure for Krenz to move further and faster, and raises a prospect that the SED may either fragment or radicalize before the New Year.

NOVEMBER 9 (8:00 P.M.)

An hour ago and almost offhandedly, at the end of his briefing, Schabowski made the sensational announcement of virtually free travel for East Germans. Details are unclear because he was uncertain and ill-prepared himself, but it could start tomorrow.

Schabowski began by announcing that he had to break off punctually after an hour, and he dropped his bombshell just before 7:00 P.M., in response to a last question. Partly reading from a paper he pulled out of his pocket, partly speaking freely, he said that pending a new law, the caretaker Stoph Cabinet had approved interim travel regulations, effective immediately. It appears the regulations stipulate that applications for private travel need no justification, that permission will be forthcoming "in short order" (*kurzfristig*) and denied only exceptionally, and that the police have been instructed to issues visas for permanent emigration "immediately" (*unverzüglich*) without applications.

My phone began to ring at once. Dick, who like me had watched on television, wanted to be certain that we informed Washington. By the time I had promised Pete Ito a telegram, Harry Gilmore was on the line from West Berlin. He was in touch with Governing Mayor Momper, he said. It would be a big challenge to public order, but plans had been ready since Schabowski advised Momper more than a week ago to expect large numbers of visitors soon. When will it begin? Harry asked. Schabowski indicated East Germans needed documents, I said. It seemed odd that permanent emigrants would be processed more quickly than visitors, but that might mean a day or two respite before the flood. It could be as early as the opening of police pass offices tomorrow morning, however.

By then, Imre was back to compare notes. We agreed there were unanswered questions. If travelers required passports, there could be a long wait, if only because millions would have to be issued, and financial aspects had still not been addressed. But it was clear that the West would need to brace for a torrent of tourists and emigrants. As Schabowski spoke, Imre recounted, the normally unflappable Ständige Vertretung press spokesman had grasped his head, moaned, and dashed from the room to sound the alert.

Krenz is trying to make up for the opportunity he missed Monday with the draft law. His quick response is meant to signal that, unlike Honecker, he takes popular and Parliamentary will seriously and that when the bill finally emerges it will indeed be a vast improvement. He is also still seeking desperately to halt the hemorrhage to the West. He hopes this extraordinary measure will encourage people to give reform a chance.

If the authorities process applications as promised, the question will quickly arise: What purpose the Berlin Wall? Schabowski was asked that and ducked. Nevertheless, unless Krenz acknowledges the Wall is rapidly becoming an anachronism, many may conclude that the new liberalization is a gambit that could be withdrawn as quickly as it was introduced. Until he does so, he works at psychological cross-purposes to his high-stakes gamble.

Gaby called to ask whether I had heard Schabowski and to report a worrisome experience she had minutes ago on returning to East Berlin. As she was waved through the checkpoint, a dozen men, gesticulating and shouting unintelligibly, blocked Bornholmer Strasse. She first thought they were drunk, but no bottles were visible. As they let her pass, she saw more people coming out of the nearby apartment buildings, apparently to join them. Nerves are stretched taut tonight. Hopefully the restraint that has carried East Germans so far will not fail them just when their demands for free travel and political and economic reform are so close to realization.

NOVEMBER 9 (9:00 P.M.)

Twenty-four hours after it was selected, Krenz's Politburo is coming apart at the seams. Local Party organizations have voted no confidence in Halle's Böhme, Cottbus's Werner Walde, and Neubrandenburg's Chemnitzer. It is the clearest sign yet of how bitter the feeling at the SED's middle and grassroots levels is. Krenz is in for a difficult time at next month's conference.

NOVEMBER 9 (10:50 P.M.)

We have finally sorted out the day's stories. J.D. has left, and I am about to follow. As always, the communicators, Duane Bredeck and Larry Stafford, stay the longest. Political Officers go home when we give them our telegrams. On this night and many others, they work alone to midnight and beyond to process them, but they make no complaints. Like everyone in the embassy, they are excited and a little awed by the history they are a part of.

Last notes: Schabowski, asked about responsibility for the Honecker personality cult when he ran *Neues Deutschland*, replied that he had been both object and subject of those policies. The experience could make one either insensitive or determined that it should not happen again, he argued, much as being beaten could make a child a worse or better parent. He himself, he said, had become more committed to open media. Earlier this week, Günter Gaus, the SPD writer who opened the Ständige Vertretung in 1974, had called for a Four Power conference on Germany. We mean to succeed, Schabowski said, and will not act on a worst-case scenario.

This press conference will be remembered for the announcement at its end, but Schabowski the politician is fascinating, not least because he acts at home in a milieu for which an SED career scarcely trained him. He knows his party and state are in trouble, and only cures that have a good chance to kill the patient are conceivable. The admission of co-responsibility for a disastrous media policy is a marked contrast to Krenz's obfuscation of his role under Honecker.

Except for the travel sensation and the swelling SED grassroots revolt, this was a "routine" day, the midpoint of the Plenum when most activity was focused on debate. The program of action that Krenz has outlined and Modrow must implement should be finalized tomorrow. Then we shall have to ask what chance it has to brake the escalating pace of events and demands.

NOVEMBER 10 (1:00 A.M.)

One August morning twenty-eight years ago, Berliners awoke to learn that the border was closed, and the Wall had become the central fact of their existence. On this morning, when many will not sleep, the Wall still stands, but Berliners are streaming through its open gates by the scores of thousands. The signs have been there for days. Schabowski's remarks six hours ago were but the most explicit. Still, the actual moment is as much a shock as must have been that other occasion, in 1961. As then, it will take time for numbness, personal and collective, to wear off and implications to make themselves apparent. For now, there is simply the wonder.

As I drove from the embassy two hours ago, downtown was empty, though lights were burning at the Central Committee. But, as thirty-three evenings ago, the scene changed dramatically when I reached Schönhauser Allee's weathered cobblestones, in the shadow of the elevated train. This time the focus was not Gethsemane Church—that symbol of refuge and revolution was dark—but a few blocks north along Bornholmer Strasse. Thousands of pedestrians and cars were moving through the intersection toward the checkpoint. Red-faced, desperately overtaxed traffic cops struggled to keep a lane to Pankow half open, but the vast crowd was intent on reaching the border.

I was frightened for these people and, suddenly, for the remarkable process we have witnessed this fall. There were far fewer police than the night the demonstrations began, but I knew there were troops at the Wall, just hundreds of yards away. If the Berliners did not wait for morning, if they demanded to be allowed through now, how would those guards with whom Gaby and I had shared small jokes and the young soldiers in the towers react? Would orders to open the gates come in time? Could they act on their own? Was there one panicky youth with a weapon on either side of the barrier? After weeks of prudence and discipline, was there now to be a tragedy on the very eve of a great and hopeful breakthrough? Markus Wolf's warning about a Hungarian Revolution–style incident that could bring civil war was very much in my mind.

I considered abandoning the car and joining the throng pushing toward the Wall, but if I did it might be hours before I could extricate myself and reestablish contact with the embassy and Washington. Better, I decided, to go to a phone and warn of possible trouble. I crawled through the intersection and then sped home. As I entered our driveway, I could see that, unusual for this early-to-bed neighborhood, lights were burning in the windows of almost every house. Ours, however, was dark, and I had to awaken Gaby, who, knowing I would work late, had gone to bed. She stood anxiously beside me as I telephoned. J.D. came on the line at the first ring. Thousands were pushing toward the Wall, I told him, and there could be serious trouble. "It's all over," he said. "They've opened up the Wall, and the people are going through. I've spoken with Washington. Turn on your television."

And so we did, and saw the scenes of joy and incredulity. Cameras on the bridge's western end showed the East Germans, most young, shouting, waving arms or honking Trabi horns as they entered Osloer Strasse. They showed the West Berliners, gathering in increasing numbers, who offered flowers to those coming off the bridge, or champagne toasts. "How do you feel?" a reporter asked an East Berliner in worker's windbreaker whose blonde wife held an infant in her arms. "Crazy, crazy [*Wahnsinn*]," he replied. Gaby, who was in high school when the Wall went up and has known it all her adult life, shook her head and said again and again, "I don't believe it. I just don't believe it." Should I dress? she asked. Should we go downtown? I want to, I replied, but it has been a long day, and a longer one starts in six hours. And so we go to bed while Berlin celebrates. Perhaps we cried a bit first. In a few hours, I shall begin to try to understand.

NOVEMBER 10 (10:00 A.M.)

This is a holiday, of course, for the Americans long scheduled (Veterans Day), for the Germans spontaneous, but the embassy is buzzing. I marveled at how normal the streets looked on the drive in. The exception, again, was Bornholmer Strasse, where the jam now extended for blocks in both directions. As many people were wending their way wearily home after a night's exploration of the other half of their city as were queuing to cross the checkpoint. The latter were more patient than last night, cooperating cheerfully with the police, who kept traffic moving. But I also saw workers boarding the elevated trains along Schönhauser Allee, and most shops were preparing to open for business. It is different in West Berlin, where street parties continue. As in the aftermath of the great demonstrations, however, the immediate impression here is of routine and order, even if this time with a dazed touch of hangover. I cannot get to the West to experience the celebration today. Our job is to assess how different the last twenty-four hours have made the GDR—and, indeed, Germany—and to report the Plenum.

Dick convened J.D., Mike, and me. We will never have more attentive readers, he said, so we must be quick off the mark with short, well-argued assessments of the new political and economic agendas. We batted his ideas around, and then he left us to it. Janice will absorb atmosphere in East Berlin; Heather and Imre will stay with the Central Committee. I will try to escape the office to cover a large SED rally marking the Plenum's end that is called for late afternoon. Once Washington is awake, we are certain to get new requests.

NOVEMBER 10 (2:00 P.M.)

Dick is looking at our drafts. I have a moment to reflect. When there is time to read history, not just live it, we may find that Germans moved apart during twenty years of confrontation and then began slowly to come together again over an additional twenty years in reconciliation. November 9, 1989, began a new stage of the historic process that is ending the division a world war and a cold war produced. On the evening of that remarkable day, as people streamed freely between East and West, the Berlin Wall lost its meaning. It is either the beginning of the end of the GDR as an illegitimate state held together by force, or the beginning of a new GDR with a chance to draw its justification from the consent of the governed. It is possible to differ as to which is more probable. History, as Gorbachev is fond of saying, will decide the German Question, but history is coming faster than usual. A half year from now, the GDR of this November will seem as light years distant as the grim, Berlin-Wall-visage, stodgy, conservative, petit bourgeois neo-Stalinist state of late summer does today.

By amnestying prisoners last month and opening the border yesterday, the GDR has essentially met its CSCE human contacts obligations. There has been notable progress toward satisfying other Helsinki commitments to freedom of press and association, legal reforms, and elections. The power-sharing issue will determine how closely the GDR comes to resemble a Western European state in the next six months, but agenda and compass-setting are clear. Egon Krenz and the SED have crossed their Rubicon. They are committed to reform that is more radical for pace and stakes than anything yet seen in Eastern Europe. They are betting their existence and their country's on the proposition that the GDR has a chance to survive and prosper as a second German state by pursuing thorough revision of its political, social, and economic culture. They may be wrong to believe the chance is realistic, but they know it is the only one. There is no going back.

Krenz, Schabowski, and Modrow are improbable, even unwilling, reformers who at the decisive moment acted courageously and rationally. They hope that by at last taking a bold, full measure, instead of reluctant half measures, they can get ahead of their people. They seek a respite in which to consolidate their position and implement the program they believe gives them a chance of survival, but they face possibly insurmountable challenges. The revolt within the SED, which has already brought down a quarter of Krenz's new Politburo, is almost as bitter and extensive as the citizens' revolt against it. This will come to a head in five weeks at a special Party conference that may throw out Krenz—it will certainly turn over his Central Committee—and split the Party. The internal struggle is between Stalinist traditions of the prewar Communists and the Social Democratic branch of the German Left tradition, which was submerged in the SED after the 1946 shotgun marriage and is now resurfacing. Krenz (least likely), the tactically well-positioned reformer Modrow, and the intelligent, populist Schabowski may ride out the fight, but if the SED survives to summer it will probably be more Social Democratic than Communist—though closer to the old West German SPD before it threw Marxism overboard in the late 1950s than the current version.

The second front is with the emerging political forces, those in the newly assertive Bloc Parties and those in the Opposition. This struggle will become more open when Parliament convenes Monday. Krenz has pledged that Bloc Parties and legislature will have new roles, and they are ready to take him at his word. The urgent need is to come to grips with the demands for new laws, especially one that mandates free, contested, secret elections in which the SED will have to risk much, if not all, of its claim to further power. The SED hopes to spin this out—Krenz said yesterday that he believed elections could be put off to 1991—but there is no reason to think it will be more successful at delaying the bills on elections, free press, free speech, and the other democratic requirements than it was on travel and the Wall.

It is an irony that the GDR created and maintained the framework of a democratic system for wholly other reasons. Each Bloc Party has begun to profile itself as a genuine representative of interest groups. It will be hard to succeed, since each is tainted by decades of subservience, but they have advantages, including organizations and newspapers. The best positioned is the LDPD, which has always cultivated some of the same liberal, small entrepreneur constituencies as the West German FDP. Its chairman won respect by criticizing Honecker weeks before it became fashionable. The CDU will have a tougher time because it was more co-opted and is scorned by most of its natural supporters around the church. It pins its hopes on a new leadership to be elected soon. The NDPD and the Peasants Parties, with no West German equivalents, target traditionally conservative elements. The Bloc Parties will stress independence as their only path to credibility. This dooms SED hopes of saving the old National Front. Coalitions are possible, but the SED will have to pay a real price as no longer automatic allies try to win votes by pushing it in new directions.

The half million who marched in the Leipzig rain showed that street protestors will remain important. Their function, however, is to keep the reform process honest. They cannot develop and implement the programs on which attention will increasingly focus. In a society that harbors so much resentment, Opposition groups obviously have potential. Locally—for example, in Dresden—they are developing genuinely representative mechanisms, but national entities like Neues Forum and the SDP suffer from lack of forceful leaders and organization, too much theory, and too little experience. They cannot yet hold up their side of a roundtable.

The West Germans are the other vital factor. They will be all over this country, aiming to influence policy and foster democratic institutions. Whatever reservations Krenz has will yield to the realization that there is no alternative to the assistance Bonn will give if its price is met. The SPD will have difficulty because it is torn between trying to reclaim the SED's soul and helping the SDP. The CDU will court the SED as long as it is in power, but will also develop virtually nonexistent ties to the local CDU. The Greens will school the Opposition's "alternative" potential.

The process can still go seriously wrong, especially if rising demands force a pace that overwhelms the capacity of system and participants to adapt, or if there is an ugly incident. The odds, however, are that, just as GDR newspapers today printed television rating polls for the first time, they will within six months be printing voter preference polls—and perhaps even results.

Before I leave on Monday, I need to talk with J.D. and Dick about bilateral relations. Dick will address them in his own channels, but perhaps I can help when I am in Washington. SED dictatorship is finished. Bonn will give financial and technical help, but it is not money the GDR wants from us at this time. It is a dose of the political legitimacy Honecker was denied but that now might contribute to keeping this revolution on track.

NOVEMBER 10 (5:00 P.M.)

Janice had tales of wonder about how average East Berliners are responding to the first day of open borders in twenty-eight years. Their discipline and steadiness in the midst of intoxicating new freedom is remarkable. We can no longer say that no time has been lost from the workplace in this revolution. Many have taken the day off to explore West Berlin, but on television, as the sun rose, I saw checkpoint interviews with workers who were returning to their factories and youths who were going directly to school. Janice talked with shopgirls who were waiting for their relief. Only then would they cross to see the West for the first time.

Gaby brought pizza for those of us too busy to get lunch. "The whole city is crazy," she said. "There isn't a bottle of champagne left in West Berlin." She carried the last one, however, so we drank it: the ambassador's secretary, Margie; Carolyn from Admin, who was helping with typing; Heather; and I. Checkpoint Charlie had been thrown open to all, and it had taken Gaby an hour to get through, so the pizza was cold—but no one minded.

"Nightline" wants to interview Dick from his office this evening. Meanwhile, I gave my own "on the record" interview to a reporter from the *Wilkes-Barre Times-Leader*, my hometown paper, whose editor wanted a local angle in the big story. All my talks with journalists here have been on background, with the understanding that what I said would not identify the embassy, but, I reasoned, the *Times-Leader* is not read in Washington. It is the kind of paper that considers "foreign news" something happening in Harrisburg. For it to track me down is a good indication of the impact the Wall's opening is having at home. I mentioned this to Tom Praster, an economic officer, also from Pennsylvania. Yes, he said, the Williamsport paper had just called him.

NOVEMBER 11 (1:00 A.M.)

What of the Plenum that has just closed? Its final day began with embarrassing bloodletting: the resignation, as a consequence of local revolts, of four of the seventeen Politburo members or candidate members elected two days earlier. Mittag was expelled from the Central Committee "for grossest violations of intra-Party democracy" and "damaging the Party's reputation." A commission is to probe responsibility for the economic situation. The program adopted at the end had been foreshadowed by Krenz's two speeches. It was heavier on promises than on detail, including a pledge to hold free, contested Parliamentary elections and accept "new political associations."

I saw the SED's grassroots unrest firsthand when, just after dark, I crossed the Schlossbrücke to the Lustgarten, the open area off Unter den Linden that was part of the grounds of the Kaiser's city palace. The faithful and the curious who mingled under the stern-visaged statues of Prussian generals were fewer than the officially estimated 150,000, and their placards expressed both old ("In Unity There Is Strength") and new ("Listen to the Grassroots") themes. I worked my way nearly to the museum steps on which the speakers stood and was surrounded by factory workers who offered a running commentary on lost faith in the leadership. With that crowd, Krenz has barely begun to make the deficit good.

Remarkably, they wanted to hear the activists of the GDR's first hours—Ruth Werner, for example, an underground fighter against the Nazis and Soviet spy, later a writer. Most could have had little or no personal memory of those times, but these were the speakers whose call for a reformed, honorable Party rang true to them. The demand for more workers in the Central Committee was particularly popular. However, my neighbors were not undiscriminating when they heard calls for the rehabilitation of those who had fallen afoul of Honecker. One orator praised Konrad Naumann, banished from the Politburo a few years ago. That drunkard and autocrat, they hooted, had no place in their Party. Speaking last, Krenz was innocuous and earned at best polite applause. Indeed, he was jeered when he argued that Party renewal had gone far enough for now. Comrades, he said, should read the Plenum speeches to see how thoroughly new the old Central Committee had become. He did not persuade those near me.

The rally ended traditionally with the "Internationale." The singing had fire, but the clenched fists were raised as much against Krenz and those about him, so many of whom are the familiar faces, as they were against the Honecker clique or the outside world. There may be more in common than we think between a Party crowd such as this or the one that heckled Krenz and Schabowski Wednesday and the Leipzig marchers. The SED is far from a 2-million-plus bulwark for Krenz. Its total control of society is shattered beyond recovery, and its disgruntled membership may be the greater immediate threat to his position.

NOVEMBER 11 (11:00 P.M.)

I left the embassy early in the morning meaning not to return for a month. For most of today, I soaked up Berlin's new atmosphere. Gaby and I went West in the afternoon. At Checkpoint Charlie, we inched forward among Trabies for a half hour until a harried but cheerful police officer waved us through with an assurance that "after the weekend, we'll get this regularized." We said we did not mind waiting on such an occasion, and he laughed in agreement. The guards were relishing a new status as officials who say "yes." Many wore flowers—gifts from fellow citizens—self-consciously on uniform caps.

Just beyond the checkpoint were new lines, at a post office where East Germans could pick up the DM 100 "welcome money" ($60) an adult is entitled to once a year. It gives visitors whose government permits them to exchange only 15 Marks at 1 : 1 enough to make small purchases independent of relatives. This act of generosity and pump-priming—the money flows back into West Berlin's subsidized economy—has always been a large charge against Bonn's budget, but nothing like this weekend's demand had been foreseen. The payout offices are usually the initial stop for East Berliners, who then face the stunning dilemma of how to spend their stake in the consumer cornucopia.

We saw families exhaust their allotment in the first block, buying liquor, fast food, or household items in small Kreuzberg shops. Most, however, wanted to visit the Kurfürstendamm, West Berlin's up-market shopping heart that for the weekend was converted into a pedestrian zone—one vast mall, its six lanes and median strip given over to strollers. It was hard to say which Berliners had wider eyes: the *Ossies* as they confronted the shopwindows and glitz, or the *Wessies* as they marveled at a sight most did not expect to see in their lifetime. Berliners cultivate a sassy style that goes beyond the rude shell common to large cities and is best compared perhaps to a New Yorker's self-image. Public friendliness is uncharacteristic. Gaby perversely smiles occasionally simply to disconcert shop clerks. For today, however, the city was transformed. Not everyone was a philanthrope, of course. There were businessmen who offered to take the GDR Marks many Easterners "illegally" carried at half the free-market bank rate. The overwhelming response, however, was generosity. Many stands offered free refreshments. There are countless tales of taxi drivers who refused payment. No one yet complains about the traffic chaos or the smoke pall thrown up by the noxious GDR cars.

Two incidents illustrate the good-hearted wonderment. The Tauentzienstrasse, just off the KuDamm, is frequented by elegant ladies who refresh themselves at its cafés. We witnessed a three-year-old East Berliner relieve herself on its grassy median strip under the direction of her mother, to amused *Wessi* smiles. The Avus, the segment of the City Autobahn that before the war was one of Europe's great racetracks, is used by West Berliners otherwise frustrated by their city's narrow confines to satisfy the national love of speed. The unwritten code is that Volkswagens and Opels go as fast as Americans only dream about, up to 100 miles per hour, while bullish Mercedes are kings of the road that force others out of the passing lane and are only rarely challenged by the rogue Porsche or BMW. As we dissolved in laughter, a Trabi, which can barely do 70 mph downhill, came up, lights flashing in the traditional and rude "pass" gesture, on a $50,000 Mercedes. Whether from shock or awareness of the occasion, the West Berliner yielded to the East Berliner, who was kicking up his heels with enjoyment of a new liberty.

Only a quarter of 40,000 soccer fans in the Olympic Stadium paid. The remainder were East Berliners using their first day of free travel to resume a love affair. Hertha, the Berlin club whose old grounds were a few hundred yards west of the Wall, threw open its gates to anyone with a GDR ID card. The team did not rise to the occasion, managing only a draw, but the crowd, by a factor of three the year's best, gave tangible form to speculation about the heights a Berlin without borders can regain. Two-thirds of those in the KaDeWe, the elegant department store, were, we judged from dress and speech, *Ossies*. Many used precious "welcome money" for more serious purchases than a Western version of a Thüringer sausage or an electronic gadget. Heinz Kosin told me last month about the memoirs of Walter Janka, a victim of Stalinist injustice in the 1950s—*Difficulties with the Truth*—which had just been published in the West. "You got the last copy," the clerk said. "The East Berliners have been asking for it all day."

An incongruous image of how once-colorless GDR broadcasters covered the giant Berlin street party will last. A reporter from the brash youth show "Elf 99," which was one of the first to break the mold last month, stationed himself at a notorious corner near the KuDamm to interview those emerging from the Beate Uhse Sex Shop, the kind of consumer paradise absent from the not-prudish GDR. Embarrassed East Berliners stammered excuses like "I was just looking for my friend" while the reporter asked innocently why the friend might be in the store on the first weekend of the open Wall. The broadcast had no hint of the censorious, as would once have been obligatory. Is anything this fall more astonishing than GDR television with a sense of humor?

NOVEMBER 12

Gaby packed, and I worked at home on the opinion-page article I had promised the *Los Angeles Times*. I wrote:

SEVEN QUESTIONS, NO ANSWERS ON EAST GERMANY

"A West Berlin newspaper described it laconically as the day 'The Wall lost its function.' In fact, it was a festival of freedom. My Berlin wife commented joyfully as crowds streamed East and West that she had seen the Wall built in 1961, heard John Kennedy proclaim 'ich bin ein Berliner,' and queued six hours on a cold 1972 day to get first Christmas passes to visit her relatives. Now the dream had come true. Berliners moved freely, and East Germany was undergoing extraordinary change.

"How did it happen, where is it going, what does it mean? Is one Germany reemerging before our eyes and the uncomfortable but stable postwar order ending? A word of caution: we need to locate a few fixed points in the radically changed landscape because the issues are vital, but believe no one who says he knows. These are questions one observer asks and his tentative answers.

"*How Could the Wall Fall so Fast?* A few months ago, East Germany—the GDR—seemed stodgy and predictable, with Eastern Europe's strongest economy, most efficient security forces, a government determined to hold reform back. It was never truly that comatose. A consensus had developed that society had matured, people would have to be treated as adults, not children, by a paternalistic, often arbitrary Father State. Erich Honecker, who built the Wall and ruled for 18 years, badly misjudged this temper. A people whose expectations rose each time Gorbachev indicated anything was possible in the new Eastern Europe ground its teeth when Honecker showed distaste for the Soviet leader and said the Wall 'could last 50 or 100 years.' That the break came so suddenly was circumstance—Hungary's decision to open a gate behind the Wall and Honecker's illness, which paralyzed the government for a crucial half-summer. But it was bound to come, as in any family.

"*Is It for Real?* Yes. The once grim-visaged GDR of the Wall and petit-bourgeois neo-Stalinism is committed to reforms more radical for the enormity of the stakes than those being attempted anywhere else in Eastern Europe. It can go tragically wrong if there is an ugly street incident or if change comes too rapidly to absorb, but the old ways cannot be resurrected.

"*What Do the Reformers Want?* Essentially the democratic, human rights standards of the Helsinki Final Act. Substantial progress has been achieved or is under way. Freedom of travel is the most dramatic, but the change in the once insipid, polemical media is almost as remarkable. Suddenly East Germans are watching their own television more than Western programs. That is symptomatic for other change. Lawyers demand the criminal code be purged of 'rubber paragraphs' aimed at dissidents, and mass public protest is now part of political life.

"So much could be done so quickly because it was part of the consensus Honecker ignored. Its outer limits are now being reached. A new consensus will be more difficult. Reformers must decide how to shore up an economy buffeted by emigration and threatened by Black Markets. Most fundamental is whether and in what measure Communists are willing to yield power in elections.

"*Are the Communists Doomed?* Not necessarily. Their senior leadership is discredited, and the Party bears the brunt of human rights violations and arrogance of power. The Communists alone possess a strong organization, but quick elections likely would validate Polish President Jaruzelski's Rule: 'A donkey with a Solidarity sign around its neck could have beaten our best man.' East Germans want the satisfaction of saying 'no' to old rulers. In six months, if the party reforms, and the government builds a record, the situation could look different. The odds are long, but by opening the Wall, Party Chief Krenz acted boldly to get in front of the people. He shows unexpected foot speed and learning ability. Prime Minister Modrow, one prominent Communist with some credibility, has an ambitious reform program.

"Standing among 100,000 at a rally one day after the Wall was opened, I could see that Party rank and file are nearly as radicalized as the rest of the country. They have forced an extraordinary Party meeting, December 15, to clean out Honecker's Central Committee. Krenz must fight to persuade even Communists he is the man to execute reform. The struggle within the Party is between Social Democratic traditions submerged but never destroyed by the 40-year shotgun marriage with the Communists and the Stalinist tradition. If the former wins, the new-style Party could contend for power. If it loses, the Party could splinter and almost surely would be washed away. Surprisingly, many are excited by the challenge. 'At last,' one think tank official said, 'we are on the same wave length as Gorbachev. Now we just have to do Glasnost and Perestroika faster and better.'

"*Are There Alternatives to the Communists?* Of course, but each has problems. Demonstrators keep the politicians honest but cannot develop complex programs. The four 'Bloc Parties' suffer from histories of subservience. They can probably be more influential pushing the Communists in directions they may not want to go than by leading. The Opposition remains largely unorganized. It has great potential, obviously, but to do more than articulate frustrations, it needs leaders with political skills. No Lech Walesa is apparent, nor is the Opposition ready to support its position in a Polish-style roundtable negotiation.

"*Can the Reforms Succeed?* The GDR has tangible advantages. A Polish Minister called radical reform 'like operating on a patient without anesthetic: it hurts.' The GDR economy, not as good as it once looked, is still stronger than that of other reformers. To the extent it needs infusions of capital, not just wiser policies and freeing of creative forces by loosening controls on its private sector, it can count on the West Germans to apply at least local anesthetics. The GDR also has educated, motivated people, who can quickly learn to run a choice-oriented society. One Party member, asked if Modrow was assembling reform protégés, said 'of course, like Gorbachev. The difference is, it is easier to find them in the GDR than the Soviet Union.' The suspicion is Gorbachev spoke from the heart when he told Berliners, 'Don't panic. Your problems are nothing compared to ours.' If he could, he would probably trade his hand for the GDR's.

"*Will Germany Reunite?* No one knows, but it is the wrong question. The current insistence is on self-determination, not reunification. They are not necessarily equivalent. The German Question must be faced, as was assured once the East-West confrontation began to recede. In a Europe increasingly guided by Helsinki CSCE standards, it can only be answered, ultimately, by the citizens of both German states. As non-Germans watched the joyful reunions in Berlin, many assumed that reunification was coming and quickly. The immediate impact, however, has been that some who fled in summer have returned, and Germans East and West are beginning to face realistically the complexities of their national question.

"How much do West Germans want reunification? Polled in a crisis, they will answer 'yes,' but are they prepared to accept the real decline in living standards early reunification would involve? How much do East Germans want reunification? They are more interested than their cousins, but in proportion to hardship at home. With prospect of a freer society, the attractions of reunification may be less, the self-defense mechanism against patronizing by rich Westerners more powerful. A unified national state is the not happy exception in German history.

"How much would Germans, East and West, be willing to adapt their institutions and structures? An early poll (West German) taken under the new circumstances showed 60 percent of East Germans supporting eventual reunification but 66 percent saying they wanted to retain 'Socialism.' Would that be acceptable to West Germans, not to mention Europeans fearful that Bonn could lose its orientation in pursuit of a nationalist identity?

"Can the GDR make a success of Socialism? No one has, leading many to conclude that the new GDR will either dissolve into chaos or so mirror West Germany that there would be no alternative to reunification. The full political spectrum says, however, that it wants to reform Socialism, not consign it to the history books. They may be kidding themselves, but one close observer concluded after touring the region's reform tier, 'Polish and Hungarian Communists talk as if trying to persuade themselves. East Germans are serious.'

"In 1949, West Germans decided freedom was more important than unity. Might this judgment be reinterpreted if the GDR becomes free and democratic? Were artificial barriers removed, would Germans accommodate neighbors' reservations about German unity because the existence of two states was no longer painful?

"Neither the Four Powers—the U.S., U.K., France and Soviet Union—with residual responsibilities for Germany nor the rest of Europe could easily forge a consensus on final settlement of the questions left over from World War II or the relationship of the two German states to NATO and the Warsaw Pact. The point to focus on immediately is the process of change in the GDR itself, not where it might ultimately lead. All parties, including the Germans, share an interest that the reform process succeed. If the GDR descends into chaos, the ultimate issues of the postwar order would have to be resolved in a crisis atmosphere before participants were physically or psychologically prepared. If the reforms proceed concurrently with the build-down of the East-West confrontation, the Germans will have time to settle the degree of greater affinity they want and the rest of us time to accommodate constructively.

"East and West share a need to engage the new GDR in a manner that assists, each according to circumstances, reforms to take hold. If we do, History, as Gorbachev is fond of saying, not crisis management, will decide the German Question. That is the surest bet for both those who think they want reunification and those who worry about it."

Afterword: The Year of German Unity November 13, 1989— October 3, 1990

INEVITABLE UNIFICATION?

Washington was under Berlin's spell. West Indian taxi drivers and Foreign Service colleagues alike wanted to discuss the "wonderful" scenes the television had been showing and to ask how soon—not whether—Germany would be united. Their enthusiasm left little room for the agnosticism we carried across the ocean. My consultations were pleasant if not very productive. As the first eyewitness to the "Peaceful Revolution's" climax to return, every door was open to me. Especially the many who had served in Berlin wanted to hear tales and ask if I had brought them pieces of the Wall. Gaby said we should have carried rocks from our garden; no one would have known, and we would have made friends happy.

In the European Bureau and the National Security Council, I found an awareness that a complicated new phase of relations with the Soviets was beginning, and considerable concern that German developments be managed without prejudice to Bonn's NATO commitments. Over pizza, Pierre Shostal brainstormed how the United States might retain influence on events, perhaps by restoring life to the Reagan Berlin initiative. Jim Holmes of the Secretary's policy-planning staff shared a draft that four weeks later formed part of Mr. Baker's "New European Architecture" speech in Berlin. He was noncommittal as I urged emphasis on the right of self-determination, not the necessity of unification, lest a matter be prejudged that, to me at least, was less than clear on the ground and could yet place the Soviets, much of Europe, and the Germans themselves before tough choices they were not ready to make. Jim Dobbins of the European Bureau authorized me to pass my article to the *Los Angeles Times* out of generosity and the belief that events would soon overtake it, not because he agreed. He saw no reason, he said, why East Germans would try to solve problems their own way when they had the West German model. (He was right, of course. Before the *Times* could edit the text, it was significantly behind the headlines. I agreed with Deane Wylie that the situation was developing too rapidly and withdrew from the public prophecy field.)

Nowhere did I encounter more than politeness for my argument that regardless of how the German Question was eventually resolved, it was in everyone's interest to help the GDR. I suggested that political gestures and economic support withheld from the old regime should be offered generously to confirm the democratic process and gain time that all could use to become accustomed to the new contours of European politics. There was preoccupation with the need for the drama in Europe's center not to turn violent, and still doubt about the Soviet Union's capacity to accept the collapse of its political and military positions, but there was little interest in, and certainly no sense of urgency about, assisting the GDR.

I still wonder why. Certainly an element of shrewdness was involved. President Bush and Secretary Baker recognized the probability (inevitability?) of unification and acted forthrightly to facilitate it sooner than Moscow, London, or Paris, for which they deservedly received German gratitude. With the more comfortable perspective provided by an ocean and a less terrible war experience, Americans were more ready to accept the implications of forty years of rhetoric and come to terms with a unified Germany.

Nevertheless, I suspect that old habits played a part. The GDR was always unloved, without even the ambiguous domestic constituency other Communist states could play to. It was merely the Soviet Union's Germany, with whom we were too idealistic or naive to play power politics. We could not conceive that, freed of the constraints of dictatorship and cold war, there might be any desire on the part of its citizens, or other reason, to see it preserved, even provisionally, and we acted accordingly. Secretary Baker showed political courage in visiting the GDR in December to meet Modrow before it was certain the revolution would remain peaceful. But little more was done with East Berlin. A full half-year after the GDR opened the Wall, our embassy was asked to obtain formal assurance that it would adhere to free emigration as a prerequisite for obtaining Most Favored Nation status. When unification came, the United States had not yet awarded that status. To the end, the GDR was a problem to be managed with the Soviet Union and especially Bonn, never a subject in its own right, not even after it had in place Eastern Europe's first democratically elected non-Communist government.

There was goodwill toward Germany wherever we traveled that month. If anything, the Berlin Wall had symbolized the cold war more intensely for Americans than for Germans. Berliners had accommodated of necessity to that scar through their city and took advantage of the structure's increasing porosity. Americans, who often knew nothing else about the state that had built and sheltered behind it, retained a purer if more abstract horror. Only in the understandably sensitive Jewish community, and then mostly among older members, did I sense true anxiety that Germany united could again be a problem. Even then, the view was advanced only by a minority, with embarrassed recognition that it would be unjust, and more dangerous, to deny Germans the right to decide their national question. That Germany was about to unify was assumed. I tried my article's theses with an audience that filled an auditorium at Wilkes University in Wilkes-Barre despite a cloudburst and Monday Night Football competition. It, and students the following day, were as polite and dubious as my Washington discussion partners.

How ephemeral the analysis I carried from Berlin was had been shown almost before our flight landed. In those weeks, sensations tumbled out one after another: revelations that Mittag had concocted statistics even more extensively than believed and that the economic crisis was grave; the opening of Wandlitz to the public with the consequent if rather naive outcry against leaders who preached socialist ideals while enjoying middle-class Western luxuries; the arrest of senior SED figures; and, above all, the escalating demands of the people, in the streets by the hundreds of thousands, and of the SED grassroots as well, for ever more radical change.

At the New Jersey home of Gaby's cousin, we learned of Kohl's ten-point program for the next decade, which aimed first at a confederation then a more organic federation of the two German states. That initiative seemed bold but not irresponsible after we bought *Der Spiegel* at Princeton. As Gaby drove on to Philadelphia, I read to her the account of the latest Monday demonstration in Leipzig, where "We are one People" and "Germany, United Fatherland" cries, and West German flags had overwhelmed the calls for GDR reforms. "We better get back soon or we may miss it all," she said.

Before we could return, there was a week of Florida holiday to be endured. Every morning we pored over a *New York Times*, more than once finding that the reporter had sought out a friend of ours from the church or the Jewish community to interpret a crisis that looked like it would climax even before the Party Congress (no longer just a conference), for which we had timed our return. Afternoons, we came in early to catch news broadcasts. The weather was good, the fishing better, but the seven days were among the most frustrating we have experienced. During a stopover in Philadelphia with my brother and family, we learned that Krenz and the entire Politburo and Central Committee had resigned. Gregor Gysi, my luncheon partner a month earlier, was the new Party head, but the once-mighty SED was clearly rent, possibly fatally. Modrow was safe as prime minister for the moment, but the New York and Washington press were reporting that public order was breaking down. What would we find when we returned on December 13?

At first, surprisingly, near normality: The "welcome money" lines were gone, and the flow of people back and forth through the checkpoints disturbed traffic no more than a regular rush hour. In East Berlin the stores were open, buses were running, and workers were in the factories. Fewer police and military were about, and there was no hint of the incipient chaos heralded in the American press. Colleagues told me how, twenty-four hours earlier, Modrow had pledged to the secretary of state that he would submit his government to the electorate's judgment on May 6—a year after Hungary's decision to snip the barbed wire at its border and the falsified communal vote had started the snowball rolling down the mountain.

Not least of the changes from our parochial viewpoint was that over the night of November 9 East Berlin became the most popular stop for traveling U.S. Congressmen. The phenomenon lasted well into 1990, until near quorums of Senate and House had come. With the diversity and mixed motives of such visits, some were serious, all-work occasions, like Stephen Solarz's return and Bill Bradley's diversion from Moscow carrying his own suitcase and without aides. A few were political photo-ops. One senator was in Berlin three times in as many months. On the last occasion, he jumped expertly into the breach to give a half dozen colleagues his own tour of the classical antiquities in the Pergamon Museum, and on the way picked up four more senators from a separate group. Everyone wanted to be a part of history, and get their own piece of the Wall.

The Last Leipzig Demo: End of the Revolution

To plug back into the electricity, Gaby and I drove to Leipzig on our first Monday back. On the Autobahn, we listened to radio reports from an early session of the Roundtable convened in Berlin to put the old and new political forces into formal dialogue. In what Christoph Hein had named the "Hero City of the GDR," however, we found a touch of nostalgia, almost the last of the old revolution.

Christian Führer, pastor of Nikolai Church, had for years offered refuge and a weekly service to the handful of emigration activists, until suddenly, in September, the frustration of an entire city, then a country, boiled into the streets. He was now a media figure who budgeted time to Japanese and West German television crews before sitting down in a corner to discuss with us the miracle he had midwifed. Leipzig Mondays were changing, he said, and not only in theme. The core of engaged citizens who first marched to reform the GDR was pulling back, less because their objectives were achieved and more because others now set the tone. On the fringe of the demonstration, a harder, even a right-wing and nationalist, accent had appeared, he said. Many couples now kept children away for fear of rowdiness or a clash between demonstrators. Much remained to be done, he said. The people must keep the streets as their control mechanism against the politicians; the SED was wounded but not safely removed from power. Nevertheless, it was time to pause and reflect. Führer's superior, Superintendent Magirius, and Kurt Masur had appealed that on this last Monday before Christmas the people should march silently and without posters to remember the victims of Stalinism. The holidays must be used, Führer said, to consider what purpose the marches might serve in January.

After Magirius spoke to an overflowing congregation, we filed out to join those waiting in the evening gloom to begin the march from the Karl-Marx-Platz around the Ringstrasse. West German flags were prominent, but there were indeed few posters and no speakers. The families were back, and every third or fourth person carried a candle. The circuit was completed in virtual silence. Many detoured to approach the massive building that until a few weeks earlier was Stasi headquarters. As Gaby noted wonderingly, they used the gravel footpath. "We Germans," she said, "even make revolution without walking on the grass." There was never a hint that the crowd might demand entrance from the unarmed Citizen Committee guards, but many placed candles against its walls.

We returned to Berlin with an exaggerated notion of the extent to which East Germans would still follow those who set the first agenda for their uprising. Such clerics as Führer and Magirius, the musician Masur, who briefly seemed to have the unifying charisma of Czechoslovakia's Havel, and human rights activists from the citizens groups—for all of whom the street protests were a way to improve the GDR—retained respect. Demonstrations in the new year, however, were rallies for unification and elected office, dominated by parties, the famous Bonn politicians, and Eastern protégés. The marches that set Germany on fire effectively ended that Monday before Christmas, when we witnessed the final great tribute to the moral force of the Lutheran church.

The Communists Lose Their Power

It was not always easy at first to recognize how basic the changes already were. The SED seemed to have a fair chance of survival. Like others, I had difficulty shaking the habit of believing Party and Government were indistinguishable. Shortly after our return, Gysi proposed that the two German states make parallel military cuts. That morning I saw Wolfgang Herger, who had won and lost a Politburo seat since Les Aspin's visit. He still chaired the Defense Committee, however, and after he filled in some details, I drafted a report on the "GDR's arms control initiative." Dick asked whether I was certain it was a "GDR" initiative, not just a partisan gambit. For a moment, I was nonplussed, but there was no longer automatic identity of views between the SED and the Cabinet. Foreign Ministry contacts criticized Gysi's "amateurish and flawed" proposal. It was my introduction to a new political fact: The prime minister was an SED member, and that Party theoretically had majorities in Cabinet and Parliament, but the Modrow Government was no longer "Communist-controlled." It was an increasingly fractious coalition that struggled to carry the country to election day while parties jockeyed for advantage. In this case, it took Washington much longer to escape the old thinking.

Still, for weeks it looked as if the SED could do well in an election. A Leipzig institute that formerly surveyed youth attitudes for the Central

Committee published polls that put the Communists in front, with a projected vote that rose from 31 percent to 34 percent in the second half of December. My inclination to reject this as flawed by methodology or partisanship was called into question at a holiday party Heather threw. Many of the leading new politicians came to say good-bye to her, and their nearly unanimous pessimism shocked me. They despaired of countering SED advantages in logistics and political experience. If the election were today, predicted one young lady who had driven from Leipzig, where she was organizing Saxony for Neues Forum, the SED would get 40 percent.

In fact, the Modrow Government's popularity was already at its zenith. By late January, it was so low that Modrow had to bring the Opposition into the cabinet and advance elections to March 18. Some decline was inevitable, as people realized that they could oppose the Communists without retribution, and the West German parties moved massively into the GDR. But Gysi and Modrow's miscalculations were also responsible. The former tried to place himself at the head of an "anti-Fascist" coalition when the Red Army's imposing war memorial in Treptow Park was mysteriously sprayed with anti-Soviet slogans. The intellectual lawyer looked ludicrous in the black worker's cap he wore on the platform of the SED-orchestrated rally and awakened unhappy memories of earlier "unity" demonstrations.

Much worse was Modrow's insistence on reconstituting the Stasi as an "Office for National Security." He was literally right that every state has some such office, but he ignored the passions the issue aroused. Jens Reich told J.D. and me he was convinced the storming of Stasi Headquarters in the Normanenstrasse in mid-January had been arranged by the Stasi either to permit its people to reenter the building to recover files or to show the need for law and order. Nevertheless, it reflected the bitterness at any hint something would be left of the repressive Stasi machinery. The belief that Modrow wanted to preserve a part of the Stasi—whether out of Communist habit or to curry favor with a numerically not insignificant part of the electorate—cost him dearly. Though he subsequently promised to dissolve the organization and delay consideration of a successor until after March 18, Modrow's credibility, and especially that of his Party, never recovered.

I held several conversations in late January to ascertain the Party's health. Rolf Reissig, earnest, idealistic, and honest as always, told me that he had rejected an offer to be Gysi's deputy and was withdrawing from politics. The effort to turn the SED into an effective, democratic force was probably futile, he said. It carried too much baggage. It would be more realistic to make it a vehicle of transition to assist hundreds of thousands of Communists to feel at home with Social Democratic values. He would keep his membership because he could not deny his career, he said, but he could aid that transition best by finding work for the finest of the SED's political scientists. The Berlin Institute for Social Science Studies (BISS) he later founded offers such scholars the chance to contribute both to an understanding of the GDR's failure and to the solution of the new Germany's problems.

André Brie, who did become Gysi's number-two, is another fascinating case study of what might have been had the SED dared Glasnost and Perestroika in the first Gorbachev years. I met him in Fall 1988 at a cocktail party for a Rand Institute delegation, where he was considerably more outspoken than the usual East German bureaucrat, but for the next year, whenever I called, he was "unavailable." Only after the revolution began was he free to meet. Because he had protested the ban on the Soviet magazine *Sputnik*, the SED had forbidden him to have any contact with Westerners. Now he was at the forefront of the effort to reform and preserve that Party.

Tall, eloquent, with a wide-ranging intelligence, the French Huguenot–Jewish descended Brie can do anything he sets his mind to, said a mutual friend. That applied to running the Party from just off the stage, which he avoided from a lingering desire not to break ties with the academic world. That winter, he managed its campaign for votes with wit and imagination, putting a parachute harness on a bemused (if not terrified) Gysi so he could jump into a rally from an airplane, and blanketing the GDR with clever slogans. His best, a call for East Germans to approach Western cousins as equals, was a takeoff on both the Leipzig demonstration unification call and the demand for West Marks: "We are one people at 1:1." Like his stunts—covering the facade of the Central Committee building with pop art, and holding children's fairs at the same time as electoral meetings, for example—it won over few hostile voters. He lent a welcome light irony, however, to a season of heavy politics.

In January, Brie, as well as Gerd Basler, who had joined the Social Democratic Party, described the SED's bitter divisions. At least four platforms contesting its future had been developed by rivals. The prescriptions ranged from virtual restoration of old ways (Willi Stoph's son led that wing) through dissolution of the SED and a new start. Reformers won, but only after making debilitating compromises with the functionaries. The half-renaming of the Party was symptomatic. Even after the radical proposal to declare legal as well as political bankruptcy was defeated, its proponents hoped to scrap the discredited "SED" title. Gysi, ever the lawyer, advised against a step that, he said, could weaken the Party's claim to bank accounts, real property, and business enterprises, assets that were a foundation on which to base plans to retain political influence. And so Honecker's SED became Gysi's SED-PDS, the "Socialist Unity Party of Germany–Party of Democratic Socialism." Only months later was "SED" dropped. By then, a Parliamentary Control Commission had begun to divest the Party of those assets anyway.

At the time, I believed the ethical course was to retain "SED." The Party could not escape its heritage simply by shifting a few letters, and it seemed more honorable to ask for votes on the basis of personnel and policy change, not semantic change. I did not fully appreciate the symbolism in that struggle. The fights over name and money were rearguard actions of a party that understood neither what had brought it down nor how to claim a modest place in the new political spectrum. In that early winter when it was reluctantly becoming the PDS but refusing to face up to the full implications of its legacy, the SED threw away its last chance to retain influence on what the GDR and Germany were becoming.

At the end of January, I wrote a final long assessment of the Communists. Their power was gone, I knew. A few of the old, such as Stephan Hermlin, were serene enough to say they were glad and that a handful of honorable idealists could do more good by stimulating the new establishment from the left than could a mass party contending for a role in government. Whether the PDS can perform such a function, of course, is doubtful. It still has many apparatchiks, who regret the SED's collapse. It faces massive distrust in the old GDR and almost total rejection in the West. Other than the appeal Gysi and Brie can exert on a romantic segment of German youth, the PDS has few assets that translate into a future. The money and other tangibles Gysi fought to save have largely been dissipated or mire the Party in legal disputes about its past. Probably Reissig was right: The service the PDS performs is to offer a halfway house to those not yet psychologically able, and to those with too many outward blemishes from service to the old regime, to complete the journey into a new political culture. By mid-winter 1990, that party had become irrelevant to what was happening in Germany. The election, and its great issue—unification—would be decided elsewhere, and I had to refocus my attention.

Keeping in Touch with the Soviets

The Soviet Embassy, always a place to which one looked to anticipate political developments in Honecker's GDR, was important for sorting out the jumbled events of Winter 1989–90 as well, but in a new way. Where we had once courted every shared confidence, the situation was nearly reversed. Our Soviet colleagues retained excellent sources within the Modrow Government and the country at large, but increasingly they sought us out, though not so much for information. It was important for the Soviets to be seen as working demonstratively with the West, and especially with the United States, on German questions. They had been granted one early Quadripartite ambassadorial meeting that showed the World War II victors at least consulting to influence events, if not in control. There was never another such meeting, but the Soviet Embassy was eager for regular bilateral conversations.

The Soviets had respected vestigial elements of Berlin's Four Power status, both to avoid offense to the West and to have more leverage over the German situation. How much respect was afforded at any time depended on the East-West climate. For several years, they had gone out of their way to avoid incidents.

Shortly after I returned in 1987, I was involved in a bizarre and tragic affair. A retired American military officer died of a heart attack on Alexanderplatz. An East German ambulance brought the body to our embassy and requested instructions. Then Berlin-status issues intervened. While the widow waited in the lobby and the ambulance driver, a doctor, and I stood aside, Soviet and American officers negotiated transport of the body through Checkpoint Charlie. On a deserted street in front of the embassy at midnight, the Four Power role in Berlin was played out more explicitly than it had been for years. Now every sign of Quadripartite cooperation implied that the course of GDR events was not left solely to demonstrators or even to German politicians. We had to balance our desire to learn Soviet perspectives against the risk of appearing to be conducting a Great Power condominium over German heads.

Believing Gorbachev

Keeping in touch with the Soviets was especially important, because for months no one could be certain Gorbachev meant it when he said GDR decisions would be made in Berlin, not Moscow. Both Honecker and the demonstrators welcomed that ambiguous statement in October, and it was some time before it was appreciated how consequential Gorbachev was. Only when East Germans were convinced Soviet troops would not leave barracks, that the external restraints against self-determination had been unilaterally removed, did they escalate their demands to early unification.

That moment of revelation came sometime in late fall or early winter. I believe that throughout the crucial period the Soviet Embassy reported accurately and cautioned against a Moscow tendency to believe East German discontent could be tamed into reform communism. G. and his superior told J.D. and me repeatedly about their frustration at Moscow's inability to appreciate the full extent of the crisis. Over time, however, their embassy's reporting seems to have played an important role in convincing Gorbachev of the need first to recognize that unification was coming fast, and then to accept it on largely Western terms.

Bonn Sets the Fast Track to Dissolution

In early January, the new politicians unanimously described unification to Stephen Solarz as desirable but dependent on circumstances that would delay its realization for several years to a decade. By the end of that month, there was consensus that a single German state was coming quickly—certainly no later than 1991. It is symptomatic that Neues Forum's first national conference opened with consideration of a draft plank that assumed continued existence of two states. Heated floor debate left many early leaders of the movement in the minority and produced a position favoring a united country as soon as practicable. Any remaining doubt that a new Germany was inevitable was removed on February 1. A day after returning from Moscow, Modrow announced his own "United Fatherland" proposal. Heavily caveated with conditions that both states leave their military alliances, it nevertheless signaled that Gorbachev had written off an independent GDR. The only remaining, though serious, questions involved timing and terms.

What shifted the GDR irreversibly onto the fast track to dissolution, and whether this was prudent or foreordained, will be debated for years. My impression, then and now, is that the psychology of East Germans was the decisive factor. Throughout fall and early winter, they gathered nerve to push for what a majority clearly desired—one Germany—but in the revolution's early stages scarcely dared hope was attainable. As we in the embassy documented, each passing day convinced more people that Gorbachev would not put up a "Stop" sign.

GDR parties sought to keep up with this internal process of self-education and persuasion, but neither instigated nor guided it. West German politicians, above all Chancellor Kohl, did play a significant and creative role.

They transferred to the GDR the start of their own 1990 campaign (ironically, in view of the outcome, the SPD was quickest off the mark). Their overwhelming physical presence in campaign headquarters and on television and speakers' platforms accustomed GDR citizens to a single polity. And there is no doubt that Kohl, especially, recognized the opportunity for unification and deliberately forced the pace.

There were hints soon after the turn of the year. In the first days of January, André Brie told me that in 1990 at least 500,000 would emigrate across the open border to the Federal Republic. Neither German state could do anything about it, he said. His prediction, substantially accurate, was shared by every other serious politician with whom I spoke. Bonn's public line during the winter, however, was that a forced pace of unification, in the first instance of economic and currency union, was necessary precisely in order to prevent such an outflow. The claim was backed with reference to daily emigration rates of 2,000 to 3,000 and to the demand for hard currency. ("Bring the West Mark to us or we go to it" had become a familiar chant in Leipzig.) In fact, emigration averages were generally about half that, roughly in line with what observers regarded as unavoidable regardless of short-term policies. A decision once the Berlin Wall was open to treat Germans who moved to Munich from Leipzig no more favorably than those who moved from, say, Hamburg might have built a simple earthwork against a greater emigration flood. Only after economic and currency union was in force, however, did Bonn end job and apartment subsidies for those who went to the West.

The decision to create rapid economic and currency union clearly resulted from a Kohl Government power-play. In mid-February, Modrow, accompanied by ministers from the new democratic groups and supported by Roundtable resolutions, went to Bonn to ask for emergency economic assistance. His request—nearly $9 billion—was steep, and it would not have been the last, but it was accompanied by pledges of economic reform and proofs of political change that would have been literally beyond price in the inner-German context of only a few months earlier. He was met by a stony refusal to transfer meaningful sums unless the GDR renounced control of its economic and fiscal policies by summer.

The clearest example of Bonn's tactical efforts to foreclose even provisional alternatives to rapid unification that we in East Berlin witnessed came later in February. Gaby and I had traveled much of that week, first to Wittenberg, where Friedrich Schorlemmer put us in touch with a range of activists. From there, after visiting with Cottbus friends, we moved on to Magdeburg, where over several days we spoke with the main new parties and groups and several of the old (including a local Communist chief, a month in Eberlein's chair, who hesitantly asked if he could invite us to lunch). In gathering twilight, we took coffee and cakes with the GDR's senior Lutheran bishop, Demke, and his wife in their apartment across from the great cathedral. The next day—a Saturday—we drove back to Berlin, stopping in a village near Brandenburg to interrupt a Social Democratic Party organizer's lunch and chat in his living room.

The phone rang as we arrived home. It was Dick to say I was needed urgently. When Mike Mozur and I reached his office, he explained that Washington was asking if the GDR was but days from collapse. Behind this startling question was new speculation about imminent disorder. The West German press carried a story sourced to Horst Teltschik, Kohl's security adviser. Bonn allegedly believed the GDR was bankrupt and would default its financial obligations before month's end. Major public-sector components were already unable to function, the story went, and chaos might be only hours away. Embassy Bonn and the West Berlin Mission contributed to a sense of looming anarchy with their own reporting sourced to other senior federal and city government officials.

Mike, just back from his own extensive trip to the provinces, and I looked at each other in astonishment and sat down to describe the true situation: considerable upset to normal routine, but no breakdown of basic services; ongoing political ferment, but a sense of business as usual between 8:00 A.M. and 5:00 P.M. Bishop Demke had described towns where pastors were plugging gaps caused by the withdrawal of especially tainted Communist officials. In the cities we visited, the new political forces had informally assumed a share of governmental responsibility in advance of electoral legitimation. In Magdeburg, for example, the SED district chairman and the mayor were soliciting help. Twice during our talk, the young labor activist who led the city's Social Democrats took calls from an SED deputy mayor. In between, he told us Magdeburg's industrial output had stabilized in January and was up in February, a picture that Mike confirmed was not abnormal. It was vital for the GDR to get through democratic elections, we argued. The legitimacy they would give was needed to stabilize a still-serious political situation. The economy was on autopilot, and fundamental decisions about market orientation were required to keep it from losing altitude rapidly. But the GDR was not about to crash, at least not for objective reasons. We hedged that if there was enough talk—especially in the Western media, which was still the main source of trusted information—the prediction could create its own reality.

Our analysis dampened Washington speculation, I believe, and of course the dire scenarios never came to pass. There would be similar alarms almost until the day of unification, however. The most common variant throughout the spring and well into the summer was that Parliament, or individual regions, would simply declare themselves unable to cope and apply for immediate acceptance by Bonn—an application the West Germans could not constitutionally refuse. Senior members of the new political elite did toy with such ideas, though apparently more to explore their political impact than for lack of practical alternatives. My Soviet contacts expressed bafflement: they worried about anything that would present Gorbachev with a fait accompli before he could negotiate an acceptable retreat from Germany, and they wondered what the fuss was about, because they too had their finger on the country's pulse and knew talk of imminent collapse was unfounded.

Diplomats in East Berlin did not always see matters clearly in 1990, of course. Historians must do more work before a reliable balance can be drawn between the situation as it appeared to us on the scene and as it was regularly portrayed in the West. Several factors, however, help explain the less-than-full objectivity of the latter accounts. Once again, it was virtually impossible, without living there, to conceive that the buses ran and the shops opened amid the remarkable change that swept the GDR.

Americans and West Germans alike can be excused for assuming that the collapse of the SED political system must have had equally devastating implications across community life; that is often the way of revolutions, but not of this one. To select one example: Despite the loss of police authority and the widespread anger against many SED (and especially Stasi) functionaries, there was no vigilante justice. The same discipline that allowed East Germans to bring down Honecker and the Wall without violence preserved civilized behavior. Natural skepticism that this could happen was reinforced by decades of cold war crisis-planning. Scenarios developed by think tanks for a slide into East-West conflict often began with GDR political instability that deteriorated into domestic chaos and revolutionary violence. Long after it was clear that Soviet tanks would not impose a political solution, there were twinges of reflexive worry at any hint of East German civil breakdown.

Other factors had more to do with politics, both the grand and partisan variety. Indeed, it is probably impossible to distinguish the two. Germans are no less inclined than other politicians to believe advancement of their own and their country's interests are linked. That the Bundestag campaign was under way did not help to produce disinterested assessments of the GDR. Not all Westerners believed that a forward position on unification was advantageous. Oskar Lafontaine, the SPD Chancellor candidate who lost badly in December 1990, was an exception who proved the rule. Most West Germans, however—and again Helmut Kohl is the preeminent example— were eager both to profile themselves and to seize a historic moment.

West German leaders voiced private concern that unification might be delayed indefinitely if the nation did not use its window of opportunity. This was frequently phrased as doubt that the Soviet Union would remain benign about German events. Americans were often reluctant to test statements and actions against a politician's objectives. Walter Momper, West Berlin's SPD governing mayor, had at least one eye on freeing himself from Allied constraints when he warned of imminent paralysis in East Berlin. Teltschik and his political master were as surely attempting to persuade Gorbachev, whom they were about to visit, that he had no choice but to accept quick unification when they put about the story of GDR bankruptcy. When they were accepted as inside information free of special pleading, these claims made their own contribution to the political dynamic.

But again, only historians with equal access to Bonn and Berlin perspectives can tell us how much unification's pace in those decisive months was set by West Germans pursuing personal and national agendas and how much it was set by objective conditions in the GDR.

THE ELECTION CAMPAIGN

Did Neues Forum Want Power?

When the GDR campaign began, it was widely believed that the new political forces, and foremost Neues Forum, would win. The Communists had organizational advantages, but it was assumed they could not overcome their legacy. That was correct, but the complementary assumption—that the citizen groups would take power once they had broken the SED—was badly off the mark. There was a similar miscalculation about the Social Democrats—a new party, to be sure, but one with ties to a major West German political force that, it was believed, could draw on prewar traditions of support in eastern Germany. How in three months did the revolutionized

GDR electorate give a landslide victory to the CDU, a party that had seemed almost as crippled by its collaborationist past as the SED?

Before the CDU won the March vote, it was lost by its competitors. For Neues Forum, this was close to a willful failing. The disparate individualists, romantics, and reform socialists who dominated the small activist minority that set the revolution in motion were ill-suited to compromise on a broad-based political program. The tendency toward particularism already visible in September was never overcome. The original leaders were admired but never fully trusted: They looked and acted too differently, both from the man in the pub and from the West Germans the man in the pub took as his politician models. "I don't want to be governed by such a woman. I don't even want to be painted by her," said one typically of Bärbel Bohley, who more than any other rebel symbolized the revolution's origins. It is possible, of course, that more pragmatism—even a thirst for power—would have developed, but in that winter, time was the scarcest of commodities. Throughout December and January, I received rambling responses when I asked why Neues Forum would not convert into a true party. Reluctance was understandable given unhappy experiences with the deformed versions of parties during the SED's hegemony. It was also symptomatic of a fatal reluctance to accept that the challenge was now to organize for governing, not opposing.

Neues Forum's late January convention was a nostalgic affair. The walls were lined with posters and banners from the November 4 demonstration in Alexanderplatz, which already seemed very long ago. It was also depressing because delegates were unable to agree on the smallest point without enervating squabbles that threatened schism. "It's like 1968," Gaby said as we walked to our car, parked a stone's throw from the breach in the Wall that led to the Reichstag. "They sound like students at the Free University when we were listening to Rudi Dutschke." Many citizens concluded that the GDR did not have the luxury of waiting for an experiment in grassroots democracy to sort itself out. Neues Forum's opportunity had existed, but it passed in a blink of the eye.

Months after it was clear that Neues Forum could be at most a gadfly in the new Germany, I discussed that opportunity separately with two men. Stefan Heym had never belonged to a party, but the old socialist was an intellectual father figure of the revolution. By early winter, he feared that history was repeating and that a new Germany could again threaten itself and Europe. He regretted the lost chance for a genuinely democratic and socialist reform of the GDR. There had been, he suggested, a failure of revolutionary nerve, his own not least. He recalled the feeling he experienced on Alexanderplatz that November afternoon when a half million had stood up in their own cause. After the speeches, they went quietly home. Within days, the Wall was opened, and then the West Germans took control. But, he wondered, what if that day he had pointed to the Council of State building a block away, had urged the people to seize power and complete their revolution? "Perhaps I would have made a fool of myself. Perhaps they would have laughed at the old man," he said. "But there were good people on the platform like Schorlemmer and Reich. We could at least have spared everyone the farce of Krenz. I will always wonder what would have happened." Remember that troops were nearby, I told him, there could have been bloodshed; it was best you never took the risk. Of course, I also wondered what might have been had the revolution found one bold leader when everything hung in the balance.

The second conversation was weeks later on a hot summer day over lunch in the wine cellar of the Red City Hall with Jens Reich, one of those Heym had wanted to fit for the revolutionary mantle. More than any other in the new groups, Reich had charisma, the aura of a politician who could inspire. He was in distress during much of that pivotal January convention when Neues Forum opted out of mainstream politics. Again and again he waved his hands over his head to claim the floor and strode to the microphone to urge that delegates not make the movement an object of ridicule. Why, I asked, did Neues Forum lose control after those heady November days, when it not only overturned the GDR's old order but also became the model for the Velvet Revolution in Prague? Why did you and your colleagues not do what Havel and his intellectuals had done?

Reich struggled to respond to a question he obviously had asked himself. Power was there for the taking, at least briefly, he acknowledged. Individual character and the activists' antipathy to traditional politics were partial answers. Above all, however, he said, the special circumstances of the GDR were responsible, not so much that there was a West German model but that Germany was sensitive for the Soviet Union. Many in Neues Forum had been deliberately discreet, had emphasized their desire to build on the foundations of the second German state and downplayed nationalism lest they alarm Moscow. That was a situation with which Havel never had to contend. Within months, if not weeks, this constraint was astonishingly removed from GDR politics, but by then Neues Forum was on a downward slope. Still, Reich said, its members could be proud of the responsible and indispensable role they had filled. A convenient explanation, perhaps, but credible from the decent and thoughtful Reich, who added that he did not want further political responsibility. Nor did he particularly want Neues Forum to take on government functions. He found a legislator's life uncongenial because it included little time for reflection. He would be interested in Bundestag service only if partisanship were suspended for a term to form a ticket of wise men across party lines. He knew the idea was impractical.

I heard echoes of Hermlin's hopes for a reformed Communist Party in Reich's concept of Neues Forum's future. Both men preferred for their movements the purer role of political conscience. There were differences between the honorable Communist and the best activists in the citizens groups, but their idealistic approaches to socialist society might have found common ground had the old SED leaders been less blind. It was the GDR's tragedy that both reform Communists and left-of-center non-Communists were marginalized in the years that led up to its revolution, the latter virtually criminalized. Otherwise, we might have learned whether the dream that many Germans harbored throughout the cold war of a third way—a Western and German path to socialism, rather than a Stalinist and Russian model—had basis in reality. But well before March 18 such theorizing no longer interested many in the GDR.

The Social Democrats' Failure

The failure of the Social Democrats, who did want power, was more puzzling. Originally, Neues Forum was the umbrella beneath which most SED opponents sheltered. The attitude toward practical politics, toward organization and governance as opposed to the art's more abstract side, was what distinguished the activists who soon enrolled as Social Democrats from those who remained with the citizens movements. By year's end, the politically committed were headed in different directions. A handful rejoined the Bloc Parties from which they were estranged in the final Honecker years. I met such CDU officials in Görlitz and Erfurt during 1990, but most with a taste for party politics became Social Democrats.

In January-February 1990, much evidence, including the few polls, suggested the Social Democrats were almost certain to form the GDR's first democratic government. They had gathered a cross section of early Honecker opponents. (One they failed to recruit was Gregor Gysi. The party founders had expected to be arrested when they went public on October 7, and had arranged for Gysi to represent them. Weeks later, I was told there was hope

Gysi would join the leadership; no one imagined that the lawyer and regime critic would accept the tiller of the foundering SED ship instead.)

In the matter of their name, the Social Democrats showed a sense of practical politics and a feel for public opinion that set them apart from Neues Forum. The initials they chose at the beginning, it will be recalled, were "SDP"—just different enough from the West German model to rebut the SED charge that they were an all-German stalking horse and to appeal to the then majority view that the priority was GDR reform. Once the demand for unification was clear, however, the name was changed to SPD, as in the West. The SPD was also first to rely on a West German connection. Much of their early attraction for East Germans was the tie to the sister party in the Federal Republic, which offered expertise as well as fiscal and administrative support. In February, I met Western pros—often retired "old pols"—in SPD headquarters all around the GDR. One Magdeburg talk was interrupted by the arrival of a badly needed copying machine donated by the organization in Braunschweig, just across the border.

Youthful Social Democrats were usually the most dynamic, optimistic, and confident campaigners Gaby and I met. They expected to win and welcomed the challenge. At their first "national" convention, in Leipzig over a late February weekend, they were introducing themselves to one another at the same time they discussed who from other parties might be included in their cabinet. The city was bedecked with SPD banners. I encountered Willy Brandt, the old Chancellor, at breakfast. "Who would have believed this possible?" he asked. Brandt got a hero's welcome that day at the convention and in the city square. Like others, I believed victory was in the air.

The party's nuanced stance on unification was probably one of the least important reasons this was not to be. As its name change indicated, and its Leipzig Platform documented, the East German SPD was for German unity before the campaign home-stretch—and before it lost its lead in the polls. True, it footnoted this support with "as soon as practicable," by which it meant as soon as special East German interests could be negotiated with Bonn and the Four Powers, who were believed to retain a substantial say. Every sign, however, was that this caveat was widely accepted, at least in the abstract. As late as April, a month after CDU victory, polls showed that a plurality of East Germans believed unification was coming too fast, and with inadequate attention to detail.

A larger share for failure is due the reciprocal of the SPD's early advantage: It truly was a new party. That helped it avoid the inheritances that burdened the former Bloc Parties and the SED-PDS, but no organization, no logistical infrastructure, existed. In the short, decisive race to choose Parliament on March 18, the SPD suffered from lack of offices, membership lists, and telephones; it never had a presence in many rural areas. The West German SPD probably sent in as many slick posters as the CDU. I saw trucks from West Berlin deliver neat bundles to both headquarters in Potsdam on the same day two weeks before the election. The difference was that the city's Social Democrats ran a learn-as-they-went operation out of the Stasi jail, which had been converted to offices for the new parties; the CDU machine was run with professional organizers and word processors from the elegant villa that was a Götting-era legacy. (The villa, though, was freezing that late winter morning; an overnight storm had felled a tree and left a large hole in the roof.)

The SPD's choice of leaders was a self-inflicted wound. Evidence strongly implicating its first chairman, Ibrahim Böhme, as a Stasi informer surfaced only later. Preelection rumors were no stronger than those that swirled around Lothar de Maizière, the successful CDU candidate. More damaging was an impression that Böhme was too indecisive and shallow, or at least inexperienced. I understood the concern. He was an uninspiring, untelegenic campaigner. Up close, he lacked self-confidence, at times to the border of panic. He certainly panicked me once by forgetting a private lunch I had scheduled him for with the ambassader. If that gaffe was due to lack of organization, the man who sat nervously on an embassy couch and asked disarmingly for advice on dealing with dignitaries days before he expected to become prime minister betrayed real anxiety. I still wonder whether these were momentary weaknesses he would have grown out of had the SPD won, or whether they reflected the torment of a man who knew his past would catch him if he continued on a path he could no longer leave gracefully.

The Stasi Nightmare

The dark side of Böhme's character was symptomatic of a problem that has haunted eastern Germany well past unification. The involvement of so many with the Stasi, the old regime's omnipresent control organ, was rarely black and white. The degrees of guilt, the fact that the same individual was often victim and perpetrator, are complexities observers fortunate enough to lack firsthand experience of a highly organized and efficient domestic spying system have difficulty grasping.

The political implications are not partisan. A sadder case than Böhme's involved Wolfgang Schnur, who wrested leadership of Democratic Awakening from Friedrich Schorlemmer, then moved it into Helmut Kohl's Alliance for Germany to contest the election on Christian Democrat lines. The revelation a week before the vote that he was a paid Stasi informer destroyed Schnur's career and crippled his party. Was he a villain? I doubt it, and not just because I knew him before the revolution as the lawyer most ready to defend otherwise helpless victims of a repressive legal system. I remember Imre's description of an evening in 1988. Long after an emotional service in Gethsemane Church for arrested activists had ended, Schnur sank to his knees at the altar. With hands clasped and tears running down his face, the lawyer was unaware he was being observed. At the time, I thought the incident showed piety. Now I wonder if we did not glimpse an agonized soul caught between ambition and faith, sordid compromise and ideals. Whatever the moral judgment, such vulnerable human beings should abstain from politics, but that is easy for an outsider to say. It is not the least of the GDR's sins that it produced, or at least exploited, so many weaknesses in men and women no less decent than most. Nor perhaps is it the least of current problems that the new Germany arrived so quickly that GDR citizens had no time to sift the layers of wounds on their own to decide who, and in what measure, was worthy of trust. It was too easy to cast the first stone at those whom ambition or circumstance brought into prominence but otherwise ignore one's own compromises and move on.

While Social Democrats had no unusual share of Stasi ties, a different personnel weakness did sap their early lead. Subjective impressions played a part. All parties except the SED-PDS relied heavily on church figures. There was no alternative pool of talent that could be presumed to be mostly free of collaborationist taint. But pastors with long beards, and fiery young women, were especially numerous in the SPD. Markus Meckel grew into a Foreign Minister who handled himself well with Genscher, Shevardnadze, and Baker. When he was elected Deputy SPD Chairman in Leipzig, however, admirers gave him a tie and scissors. Only much later did he use either. Thomas Krüger, an activist who was staging church plays when we met in 1988, became an effective member of the first all-Berlin Cabinet. His beard is neatly trimmed now, and he wears a tie, but he did not in Winter 1990, when he lost a vote for East Berlin Party Chairman to a young lady shorter of thirty than he. "They will never get the man-in-the-street's vote if they offer choices between Teeny and Topsy," exclaimed one contact in prophetic exasperation. Many who came to prominence in the early days looked the part of the radical individualists they were when they broke the Honecker regime. Voters found them too exotic to carry the GDR into union with Bonn. Unification's pace left no time for them to evolve into the new-type candidate who could win the confidence of an electorate that believed only West German models had value.

De Maizière: An Unlikely Victor

Conservatives were no better at finding candidates who inspired confidence. It could hardly be otherwise. They wore suits with more ease, but many had associations with the Bloc Party past. Christian Democrats said they had cleaned house, and certainly the worst of the old leadership were retired, but in every CDU office I found "professionals" who had run the machine when it swore fealty to the SED. Left to its own devices, that party would never have swept the boards in a democratic election.

I did not know the new CDU leader, de Maizière, well. Before the revolution, he had a reputation as an attorney who fought for his clients and as a man of faith who was in the leadership of the Lutheran church but not Götting's CDU. I first met him in Gregor Gysi's office in 1988 but failed to follow up. (Gysi was chairman of the Lawyer's Association, de Maizière was his deputy, and they were professionally close.) Once he became Prime Minister, I observed him only in larger gatherings or as the ambassador's notetaker. Imre knew him for three years, however, and breakfasted with him on election day. Prime Minister de Maizière had few cards to play, but I thought him a man of some courage who did his best in difficult circumstances to represent East German interests. There was more ambition, drive, steel, and stubbornness in this cellist-turned-lawyer-turned-politician than a meek appearance and slight speech defect suggested on first impression. But his own strengths would have been no more adequate to save the party that turned to him in desperation than those of his friend Gysi.

Small Parties of the Right

The minor conservative parties were even less masters of their fortunes. Rainer Eppelmann stepped in at Democratic Awakening when the past caught up with Schnur, and became another casualty of fast-forward politics. The SED regime, of which Eppelmann had been a prominent critic, did not doubt his moral courage, but he never found his footing as party chairman and then Europe's first pacifist minister of defense and disarmament. Eppelmann won the respect of East German professional soldiers by trying to make the transition to the new order as humane as possible for them. To many in the West-CDU, his social views were suspiciously close to those of the SPD's; to security professionals, his dislike of military alliances, NATO included, branded him a dangerous dilettante. His vanity and taste for the pomp and circumstance of office made him easy to satirize and belittle, but Eppelmann was a man of real depth whose natural home may have been politics. During the campaign, he was asked why he had chosen a church career. "I was always interested in public life," he explained, "and when I became twenty I asked myself how I could become old honorably. The only path in the GDR was into the church." Had he more time to learn the new craft, he might eventually have practiced it with the imagination and panache that won him respect on the pulpit. But again, no one had time in the 1990 GDR, and Eppelmann was never an electoral factor.

The third Alliance party, the DSU, polled more votes than Democratic Awakening, particularly in Saxony and Thuringia, but from the start it was too obviously a stalking horse for Bavarian conservatives. Todd Becker, who came from Washington to assist us invaluably in covering the campaign, met all his old Munich contacts (where he had recently served) within an hour at the DSU convention. The West-SPD prowled the corridors at its sister party's convention; the West-CDU stood just behind de Maizière while dictating policy and tactics. The Bavarians were on the platform, arms around protégés.

The DSU's most striking figure, Peter-Michael Diestel, later interior minister, was its most controversial. There was something a bit too determinedly macho about him for confidence. A child of an SED family who became a lawyer, he owned two villas and lived well without documented connection to the old system. He strove for effect, whether as a passionate body builder or a cabinet minister who claimed to be the target of death threats and proudly carried a gun. (When J.D. and I sought protection for American facilities during the Gulf Crisis, he asked if we had our own pistols.) Doubts about Diestel's constancy were not relieved when he left his party after the election for the more successful CDU. He was one of the ablest in de Maizière's cabinet, and he won private respect from Social Democrats who worked with him during the Grand Coalition. But long before Diestel's term saddled him with further questions about his commitment to uncovering Stasi influence in bureaucracy and economy, it was clear that he was no vote-getter.

The DSU's nominal founder and first chairman, Pastor Ebeling of

Leipzig, was even less successful. I remember him best for the April morning after he had failed to appear at Dick's sit-down dinner for six U.S. Senators. The coalition parties had met past midnight to hammer out their program and apportion cabinet posts. Ebeling was needed there, and Dick had understood his no-show. As I left the embassy at 9:00 the following morning, however, Ebeling was explaining to the doorman that he wanted to apologize. I assured him there had been no offense and wondered how long it would take senior East German politicians to acquire the hard shell of their colleagues elsewhere. But Ebeling was only a figurehead in the DSU. His pulpit was in Leipzig, the "Hero City," but at Thomas Church, not Nikolai Church. While Magirius and Führer sheltered the groups whose anger incited the great demonstrations, Ebeling gave unto Caesar. He and his party called loudly for unification by tomorrow, if not yesterday, and condemned every aspect of the old GDR—in 1990. Friedrich Schorlemmer's comment struck home: "Before the revolution, I knew Pastor Ebeling as a conservative man, but not as a brave man." In March he was no more the leader to mobilize East Germans behind him than he was during the revolutionary autumn.

The West Germans Take Over: Kohl vs. Brandt

The conservative parties won the election and set the tone for the Year of Unification not from inherent strength but because the contest became one between Helmut Kohl and the West-SPD. The Chancellor fought brilliantly, recognizing the historical moment and making full use of the incumbent's power, but it was a near-run thing. For weeks, the West-SPD was alone on stage while Kohl agonized about the East-CDU he had belittled as collaborationist. Was it wiser to use its assets or to put all hopes on the minuscule new center and right parties? Not until February 5, less than six weeks before Election Sunday, did Kohl hammer together the uneasy coalition of old and new, of CDU, Democratic Awakening, and DSU, that as the Alliance for Germany won a landslide. The Leipzig pollsters documented how far behind it started. On February 9, the SPD was the choice of 53 percent of East Germans, and the Alliance was the choice of 17 percent (of which the CDU claimed 13 percent, up three points from late November). To the query "Which [West German] politicians do you trust to pursue a 'Germany policy' in the interests of the people?" 28 percent responded Oskar Lafontaine and 24 percent said Helmut Kohl. When Kohl and the West-CDU took over the campaign, they set new parameters for the unification issue more than they responded to a trend the SPD ignored.

The Chancellor forced the pace of GDR economic collapse and international acceptance of early unification as both possible and essential. But he did more. His appearances at election rallies in the final weeks changed the psychological climate in a way the SPD could not match. Only Willy Brandt had comparable name-recognition and charisma, but the Nobel Peace Prize winner spoke in almost nonpartisan tones. He had little choice: The West-SPD had neither policy consensus to make promises nor governmental authority to keep them. By contrast, authority emanated from Kohl's physical presence—and Helmut Kohl on the stump is an impressive sight, especially to an audience wanting desperately to believe in a short path to prosperity. When he promised the West Mark would be introduced quickly into the East—and even more when he pledged that no one would be worse off with unification and that almost everyone would be better off—he was believed. His hand was on the levers of power. Indeed, Kohl personified power—the politician who got things done.

"This Country Needs Money"

Kohl's engagement changed the campaign's terms, and it was apparent by late February that the election was a horserace. The final survey, a week before the vote, showed the SPD's lead at 34 to 31 and shrinking. About then, I gave a ride home to Pflugbeil, Neues Forum's representative in the Modrow Cabinet. He spoke of a conservative groundswell and predicted the citizens groups (united as "Bündnis '90"—"Coalition '90") would be nearly shut out. "You have always been a pessimist," I said. "This time I really have something to be pessimistic about," he rejoined. At lunch the next day, Thomas Krüger confirmed that the SPD hoped to break even nationally and win in Berlin, but he was nervous. In a circle of election-morning intimates, Imre said, de Maizière expected a narrow victory. At the end, that was what I tipped.

Harry Bergold, who had been my ambassador in Budapest, and his wife, Karlene, visited on election weekend. On Saturday, half of Berlin was strolling through the Brandenburg Gate and along Unter den Linden as a multihued hot-air balloon was launched from once-austere Marx-Engels Forum. We joined Henry Kamm, the *New York Times* correspondent, for a drink on the Palast Hotel balcony. "The Alliance will win big," said Henry, just back from Saxony. "Even in Brandt's crowds I couldn't find SPD voters."

My own tip-off was a chat a few days earlier on a train to Frankfort on the Oder. Two young men explained their first free ballot. "We are workers," one said. "We should vote SPD. Next time we probably will. But this country needs money. The West controls the money, and the CDU controls the West, so we will vote CDU." Many shared their pragmatism.

The Chancellor's Victory

On election day, the Bergolds and I stopped at polling stations in Berlin and neighboring villages. We were welcome everywhere, mostly without showing the "CSCE Observer Delegation" card I had obtained for U.S. Congressmen who came to certify the vote's fairness. I could not help but compare my experience ten months earlier, when East Germans dropped ballots into boxes while nervous officials watched me watch. That evening, at the open house Gaby and I held for East German friends, Uwe and Marianne Haus brought a just-published volume of Stasi documents. "Look here," they said, pointing to the description of how "U.S. Embassy Counselor Greenwald visited an election polling station in Pankow and asked questions especially about the use of voting booths." This time we saw voters and officials alike take pride in a fair, free, and secret choice. At 6:01 P.M., one minute after voting ended, results of exit polls were broadcast, and all suspense was gone. The extent of the Alliance victory was a shock, but for that evening our friends cared little who won or lost. They celebrated democracy.

After a few hours, I returned to our embassy. With the sober analysis we put into the cable that evening, I hardly dared suggest one factor for fear it would be deemed frivolous. I believe, however, it was significant. Almost every East German I talked with in the months leading up to that watershed election had a divided political soul. Half of him (or her) wanted to move boldly into the united Germany that Helmut Kohl attractively portrayed, and half feared hasty loss of familiar values and security. Broadly speaking, the Communists and the Bündnis '90 emphasized that latter side of the equation, though with different nuances. The SPD sought the middle ground. Many voters were still undecided that final weekend.

Most who expressed a preference were only lightly committed and could easily change at the last minute. What moved virtually every undecided vote into the Alliance's fold? It can never be proved, but I will always believe that weather made a difference. March 18 was a warm, sunny spring day, the kind that stirs any but the deadest soul. There could be no better omen for optimism, for a gamble on the future. Had the day been dark and rainy, as often in Germany in March, would 10 percent fewer East Germans have dared the leap? Perhaps, but once the votes were counted, the GDR's first democratic government had a mandate to do only the minimum necessary to work itself out of office. As I let myself into the house at midnight to have a drink with the last guests, I knew de Maizière would be less a free actor than Honecker had ever been. Kohl was the real winner, and decisions concerning the GDR's short remaining history would be made in Bonn.

200 DAYS

Important political matters were resolved in the half year remaining to October 3, 1990, the day unification was legally consummated: the international arrangements—including Gorbachev's acceptance in July of a unitary Germany's NATO membership, for example—and the domestic terms on which the two German states came together. The election campaign, however, spanned the revolution's second phase. When it began, the Roundtable had just been initiated, and the new democratic forces, with Neues Forum most prominent, were ascendant. By the time East Germans voted, the Roundtable was irrelevant. It was important in helping the Modrow Cabinet limp through its term without chaos, but as the GDR assumed the political texture of the Federal Republic, its political prescriptions were ignored. At its final session, March 12, the Roundtable recommended a draft constitution for a united Germany and a plebiscite on June 17, the anniversary of the 1953 uprising. The draft was set aside by the party politicians who dominated the Parliament that convened in April. Under pressure from Kohl, unification was pursued through simple accession to West Germany's laws and structures. The political maneuvers and negotiations on two state treaties that preceded the late summer accession vote were over an infinite number of technical details. The decision on unification's basic nature had long since been made.

Did Unification Come Too Fast?

The decision—that unification would not be the act of partners but in effect annexation of East by West—explains much that has happened in the new Germany's first years and will carry serious implications for decades to come. It was widely welcomed in the Federal Republic and by most of its friends.

West Germany was a successful democracy; East Germany was a failed tyranny. Even isolated areas where GDR practices appeared equal, much less superior, were hard to find. Germans on neither side of the border wanted to experiment. To West German pride in accomplishments was added East German loss of confidence provoked by the political and social system's obvious shortcomings. It seemed self-evident that the GDR should close the deal quickly by taking the working model without reservation. This reassured Bonn's allies that the new Germany would retain a democratic and Western orientation.

The theme needs its own book, but two anecdotes may illustrate my reservations. Shortly before the election, I attended a seminar for the GDR's inexperienced democratic politicians. Good advice was given about building organizations, using volunteers, getting out pamphlets, and other aspects of practical politics, though some comments reflected unfamiliarity with local conditions. "Make sure they write the check" had little relevance to a society where checks were essentially unknown; nor was it helpful to recommend mobilizing housewives in a country where more than 90 percent of women worked. But a late-evening exchange took me aback. An American consultant told his audience never to forget that "politics is about power." Wolfgang Ullmann of Democracy Now, a Roundtable minister in Modrow's Cabinet, interrupted. That comment, he said, speaking English for emphasis, reminded him of SED philosophy. "We did not go into the streets to get power, but to achieve freedom and justice." A moment of embarrassed silence was followed by efforts to smooth things over. Of course, the American explained, he did not mean politics was only about winning power; it was also about how power should be used, but he had addressed the professional's craft, not substance.

Perhaps Ullmann—lawyer, teacher, and church layman—and those he spoke for were naive. Nevertheless, it was hard not to sympathize with the belief that, at such an early stage in their society's adjustment to democracy, time to consider first principles was more important than the nuts and bolts of wooing voters. East Germans were introduced to politics' hard-shelled cynicism before they could acquaint themselves with its foundation. Is it surprising that disillusionment with Parliament and leaders came quickly, or that they soon thought themselves incapable of using their new democratic institutions to help themselves?

At about this time, I dined with Martin Kirchner. A minor figure in the East-CDU before he signed the "Letter from Weimar"—its first sign of dissidence—in September, he was now the party's secretary general and regularly taking the Bonn line in public. He urged the CDU to distance itself from Modrow so that it could run as "Opposition." He was also one of the first to adopt the mannerisms of the pros from the Rhine and their patented phrases (such as beginning every other declamation with "ich gehe davon aus, dass . . . ," I proceed from the view that . . .). We fell into serious talk over brandies. It was my impression, I said, that people were losing confidence in their revolution. They sensed events were moving beyond their control again; they had destroyed SED power, but they had difficulty reorganizing and reforming society. Increasingly, they sought a single, quick answer that would absolve them of responsibility for tough choices. This seemed to underlie the drive for ever quicker unification, I said provocatively, and most GDR politicians encouraged the trend.

Was this so bad, Kirchner wondered? Perhaps, I said. There would be a united Germany soon, but how the parts were stitched together was important. If East Germans confined themselves to expressing support for inevitable unification without doing their share to ensure that the GDR that went into union with the West retained a certain sense of itself, eastern Germany would at best suffer from a vast inferiority complex for a generation. At worst, if something went badly wrong with Germany's economy, and expectations were disappointed, the ensuing bitterness could debilitate the entire body politic with consequences that must be considerable, even if they could not now be precisely described.

East Germans had always felt disadvantaged by their Western cousins, I argued, but with their Peaceful Revolution they had for the first time done something no Germans—indeed, few people ever—had achieved. They, not the West Germans, had produced a political miracle that impressed the world. Scant weeks after the Wall was opened, however, they began to lose control of their creation. Within months, the self-confidence and pride that should have been their political dowry had all but dissipated. If this continued, I worried, they would go into the new Germany on their knees. So little sense of self-worth was unhealthy; there would be mutual resentment if unification and the substantial material support that must in any event flow West to East for years was seen as a gift to supplicants who exercised little control over their own destiny. An *Anschluss* (annexation) mentality would be a heavy mortgage on German unity, I offered. Slower unification might be better for everyone if the time was used by East Germans to consolidate the gains of their revolution, acquire experience with managing their own affairs, and make considered judgments jointly, as partners with the West Germans, about the terms of the new relationship.

"Intellectual moonbeams!" Kirchner scoffed. "I hear the same from the church," he said with a nod at a pastor from Gethsemane Church, who had played a pivotal role in October. He went on: "A politician's job is to listen and respond to the people. Our people want to live as well as the West Germans immediately, not in five or ten years. They have been waiting forty years and want no experiments. The West German system works, and we shall take it over. It will be like the 1950s in the Federal Republic. Then too, a lot of the so-called finer values were set aside to concentrate on learning a new way and building up the economy. The West Germans studied you Americans to become better *Spiessbürger* ["Babbitts" is the best translation someone who has read Sinclair Lewis can use for this term] than you. We will study the West Germans and be better *Spiessbürger*, at least for a generation. Is that so bad?"

Perhaps he is right. Kirchner did not make the transition to leadership in the new Germany. Charges of Stasi complicity brought him down. I do not know their truth, and I am reluctant, as with Schnur, to condemn him unreservedly even if they are proved. Those who did not have to survive in the deformed society SED and Stasi created are poorly qualified to evaluate the accommodations nearly everyone made in some degree. Kirchner is intelligent and complex. Much worse can be imagined than a society as free and dynamic, if perhaps overly materialistic, as West German society in the years of its Economic Miracle. If that is what East Germany becomes this decade, probably only a handful of intellectuals will begrudge the spiritual cost of the rejected opportunity in Winter 1990. But at least until East Germans break free of the apathy, amounting to paralysis, that has characterized many in unification's first stage and that is a consequence of how that unification came, I suspend judgment.

Negotiating Germany

The international aspect of unification formally paralleled the inner-German aspect but in fact was driven by it. Unlike postwar Four Power conferences, the Two-Plus-Four was never truly charged with resolving Germany's division. That, properly, was left to the Germans. It satisfied legal form and allowed Moscow a graceful retreat from Central Europe. At least the Soviet Embassy in Berlin never harbored illusions that negotiations could affect the reality being created daily on the ground.

The American position was clear. We wanted unification to come quickly in order to minimize distraction of our Bonn ally. Senior State Department officials were uneasy when, that winter, I jokingly told them Germany could not be whole before autumn. Why? they asked, perplexed. The West Germans expected to win the soccer World Cup in summer but would have to play East Germans on the national team if unification came too soon, I explained. In 1938, a favored German team lost the Cup because Austrians weakened its cohesion. No one would risk a repetition, I said.

More seriously, Gerry Livingston of Johns Hopkins University identified a potential policy contradiction. Secretary Baker had said in December, he noted, that unification must be in the context of continued German participation in Western institutions. But what if the Soviets refused to accept incorporation of their most important ally in NATO? Would the United States block self-determination if the German states chose neutrality? I discouraged speculation that ours was a Machiavellian formula to slow unification by setting impossible terms, but many shared Livingston's doubts that Gorbachev could accept Germany's unrestricted NATO membership. East Germans had no enthusiasm for trading alliances. Even if they knew there were differences between NATO and the Warsaw Pact, their preference was for a clean break with cold war structures and development of the CSCE into a new pan-European security system. That was the view of every politician Stephen Solarz quizzed in January, and I heard it throughout my subsequent travels.

Several factors produced the result that initially seemed so problematic. The firmness of Western negotiators was vital, especially that of Kohl, who ignored the neutrality card when Modrow played it. So was the fact that East German reluctance was as shallow as it was broad. A plebiscite would have rejected NATO, but unification and associated economic issues were what people cared about. On NATO, to them a secondary matter, they were prepared to follow Bonn whatever their doubts. In the end, Gorbachev's remarkable ability to adjust to reality was decisive. When he concluded that a strong, well-disposed Germany could be more help than anything that could be retrieved from the GDR failure, he cut his losses and made the best deal he could with Kohl.

Our embassy played little part as the Two-Plus-Four dotted "i's" and crossed "t's." The exercise was handled at senior levels from Washington. We were involved, primarily as facilitators, when the negotiation came to East Berlin, but our major contribution was between sessions, when we maintained a dialogue with the new GDR policy-makers. To be honest, the United States never took the East German voice at the negotiating table seriously. Diplomacy respects power and leverage, and the internally divided de Maizière government, which could only negotiate itself away, had neither. Nevertheless, we sought to influence its thinking since East German positions were potentially disruptive.

Dick concentrated on de Maizière, who generally supported Western positions, particularly after lunching with President Bush in Washington. J.D. kept in close contact with Hans Misselwitz, the pastor who as number two in the Foreign Ministry was the official most closely engaged in the negotiation. I had long talks with my old Potsdam acquaintance, Helmut Domke (who had become a State Secretary), and SPD Foreign Minister Meckel's adviser, the West German Christian von Braunmühl, brother of a senior Bonn diplomat assassinated by terrorists a few years earlier. He and Meckel had met at a peace seminar before the revolution.

The Foreign Ministry and to lesser extent Eppelmann tried to shape a real policy. They did so neither from fealty to Moscow nor, despite the imputations of Bonn-inspired press stories once partisan jockeying began, out of an overdeveloped sense of grandeur. They believed there was need for a new beginning in Europe's security relations; they considered it prudent and appropriate for Germany to respect the interests of a Soviet Union that feared isolation, and they felt strongly that, with its ideological division overcome, the continent must not be divided at the Oder-Neisse between a rich West and a poor East. They thought they could make a unique contribution as Germans who understood the moribund Warsaw Pact, and they did their best to do so honorably. It was not always so understood by professionals in the chanceries of other Two-Plus-Four powers, but theirs was an authentic, if alternative, German voice that fairly reflected the sentiments of many East Germans. It was only that in this, as in much else, they had neither time to master nuances nor, in the end, the political backing from impatient GDR citizens that might have allowed them to put weight behind their concepts. It is hard to say it without being patronizing, but they were idealists whom history was too busy to give the hearing their commitment deserved.

Bonn Politics Come to Berlin

In the months following investiture of the de Maizière government, the U.S. Embassy chronicled the unification story while continuing to receive Congressional visitors. Affairs of state, however, were disappointing, often depressing. It was perhaps inevitable that for the remainder of the year GDR politics was little more than a skirmish line between West German parties positioning themselves for the coming election in the Federal Republic. By

June, Wolfgang Thierse, the new East-SPD chairman, admitted to us that the Grand Coalition was dead, though neither side could be certain which would benefit from forcing collapse. By August even that uncertainty was gone, and under pressure from de Maizière, in concert with Kohl, Thierse's colleagues withdrew from the Cabinet. No political grouping believed the best politics might be a moratorium on partisanship. It was a disconcerting introduction to democracy for East Germans, who asked what the posturing had to do with an increasingly shaky economy.

An Unusual Foreign Minister

Exchanges with the Foreign Ministry took on a new quality. I recall with pleasure a long breakfast to which von Braunmühl invited me in the private ministerial suite, once off-limits for us. Over coffee, rolls, and an assortment of sausages, he and his staff tried to explain themselves while I did my best to convey to them why their initiatives made traditionalists in Washington nervous. We settled nothing, but I think we came to understand each other. None of this was conventional, but it was in the spirit of our first official encounter with Meckel in the office he inherited from Oskar Fischer. He confessed that he was not a professional and would undoubtedly make mistakes; therefore, we should talk all the more frankly and often, he said. I never doubted that goodwill was present in the fullest measure from Meckel and his team. I hope they knew it was mutual.

I saw more of Meckel after he left office. The SPD ministers withdrew from the Cabinet in August. A few days later, we were dining at a pub in Prenzlauer Berg with Gaby's niece Karen, a new Harvard graduate. Meckel walked over from the bar with his beer to join us, and we chatted for an hour about politics and his life. He and his wife later came to our house for a private dinner.

Meckel was criticized during his brief incumbency for meddling in high policy beyond a temporary player's competence. I kept the following example of the backgrounder journalism that typified the savage infighting. In June the *Herald Tribune* reported:

> Irritation and alarm are mounting in Bonn and East Berlin about these Social Democratic cabinet ministers' lavish official life-styles and their political maneuvers to delay reunification and perhaps even prolong the presence of Soviet troops in East Germany. . . .
> "They are globe-trotting pointlessly and spending money like people

who have been given only short months to live," the West German official said, "but we expect a letter within the next weeks on reunification or else there is going to be trouble." Singled out for criticism are two Social Democrats [sic] in particular, Markus Meckel, the foreign minister, and Rainer Eppelmann, the minister for defense and disarmament. Both are clerics, and both now travel in private jets, with large entourages, making pronouncements about East-West relations that Western officials find both comic and pernicious. . . . "These Social Democrat ministers represent a defeated party, in a caretaker government committed to folding their country cleanly into the new Germany," a former U.S. official said, "but now they are starting to carry water for Moscow's hard-liners. . . ." Privately West German officials are indignant about the East German leaders' frenzy to travel abroad and beat the air politically. And an East German official who was loyal to the Honecker regime and who remains in government said, "Those ministers have four times higher salary than their predecessors, they travel now in private jets like no minister used to and they bring their women to help them spend. . . ."

That was unfair. Meckel traveled no more than many foreign ministers. His policy prescriptions often could be faulted as naive, or at least not well staffed, but he was at a disadvantage: He admitted inexperience, but he had neither time nor inclination to develop ties with the professional foreign policy bureaucracy he inherited from Axen and Fischer. Meckel's real sin for many, as the article hinted, was that he did not act as if Bonn already represented all Germans at the negotiating table.

To be sure, the attacks had an element of accuracy. Meckel did not back down in the face of realities to which a more experienced politician would probably have accommodated. His SPD and its Western sponsors were as partisan as the Christian Democrats—a point not lost on the man in the street. However, CDU leaders used Bonn and Berlin incumbencies to play the game more effectively. Ad hominem criticism of SPD Finance Minister Romberg, who accurately claimed that the new East German federal states were not financed adequately in the agreements the Kohl and de Maizière teams negotiated, finally forced the breakup of the Grand Coalition.

The criticism to which Meckel was sensitive when we talked, probably because he recognized it as substantially justified, came from within his party. It said he neglected the grassroots to pursue the statesman's role. The party stripped him of leadership and forced him to contest a marginal seat for the all-German Bundestag. He won, and he may become again a spokesman for East Germans and the SPD. I hope so for his own sake—like many of the revolution's political pastors, he admittedly would find it difficult to return to a pulpit—and for Germany's. A country more easily risks challenge to comfortable foreign policy assumptions than it casts aside a man of courage and commitment.

The U.S. Air Force Goes to Görlitz

I had more uplifting experiences outside politics. Young East Germans recounted how a new world of travel and intellectual challenge was opening for them. We saw daily change, large and small, in Berlin's physical appearance that showed some East Germans were learning to cope. Hardly a restaurant or shop did not soon sport at least a more colorful awning or window display.

Shortly before the May 1990 elections that democratized local councils, we traveled to Görlitz. Gaby's mother, seeking refuge from the bombs, gave birth to Gaby in that small city and six weeks later took her back to Berlin one step ahead of the Red Army. When a church synod brought us there in 1987, Gaby discovered that the Number 2 trolley still ran from the market square to the Landeskrone, the hill overlooking the triangle where the GDR, Czechoslovakia, and Poland come together, and to the church home where she was born. Görlitz was beautiful and sad. The medieval core was protected as a national treasure, but there was little money for restoration. Architectural treasures were crumbling. Even more than most East German cities, Görlitz bore an air of neglect and decay. Divided in 1945, the portion east of the Neisse River became Polish. The GDR gave few resources to this easternmost point of German territory. Deprived by geography of Western television, residents knew theirs was the most isolated city in an isolated land.

In Spring 1990, however, Görlitz had new vibrancy. People talked about the election and the city's prospects. While there was worry that industry would be unable to face Western competition, tourism offered good chances as, suddenly, did geography. Görlitz, many said, would be Germany's gateway to the East. Omnipresent yellow and white flags symbolized the new spirit. The flag was Silesia's, an entity the GDR had attempted to force from the region's memory because the rest of that ancient German province now lay across the river border, and the Poles were sensitive. With restrictions removed, Silesia was on everyone's lips.

Most said it was simply local pride asserting itself, that it had less to do with nationalism than with making Dresden, the Saxon capital, remember Görlitz and give it autonomous status. There had been unfortunate incidents, it was agreed, including meetings of "Skinheads" and neo-Nazis, as well as imprudent discussions with Silesian associations in the West whose members dreamed of recovering homes from Poland. Every politician said he (or she) backed the Silesia movement to keep it from being seized by "someone worse." The Communist mayor left office to chair the Silesian cultural society. Members wanted friendly ties with Poles and were a bit puzzled, he said naively, that invitations were not accepted. In fact, he said, Polish Görlitz appeared to be withdrawing into itself in reaction to German assertiveness.

We left Görlitz slightly uneasy, feeling that as in much of Eastern Europe ethnic problems dormant under the cold war blanket could revive. But that worry was diminished by the final evening's exuberance. The formal occasion for our visit was to represent the embassy at an astonishing event. Just as the Wall opened, the Görlitz mayor visited Wiesbaden, in West Germany. Impressed by a U.S. Air Force Band concert, he invited the musicians on the spot. Our embassy supported this as a people-to-people opportunity; to its credit, so did a startled military bureaucracy. I have never seen better natural ambassadors than the young Americans who put on a two-hour virtuoso performance ranging from Dixieland through symphony, to Broadway. For the finale, they accompanied the local CDU chairman, who sang Schiller's "Ode to Joy" to the music of Beethoven's Ninth. The audience, including a game Soviet base commander, gave a standing ovation. Görlitz's isolation was over.

Return to Bad Salzungen

In late summer, we drove again to Thuringia. Of politicians, churchmen, and journalists we interviewed in Erfurt, the most interesting was Sergei Lochthofen, a Russian citizen but lifelong GDR resident whose colleagues had chosen him in November to run the former SED regional paper. At lunch, he described proudly how it had been the first to print West German television listings. "Who authorized it?" astonished editors around the country wanted to know. "I did," Sergei said, laughing. He was among the most optimistic of our interlocutors, though one incident troubled him.

"Erfurt makes wonderful beer. You must have some," he had said. Soon bottles from Herford, in West Germany, stood before us. "You misheard," Sergei reprimanded the waiter. "I ordered Erfurt, not Herford, beer." "I'm sorry," was the response, "but we carry only West German brands." It was symptomatic of what happened throughout the economy. Consumers demanded Western products, and West German merchandisers not infrequently compelled retailers to give exclusive rights as a delivery condition. This undermined the already shaky competitiveness of many firms and the self-confidence of East Germans, who saw familiar products disappear from shelves.

We proceeded toward Bad Salzungen, stopping on a sunny day in tiny Dietzgenhausen, where we found Landolf Scherzer on the terrace of his cottage, halfway into the woods, bidding farewell to the West German publisher of a new edition of *Der Erste*. The author plied us with sausage and the well-remembered Rhön beer and talked of the changes in his life. He had learned of the revolution in the Volga village where he was researching his Perestroika book, and had hurried home to throw himself into reform of the SED. At the December emergency congress, he was elected to the governing board, successor to the Central Committee, but disillusionment set in quickly. The Party, he said, was still run by those who set greatest store on careers and privileges. He remained in the PDS because socialism was his political creed, but he would focus on local issues where an honorable man might make a difference. Could our embassy, he asked, finance a traffic light for Dietzgenhausen as a goodwill gesture? The once quiet road was now a through route from the border and dangerous for schoolchildren.

We missed Fritschler and Stumpf. The former had been one of a handful of county chieftains to survive the turmoil at the top of the SED-PDS, but, discouraged by the election results, he had resigned and, after a short vacation, would join a new automated carwash venture. Stumpf had sent me a melancholy letter. He thought often of our August visit and the questions we discussed so frankly, he said, and would have more time to ponder their implications in forced retirement. We rang his gate bell in vain. Subsequently another letter from him regretted he had been traveling.

After losing our way between modern apartment blocks on the edge of town in search of the PDS's modest new office, we found Fritschler's successors. A year earlier, the young man had been Second Secretary and the young woman had been in charge of culture. They told us our first visit had created a sensation. The Stasi prepared for days, and Fritschler had to write detailed reports. If we had ever doubted, it was clear now why he tried to say much with body language rather than words, and why Scherzer conspiratorially whispered his last comments about Perestroika as we departed. The pair was sober about prospects in Bad Salzungen. They hoped the membership hemorrhage was stanched and spoke of a few young people who had joined. They were introspective about the past, but we left unsure of their conversion to grassroots democracy. Was their decision to remain when many had jumped ship idealistic, or were they compromised apparatchiks? As with so much in 1990, rush to judgment was imprudent.

We also called on the new political elite. Bad Salzungen was now a CDU stronghold. The engineer who succeeded Stumpf as county commissioner described his difficulties much as had Erfurt's mayor the day before. Parliament, he said, was taking over volumes of West German law at a sitting. He received telexes from Berlin but no money, and he had few advisers to help him understand the new system. Still, he exuded a calm, problem-solving competence.

Mayor Bormann received us at the town hall flanked by cabinet and reporters. She apparently believed I was the U.S. Ambassador—and from Bonn, not Berlin. Not wanting to embarrass her, I whispered my identity. Unfazed, if understandably not pleased, she carried on, presenting me a leather-bound plan to utilize Bad Salzungen's location on the old inner-German border to make it a goods-transshipment center. At last, she said, she could root openly for the Bayern Munich soccer team. She had led the city CDU for nearly twenty years, she acknowledged, but had always disliked Communists.

Did the GDR Ever Have a Chance?

August 13 was the Berlin Wall's 29th anniversary, and the first since the revolution. *Neue Berliner Illustrierte*, a weekly trying to survive in a suddenly competitive world, marked the occasion by inviting politicians and Four Power representatives to a public forum. I was the only diplomat to accept, in the expectation that I would finally meet Markus Wolf, but the spymaster withdrew at the last minute.

Despite oppressive humidity, Berliners packed an art gallery the walls of which displayed photos of the infamous structure that still stood a few hundred yards away. Our panel included the Countess Dönhoff, the octogenarian publisher of the West German weekly *Die Zeit*, whose mind was as sharp as when I first met her a dozen years earlier; Antje Vollmer, a West

German Green; and Dietmar Keller, Modrow's culture minister and still a controversial PDS leader. The debate was whether the GDR ever could have been more than a creature of Soviet power. Had the Wall, cruel as it was, offered a weak entity that was bleeding to death in struggle with West Germany in the early 1960s, a last chance to consolidate and develop its own identity? Or had the fateful August 13 sealed a spiritual bankruptcy that made political collapse inevitable? Panelists and audience tended to the latter view. Even Keller professed to have recognized the unpardonable sin a few years earlier when he viewed the metropolis from the thirty-eighth floor of the Hotel Stadt Berlin. He realized then, he said, that the Wall cut through flesh of a living organism and could not last.

Most intriguing was a witness I could not have met before. The recently retired commander of border troops, who had controlled the Wall, said that within months of that 1961 Sunday, East Germans had reconciled themselves to its existence, however reluctantly. As defenses were perfected, escape attempts declined and remained low for years. Suddenly, in a single month, they tripled and then rose steadily. Could anyone guess that date? he asked. We could not. It was Summer 1986, he said, after the SED Congress. Gorbachev was in power, and Honecker had made clear that the GDR would have nothing to do with Glasnost (Perestroika was not yet born). Until then, East Germans, whatever their true feelings, had grudgingly gone along. They saw no alternative and were prepared to believe that their leaders were doing the possible in a restrictive environment, the limits of which were set by the Soviets. Once it became apparent that the GDR Politburo, not Moscow, was braking reform, something happened in the East German psyche, the general hypothesized. Demoralization took many forms, but by last fall there was a consensus, even among border troops, that the regime had lost all legitimacy. His troops were also of the people, he said, and they would not have fired if ordered. There was no way for Wall or regime to stand any longer.

Farewell to the Opposition

And then, more quickly than seemed possible, it was October and the GDR's final hours. The month's second day was the last for the American Embassy in Berlin. Unification was marked at midnight before the Reichstag, just west of the Brandenburg Gate. Before then, "final" ceremonies were held around East Berlin. A street festival was beginning along Unter den Linden. J.D. wrote and Dick signed one more cable, advising that Embassy Berlin had completed its work. In late afternoon, we gathered in the basement, the *Keller*, site of so many farewell parties. Dick distributed departmental awards to the entire staff, and J.D. read to him the secretary of state's message that accompanied his own. Janice—in Brussels since summer but back for this day—sang a song with the refrain "It's been great, but why did they have to take our embassy away?" There were tears and laughter before people wandered into a night everyone knew would belong to history.

As Gaby and I departed, we encountered young people with a petition. Its burden was that the nation being born that evening must not be like the old Reich; Europe must have a peace of reconciliation and a new beginning. I accepted it in Dick's name and their invitation in my own to join them at the House of Democracy in the Friedrichstrasse where many from Neues Forum and the other citizens groups would count down the hours until midnight.

We pushed through the thickening crowd to the building that had offered democratic forces their first office space the previous winter. Beer and snacks were available, but the purpose was to allow friends to catch up with each other. For the first time in months, we spoke with Stefan Bickhardt, who was leaving politics. He had completed theological studies and would lead a congregation in a small town north of Berlin. He was disappointed in much that happened after the revolution became a competition about who could produce unification most rapidly. His group, Democracy Now, was barely represented in the new parliaments. Perhaps his true calling was the pulpit, but perhaps he would write and crystallize his thinking. He needed time, he indicated, to decide.

Ceremonies were brief. Ullmann spoke, and Bohley tried, but emotion or fatigue made her almost inaudible. Stefan introduced me as one who was a friend of the Opposition before it had been fashionable. I spoke from the heart and hope it was recognized as such, though Gaby said sternly that I had made even more grammar mistakes than usual. I was proud to be with them that evening, I said, and they should be proud of achievements that could not be measured only by votes in the elections they had made possible. Germany needed their idealism and commitment. I sat down knowing I had been near the line that divides objectivity from involvement. Perhaps on that night when there was no longer an embassy and would be no more telegrams, diplomatic reserve could be set aside.

Midnight, East of the Brandenburg Gate

As midnight neared, Gaby and I bade farewell and made our way through enormous crowds toward the Reichstag. A siren wailed in the distance, but only a handful tried to provoke the numerous police. I was reminded of May Day in the old GDR—not the formal parade, but the city-fair atmosphere after the ceremonies. There were great differences, of course. Many trying to pass the Brandenburg Gate were Westerners, often recognizable as tourists from outside Berlin. Booths along Unter den Linden offered more goods than were ever at a GDR festival. A giant mock Coca-Cola can stood on the spot where one year earlier Honecker had reviewed the FDJ by torchlight. Opposite were billboards with cigarette slogans urging "Come together, Try the West" (a cheap filter brand, actually). But there were few flags and virtually no political demonstrations. No observer could fear an upsurge of unhealthy nationalism. Germans were relaxed, curious, good-natured.

But there were so many. At Pariser Platz, progress stopped. "This is the Police speaking," called an authoritative voice. "There is a dangerous situation because of the press of people near the Reichstag. Please move to the right to make room." In orderly fashion, everyone did, but it became so uncomfortable that we abandoned efforts to reach the ceremony and with difficulty turned back up Unter den Linden. At midnight, as the haunting Haydn tune the world knows as the "Deutschlandlied" sounded, we were still east of the Brandenburg Gate.

Good Morning, Germany

October 3 was a holiday. Gaby and I drove out early, south of Berlin, to Zernsdorf, a village where her parents built a simple vacation cottage just after Hitler came to power. Though they had paid a special tax in 1933 to finance a paved street, the tarmac still stopped yards short of the property. Gaby spent summers there until she was seven, not realizing the vegetable gardening she loved was a life-and-death matter for the family after the war. She recalls the day when her mother told her they could not return. The GDR seized the property of West Berliners but did not formally confiscate it. Instead, it kept books, debiting against taxes and repair costs the nominal rent paid by the new tenants. There was a good chance that her mother could recover the property now, and Gaby wanted to see it on this day.

The villages through which we passed were quiet, almost deserted, as on a Sunday. There was certainly nothing to indicate they belonged no longer to the German Democratic Republic but again to something called Germany. Gaby had gone to Zernsdorf several times in the past three years, always remarking afterward that the plot seemed so much smaller than in childhood memories. There were a few, ambiguous signs that the economy was stirring: the first state restaurant privatized in the GDR after the revolution (actually an ice cream parlor) was in Zernsdorf, but it was closed; villas were under construction for West Berliners, but neighbors said there were still no plans for a sewage system. We did not disturb the family at the cottage. (Gaby later confirmed to the elderly couple that they could use it for their lifetime. Her mother wanted title confirmation, which the mayor's office provided, but was content with being able to complain again about the unpaved road.) It was warm, and we wandered into the sun-dappled woods to pick mushrooms. There were no *Steinpilze*, but we filled two bags with prime *Maronenpilze* before heading home. Gaby found them, of course, but she had the advantage of home territory. Her grandmother had taught her on that spot.

That evening, I sat at the typewriter to organize my thoughts once more. I had found troubling the refrain from colleagues in Bonn earlier in the week that the new Germany would be merely the old, familiar Federal Republic writ large. The GDR was gone—taken over by its irresistibly attractive Western neighbor, to be sure—but the loyal little Bonn Republic had died just as certainly at midnight, even if the realization might be longer coming. I wrote:

"Last entries normally discuss lessons learned, but by definition an embassy closing is different. German unification is a watershed. Little of what the United States has done—successfully—in the GDR, Berlin, or even Bonn for the past forty-five years will be relevant to what we must do in the future.

"I. *The Past Is Not Prologue.* Of course, nothing is fully without antecedent, uninfluenced by what has gone before, but unification projects us into a new era. We shall do better by freeing ourselves of most of the intellectual baggage we have acquired in the postwar era than by assuming it provides reliable guidelines, much less operational assistance, for what lies ahead.

"U.S. prestige is high in Germany today. We are not regarded as the all-powerful Superman / Santa Claus who keeps the Red bogeyman from the door and has the recipe for prosperity and respectability, as when our troops were passing out chocolate bars in a devastated land, but that age is lost in the mists of half-memory for almost all Germans. Never since the Federal Republic and GDR started down different paths of reconstruction, however, has the U.S. been viewed more positively in both halves of Germany. We should enjoy it while it lasts—about as long as the hangover from the all-night unification party at the Brandenburg Gate and Unter den Linden.

"Our popularity in the old GDR was a factor partly of our human rights stand, partly of our distance, and partly of the contrast with the other superpower. In that sense, the GDR was never very different from the rest of Eastern Europe, where the United States was the unobtainable, opposite pole to repressive and generally boring Soviet-modeled life. Familiarity should not breed contempt, but there is every reason to expect that the opening of this society means that we shall not long enjoy special advantages. East Germans already are taking on the worldly outlook of the West, and the trend can only accelerate.

"Nor should we be misled into believing that we can maintain our present high standing in West Germany. We held the line until the Soviet Union lost its expansionist character, and the weaknesses of its economic and political structures compelled it to accept withdrawal from the empire it gained at the end of the Second World War. More promptly than the Europeans, the United States accepted the consequences of its postwar policy, welcomed unification as inevitable, and facilitated the last stages of its accomplishment.

"Gratitude, however, has an even shorter half-life with nations than with individuals. Germans will soon and naturally come to see unification as both a normal state of affairs and one that they, not outside powers, did most to produce. The very success of our postwar stand against the Soviet Union means that the aura of threat, which did so much to make heavy American influence in German affairs acceptable even to the most nationalistic or insular, is gone. To put not too fine a gloss on it, at this moment of triumph, joy, and satisfaction, we lose both the exotic distance that made us attractive to the East of Germany and the status of largely unquestioned protective power that made us necessary to the West of Germany. We can expect to be judged by new standards, by what we offer a more self-confident, more powerful Germany that will increasingly see itself as our equal and be unwilling to yield to our wishes out of deference or need.

"II. *An American Role Beyond Containment.* We can help ourselves by recognizing that the change is inevitable, by wasting no time on nostalgia or recriminations, and by doing our best to build up more traditional sources of influence with the new entity. East German opinion is at its most malleable now. We should embark on a program of exchanges, cultural contacts, English teaching, and the like that is as substantial as possible. These person-to-person links will ultimately be stronger than the already dated, secondhand fascination for an unknown America. We will also gain time, thereby, for East Germans to judge institutions important to us, such as NATO, on their merits instead of against the prejudices imposed by constant exposure to Warsaw Pact style and propaganda.

"This will help ensure that the security structures that have won the peace and made unification possible will not be lamed or even cast aside before there is a reliable replacement. But the end of our Berlin rights and responsibilities, more than anything else, will be seen by Germans as marking the end of their need to yield pride of place in policy councils to the United States. We risk being treated by Germany as increasingly irrelevant if we henceforth stress the security guarantor aspect of the relationship. We need instead to adjust our thinking to a Germany where our influence, our ability to win acceptance for viewpoints and accommodation to interests, comes not from holding the security umbrella but from political, diplomatic, cultural, and above all economic engagement. Increasingly, we shall have to work with and help shape the evolution of civilian institutions at hand, the EC and especially the CSCE. Both because it is good business, even in the relatively short term, and because it offers new entrée where it matters for Germans, we must put greater weight on advancing American commercial interests in the former GDR.

"We shall need also to think harder about our true interests in Europe than we have for decades. Achieving our postwar objectives is not, after all, the "end of history." Germany will have carefully thought-out plans balancing firm commitment to the building of Western Europe with traditional fascination for expansion into Eastern Europe's new markets. In turn, we must weigh priorities more carefully, now that the overwhelming requirement of defense against an imperial Soviet Union has been relaxed. We have the advantage of being wanted here by all the Europeans, but their reasons are not always compatible. We are welcome to many, even to the Soviets, as the most plausible balance to German domination. The Germans are aware of that anomaly, of course, and prepared to accommodate it. Psychologically, however, it must be questioned for how long.

"Our challenge will be to define a role beyond containment, whether of Russians or Germans, and to persuade the Continent that we truly are longterm players who share democratic values and economic and political stakes. Even if we can, there will still be rocky patches. When we experience our first serious disagreement and discover that Germany "no longer loves us," a mini-crisis in relations is probably inevitable. But we should be able to weather such storms the more easily by recalling that they are preferable to the cosmic ones we faced for the forty-five years of Europe's military and ideological division.

"III. *The New German Problem.* This is essentially a positive scenario, even if it requires to make it work a great deal of the kind of rethinking that is never comfortable. A few lines should be added, however, about less-sanguine scenarios, because the emergence of a united Germany evokes anxieties even among that country's best friends.

"Potential problems should not be overly personalized. Whatever the momentary significance of differences between Government and Opposition, German politicians across the responsible spectrum are attuned to democratic exigencies. They are likely to continue to adjust to their readings of the public will in a manner that maintains considerable national consensus. No one party or leader will make the process of adjustment for Germany's allies much easier or tougher.

"Nor should time be lost worrying about a cartoon-style resurgence of a too strong, too militaristic, too prejudiced Germany. As much as it can be said of a people, Germans—East and West—have learned that lesson. They watch themselves because they know they will be watched more carefully than any others. West German democratic institutions, as well as those of Western Europe and NATO, within which Germany will continue to operate, offer further specific guarantees that history will not be repeated. Indeed, the most plausible bad-case scenario is not of a Germany too strong but the opposite: a Germany too weak, too distracted by its own problems to meet its responsibilities in the world, even in Eastern Europe. The proximate cause of such a scenario, of course, would be the burden of making unification work.

"Unification is surely a doable proposition. West Germany's population is four times that of East Germany. Its economy and social institutions are more potent in a probably higher proportion. Ultimately, the Germans will get the mix right. But the situation in the GDR is already characterized by economic depression and psychological anxiety. It is almost certain to get worse on both fronts. The upturn will come, but it makes a difference how long and how painful the transition is. Until the Germans are well along toward equalizing living standards, their attention will be focused inward. With best intent, and probably for much of this decade, they will have little time, energy, and psychic or financial capital for other problems.

"The tasks are indeed daunting. The East German economy was in worse shape than believed when the Communist regime collapsed; the pace of unification, especially the sudden and total exposure to the D-Mark, has pushed it further into receivership. The psychic burdens from three generations of totalitarianism are great, and the self-esteem East Germans gained from their democratic revolution has largely been washed away by the flood of events. Most East Germans go into unification, figuratively speaking, not with their heads high and a smile on their lips but with sunken shoulders and anxious hearts. They worry that they cannot compete, and they are not a little resentful of the schoolmaster mannerisms of their sophisticated, hard-charging cousins, who denigrate every aspect of the GDR experience, no matter how apolitical, that differs from their own.

"East Germans still want unification, of course, but they are nervous, irritable, and scared—not idealistic or grateful—as it comes to them. They desire a quick fix to deprivations of forty-five years; they did not get it with the March elections or the introduction of the D-Mark in July, and they did not get it last midnight. The ingredients for some erratic, even irresponsible, political behavior are here, as is already hinted occasionally in unrealistic economic demands, the ugly antiforeigner feeling that is fairly widespread, and the mindless right radicalism of small numbers of young people.

"It is fortunate that West German institutions have proven themselves so strong over the years, and especially that, as Chancellor Kohl has repeatedly stressed, the Federal Republic's economy has never been more soundly situated to finance unification. It belongs to worst-case scenario setting, however, to ask what might happen if something untoward should put sand in the gears of that economic machine precisely at the time of greatest East German vulnerability and volatility.

"Once again, it would be prudent not to paint even such scenarios in the darkest tones. There are real and apparent strengths to overcome setbacks in West Germany, latent strengths in the people of the former GDR. It would be conceivable, however, for German domestic preoccupation, and even a certain internal political unpredictability, to become more durable phenomena. Were that to happen, the implications would be felt wherever Germany's dynamism, prosperity, and commitment to democratic values is needed, from building the institutions of European integration through assumption of a world role in keeping with the country's stature. It would probably be most serious, however, in Eastern Europe, which needs a strong, stable, prosperous Germany to fortify emerging democracies and provide the wherewithal for economic recovery. The Soviets also need such a Germany to help them make the last stage of imperial decline the prelude to freedom and prosperity, not to chaos, even civil war.

"IV. *Conclusion and a Modest Recommendation.* In other words, the realistic if not high probability risks are not of Germany resurgent in the nature of World War II horror movies but of Germany too weak, or at least too distracted, to take the major share of responsibility for preventing the Oder-Neisse from becoming the barrier between Western European stability and perhaps dangerously infectious Eastern European instability.

"We can, of course, help ourselves by helping the Germans shoulder this responsibility. We shall certainly help pay the costs if the worst-case scenario should come about. If we can be part of the prevention by engaging in the now substantially economic and cultural process of stitching united Germany together, just as we have been constructive in the diplomatic phase, we shall not gain eternal gratitude. We shall, however, have achieved a solid basis for give-and-take with a largely like-minded, powerful ally to obtain mutual benefits and hold back mutual terrors."

Glossary

The listings below are meant to help the reader keep track of the individuals, terms, and abbreviations that appear most prominently in the text or that may not otherwise be adequately identified. Members of the U.S. Embassy are alphabetized by first name, e.g., "Dick" Barkley.

ACADEMY OF SOCIAL SCIENCES (Akademie für Gesellschaftswissenschaften): Senior institute of the SED Central Committee.
ADAC: West German automobile association.
ADN (Allgemeiner Deutscher Nachrichtendienst): Official East German news service.
ALLIANCE FOR GERMANY: Center-Right coalition (East German CDU, DSU, and Democratic Awakening), which won the March 1990 election.
AUSWEIS: Identity card or document.
AXEN, HERMANN: Member of the Politburo, responsible for foreign policy ("Honecker's Kissinger").
BAHR, EGON: West German politician (SPD), associated with Willy Brandt's *Ostpolitik*.
BASLER, GERD: Rising star at a Central Committee think tank.
BERGHOFER, WOLFGANG: GDR politician, Mayor of Dresden.
BERLIN: Capital of the German Reich, in 1989 legally still under quadripartite military occupation, divided for most practical purposes by the Wall into West Berlin (U.S., British, French Sectors) and East Berlin (the Soviet Sector, which the GDR considered its capital).

326   Glossary

BERLINER ZEITUNG: SED Berlin daily newspaper.
BICKHARDT, STEFAN: Dissident, co-founder of "Democracy Now."
BLOC PARTIES: The four political groupings (CDU, LDPD, NDPD, and Peasants Party) permitted to function in the GDR on condition that they loyally supported the Communist SED.
BOHLEY, BÄRBEL: Dissident, co-founder of Neues Forum.
BÖHME, IBRAHIM: Historian, co-founder of the Social Democratic Party (SDP, later SPD) in 1989, candidate for prime minister in March 1990; subsequently accused of Stasi collaboration.
BRANDENBURG: Heartland of old Prussia, traditionally including Berlin and environs; established as a state (without Berlin) when the GDR was reorganized along federal lines in 1990.
BRANDT, WILLY: West German politician (SPD), former Chancellor.
BRIE, ANDRÉ: Academician, Gregor Gysi's deputy in the SED-PDS leadership after collapse of the Krenz Politburo.
BRONFMAN, EDGAR: President of the World Jewish Congress.
BÜNDNIS '90 (Coalition '90):   Alliance of three early opposition groups (Neues Forum, Democracy Now, and the Initiative for Peace and Human Rights) that contested the March 1990 election.
CDU (Christlich-Demokratische Union Deutschlands, Christian Democratic Union of Germany):   In West Germany, Chancellor Kohl's party, in East Germany, a Bloc Party.
CENTRAL COMMITTEE: In theory, the highest organ of the SED; in GDR practice, subordinated to the Politburo.
CHEMNITZER, JOHANNES: SED First Secretary in Neubrandenburg.
CHERNENKO, KONSTANTIN: The elderly, sick man who was briefly the Soviet leader between Andropov and Gorbachev.
CLAUS AND CLAUDIA: The 1989 novel by Erich Neutsch, a sign of intellectual ferment on the eve of the revolution.
COUNCIL OF STATE (Staatsrat):   Highest organ of the GDR state, chaired by Honecker, then by Krenz.
CSCE (Conference on Security and Cooperation in Europe):   Diplomatic process begun with the 1975 Helsinki Final Act to facilitate peaceful change in the Soviet Union and Eastern Europe.
DANZ, TAMARA: GDR rock star and outspoken reform supporter.
DCM (Deputy Chief of Mission):   Deputy to the Ambassador, the number-two position in an embassy.
DE MAIZIÈRE, LOTHAR: GDR lawyer chosen to lead the CDU in Decem-

ber 1989, chief victor in the March 1990 election, Prime Minister until unification in October 1990.

"DEMOCRACY NOW" (Demokratie Jetzt): Opposition group formed in Fall 1989; later a member of Bündnis '90.

"DEMOCRATIC AWAKENING" (Demokratischer Aufbruch): Opposition group formed in fall 1989; later a member of Alliance for Germany.

DER ERSTE (Number One): Landolf Scherzer's best-seller about an SED county chief, a hint of GDR Glasnost in early 1989.

DER MORGEN: LDPD daily newspaper.

"DICK" BARKLEY: Richard C. Barkley, the last American Ambassador to the GDR.

DIESTEL, PETER-MICHAEL: Lawyer, DSU co-founder in 1990, later switched to the CDU; Interior Minister after the March election.

DIETZEL, DR.: Deputy Editor of the *Berliner Zeitung*.

DIE ZEIT: West German weekly newspaper.

DISTEL (the Thistle): East Berlin political cabaret.

D-MARK (*Deutsche Mark*): West German "hard" currency, contrasted with the soft, nonconvertible GDR Mark.

DOBBINS, JIM: Deputy Assistant Secretary of State for European Affairs.

DOHLUS, HORST: Member of the Politburo, responsible for cadre policy and intra-Party discipline.

DOMKE, HELMUT: Physicist, lay Lutheran churchman; in 1990, State Secretary in the GDR Foreign Ministry.

DSU (Deutsche Soziale Union): Political party formed in 1990, furthest right member of the Alliance for Germany.

DUTSCHKE, RUDI: Radical student leader in West Berlin in 1968.

EAGLEBURGER, LARRY: Deputy Secretary of State in 1989.

EBELING, HANS-WILHELM: Lutheran pastor of Thomas Church in Leipzig, co-founder and first Chairman of the DSU in 1990.

EBERLEIN, WERNER: Member of the Politburo, SED First Secretary in Magdeburg.

EPPELMANN, RAINER: Lutheran pastor, dissident, co-founder of "Democratic Awakening" in 1989, Minister of Defense and Disarmament after the March 1990 election.

ESCHE, ANNEMARIE: East German academic, Asia specialist.

FDGB (Freier Deutscher Gewerkschaftsbund): East German trade union organization, member of National Front.

FDJ (Freie Deutsche Jugend, Free German Youth): East German youth organization, member of National Front.

FDP (Freie Demokratische Partei): West German Foreign Minister Genscher's political party.
FINK, HEINRICH: Dean of the Theology Faculty, Humboldt University (East Berlin).
FISCHER, OSKAR: GDR Foreign Minister.
FORCK, GOTTFRIED: Lutheran bishop of Berlin-Brandenburg.
FRG: Federal Republic of Germany, West Germany.
FRICK, HELMUT AND PETRA: West German diplomatic couple in East Berlin.
FRITSCHLER, HANS-DIETER: SED First Secretary in Bad Salzungen County, central figure in Landolf Scherzer's best-seller, *Der Erste*.
FUKUYAMA, FRANCIS: Author of "The End of History," Deputy Director of the State Department's Policy Planning Staff.
"G.": The author's opposite number in the Soviet Embassy.
"GABY" GREENWALD: The author's wife.
GAUS, GÜNTER: West German politician (SPD) and author, first head of the Ständige Vertretung.
GDR: German Democratic Republic, East Germany.
GENSCHER, HANS-DIETRICH: Foreign Minister of the Federal Republic of Germany.
GERLACH, MANFRED: LDPD (East German Bloc Party) Chairman.
GERMAN QUESTION: Interrelated issues pending since 1945: Would Germany be reunited, what would be its position in the East-West confrontation, and how could Europe avoid domination by it?
GERZ, WOLFGANG: West German diplomat in East Berlin.
GLASNOST: Initial phase of Gorbachev's reforms in the Soviet Union stressing candor about problems.
GORBACHEV, MIKHAIL: President of the Soviet Union.
GÖTTING, GERALD: CDU (East German Bloc Party) Chairman.
GREENS: West German environmental political party.
GROUP OF 20: Ad hoc body formed from demonstrators to negotiate with Dresden authorities in October 1989, briefly the leading opposition political grouping in that city.
"GUNNAR" AND "GABI": East Berlin couple, friends of the author.
GYSI, GREGOR: Lawyer, reform advocate, SED-PDS leader after the collapse of the Krenz Politburo; son of Klaus Gysi.
GYSI, KLAUS: Retired GDR official (State Secretary for Church Affairs, Minister of Culture, Ambassador); father of Gregor Gysi.

HAGER, KURT: Member of the Politburo, responsible for culture, science, and ideology.
HAUS, UWE AND MARIANNE: East German theater director with dissident political views and his physician wife.
"HEATHER" TROUTMAN: Political Section, U.S. Embassy.
HEIN, CHRISTOPH: East German writer who championed reform.
HEMPEL, JOHANNES: Lutheran Bishop of Saxony.
HERGER, WOLFGANG: Political ally of Krenz, elevated to the Politburo in November 1989.
HERMLIN, STEPHAN: GDR author and poet, an elderly SED man who lost patience with Honecker in fall 1989.
HERRMANN, JOACHIM: Member of the Politburo, responsible for agitprop and media policy until deposed with Honecker.
HERZIG, WERNER: SED Mayor of Magdeburg.
HEYM, STEFAN: Prominent GDR writer, outspoken Honecker critic.
HOMANN, HEINRICH: NDPD (East German Bloc Party) Chairman.
HONECKER, ERICH: Communist (SED) leader of the GDR, 1971–89.
HONECKER, MARGOT: Minister of Education, Erich Honecker's wife.
HÖPCKE, KLAUS: DEPUTY MINISTER OF CULTURE.
IG-METALL: GDR industrial union, part of the FDGB, distinguished from West German union of the same name.
"IMRE" LIPPING: Political Section, U.S. Embassy.
INNER-GERMAN RELATIONS: Relations between the two German states, the GDR and the Federal Republic of Germany.
INTERFLUG: GDR airline.
"INTERNATIONALE": Traditional socialist and Communist anthem.
IPW (Institut für Internationale Politik und Wissenschaft): SED Central Committee think tank.
ITO, PETE: State Department's desk officer for the GDR.
"JANICE" WEINER: Political Section, U.S. Embassy.
JAROWINSKY, WERNER: Member of the Politburo, in charge of church affairs and domestic trade.
JARUZELSKI, WOJCIECH: The Communist President of Poland.
"J.D." BINDENAGEL: Deputy Chief of Mission, U.S. Embassy.
"JERRY" VERNER: Press and Cultural Counselor, U.S. Embassy.
JUNGE WELT: FDJ newspaper.
KÁDÁR, JÁNOS: Hungarian Communist leader.
KAMM, HENRY: Correspondent for the *New York Times*.
KAMPELMAN, MAX: American political figure and diplomat.

KANT, HERMANN: GDR author, President of the Writers Association, member of the SED Central Committee.

KIRCHNER, MARTIN: Lawyer, lay Lutheran churchman, co-signer of the "Letter from Weimar" in 1989, CDU Secretary General before March 1990 election, subsequently accused of Stasi collaboration.

"KIRSTEN" CHRISTENSEN: Author's secretary, U.S. Embassy.

KOHL, HELMUT: Chancellor of the Federal Republic of Germany.

KOMBINATE: GDR economic conglomerates.

KOSIN, HEINZ: Senior academic at Central Committee think tank.

KRENZ, EGON: Member of the Politburo, replaced Honecker on October 18, 1989.

KRUSCHE, GÜNTHER: Lutheran churchman, deputy to Bishop Forck in Berlin-Brandenburg.

KUCZYNSKI, JÜRGEN: Iconoclastic GDR economist and historian.

LDPD (Liberale-Demokratische Partei Deutschlands): East German Bloc Party theoretically appealing to the same small business/entrepreneur constituency as the West German FDP.

LEICH, WERNER: Bishop of Thuringia, senior Lutheran churchman in the GDR during 1989.

LETTER FROM WEIMAR: Protest document issued in September 1989, the first sign of unrest within the East German CDU.

LIEBKNECHT, KARL: Pioneer German Communist, murdered 1919.

LIGACHEV, YIGOR: Conservative member of the Soviet Politburo.

LORENZ, SIEGFRIED: Member of the Politburo, SED First Secretary in Karl-Marx-Stadt.

LUXEMBURG, ROSA: Pioneer German Communist, murdered 1919, saint in SED pantheon, symbol of socialist democracy to many dissidents.

"MARY ROSE" BRANDT: Consul, U.S. Embassy.

MASUR, KURT: World-famous orchestra conductor, co-signer of appeal to keep the Leipzig demonstrations peaceful in October 1989.

MAXIMYSCHEV, IGOR F.: Deputy Chief of Mission, Soviet Embassy.

MCADAMS, JIM: American academic, specialist on the GDR.

MCCARTNEY, BOB: Bonn correspondent for the *Washington Post*.

MECKEL, MARKUS: Lutheran pastor, dissident, Social Democratic Party (SDP, later SPD) co-founder 1989, Foreign Minister 1990.

MECKLENBURG: Northern, mostly rural region, reestablished as a state when the GDR was reorganized along federal lines in 1990.

MIELKE, ERICH: Member of the Politburo, Minister for State Security, and head of the Stasi (Secret Police).

"Mike" Mozur: Economic Counselor, U.S. Embassy, from July 1989.

Misselwitz, Hans: Lutheran pastor, dissident, co-founder of the Social Democratic Party (SDP, later SPD) in 1989, State Secretary in the Foreign Ministry after the March 1990 election.

Mittag, Günter: Member of the Politburo, czar of economic policy until deposed with Honecker.

Modrow, Hans: SED First Secretary in Dresden, became Prime Minister the week the Berlin Wall fell.

Momper, Walter: SPD Governing Mayor of Berlin (West Berlin).

Most Favored Nation status: Term of economic art meaning that imports from a state are subjected to tariffs no higher than those imposed on imports from any other state.

National Front: GDR political "alliance" that allocated positions on a single uncontested election list and ensured that Bloc Parties and social organizations supported SED policies.

NATO (North Atlantic Treaty Organization):   Western political and military alliance.

NDPD (National-Demokratische Partei Deutschlands):   East German Bloc Party.

NEUE ZEIT: East German CDU newspaper.

NEUES DEUTSCHLAND: The "Organ of the Central Committee of the SED," the GDR's newspaper of record.

NEUES FORUM (New Forum):   Largest opposition group formed in Fall 1989, later a member of Bündnis '90.

Nier, Kurt: GDR Deputy Foreign Minister.

"Nina" Barkley: Wife of the American Ambassador.

NISCHENGESELLSCHAFT (Society of Niches):   Günter Gaus's term for East German society's inclination to atomize into apolitical units of family and trusted friends that inhibited civic activism.

NVA (Nationale Volksarmee, National People's Army):   The GDR army.

Ossies/Wessies: Easterners/Westerners.

Ostpolitik (Eastern Policy):   West German policy of extensive diplomatic relations, economic cooperation, and human contacts with the Soviet Union and Eastern Europe introduced by Willy Brandt in part to gain Soviet acceptance of improved inner-German ties.

Party Congress (*Parteitag*):   Normally convened by the SED every fourth or fifth year and empowered to make all policy and personnel decisions; contrasted in November 1989 with a Party Conference, a special forum with less sweeping powers.

PDS (Partei des Demokratischen Sozialismus, Party of Democratic Socialism): Name adopted by the former ruling Communist Party in 1990 after a brief period as SED-PDS.

PEASANTS PARTY (Demokratische Bauernpartei Deutschlands): East German Bloc Party.

PEN CLUB OF THE GDR: East German branch of an international association dedicated to protecting writers and artistic freedom.

PERESTROIKA: Second phase of Gorbachev's reforms in the Soviet Union stressing major systemic changes.

PFINGSTTREFFEN: Youth festival held by the GDR in Berlin over the Whitsun holiday in May 1989.

PFLUGBEIL, SEBASTIAN: Scientist, co-founder of Neues Forum in 1989, Minister in the Modrow Cabinet in 1990.

POLITBURO: Effectively the ruling body of the SED and thus of the GDR, led by Honecker as General Secretary, then by Krenz.

PRAVDA: Communist Party newspaper in the Soviet Union.

"PROFESSOR": The author's guide along the Baltic Coast, "Gunnar's" father.

RECHTSSTAAT (State of laws, constitutional state): Contrasted with the arbitrary and politicized practice of the GDR.

REEMER, NORBERT: U.S. Section Chief, GDR Foreign Ministry.

REICH, JENS: Scientist, co-founder of Neues Forum in 1989.

REICHSBAHN: GDR railway system.

REICHSTAG: Parliament building a few yards west of the Wall the burning of which in 1933 marked the onset of Nazi dictatorship.

REINHOLD, OTTO: Director of the Central Committee's Academy of Social Sciences and would-be heir to a Politburo seat.

REISSIG, ROLF: Senior member of the faculty of the Central Committee's Academy of Social Sciences; would-be SED reformer.

"RENO" HARNISH: Economic Counselor, U.S. Embassy.

ROUNDTABLE: Forum established in December 1989 so the SED, the Bloc Parties, and the new opposition groups could negotiate the political crisis and lend legitimacy to Modrow Government decisions.

SAXONY: Southern, industrialized region including Leipzig and Dresden, reestablished as a state when the GDR was reorganized along federal lines in 1990.

SCHABOWSKI, GÜNTER: Member of the Politburo, head of the Berlin SED organization; announced the opening of the Berlin Wall.

SCHERZER, LANDOLF: Author of *Der Erste*; after the collapse of the Krenz Politburo, briefly an SED reform politician.
SCHNITZLER, KARL-EDUARD VON: Polemical GDR journalist.
SCHNUR, WOLFGANG: Lawyer, co-founder in 1989 of "Democratic Awakening," resigned as chairman when accused of Stasi collaboration.
SCHORLEMMER, FRIEDRICH: Lutheran pastor, prominent dissident.
SDP (Sozial-Demokratische Partei, Social Democratic Party): original name of GDR opposition party founded in October 1989 with ties to the West German Social Democrats (SPD).
SED (Sozialistische Einheitspartei Deutschlands, Socialist Unity Party of Germany): GDR Communist Party.
SHEVARDNADZE, EDUARD: Soviet Foreign Minister.
SHOSTAL, PIERRE: Director of the State Department's Office of Central European Affairs.
SINDERMANN, HORST: Member of Politburo, Parliament President.
SINGER, ISRAEL: Deputy head, World Jewish Congress.
SOLARZ, STEPHEN: U.S. Congressman.
SPD (Sozialdemokratische Partei Deutschlands, Social Democratic Party of Germany): West German party; also, from early 1990, the name of the East German party originally called SDP.
SPUTNIK: Soviet magazine that championed Gorbachev's reforms and was banned by Honecker from the GDR in 1988.
STÄNDIGE VERTRETUNG (Permanent Representation): West German diplomatic mission in East Berlin.
STASI: Short for *Staatssicherheit*, "state security," the GDR ministry by that name headed by Erich Mielke and its secret police.
"STEVE" SLICK: Vice Consul, U.S. Embassy.
STOLPE, MANFRED: The senior lay Lutheran church leader in the GDR.
STOPH, WILLI: Member of the Politburo, GDR Prime Minister.
STUDNITZ, JÖRG VON: West German diplomat in East Berlin.
STUMPF, EBERHARD: Senior government official in Bad Salzungen County, a major figure in Landolf Scherzer's best-seller, *Der Erste*.
TASS: Official Soviet news service.
THURINGIA: Southwestern region of the GDR, reestablished as a state when the GDR was reorganized along federal lines in 1990.
TISCH, HARRY: Member of the Politburo, trade union (FDGB) boss.
TRABIES: Trabants, GDR-manufactured automobile.
TRIBÜNE: FDGB newspaper.

TROIKA: Markus Wolf's memoir, which raised the hopes of reformers that Glasnost was coming to the GDR.

TWO-PLUS-FOUR: The 1990 negotiation between the Federal Republic and the GDR, plus the United States, France, United Kingdom, and the Soviet Union, which set an international seal of approval on unification.

ULBRICHT, WALTER: Stalinist leader of the GDR, 1945–71.

ULLMANN, WOLFGANG: Lawyer, lay Lutheran churchman, co-founder of Democracy Now in 1989, minister in the Modrow Cabinet in 1990.

USIA: United States Information Agency, also known abroad as USIS, United States Information Service.

VOGEL, HANS-JOACHIM: West German politician, Chairman of the Social Democratic Party (SPD).

VOGEL, WOLFGANG: GDR lawyer, Honecker confidant, facilitator of spy exchanges and emigration of disaffected East Germans.

VOPO (*Volkspolizist*, People's policeman): GDR policeman.

WANDLITZ: Town and lake north of Berlin where the Politburo lived in a hermetically sealed enclave.

WARSAW PACT: Soviet-dominated military and political alliance.

WENDE (Turn): Originally Krenz's term for controlled reform, then, more broadly, the GDR revolution.

WENDEHALS (Wryneck): Bird with a flexible neck, a pun on Krenz's *Wende* applied to those who became overnight reformers.

WHITEHEAD, JOHN: U.S. Deputy Secretary of State who held three meetings with Honecker in Berlin in 1987–88.

WOLF, MARKUS: Retired master spy, would-be reform politician.

WOMEN'S LEAGUE: East German social organization, member of the National Front.

Index

Academy of Arts, 190
Academy of Social Sciences, 19–20, 222–23
ADAC (West German automobile association), 150
Adass Jisroel Jewish community, 60–61
ADN (East German news service), 141, 209, 217
  reaction to emigration crisis, 159
AFL-CIO, 159
Albrecht, Ernst, 3
Alliance for Germany, 297, 300–303
amnesty, for GDR political prisoners, 222, 253, 265
Arafat, Yassir, 175
Ash, Timothy Garton, 68–69
Asmus, Ron, 221–23, 227
Aspen Institute conferences, 19–20, 41, 42
Aspin, Les, 75, 78, 94–97
Ausweis privileges, 126–27
automobiles, poor quality of, in GDR, 5, 12, 111, 270–71
"Awakening 89—Neues Forum," 129–30
Axen, Hermann, 39, 68, 73–76, 127

Bad Salzungen (East Germany), 4, 21, 39, 117–20, 312–14
Bahr, Egon, 25, 81–82, 133
Baker, James (Secretary of State), 38, 153, 189, 197, 203, 278–79, 307, 316
  reaction to GDR revolution, 207–8

Ball, George, 76
Barkley, Richard "Dick" (Ambassador), 151, 160
  analysis of reform prospects, 3–4
  Berlin expertise of, 44–47
  Bloc Party chairmen and, 20–21
  contacts with Opposition, 220, 229, 250–51
  Dresden visit of, 182–83
  Embassy performance and, xvi, 56, 316
  Independence Day reception, 56, 58–59
  Magdeburg visit of, 3–6
  meeting with Axen, 73, 75—76
  meetings with de Maizière, 298, 308
  meeting with Krenz, 240–41
  New York Philharmonic performance, 40–41
  policy recommendations to State Department, 37–39, 77–78, 83–85, 153–54, 189, 267
  proud father, 149, 251
  receives award, 316
  responds to fall of Berlin Wall, 260, 264–65, 282
  Schabowski meets with, 227–28
  skepticism on GDR reforms, 144–49, 154, 191
  Two-Plus-Four negotiations, 308
  U.S. embassy sit-in crisis and, 66–68, 103, 162–64
  views on Foreign Service, 151–52
  Wolfgang Vogel's contacts with, 51, 88–89,

Index

102, 131, 142, 150, 165, 169, 196, 201–2, 242
Washington visit of, 197–99, 207, 219–20
Barzun, Jacques, 70
Basler, Gerd, 16, 152, 160
  joins SDP, 284–85
  post-Honecker era and, 191, 202, 221, 231
Becker, Jurek, 11
Becker, Todd, 299
Beitz, Berthold, 18
Bender, Peter, 69–70
Berghaus, Ruth, 219
Berghofer, Wolfgang (Dresden mayor), 181–83, 195, 202, 209–10
  differences with Krenz, 255
  links with Modrow, 183, 202–3
  recognizes Group of 20, 230
Bergold, Harry, 301–2
Berlin. *See also* East Berlin; West Berlin
  anti-Krenz demonstrations in, 218–19
  Four-Power rights in, 32–33, 44–47, 192, 285–86
  mass demonstration (November 4, 1989), 236–37, 242–47
  Nikolaiviertel section, 20, 117
Berlin Around the Corner, 119
Berlin Institute for Social Science Studies (BISS), 284
Berlin Wall
  escape attempts at, 104, 315
  implications of fall of, 265–67, 272–75
  as international symbol, 279
  obsolescence of, 36–37, 45–47, 217, 236, 250, 260–62
  opening of, 263–64
  28th Anniversary of, 101–2
  U.S.-GDR relations and, 28, 77–78
Berliner Ensemble, 159
Berliner Zeitung, 136, 184, 217, 237
Bertele, Franz, 156
Bickhardt, Stefan, 59, 125, 141, 316
"binational marriages," 65
Bindenagel, "J.D.," xvi, 70, 191, 203, 208, 261, 263
  Aspen Institute conference, 19–20
  monitors local elections, 10
  skepticism on GDR reforms, 154, 191
  Two-Plus-Four negotiations, 308
Biron, Jeff, 167
Bismarck, Otto von, 3, 71

Bloc Parties
  changing role of, after fall of Berlin Wall, 266–67, 273–74, 294
  "Letter from Weimar," 137
  links with SED, 20–21, 230–31
  newspapers of, 140–41, 187–88
  political power of, 146, 252–53
  role of, in revolution, 233, 240–42
Bodine, Anne, 174, 177, 180
Bohley, Bärbel, 130, 150, 220–21, 292, 316
Böhme, Hans-Joachim, 256, 261
Böhme, Ibrahim, 179, 250–51, 296
Border Commission, 150
Bradley, Bill (Sen.), 280
Brandenburg Gate, 237, 317
Brandt, Mary Rose, 103, 162
Brandt, Willy, 25, 69, 295, 301
Braun, Volker, 11, 93
Braun, Wernher von, 17
Braunmühl, Christian von, 308–9
Bredeck, Duane, 261–62
Brezhnev, Leonid, 27, 131, 172
Brie, André, 284–85, 288
Bronfman, Edgar, 66, 151
Brust, Herr, 8
Bündnis '90 movement, 301–3
Bush, George (President), 127
  attitude toward unification, 14, 278, 308
  opposition to Berlin Wall, 28, 76
  visit to GDR proposed, 24
  visit to Poland and Hungary, 73

cabaret. *See* political cabaret
Castro, Fidel, 132–33
CBS News, growing interest in GDR, 68
CDU (Christian Democratic Union) (GDR), 20–21
  changing role of, after fall of Berlin Wall, 266–67
  coalition politics of, 300–301
  Honecker's ouster called for, 191
  lack of credibility for, 190
  leadership of, 20–21, 190, 221, 228, 231, 296, 298
  "Letter from Weimar," 137, 140–41, 304–305
  links with SED, 230–31
  reforms in, 221
  revolt within, 228
  victory in 1990 elections, 292, 298, 300–303, 314

Ceaucescu, Nikolai, 136
censorship, emerging discussion of, 11–13, 237
Central Committee (SED), 47, 201–2, 280.
  See also Politburo
  potential differences with Politburo, convocation of special Plenum, 189, 194, 196, 203, 205, 206, 212–13, 216, 223, 249, 251–55, 256–58, 268–69
Chayes, Toni, 41–42
Chemnitzer, Johannes, 236, 257, 261
Cheney, Dick, 14
Child of the Revolution, 107
China
  diplomatic presence in GDR, 30, 186–87
  GDR support of, 34, 48, 59, 73, 108, 112, 158, 169
  student uprisings in, 5, 18–19, 28–30, 33–34, 48, 72
Christensen, Kirsten, 43, 231
Church of the Redeemer, 173, 228–29
churches. *See also* specific churches and church leaders
  activism of, 62, 113–15, 127–28, 137, 139–40, 143, 173, 224
  dissident activities supported by, 33–34, 41–42
  documentation of police brutality by, 218
  election fraud protests, 14–15
  emigration crisis and, 104, 127–28
  Honecker's relations with, 14–15, 35–36, 124–25
  Krenz's relations with, 208–9, 224
  protest activities and, 178–79, 182–83
  reaction to SED Glasnost attempts, 187–89
  reform movement and, 62, 163–64, 224, 281–82
  role of, in March 1990 elections, 297–98
  unification, attitude toward, 62, 127–28, 224
"civil society" movement, 124–25
claims negotiations
  Norway-GDR, 55
  U.S.-GDR, 55, 59–60, 73, 77–78, 84, 123–24, 134
Claus and Claudia, 104–5, 220
Claussen, Peter, 167
Cohen, Richard, 81
Collin, 12
Communism
  loss of power by, 282–85
  speculation about future of, in post-Honecker GDR, 273–74

Conference on Security and Cooperation in Europe (CSCE), 27, 31, 55, 59, 77–78, 88, 124, 134, 192, 199, 218, 239, 265, 272–74, 302, 307, 320. *See also* Helsinki Final Act
Congress (U.S.)
  reaction to peaceful revolution, 220
  visits to East Berlin by, 29–30, 280–81
containment policy, obsolescence of, in unified Germany, 319–20
Cultural Agreement (GDR-FRG) of 1986, 96–97
Cultural Agreement (GDR-U.S.) negotiation, 73, 75
Culture League, 190
Czechoslovakia
  author's visit to, 115–16
  GDR relations with, 9, 103
  GDR travel ban to, 162–66, 235–37
  sit-in crisis at West German embassy in, 51, 103–4, 139–40, 150–51, 155, 158–62

Danz, Tamara, 23, 49, 144
de Maizière, Lothar, 224, 296, 298, 301–3, 306, 308–9
Demke, Christoph (Bishop), 289
Democracy Now, 141, 144, 250–51, 304, 316
Democratic Awakening, 141, 163–64, 231, 297–301
Der Erste, 3–4, 21, 39, 117–20, 313
Der Morgen, 140, 155, 158, 160, 183, 210
  coverage of Neues Forum in, 258–59
  criticism of SED in, 228
Der Spiegel, 280
Dictatorship of Conscience, The, 93
Die Zeit, 69, 314
Diestel, Peter-Michael, 299
Dietzel, Dr., 136, 217, 219
Difficulties with the Truth, 271
"Dissent Channel" messages, 191
Distel (political cabaret), 44, 90–92, 222
Dobbins, Jim, 278
Dohlus, Horst, 26, 212, 242, 256
Domke, Helmut, 8, 308
Donaldson, Sam, 14
Dönhoff (Countess), 314
Dresden
  absence of Western television in, 157
  first violence in, 167
  in post-Honecker period, 222, 230, 248–49

protest activities in, 173–75, 181–82, 195–96, 202–3, 213–14
DSU (Deutsche Soziale Union), 299–301
Dynamo Berlin (soccer team), 11
Dynamo Dresden (soccer team), 11

Eagleburger, Lawrence (Deputy Secretary of State), 133, 135, 139, 152
East Berlin
  a diplomat's life in, 84–85
  protest activities in, 33, 126, 173–79, 193–95, 211, 215–16, 218–21, 236–37, 242–47
  Sunday City Hall meeting, 225–27
  Western visitors barred from, 167–68
Ebeling, Hans-Wilhelm (Pastor), 299–300
Eberlein, Werner, 3–6, 28, 58, 173, 256
economic conditions. *See also* market economy
  as catalyst for emigration crisis, 87–89, 103–4, 146–47
  as catalyst for rapid unification, 288–91, 301–2
  impact of emigration on, 87–89
  inner-German ties and, 46–47, 64–65
  post-unification problems, 313–14, 321–22
  questionable statistics on, 9, 30, 258, 279
  reform movement and, 69–70, 274
education policy in GDR, 40–41, 61
Eisenach Synod, 139–40
elections
  demand for free elections, 195, 230, 244, 247, 255, 257–59, 265–67
  GDR reforms and, 289–90
  local elections, May 1989, fraudulent conduct of, 7–15, 237
  Parliamentary campaign, March 1990, 291–303
"Elf 99" (television program), 271
emigration from GDR. *See also* Hungary; Ständige Vertretung; travel
  emergence of crisis, 51–52
  estimates of legal and illegal emigrants, 87–89
  implications for political change, 130–32, 146–49
  role of embassies in, 66–67
  sit-in crisis at West German embassy in Prague, 103–4, 139–40, 150, 155, 158–62
  unification and, 288
Engels, Friedrich, 3

environmental issues
  vs. economic interests, in GDR, 21
  GDR-U.S. cooperation on, 21, 77–78
  pollution as, 5, 118
Environmental Library, 210
Environmental Protection Agency, 21
Eppelmann, Rainer, 125, 163–64, 298–99, 308, 310
Esche, Annemarie, 10, 104

Falin, Valentin, 168, 191
Farther, Farther, Farther, 93
"Fascell Fellows," 43
FDGB (GDR trade union organization)
  calls for reform from, 258
  investigation of internal revolt in, 213, 218, 229
  Kimmel named to head, 241
  local elections, 7
  revolt against Tisch, 229–30, 233
FDJ (GDR youth organization), 104, 218
  local elections, 7
  Pfingsttreffen events and, 23
  reform efforts in, 237
  remoteness of, for GDR youth, 16–17, 218
  torchlight parade for GDR 40th Anniversary, 150, 160, 171–73
Federal Republic of Germany (FRG)
  death of old FRG, with unification, 318–23
  emigration crisis and, 86, 87–89, 95–97, 99–100, 102, 104, 112, 133–34, 141–42, 156, 158, 164, 168, 250
  GDR links with, 44–47, 62, 137–39, 221–22, 234–35
  impact on GDR reforms, 125, 267
  party politics following fall of Berlin Wall, 300–301, 308–9
  role of, in unification, 287–91, 306–8
  Soviet relations with, 39–41, 306–7
  U.S. relations with, 37–38, 44–47, 81–82, 83, 109–10, 134–35, 278, 303–4, 306–7, 318–23
Felfe, Werner, 58
Fink, Heinrich, 21, 226
Fischer, Oskar, 22, 34–35, 65, 151, 309–10
Fisher, Marc, 81–82
Five Days in June, 12
Forck, Gottfried (Bishop), 15, 41, 178, 183, 187, 217, 224
Ford, Gerald, 27, 192

Index

Foreign Service (U.S.)
  careers in, 43
  identification with host country, 37, 134
  life and morale in, xvi, 84–85
  political officer's work in, xii, 30–31
  public perception of, 151–52
  spouse's role, 30–31
"Four-Power Berlin," 32. *See also* Berlin
Frankfurter Allgemeine, 133
Frederick the Great, 3
Frick, Helmut and Petra, 28, 79, 178
Fritschler, Hans-Dieter, 117–20, 313–14. See also *Der Erste*
Führer, Christian, 281–82, 300
Fukuyama, Francis, 152–53, 189, 192–93

Galinski, Heinz, 61
Gaudian, Christian, 104
Gaus, Günter, 65, 125, 262
GDR Soccer Association, 70, 98–99
Genscher, Hans-Dietrich, 27, 115, 158
Gerlach, Manfred, 7, 20, 140, 158, 178–79, 220, 221, 240
  alliance with Krenz, 241
  on media reforms, 237
  political stature of, 253
  speech at Berlin demonstration, 245
German Democratic Republic (GDR)
  civil society in, 124–25
  dissolution of, with unification, 287–91
  40th Anniversary celebration, 168–76
  FRG push for dissolution of, 138, 148, 287–91
  international view of, xi–xii, xvii–xviii
  reform movement assessed, 142–49
  resistance to reform, 2–13, 19, 25, 26, 28, 30, 34, 36, 41, 48–49, 59, 63, 69–70, 83, 89–92, 98, 100, 112, 121, 131–32, 141, 154–55, 161, 179
  silent crisis of, 87–89, 111–15
  speculation on survival of, 75–76, 114, 133–35, 138–39, 149, 191, 265–67, 272–75, 314–15
  strategic importance of, to U.S., 6–7, 29–30, 68–69, 78, 132, 149
German-Soviet Friendship Society, 71
Germany, Four-Power rights in. *See* Berlin
Gerz, Wolfgang, 83, 103
Gethsemane Church (Berlin), 170, 173, 176–81, 183, 193, 263, 306
  demonstrations at, 215

Gilmore, Harry, 134, 260
Glasnost, GDR reforms and, 11–13, 198, 202, 208–9, 252, 273
Gorbachev, Mikhail
  appetite of, 238
  Bonn summit participation, 34–35, 39–41
  GDR 40th Anniversary visit of, 168–76, 191–92, 197
  Honecker's meetings with, 3, 52–53, 62–63, 171–72, 180, 191–92
  influence of, in GDR, xii, 3, 29, 137, 156, 163, 191, 202
  Krenz's meetings with, 211–12, 236–37
  Neues Forum letter to, 170–71
  reform efforts of, 252
  unification influenced by, 286–87, 290, 303, 307
  U.S. attitude toward, 152, 207–8
Görlitz, 311–12
Götting, Gerald, 20–21, 190–91, 240
Graham, Katharine, 31
Great Britain, relations with GDR, 24, 36
Green Party (Greens), 20, 267, 315
Greifswald, 17–18, 35–36
Gromyko, Andrei, 64
Gröpler, Helmuth, 52, 108
Grósz, Károly, 47, 86
Group of 20, 183, 230, 245
Grünwald, Siegfried, 5
Gysi, Gregor, 224–25, 238–41, 280, 282–85, 294–95
  speech at Berlin demonstration, 245
Gysi, Klaus, 57–58, 238–39

Hager, Kurt, 57, 69, 135–36, 188, 190, 216, 241–42
Hahn, Erich, 20
Harnish, Reno and Leslie, 9, 32, 50–51
Haus, Uwe and Marianne, 70–72, 302
Havel, Vaclav, 256, 282, 293
Havemann, Katja and Robert, 130
Hein, Christoph, 11, 93, 220–21, 228–29, 246, 281
Heinrichs, Wolfgang, 223
Helsinki Final Act, 27, 192, 218, 272–74. *See also* Conference on Security and Cooperation in Europe
Hempel, Johannes (Bishop), 181, 217
Henrich, Rolf, 130
Herald Tribune, 309–10

Herger, Wolfgang, 94, 97, 218, 254, 256, 282
Hermlin, Stephan, 124, 154–55, 186, 206–7, 285, 294
Herrmann, Joachim, 29–30, 47, 62–63, 86, 175, 188
  ouster of, 204–5, 212
Herzig, Werner (Mayor), 4, 237, 259
Heyl, Wolfgang, 233
Heym, Stefan, 6, 12–13, 93–94, 136–37, 187, 220–21
  Berlin demonstration speech, 246, 292–93
  criticism of emigration, 100
history, GDR-Soviet dispute about, 3, 69, 71, 107, 211–12, 284
Hoagland, Jim, 31, 33
Hoffmann, Hans-Joachim, 42
Holmes, Jim, 278
Homann, Heinrich, 20–21, 240
Honecker, Erich
  Berlin's 750th Anniversary celebration, xi
  birthday celebration, 113–15
  career assessed, xvii, 13, 119–20, 146, 203
  character of, xvii, 36–37, 52–53, 113–15
  church visit of, 35–36
  Eberlein's relations with, 4
  emigration crisis and, 87–89, 150, 152
  GDR 40th Anniversary celebration and, 169–77
  GDR microchips and, 102
  Gorbachev's relations with, 52, 168–69, 171–72, 191, 197
  Heym's criticism of, 13
  illness of, 63–64, 68, 109, 120–21, 124, 128–29
  invitation to Magnitogorsk, 3, 52–53
  Krenz and, 15, 58, 212, 257
  Momper's meeting with, 44–47
  ouster of, 201–3, 212–13, 242, 272
  Poland, relations with, 22
  possible successors to, 56–58, 82–83
  resistance to reform, 102 (*See also* German Democratic Republic)
  Schmidt meeting with, 18
  Soviet Union visit of, 52–53
  Hans-Joachim Vogel's meetings with, 25–26
  waning power of, 56–58, 82–83, 120–21, 128–32, 153–54
  Washington Post interview with, 31, 33, 36–37
Honecker, Margot, 40–41, 110, 172, 230, 232
Höpcke, Klaus, 145, 189, 214–15, 256

House Armed Services Committee, 75, 94–95
House Foreign Affairs Committee, 43
Hoyer, Steny, 59
human rights, European debate over, 27
  as centerpiece of U.S. policy in GDR, 66–68
humor, role of, in GDR politics, 44, 90–92, 222
Hungary
  border with Austria opened, 6, 194
  emigration crisis and, 51, 89–90, 96, 99–100, 126, 128–32, 194
  FRG relations with, 115
  GDR relations with, 22–23, 43, 62–63, 86, 110, 128, 135–36
  Kádár's regime in, 16
  political reforms in, 47–48, 252
  quiet revolution in, 41
  U.S. relations with, 38–39
Hutchings, Bob, 160

IG-Metall corruption case, 237
infrastructure, fragility of in GDR, 17–18, 42, 69
"inner emigration" phenomenon, 125
Institute for Contemporary German Studies, 74
Institute for International Politics and Economics (IPW), 16–17, 221
intelligence services, diplomats' experiences within GDR, xvi–xvii, 30–31, 85, 302, 313–14
International Visitors Program, 38–39
Ironside, Alfred, 11–12
Ito, Pete, 139, 207, 237, 242–44, 260

Jahn, Günther, 241
Janka, Walter, 271
Jarowinsky, Werner, 57–58
Jaruzelski, General, 22, 34, 47–48, 76–77
Jewish claims against GDR, 37–38, 55–56, 65–66, 73, 77–78, 151
Jewish community
  in GDR, 60–61, 65–66, 238
  in U.S., attitude toward unification, 279
Jewish intellectuals, in GDR, 12–13, 74, 106
Junge Welt, 140, 145, 160, 181
  protests reported in, 183, 186–88, 190

Kádár, János, 16, 22, 41, 64, 102
Kaiser, Karl, 82
Kamm, Henry, 68–69, 301
Kamnitzer, Heinz, 228–29

Index

Kampelman, Max, 124, 126
Kant, Hermann, 48, 170, 183, 185, 226
Keller, Dietmar, 315
Kennan, George, 84
Kennedy, John, 28, 272
Kimmel, Annelise, 241
King David Report, 6
Kirchner, Martin, 304–6
Kleiber, Günther, 256
Klein, Fritz, 104
Knights of the Roundtable, The, 93
Kohl, Helmut
   Alliance for Germany, 297, 300
   emigration crisis and, 142, 147
   Honecker's relations with, xi, 102, 104
   Hungarian talks with, 115
   impact on March 1990 Parliamentary elections, 300–303
   Krenz's relations with, 221–22
   role in unification, 287–91, 307–8
   ten-point confederation plan, 279–80
   U.S.-GDR relations, 38
Kosin, Heinz, 202–3, 206, 271
Krack, Erhard (Mayor), 187
Krätschell, Werner, 108–9, 113
Krenz, Egon, 15, 73
   calls for end to demonstrations, 222–23
   career assessed, 203–8
   churches' relations with, 208–9, 223–24
   election fraud and, 7–9, 13–15, 216, 217–18
   election of, 215–16
   first speech as SED leader, 204–5
   fragile position of, 253–55, 259–60, 265–67, 268–69
   Gorbachev and, 211–12
   as Honecker's crown prince, 15, 49, 56–58, 82–83, 124
   as Honecker's successor, 203, 212–13
   Kohl's relations with, 221–22, 232, 235–36
   meets with U.S. Ambassador, 212, 240–41
   Moscow visit of, 230, 232, 235–36
   Opposition and, 203, 220
   Plenum debates, 257–58
   police brutality charges, 217–18
   Politburo appointments, 256–57, 261
   political skills of, 82–83, 208–9, 249
   reform, attitude toward, 208–10, 229, 234, 239–40, 241, 249–51, 258, 265–67
   resignation of, 280
Krolikowski, Werner, 59
Krüger, Thomas, 297, 301

Krusche, Günther, 41–42, 180–81
Kuczynski, Jürgen, 40, 50
Kunze, Gerhard, 157
Kusch, Ernst, 97

Lafontaine, Oskar, 291, 300
Larrabee, Steve, 221–23, 227
LDPD (Liberale-Demokratische Partei Deutschlands), 7, 140–41, 155, 158
   links with SED, 7, 230–31
   political power of, 253, 266
   reform proposals of, 237, 240–41
Le Carré, John, 105
legal profession, calls for reform from, 224–25, 228, 239
Leich, Werner (Bishop), 137, 209
Leipzig
   protest demonstrations in, 129, 139, 151, 154, 174–75, 182–83, 195–96, 213–15, 230, 241, 252, 280–82, 284
Leipzig Fair, 124
Lenin's Death, 93
Leonhard, Wolfgang, 107
Liebknecht, Karl, 3, 53
Ligachev, Yigor, 129, 137, 156
Lipping, Imre, 7, 15, 31, 89–90, 95, 124, 127, 129, 141, 144, 151, 160, 164, 171, 174–75, 177, 181–82, 191, 195, 203–4, 208–9, 212, 214, 230–32, 236, 245, 248, 256, 260–61, 297–98, 301
Livingston, Gerry, 307
Lochthofen, Sergei, 312–13
"Lola Blau," 4
Lorenz, Siegfried, 206, 217
Los Angeles Times, 151, 157, 271–75, 278
Luxemburg, Rosa, 3, 53, 92–93

McAdams, Jim, 225, 227, 233–35
McAleenan, Mary Agnes, 167, 173–74, 178
McCarthy, Joseph, 12
McCartney, Bob, 31, 33, 105, 139, 154, 252–53
McGovern, George, 62
Magirius, Friedrich (church superintendent), 281–82, 300
Magnitogorsk, Honecker's visit to, 3, 52–53
market economy, elements of, in GDR, 62–64, 193
   reform calls for, 119, 143–44, 217, 230, 249, 258
Marx, Karl, 3

Mastny, Vojtech, 225
Masur, Kurt, 182, 213–14, 281–82
May Day celebrations (1989), 1–2
  Berlin demonstration of November 4, compared with, 244
Meckel, Markus, 297, 308–311
medical profession in GDR, 155
Meehan, Frank, xii–xiv, 4, 151, 212
Mengistu, 18
Mielke, Erich, 11, 106, 155, 188, 242
Mischnick, Wolfgang, 221–22
Misselwitz, Hans, 308
Mittag, Günter, 57, 191, 204–5, 212, 257
Mitterrand, François, 24, 36, 56
Modrow, Hans, 11, 83, 105, 151, 183, 202–3, 206, 222
  CDU and, 305
  links with Krenz, 209, 212–13, 253–54
  loss of popularity by, 282–83
  meets with Baker, 279
  as prime minister, 256–57, 265–67, 280, 288
  unification proposal of, 287
Momper, Walter, 26, 44–47, 260, 291
Montag, Claus, 197
Mormons, status of, in GDR, 43
Mozur, Mike, 85–86, 258, 264, 289
Müller, Gerhard, 256
Müller, Heiner, 93

Nagy, Imre, 41
National Defense University (NDU), 7, 56
National Front
  collapse of, 266
  local elections fraud and, 7–11, 13–14, 227
National Security Council (U.S.), 160, 277–78
nationalism
  GDR opposition to, in communist world, 5
  role of, in inner-German relations, 24, 138–39
NATO
  Bush arms reduction proposal at, 27
  impact of unification on, 133–35, 303, 307–8
Naumann, Konrad, 269
NDPD (National-Demokratische Partei Deutschlands), 20–21, 240, 266
Németh, Miklos, 47, 115
Népszabadság, 6
Neue Berliner Illustrierte, 314
Neue Zeit, 140, 190, 258–59

Neues Deutschland
  Bloc Party press contrasted with, 140–41
  as communist reference source, 31–32
  denial of crisis by, 89–90
  editorial policy of, 6, 140–42
  election fraud and, 9–11, 14–15
  emigration crisis, reaction to, 141–42, 250
  GDR 40th Anniversary coverage, 181
  Grósz, interview with, 86
  Honecker, coverage of, 68, 133, 158, 262
  Kádár's retirement covered by, 16
  Krenz's criticism of, 209
  Krenz-Gorbachev meeting covered by, 236–37
  May Day (1989) coverage in, 2–3
  Polish elections coverage in, 24, 29–34, 76–77
  protest activities reported in, 184, 213, 215–16, 219
  reform activities covered in, 190, 194
  resistance to reform from, 201–2, 209
  soccer coverage in, 70
  suspect economic news in, 9
  theater season critique in, 92–94
Neues Forum
  cooperation with SED, potential for, 170–71, 197, 206–7, 216, 294
  elections of 1990 and, 291–94
  Interior Ministry orders shutdown of, 141–42
  leadership of, 129–30, 142–44, 160–61, 196–99, 292–94
  legalization of, 163, 186, 233
  letter to Gorbachev, 170–71
  Kurt Masur on, 213–14
  media coverage of, 213, 258–59
  origins and goals of, 129–30, 142–45, 159, 166
  political strength of, 150–51, 160–61, 163, 250–51, 267
  publications by, 210
  rock musicians' support of, 144–45, 160, 190, 194–95
  Schabowski meets with, 220, 227, 233
  Solidarity, comparison with, 139, 143–44
  Stasi attack on, 155
  unification, attitudes toward, 161, 287, 293
Neutsch, Erich, 104–5
New York Philharmonic, 40–41
New York Times, 68, 82–83, 252–53, 280, 301

news media. *See also* specific newspaper names; television
  access to Politburo decisions, 216–17
  author's cooperation with Western media, xv, 105, 151–52, 268
  coverage of Neues Forum by GDR media, 258–59
  demonstrations by GDR media, 210
  dissatisfaction with GDR news media, 6, 13, 31–32, 42, 80, 90, 119, 127–28, 142, 159, 186, 187, 190, 195, 198, 208, 210, 252, 272–73
  reforms in control over GDR media, 237
  restraints on GDR media coverage, 33–34, 42
  Western media's growing interest in GDR, 68–69, 80–83, 268
"niche society," 65, 125
Nier, Kurt, 110, 220
"Nightline" (television program), 268
Nikolai Church (Leipzig), 129, 182–83, 281, 300
"1900" Cafe, 50–51
Norway, relations with GDR, 55–56
NVA (GDR army)
  loss of faith in regime of, 160, 315
  U.S. contacts with, 6–7, 55–56, 78, 94–95, 97–98, 134
  use of, during demonstrations, 169, 180, 242–43
Nyers, Rezsö, 47–48

Obituary, 12, 136
Offenberg, Mario (Dr.), 60–61
Office of Central European Affairs (U.S. State Dept.), 77–78
"One Hundred Percenters," 166
Opposition
  lasting achievements of, 315–16
  origins of, 129–30
  political power of, 220, 252–53
  prospects after fall of Berlin Wall, 266–67, 273–74
  representation of, in Modrow Cabinet, 283
  weaknesses of, 129–30, 150–51, 210, 233, 250–51
Ormos, Mária, 128, 135–36
Ostpolitik, 25

"Pan-European Picnic," 108
PDS (Partei des Demokratischen Sozialismus),
284–85, 313–14. *See also* Communism; SED
Peasants Party, 21, 266
Peenemünde, 17
PEN Club of the GDR, 11–12, 228–29, 256. *See also* Writers Association
Perestroika, 197, 236. *See also* Glasnost
Perestroika (book), 107
Pfingsttreffen, 14, 16–17, 23, 92
Pflugbeil, Sebastian, 160–61, 178, 199
  elections of 1990 and, 301
  emergence of Neues Forum and, 210, 220, 233
  meeting with U.S. Ambassador, 250–51
Pieck, Wilhelm, 49
Playboy magazine, 235
Plenzdorf, Ulrich, 197
Poland
  elections in, 24, 26, 29–34, 47–48
  FRG embassy closes in, 139
  GDR relations with, 22, 43, 76–77
  Krenz visits, 232
  political reforms in, 252
police brutality
  demonstrations against, 210–11
  during protests, 180, 217–18, 226
  legal reforms and, 239–40
Politburo. *See also* Central Committee
  domination over Party and government, 74, 254–55
  internal leadership struggles in, 73, 212, 217, 242
  Krenz appointments to, 255–57
  mass resignations of, 255–56, 280
  October 11 declaration, 187–89, 194
  purge of Old Guard from, 205–6, 212–13
  replacement appointments in, 256–57, 261, 268–69
  resistance to reform from, 130–32, 138, 147, 159, 169–70, 185–86, 201–2, 223, 227, 231, 254–55
  travel policy reforms considered, 128–29, 217
political cabaret, 44, 90–92
pollution, GDR problems with, 5, 18, 21, 62, 117–18
pop culture, in GDR, 2, 23
Pozorski, Dave, 85–86
Pozsgay, Imre, 38–39, 47
Pragal, Peter, 8, 104
Praster, Tom, 268

"Principles of Ideological Dispute" (SED-SPD), 25
private property ownership in GDR, 64–65, 317–18
Pückler-Muskau, Prince, 52

Quinzio, Tony, 211

Rand Corporation, 7, 221
Rantzsch, Roland, 98
Rauchfuss, Werner, 256–57
Realpolitik, 114
Reemer, Norbert, 24, 72, 74
"Reform" (independent trade union), 213, 218
Reich, Jens, 143, 170–71, 196–99, 206, 245, 283
  analyzes Neues Forum's retreat from power (1990), 293–94
  meeting with U.S. Ambassador, 250–51
  Schabowski meets with, 220, 233
  television roundtable appearance, 220–21
Reichelt, Hans, 21
Reinelt (Bishop), 83, 182–83
Reinhold, Otto, 19–21, 167, 185, 209–10
  meets with U.S. Ambassador, 241–42
  SED-SPD ties and, 25–26
  on socialist structure of GDR, 114, 143, 147
Reinhold, Ute, 89–90
Reissig, Rolf, 19, 25–26, 185–87
  in post-Honecker era, 222–23
  reform proposals of, 59, 255
  SED-SPD ties and, 25–26
  withdrawal from politics, 283–85
Rennert, Jürgen, 11
restaurants, in GDR, 36, 60, 85–86, 186–87, 192–93, 238–39
reunification. *See* unification
Ridgway, Roz, 151
rock music
  GDR pop culture and, 2, 17
  role of musicians in reform movement, 23, 49, 144–45, 160, 190, 194–95
Romania, GDR relations with, 136
  lampooned by political cabaret, 92
Rostenkowski, Dan, 82–83
Roundtable, 253, 274, 281, 303
Runnings, John, 24–25

Salzgitter Center, 25–26
Schabowski, Günter, 15
  announces opening of Berlin Wall, 260–61
  Beijing trip, 73, 84
  Berlin demonstration speech, 245–46
  Berlin town hall meeting, 225–27
  comments of responsibility for Honecker personality cult, 262
  Krenz, contrasted with, 57, 82, 262
  limitations as reform leader, 227–28, 245–46, 265–66
  Moscow visit by, 28
  Opposition relations with, 220, 227, 233
  Plenum debates and, 257–58
  on Politburo reforms, 227–28
  political stature of, 254
  as possible Honecker successor, 49–50, 57–58, 82–83, 124
  role in post-Honecker era, 209–11
  Soviet reform enthusiasm criticized by, 49
  Wolf compared with, 234
Schalck-Golodkowski, Alexander, 232
Schauer, Heinz, 31–32
Schauspielhaus, 40–41
Scherzer, Landolf, 39, 117–20, 313–14. *See also Der Erste*
Schmemann, Serge, 252–53
Schmidt, Helmut, 18
Schnitzler, Karl-Eduard von, 209–10, 232
Schnur, Wolfgang, 141, 231, 238, 297–98, 306
Schorlemmer, Friedrich, 17–18, 85, 104, 111–13
  role in protest movements, 141, 167, 231, 246–47, 288–89, 297, 300
  unification efforts and, 288–89
SDP (GDR)
  elections of March 1990, 295–98, 300–303
  formation of, 159, 179, 294–95
  impact of, in GDR, 159
  leadership of, 250–51, 267, 296–98
  Neues Forum ties with, 197, 294
  participation in de Maizière cabinet, 308–11
  Stasi ties of first chairman, 296–97
  unification, attitude toward, 295
SED (Sozialistische Einheitspartei Deutschlands). *See also* Central Committee; PDS; Politburo
  Central Committee, 47, 201–2, 254–58, 268, 280
  election fraud and, 7–11, 13–15
  internal conflicts in, 3, 58, 111–13, 119–20, 163, 191, 198–99, 202, 216–17, 230, 242, 254, 257, 265–69, 284–85
  loss of power by, 282–85

Neues Forum links to, 197–98, 206–7, 216, 219
Party Congress planning, 26, 47
political power of, 7, 190, 198, 206, 222–24, 226, 233, 235, 239–41, 245, 252–55, 257–58, 265–67, 273–74
reform elements within, xii–xiii, 11, 59, 125, 147–48, 153–54, 170, 181, 191–92, 198–99, 206, 216–17, 227–29, 255, 265–67
U.S. embassy relations with, 38–39
West German SPD influence on, 25–26, 202, 267
Seidel, Bernd, 241
Seiters, Rudolf, 61
self-determination, vs. unification, 135, 153, 199, 207–8, 274–75, 278–79
Semper Oper (Dresden), 247–48
service-sector, in GDR, 64–65, 192–93
Shevardnadze, Edward, 5, 34–35, 156–57
Shostal, Pierre, 77, 157, 199, 204, 242–45, 248, 278
Shultz, George, 74
Siegler, Werner, 24–25
Silesia movement, 311–12
Sindermann, Horst, 136–37, 216
Singer, Israel (Rabbi), 65–66, 151
Skinheads, 61, 243
Slick, Stephen, 103, 165
Slocombe, Walt, 41–42, 60
soccer, GDR politics and, 11, 70, 72, 98–99, 118, 235, 271
Soccer World Cup, 99, 235, 307
Social Democratic Party. *See* SDP (GDR); SPD (West German Social Democrats)
social relations, U.S.-East German contacts, 30–31, 84–85
Solarz, Stephen, 29–30, 62–63, 280, 307
Solidarity
  comparison with Neues Forum, 139, 143–44
  election victory of, in Poland, 24, 29, 33–34, 232
Sonntag, 183
Sophien Church, 143
Soviet Union
  East Berlin Embassy, 116, 156–57, 191, 201, 287, 290
  East German public's attitudes toward, 71, 191
  economic agreements with GDR, 4–5

GDR relations with, 4–5, 28, 34–35, 52–53, 129, 156–57, 168–73
Honecker's visit to, 3, 52–53
Red Army presence in GDR, 71, 94–95
unification of Germany and, 81, 133, 156, 207–8, 225, 285–87, 290, 307–8
West German relations with, 34–35, 39–41, 52
SPD (West German Social Democrats), 19
Communist ties with, 25–26, 267
elections of 1990 and, 287–88, 291, 295, 300–301
influence in GDR politics, 159, 202, 267
members' GDR travel halted, 136–37
unification politics and, 287–88, 291, 300–301, 308–11
Spira, Steffi, 247
Spitzner, 98–99
Sputnik (Russian magazine), 71, 107, 112, 211–12, 284
Stafford, Larry, 261–62
Ständige Vertretung (Permanent FRG Mission in East Berlin), 28, 65, 142, 156, 176, 178, 188, 260–61, 262
emigration sit-ins at, 51–52, 67, 79–80, 95–97, 99–100, 103, 126, 176–77
inner-German relations and, 61–62
National Day reception, 22
role of, in post-Honecker era, 221–22
Stasi (*Staatssicherheit*, GDR secret police), 11, 22, 105–8, 114–15, 203, 232, 242, 296
continuing nightmare, 296–99, 306
emigration crisis and reform, attitude toward, 41, 67, 103, 107, 125, 155, 159, 161, 165, 210
monitors U.S. diplomatic personnel, xvi–xvii, 30–31, 85, 120, 165, 302, 313–14
omnipresence of, 8, 33, 50, 72, 111–13, 116–18, 120, 125, 174
presence at political demonstrations, 1, 172, 175, 178, 193, 215, 225–26
proposal to reestablish as "Office for National Security," 283
target of political demonstrations, 214, 226, 234, 243, 245, 254, 281–83, 290
vacation resort of, 36
State Department (U.S.)
attitudes toward GDR in, xiv, 38, 77–78, 83–84, 139, 152–54
European Bureau policy review, 59–60, 77–78, 109–11

growing interest in GDR crisis, 87–89, 130–35, 152–54
reaction to GDR revolution, 189, 203–4, 207–8, 220, 237, 248
reporting to, 77, 83–84, 139, 191, 264, 302–3
unification issue, policy toward GDR and, 133–35, 191, 277–79, 289–91, 306–8
Stern, Maram, 151
Stolpe, Manfred, 186, 194, 209, 220–21, 223–24
Stoph, Willi, 47, 64, 124, 166, 242
Stralsund, 17–18
street demonstrations. *See also* individual cities
changing character of, after fall of Berlin Wall, 279–82
police brutality during, 217–18, 226, 239
as reform catalyst, 154, 174–77, 181–83, 195–98, 213–15, 234, 244, 247, 252–53, 257, 266–69
Studnitz, Jörg von, 188, 241
Stumpf, Eberhard, 117–20, 313

Teachers Conference, 40–41
Telegraph, 210
television
influence of West German television, 6, 13–14, 16, 125, 157
reform tendencies in GDR television, 194–95, 204, 209–10, 220–21, 229, 271
Teltschik, Horst, 289, 291
theater
quality of, in GDR, 4, 92–94
role of, in reform movement, 71–72, 92–94, 159, 210, 222, 248
Theater Association, 210
Thierse, Wolfgang, 309
Tisch, Harry, 2, 229–30, 232, 240–41
Trabants (GDR automobiles), 12, 111, 271
trade relations, U.S.-GDR, xii, 30, 59–60, 66, 73, 76–78, 109, 154, 279
Transition Society, The, 93
travel
draft law, 209, 211, 217, 240, 250, 255–56, 259–61
East German demand for, and GDR policy on, 6, 27, 41, 51, 62, 65, 79, 86–91, 93, 127–28, 131, 142, 146–47, 162–63, 166, 187, 195, 199, 201–2, 209, 217, 222, 235–36, 252, 260–61, 272

Tribüne, 140
Troika, 106–7
Troutman, Heather, 23, 49, 129, 142–43, 160–61, 167, 173–75, 177–78, 194, 196, 199, 208, 221–22, 229, 233, 256, 264, 268, 283
Two-Plus-Four negotiations, xv, 306–8

Ulbricht, Walter, 3, 57, 131–32, 181
Ullmann, Wolfgang, 304, 316
unification of Germany. *See also* Federal Republic of Germany; German Democratic Republic; self-determination
assessment of, xvii, 303–6, 317–23
attitudes of GDR reformers toward, 143–44, 153, 161, 163–64, 199, 216, 224, 231, 244, 274–75, 280–82, 287, 293–94
challenge to international relations and, xiv, xvii–xviii, 131–35, 306–8
FRG reactions to, 133–34, 137–39, 148–49, 156, 168, 221–22, 267, 279–80, 287–91, 306–8
future problems with, 321–23
Gorbachev's influence on, 286–87, 290, 303, 307
news media interest in, 68–69, 80–82, 133
public opinion polls on East German attitudes, 146–47, 295, 300
Soviet reaction to, 156–57, 285–87, 290, 303, 307
U.S. reaction to, 14, 133–35, 207–8, 274–75, 277–79, 306–8
unions in GDR, U.S. embassy contacts with, 159. *See also* FDGB
United States. *See also* State Department
fears for chaos in GDR, 236–37, 242, 244, 248, 263, 289–90
GDR relations with, xii, 36–39, 59–60, 67, 73, 75–78, 109–11, 133–35, 151, 154, 165, 189, 204, 207, 220, 275–79
Hungarian relations with, 38–39
military contacts with GDR army, 6–7, 55–56, 78, 94–95, 97
policy toward asylum-seekers, 66–67
United States Embassy (Bonn), 45, 133–34, 168, 289, 318
United States Embassy (East Berlin)
anniversary congratulations for GDR overlooked, 184–85
attempts to stimulate interest in GDR, xii–

xiv, 30, 37–39, 44–47, 55–56, 77–78, 82, 86–89, 109–11, 132, 134–35, 139–40, 145–49, 153–54, 197–99, 267, 277–79
  demise of, with unification, 315–16
  Independence Day reception, 59
  as sit-in target, 66–67, 96, 103–4, 142, 161–66, 170
United States Information Agency, 218
United States Information Service Library, 67–68
United States Marines, difficulties of, in GDR, 165–66
United States military forces
  East Berlin shopping visits of, 32–33
  proposed contacts with GDR military, 6–7, 55–56, 78, 94–95, 97
United States Mission (West Berlin), 45, 134, 236–37, 260, 289
universities, role of, in protests, 195, 210, 218
urban restoration, GDR efforts at, 17–18, 50
Usedom, 15–16

Verner, Jerry, 38, 41, 72, 103, 166, 189, 214
Vogel, Hans-Joachim, 25–26
Vogel, Wolfgang, 24–25, 51, 67, 88–89, 99, 102, 201–2
  comments on Honecker's policies, 131, 169
  fall of Honecker and, 196, 201–2, 242
  meeting with Kohl, 142
  on Politburo deliberations, 202, 242
  reform proposals of, 237
  role in Prague "sit-in" crisis, 129, 131, 150, 152, 155
  U.S. Embassy sit-in, 96, 142, 162–65, 170
Vollmer, Antje, 314–15

Wage Depressor, The, 93
Walde, Werner, 261
Walesa, Lech, 22, 47, 252
Walters, Vernon, 133
Wandlitz ("golden ghetto"), 9, 49, 279
Warsaw Pact, summit meeting of, 43, 63
Washington Post, 31, 81–82, 105, 192, 252
Weiner, Janice, 21, 93, 140, 144, 159, 171, 173, 177, 193–96, 210, 213, 215, 218–19, 228–29, 237, 256–57, 264, 267–68, 316
Weiss, Konrad, 141
"welcome money," 270, 280

Wendehals concept, 229
Werner, Ruth, 269
West Berlin
  GDR relations with, 44–47
  responds to fall of Berlin Wall, 260, 263–64, 268–71
Western contacts, by East Germans, 30–31
Whiffenpoofs, 72
Whispering and Shouting, 23
Whitehead, John, 53, 75–76, 134
Wilkes-Barre Times-Leader, 268
Witt, Katarina, 52
Wochenpost, 107
Wolf, Konrad, 94, 106
Wolf, Markus, 58, 105–8, 117, 155, 220–21, 314
  political standing of, 232–33, 253–54
  reforms assessed by, 233–35
  speech at Berlin demonstration, 245
Women's League, 7
workers, 159
  FDGB links with, 229
  lack of motivation among, 60
  role of, in peaceful revolution, 208, 210, 213, 218, 223–24
workers militia
  dissatisfaction among, 214
  use of during demonstrations, 169, 180
World Jewish Congress, 65–66, 151
writers, role of in GDR, 100, 124. *See also* individual authors
Writers Association, 48, 144, 183, 194, 226
Wylie, Deane, 151, 278

Yakovlev, Alexander, 232
Yao Yilin, 175
Yeltsin, Boris, 191
youth in GDR, attitudes of, 17–18, 23, 34, 40, 49–50, 53, 61, 62, 79–80, 87–88, 103–4, 108–9, 112–13, 120, 135–36, 144, 160, 162, 167, 172–73, 180, 182–84, 193, 195, 210, 218, 231, 311, 316

Zaikov, Lev, 191–92, 202
Zduriencik, Jack, xi
Zernsdorf, 317–18
Ziemer, Christoph (church superintendent), 245, 248–49